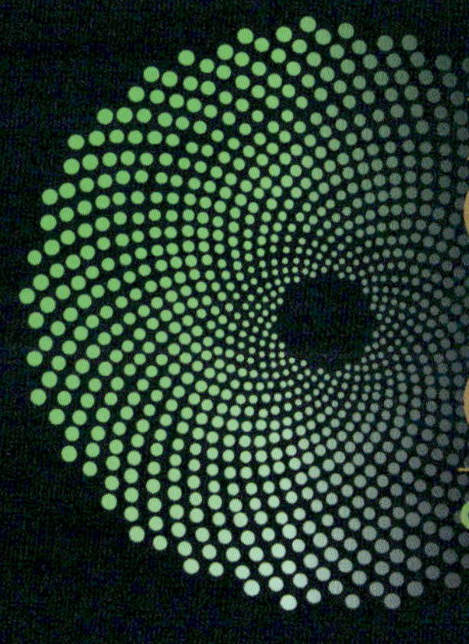

INTERNATIONAL GARDEN PHOTOGRAPHER OF THE YEAR

COLLECTION NINE

CONTENTS

Design and production: Nick Otway.
Proofreading: Richard Wilford, Gregory Brooks and James McGlinchey.
Edited by Curtis McGlinchey.
Image retouching and colour repro: Michael Moody.

A catalogue record for this book is available from the British Library.

ISBN: 978-0-9934529-0-1

The contents of this book are believed correct at the time of printing. Nevertheless, Garden World Images cannot be held responsible for any errors or omissions or for changes in the details given in this book or for the consequences of any reliance on the information provided by the same. This does not affect your statutory rights.

Printed and bound in Italy by Printer Trento S.r.l.

www.igpoty.com

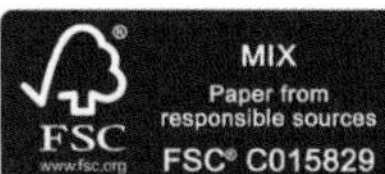

SPONSORS AND SUPPORTERS

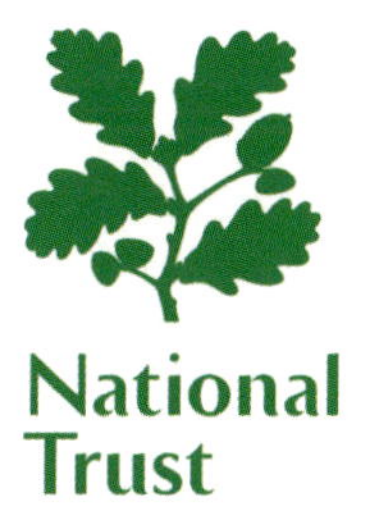
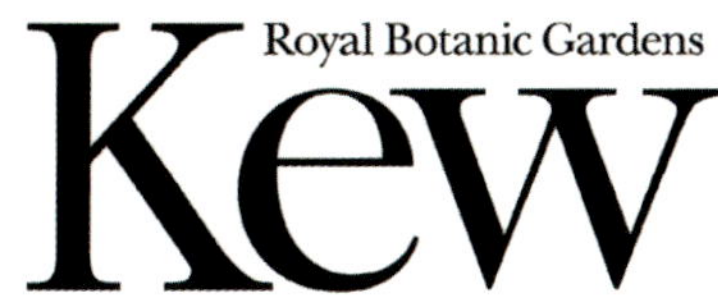
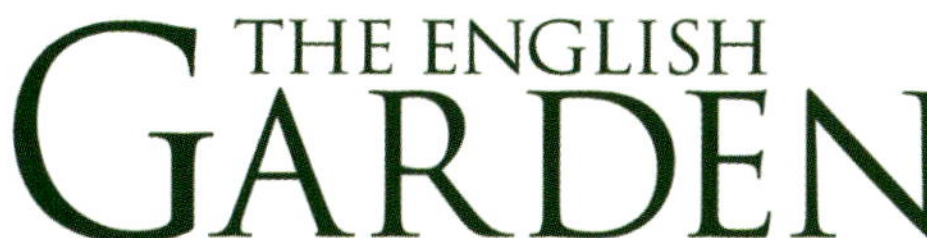
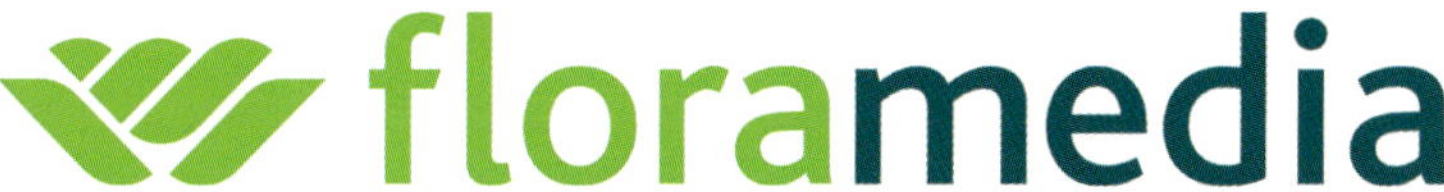
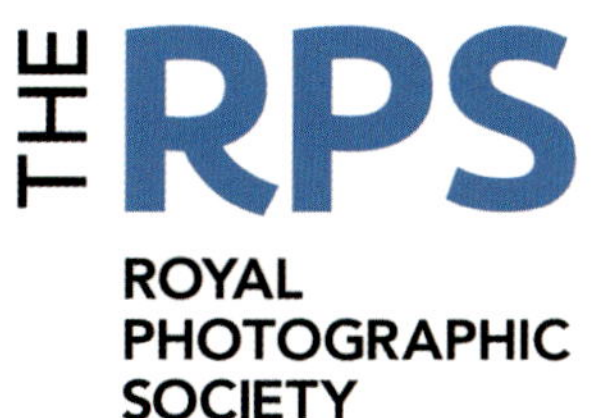
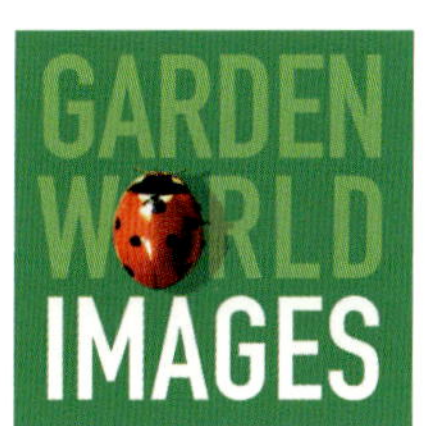
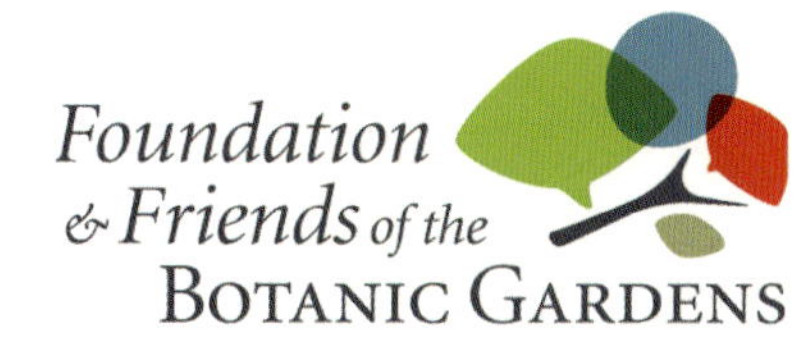
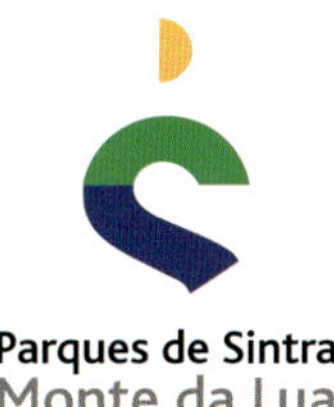
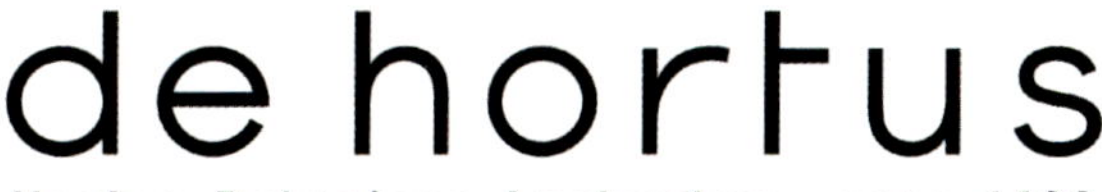
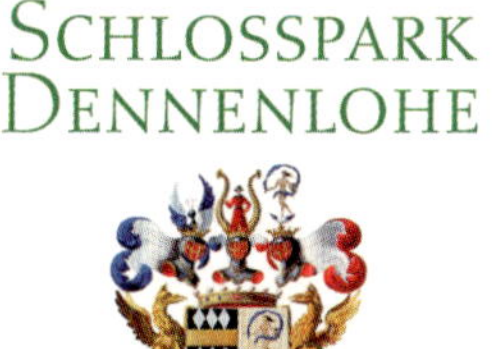
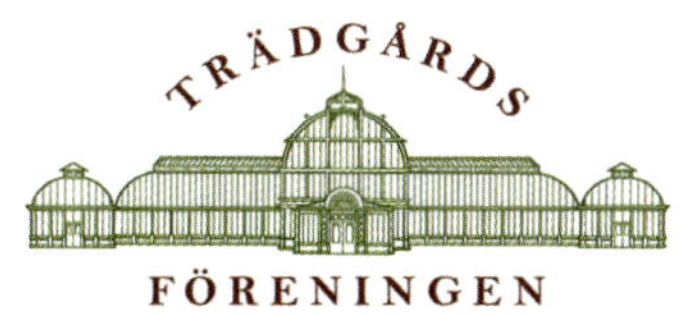
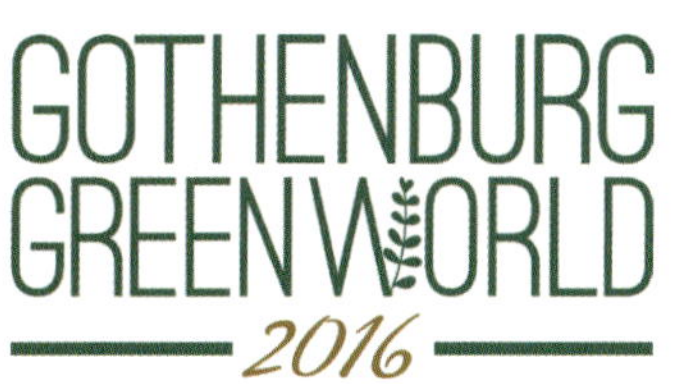
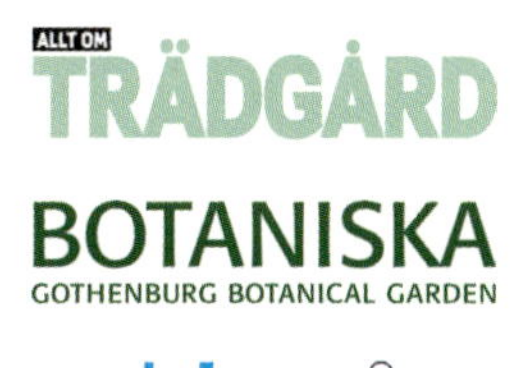
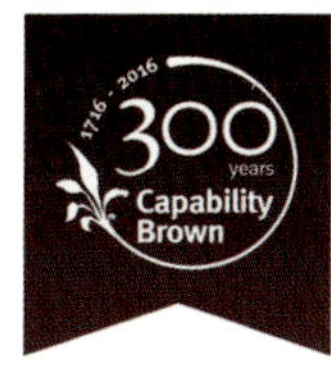
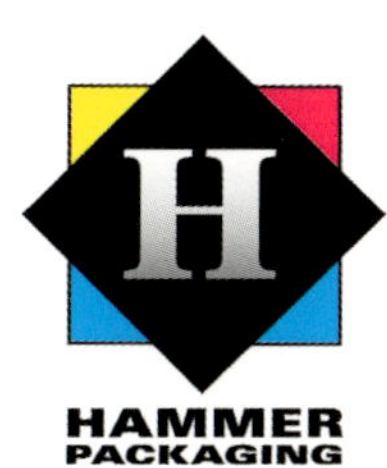
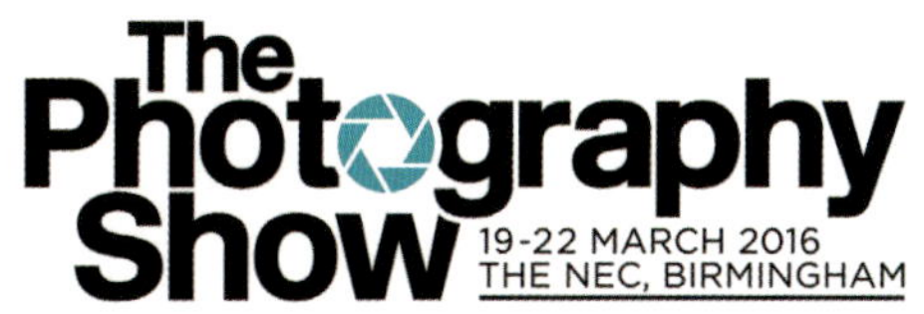
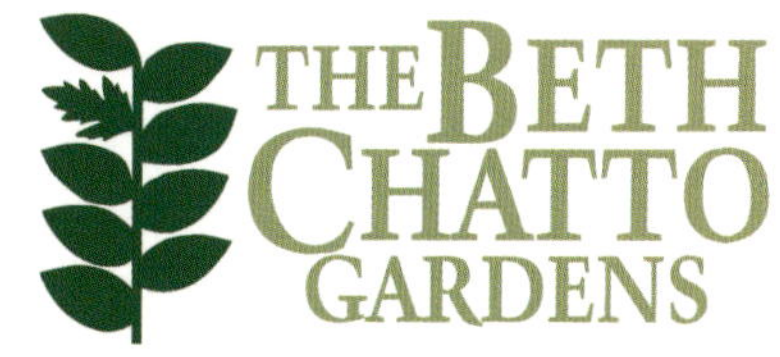

INTRODUCTION

By Philip Smith, Founder of International Garden Photographer of the Year

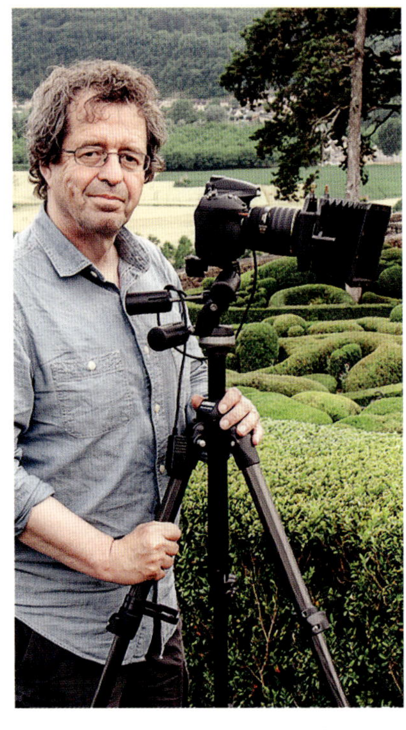

This year for IGPOTY has been one of transition and I am very pleased to be working with Tyrone McGlinchey and his team as they provide a new base for IGPOTY's future, with fresh ideas and new horizons.

What has not changed is the humility I feel when reviewing the many thousands of photographs that have been entered. It is a true celebration of the plants and gardens that are such an important part of our lives. Each one of the photographs entered is a statement made by an individual photographer in appreciation of the green environment. Today it seems ever more important for all of us to make such statements to support our natural world.

The images in this book make strong, beautiful and clear visual statements. The photographers showcased here capture the essence of a garden, a flower, a tree, a green space. They show great skill and they inspire us with the freshness and accuracy of their vision. They can pull on our emotions, and they can open our eyes wide in wonder.

When I lead an IGPOTY workshop I am always struck by the passionate interest in plants and gardens that students have, and the huge pleasure they get from their photographs whether captured on a phone or a sophisticated camera along with a bag full of the latest accessories. As you enjoy the wonderful photography in this book, remember that it stands on the shoulders of all the people who entered the competition, often without a real expectation of success, without whom this marvellous book could not be made. Everyone's contribution adds to the whole.

I know this book will refresh your view of the world of plants and gardens, and enhance your understanding and appreciation of our green planet. I am sure you will be enriched, uplifted and inspired by the dedication of the photographers whose work is displayed so beautifully in these pages.

FOREWORD

By Andrea Jones, garden photographer and author

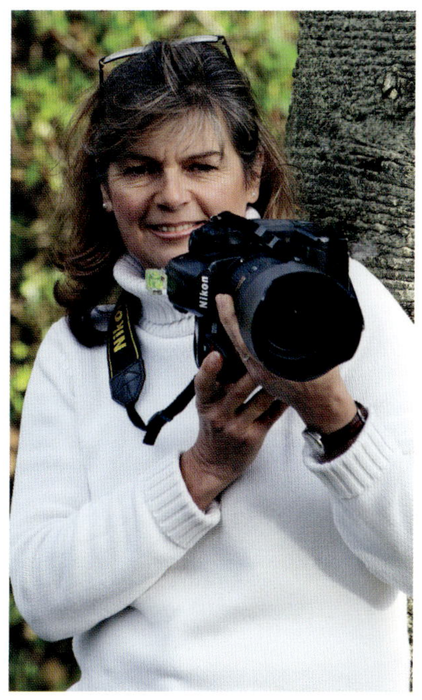

IGPOTY is more than just a competition, it is a celebration of the gardens and plants we all love so much. This is the first year I have had the privilege of judging this very prestigious event and it has been entrancing.

I've enjoyed the subject myself since childhood and writing this foreword has prompted a memory of the first art competition I ever entered as a child when I chose to draw a fir cone. I laboured over a pen and ink drawing, becoming increasingly fascinated by the amount of detail in this tiny, yet otherwise rather overlooked object of natural history.

I so enjoyed the whole process of drawing this intricate specimen it never occurred to me that I might actually win a prize. I don't even remember what the prize was, but I do remember the pure joy of exploring the minute detail of this wonder of the natural world and creating exploded details with my nib, of that tiny, somewhat insignificant cone. Had there not been a competition I may never have experienced this pleasure and focused my attention on this tiny thing of beauty. It sparked something.

Amongst all the good things IGPOTY brings I hope more than anything that someone who may perhaps not have noticed how beautiful nature can be, might be touched by these remarkable images and be inspired to look more closely at the world around them.

Some of us are lucky enough to live in the countryside and be spoilt with woodland trees, expansive farmland and scenic views but wherever we live nature exists. It might be herbs within a window box or some horseradish growing in the crack of a paving slab. Observing is the key. If more of us began to look and appreciate nature, the better chance we might have of protecting this incredible world.

The entries for this book have come from garden and photography enthusiasts of all levels from around the world. Sadly, not all the submissions could be included and although judging them has been a great joy, having to eliminate some images has been extremely hard. I hope very much that those whose entries didn't make the pages on this occasion will try again next time and not be disheartened.

So what makes a great garden photograph? A combination of being in the right place at the right time, good composition, correct exposure, spectacular colour, a lucky moment when we catch that illusive shaft of light. It's hard to explain but we know when we see it, whether it's in the viewfinder or on the page, it really feels like *magic*.

As you turn the following pages I hope each picture sparks as much delight for you as it has for me whilst judging, and by the time you reach the end you'll be itching to get out outdoors with your camera again – like I am!

The judging of International Garden Photographer of the Year took place over a period of two months from November to December 2015. Each photograph entered was scrutinised and assigned a ranking by individual judges. These were then tallied and carried forward to a series of group judging sessions held at studios in Soho, London. High resolution image files were requested from shortlisted entrants and a further set of judging decisions took place. We thank all the judges for their dedication and thoroughness in assessing a very wide range of entries from all over the world.

JUDGES

- Tyrone McGlinchey, Managing Director, Garden World Images
- Philip Smith, Founder of IGPOTY
- Clive Nichols, garden photographer and author
- Andrea Jones, garden photographer and author
- Joanna Fortnum, Gardening Editor, *The Daily Telegraph*
- Tony Kirkham, Head of Arboretum and Horticultural Services at the Royal Botanic Gardens, Kew
- Christina Harrison, Editor, *Kew Magazine*
- Chris Lacey, Head of the National Trust Picture Library
- Clare Foggett, Editor, *The English Garden* Magazine
- Ray Spence, FRPS, fine art photographer, author and lecturer

EXHIBITION

The International Garden Photographer of the Year tours to a range of venues in Britain and around the world, including the Royal Botanic Gardens, Kew, Royal Botanic Gardens Sydney, De Hortus Botanicus, Amsterdam, Palace of Monserrate, Portugal, and various National Trust venues, to name but a few.

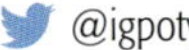

THANKS

Tyrone McGlinchey the Managing Director of The International Garden Photographer of the Year would like to thank:

- Philip Smith, Founder of The International Garden Photographer of the Year
- Royal Botanic Gardens, Kew, Katie Weaver, Festivals Team
- Foundation & Friends of the Botanic Gardens, Sydney
- The Royal Photographic Society: Liz Williams
- Floramedia: Merthus Bezemer, Robert Wacker, Christian Beer
- Garden World Images
- Spingold Design & Print
- Prodigi: Steve Levin and James Old
- *The English Garden* Magazine
- Supporters and photographers
- Special thanks to our team who contribute so much to its success: Hagar Lee, Ben Waterson, Nick Otway, Linda McGlinchey, James McGlinchey, Curtis McGlinchey and Shaun McGlinchey

WORKSHOPS AND LECTURES

International Garden Photographer of the Year runs workshops and lectures at exhibition venues throughout the UK.

The sessions are open to anyone who wants to improve their garden and plant photography at whatever level of experience. For further details visit www.igpoty.com

Photographers can enter single images or portfolios of six images in any of the following categories with the associated briefing in mind:

WILDFLOWER LANDSCAPES

Flowers that were once widespread amongst fields, meadows and woods are now extremely rare and some have become extinct in the wild. This is largely due to disappearing habitats. Landscapes that are home to distinctive species of plants or animals are under threat. Bring this to the world's attention through your photography of plants in the landscape. The wild flowers you photograph may be in gardens - which can be fragile landscapes in their own right - or in the true 'wild'. The judges will be looking to show the flowers in their right context - whether that is part of naturalistic planting or in the fields and hedgerows. They can be wide shots or close-ups of individual species. Now is your chance to seek out the wild spaces on your doorstep and to celebrate them through photography.

THE BEAUTY OF PLANTS

Achieving great images of plants and flowers requires skill, passion and commitment. This category celebrates the ephemeral beauty of the plant - from seed to compost. Plant portraiture is all about capturing the very essence, or character, of a plant. This could be a rambling rose or a humble bluebell, an exotic tree peony or the delicate flowerhead of a grass. A single bloom in isolation can be admired for its uniqueness. Take a closer look. The judges will be looking for spot-on technique and original artistic views of your subject.

BEAUTIFUL GARDENS

Visiting a garden is a great day out for many of us. We can stand and admire the work of gardeners who have dedicated themselves to creating a personal paradise for the enjoyment of themselves and others. You can enter images from gardens in any part of the world, from Tokyo to Tuscany, from Montreal to Melbourne. As the photographer you are the storyteller. The judges will be on the lookout for images that show us what is special about a particular garden, whether it's large or small, whether it's a chic design statement or a plantsman's paradise. Tell us the story.

TREES, WOODS & FORESTS

We celebrate the tree in all its diverse forms. From the gnarled old oak to the mighty redwood, we are inviting you to show us how important trees are in our lives and in the health of our planet. Winning images will reveal the treasures of our great world woods and forests as well as the beauty of a solitary tree. How do people and trees live side by side in one world? How does a tree create a sense of well-being? The judges will be looking for those images that seek to address these questions, as well as those that celebrate the simple beauty of our planet's trees.

WILDLIFE IN THE GARDEN

In a world where natural habitats are being depleted, gardens are a haven for wildlife. The wild creatures that use our gardens and parks can become familiar companions, or rare and special visitors. These may be creatures that only you are privileged to see - a nocturnal hedgehog for example - or they could be tiny insects that are easily overlooked - except by the keen photographer! They may be creatures you can only see in a wildlife reserve. This category is about all the creatures that enjoy gardens, parks and nature reserves, from beetles and butterflies to birds and badgers. Try to capture that moment where 'wildlife havens' becomes an inspiration.

GREENING THE CITY

On our crowded planet, town gardens, parks, open spaces and city nature reserves create conditions for a surprising variety of plant and wildlife to thrive. Some plants have adapted to a changing environment. The judges will look for images that celebrate the juxtaposition of the concrete urban scene with the organic beauty of plants and trees. The sheer adaptability of plants - flowers growing in pavement cracks - will be a focus of this category.

BREATHING SPACES

This category celebrates open spaces and the places where we love to relax and enjoy the feeling of well-being. It could be that people are the subject of your photography or it could be animals or plants; perhaps a landscape - a wide vista or a favourite hideaway. The judges will be looking for those images that express peace, contentment and enjoyment. Your entries can be of any open space or green location.

THE BOUNTIFUL EARTH

Mother Earth provides everything we need to live - food and medicine. We celebrate the gifts of the earth, from the allotment to the wild medicinal herb, from the crops on which we depend to the home-grown tomato plant pot on the windowsill. Judges will look for images that connect people to the earth and show the essential part that plants play in our world. This can be local or global - seed or paddy field - it's up to you to decide what to focus on.

YOUNG GARDEN PHOTOGRAPHER OF THE YEAR

Under 16s were invited to enter single images into any of the above categories. The title of Young Garden Photographer of the Year was awarded to the best single image.

AWARDS

Best Portfolio award was given to the best themed portfolio.

Runner up prizes were awarded to the portfolios judged second and third.

A first, second and third award is given for each category. In addition, a number of photographs in each category are judged to be 'Finalist'. These and the winning photographs form the International Garden Photographer of the Year exhibition at the Royal Botanic Gardens, Kew and other venues. A number of photographs were also selected as 'Highly Commended' in each category.

PREFACE

By Tyrone McGlinchey, Managing Director of Garden World Images

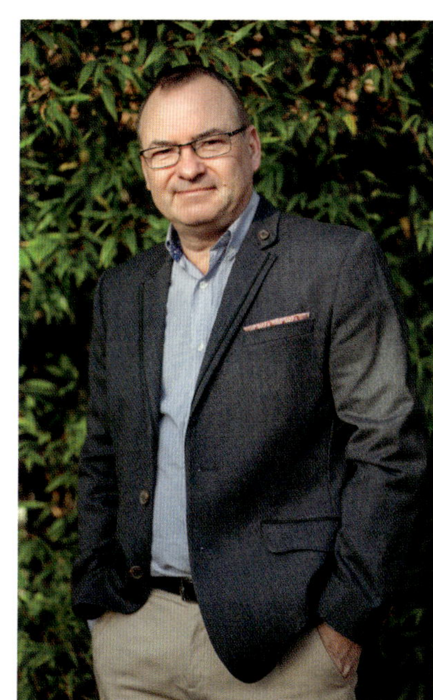

The intention and ultimate hope of this book is to thrill, inspire and immerse readers in the beautiful green world that surrounds us. Everyone deserves their own green personal space, whether a balcony, a local park or a grand garden and one of the most effective ways to better connect with these spaces is through photography.

IGPOTY has a habit of making us stop and think about things, and helps us reflect upon our own time spent in gardens and nature. For many years whilst taking pictures – and looking beyond my own best advice – rather than relaxing and pressing the shutter or cable release on an exhale, I used to hold my breath. At the time I wasn't sure why it was so difficult to stop doing this but looking back I think I now know the reasons why.

The anticipation and excitement of capturing something which could possibly form a deeper connection between myself and nature was just too great to ignore. When we judge the best garden photography on earth, I often get this exact same feeling and it is an absolute privilege.

We all lead busy lives and I believe IGPOTY is a vivid reminder for all of us stop and stare; to take some time out and just watch, observe and capture our fascinating green planet. The IGPOTY entries continue to surprise and give our esteemed judges a true sense of awe. The time and effort behind some pictures is quite amazing and the results truly astounding.

I wish to thank all of our entrants from around the world for making IGPOTY what it is today: a true celebration of photographic art and nature. I also wish to thank all the visitors to the exhibitions and workshops as well as all of the staff at the venues. As the IGPOTY message continues to grow with wonderful new venues across the globe I hope to meet even more like-minded people and partners.

With that said, if you find yourself deep in thought with distantly focused eyes, hand perched on an unturned page whilst looking at a particular photograph, you may be connecting with gardens and plants in a way you never thought possible. Just remember to take a breath.

INTERNATIONAL GARDEN PHOTOGRAPHER OF THE YEAR

RICHARD BLOOM

'This picture is totally immersive and a joy to behold. The eye is led to the horizon by the diagonals of the stream and the trees, with the cool blue notes in the foreground complemented by the warmth of the rising ground in the distance.

The cobbles of the stream and endless lupins beautifully orchestrate the picture's structure and texture whilst the trees soften the scene, making this an elegant symphony of plants and nature.'

Tyrone McGlinchey, Managing Director of Garden World Images

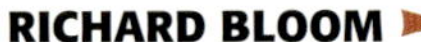

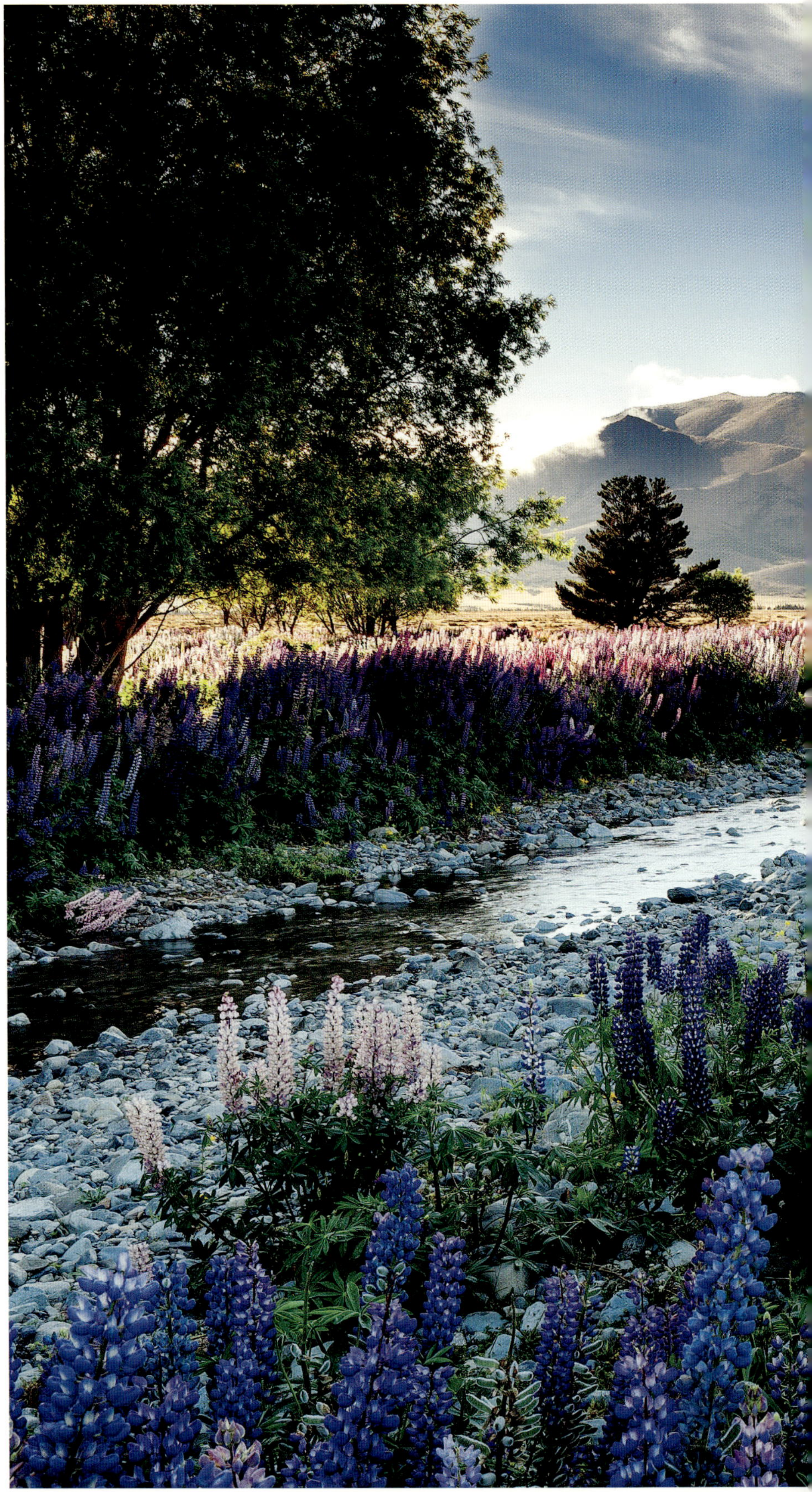

RICHARD BLOOM ►   1ST PLACE, OVERALL WINNER

Tekapo Lupins
Lake Tekapo, Mackenzie, Canterbury, South Island, New Zealand

On the way to Lake Tekapo on the South Island of New Zealand in early summer the landscape, already amazing, was scattered with drifts of naturalised lupins, which gave it an almost psychedelic, wonderland feel. The banks of this stream were bristling with masses of different coloured lupins stretching toward the distant hills and out of shot to the west, giving the sense that they went on forever.

Canon EOS 5D Mark II, Canon 24-70mm lens, 1/4sec at f/16, ISO 160. Tripod, polarising filter, graduated neutral density filter. Post-capture: basic image management.

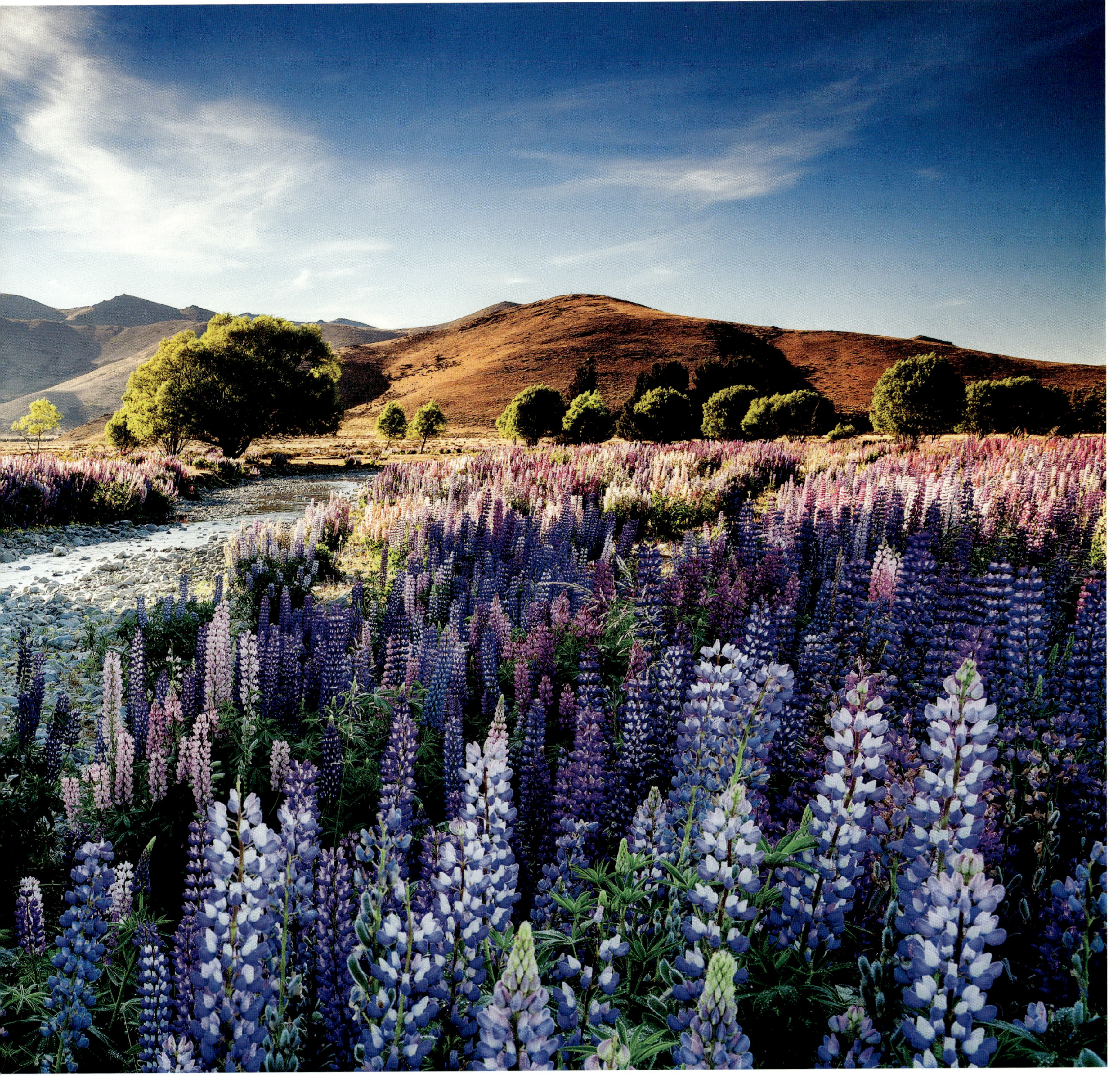

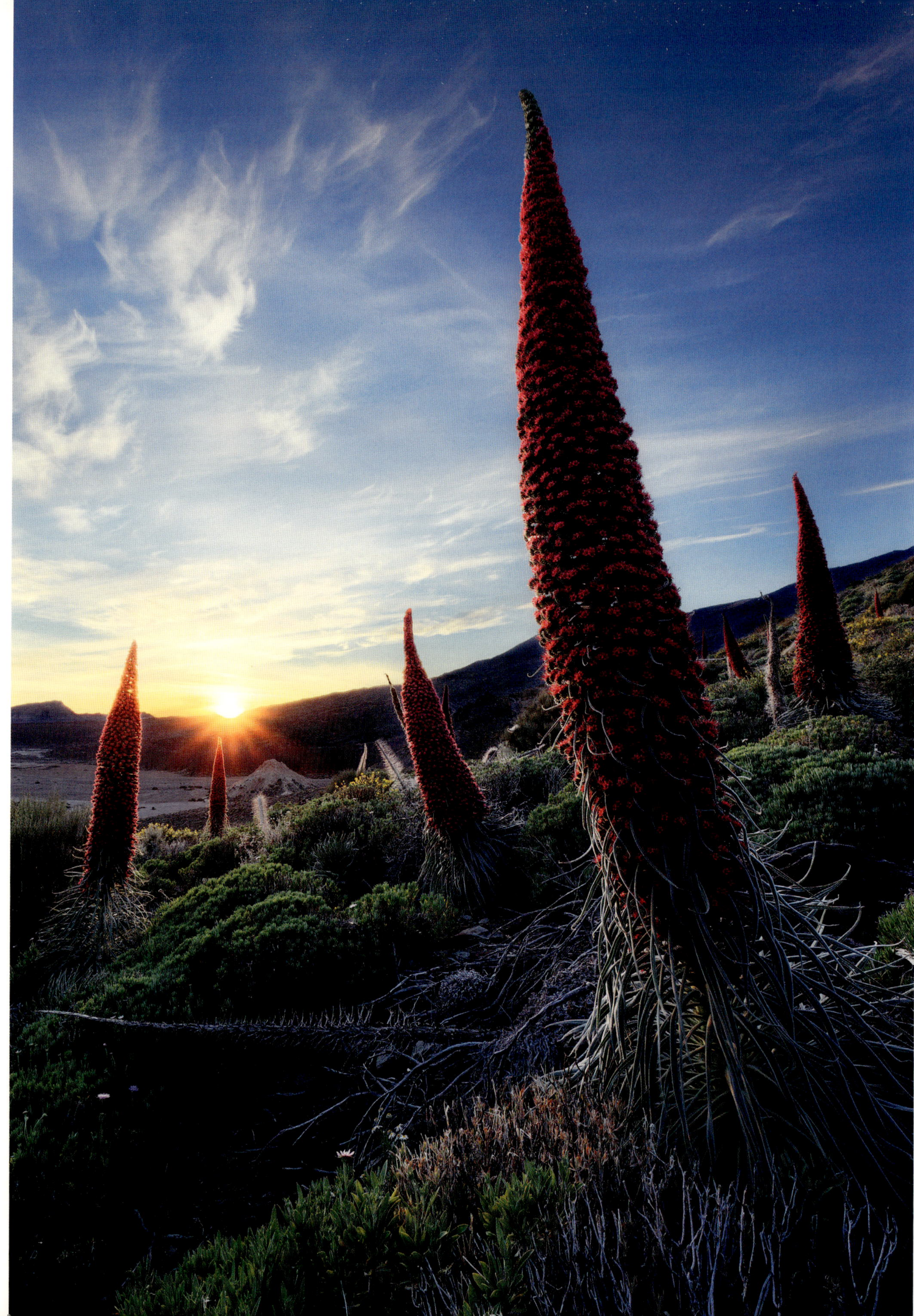

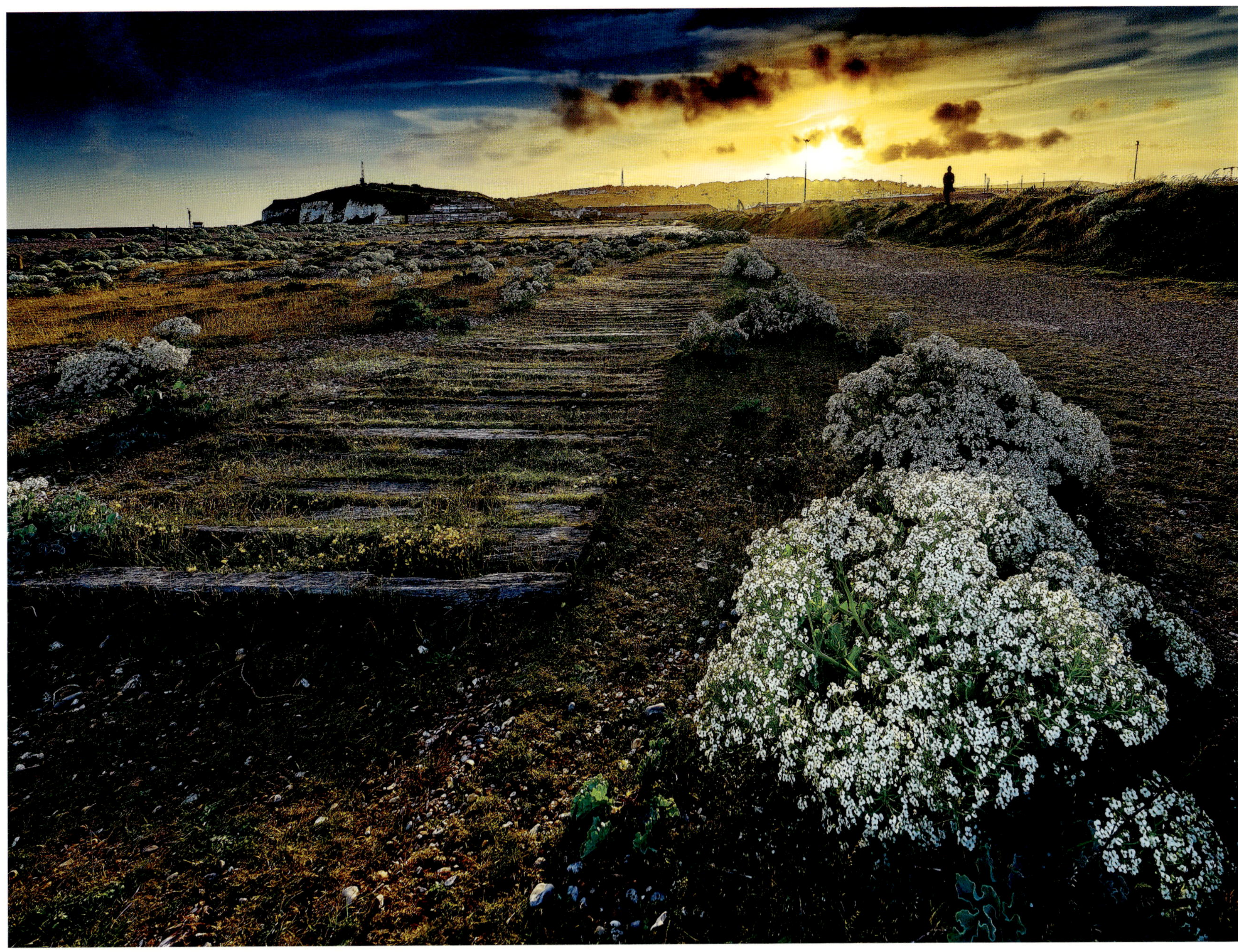

National Park Kings
Tenerife, Canary Islands, Spain

I travel to this spot in the Cañadas del Teide National Park almost every year throughout the flowering season. Because of my frequent visits, I knew when the sun would be in the exact right place for the perfect shot of this endemic biennial *Echium wildpretii*.

Canon EOS 5D Mark II, 17-40mm lens, 1/15sec to 1/160sec. Post-capture: combined four exposures.

Tide Mills
East Sussex, England, UK

Newhaven Tide Mills is one of those wild, unmanaged places that are highly valued for recreation by local people but unfortunately less so by the local council; some of the land shown in this photograph has been allocated for development. For a couple of weeks in May each year the whole area is covered in the snow-white pompoms of wild sea kale (*Crambe maritima*) in full flower. These are at their most resplendent in the evening sunlight.

Sony α7R, Nikkor 14-24mm lens, 1/30sec + 1/250sec at f/16. Tripod. Post-capture: composite image of two photographs.

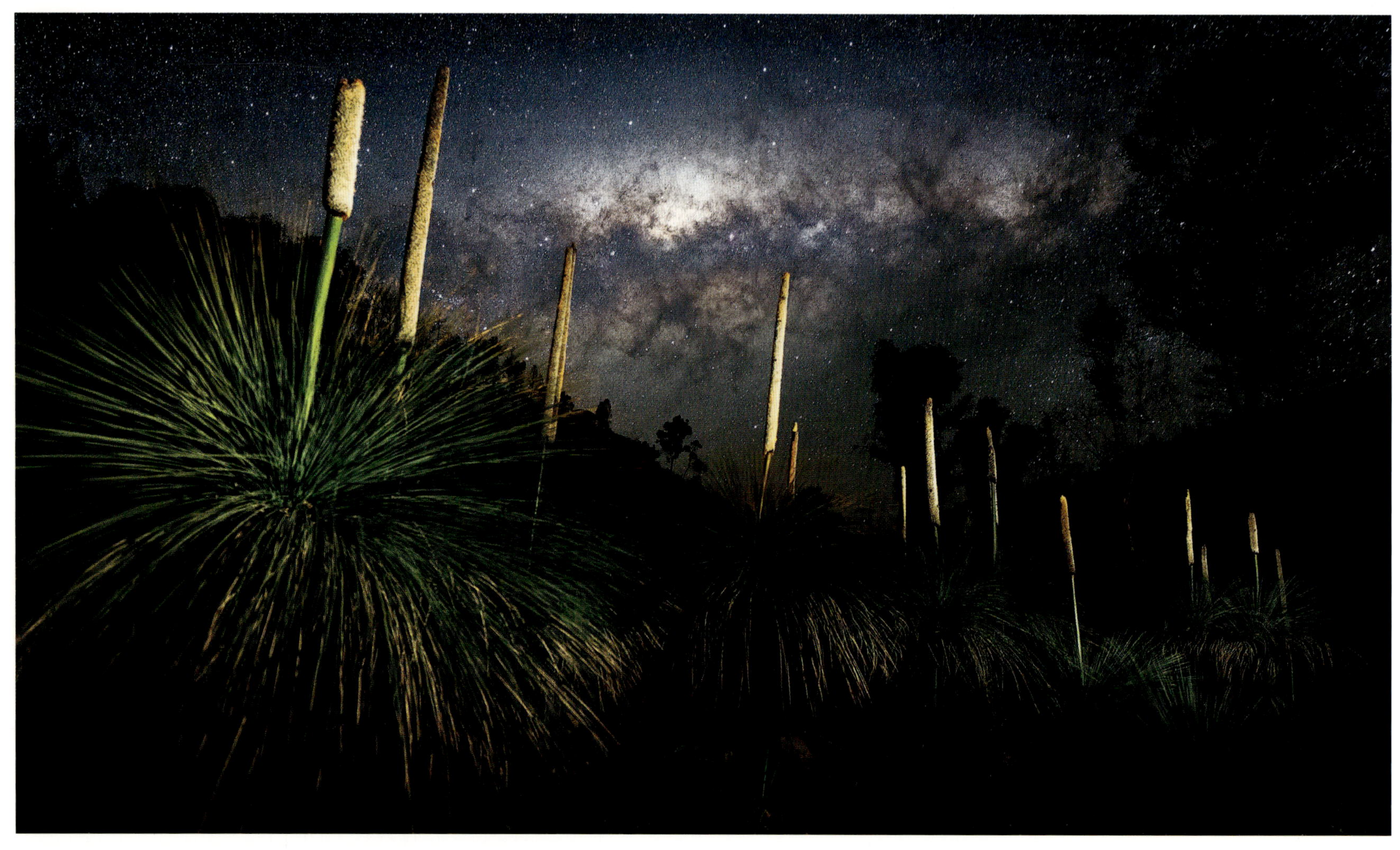

Dancing with the Stars
Warrumbungle National Park, Coonabarabran, New South Wales, Australia

What an amazing and unique sight, to find a row of ancient grass trees, and all in flower. I came across this patch several months after the area was destroyed by a bush fire. They had somehow regenerated, and the fire had stimulated them all to flower at once; I doubt that will ever be the case again. To me they looked like a magical row of dancers, dancing free under the stars.

📷 Nikon D600, Nikon 14-24mm lens, 30sec at f/2.8, ISO 3200. Post-capture: basic image management.

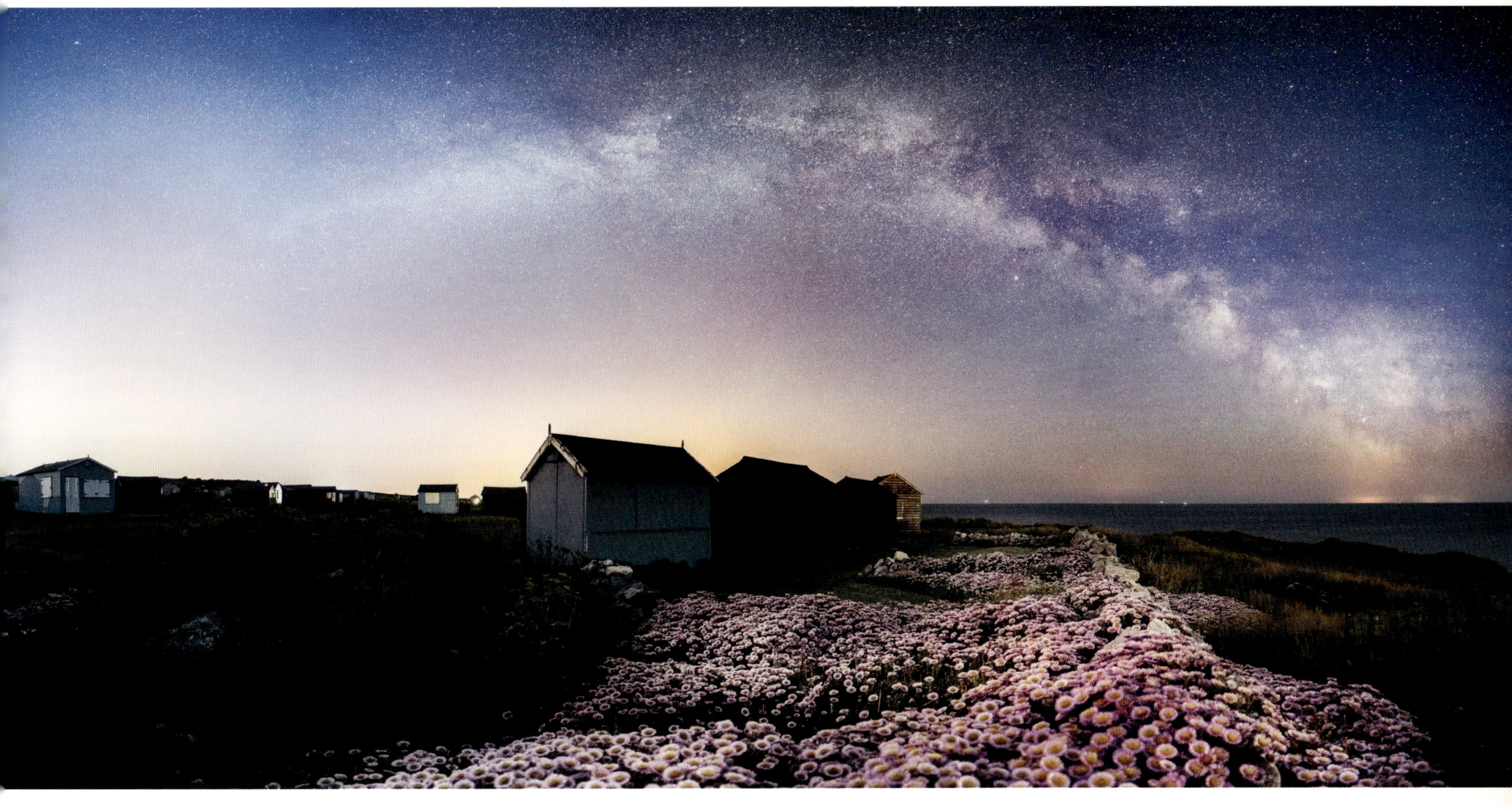

Island Sea Breeze
Isle of Portland, Dorset, England, UK

This flower is well known locally as sea breeze; however it is also referred to as beach fleabane and seaside daisy (*Erigeron glaucus*) and is part of the daisy family. It flowers in abundance on the Isle of Portland in early summer, usually in large clusters in the same location as it is a perennial. The flower looks amazing under the late spring blue skies. Portland also has incredibly dark skies facing out to the English Channel, and this image has tried to show the beauty of the flower under starlight.

Nikon D810, Nikon 14-24mm lens, 20sec at f/3.2, ISO 5000. Post-capture: four images stitched together to create the panorama, basic image management.

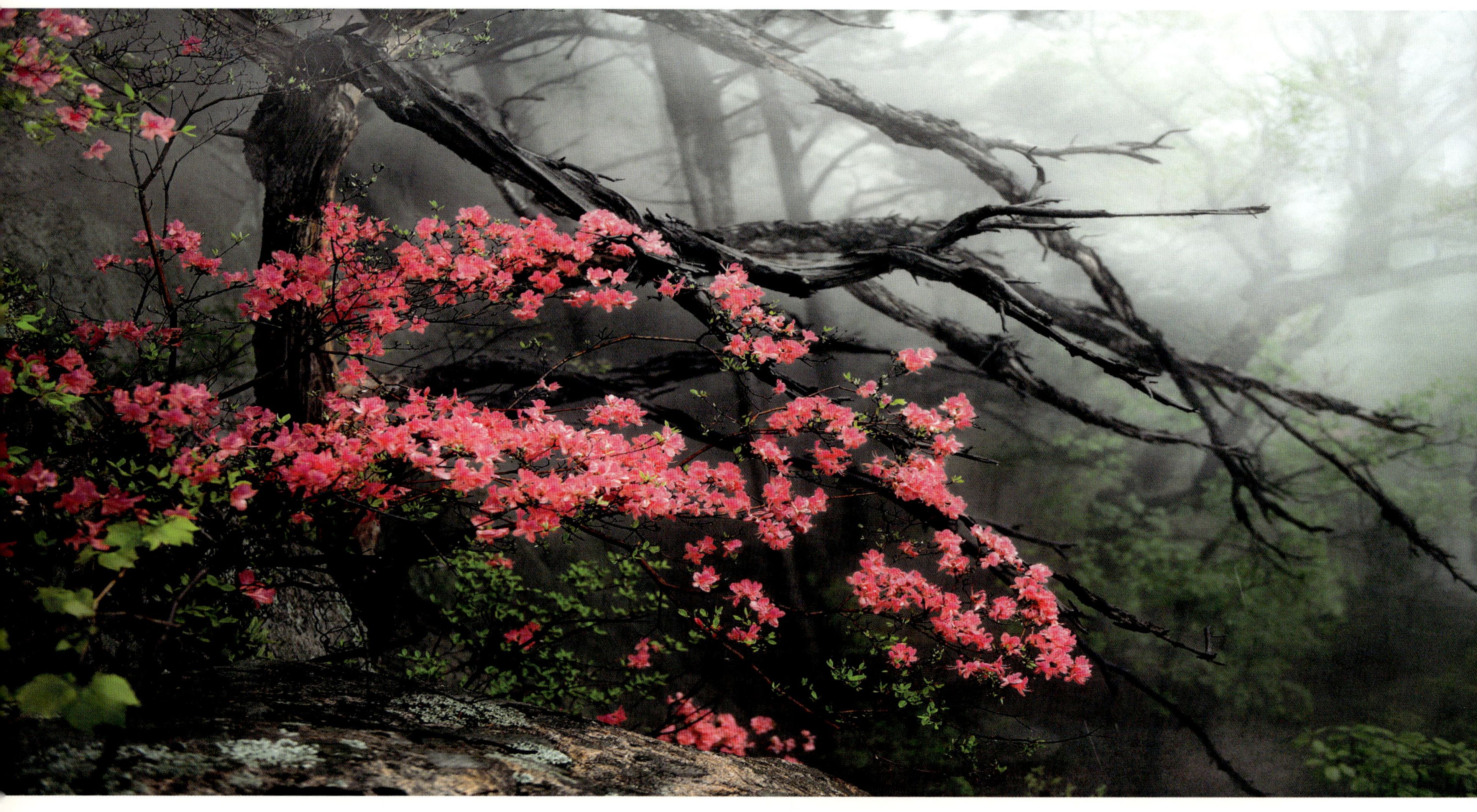

Red in Forest
Ta-pieh Mountains, Henan, China

Situated on the borders of three provinces, namely Anhui, Henan and Hubei, the mountain is a natural habitat for *Azalea* blossoms.

Nikon D700, Nikon 40mm lens, 1/50sec at f/2.8, ISO 400.

Morning Splendour
Peak District, England, UK

I started out walking in fog but the sun soon burnt most of it off leaving a carpet of dew glistening in the light. I was fortunate to come across these moorland beauties side-by-side in full bloom. Gorse bushes are usually taller and tend not to mix with the low lying heather.

Nikon D800, Nikkor 16-35mm, 1/15sec at f/16, ISO 100. Tripod.

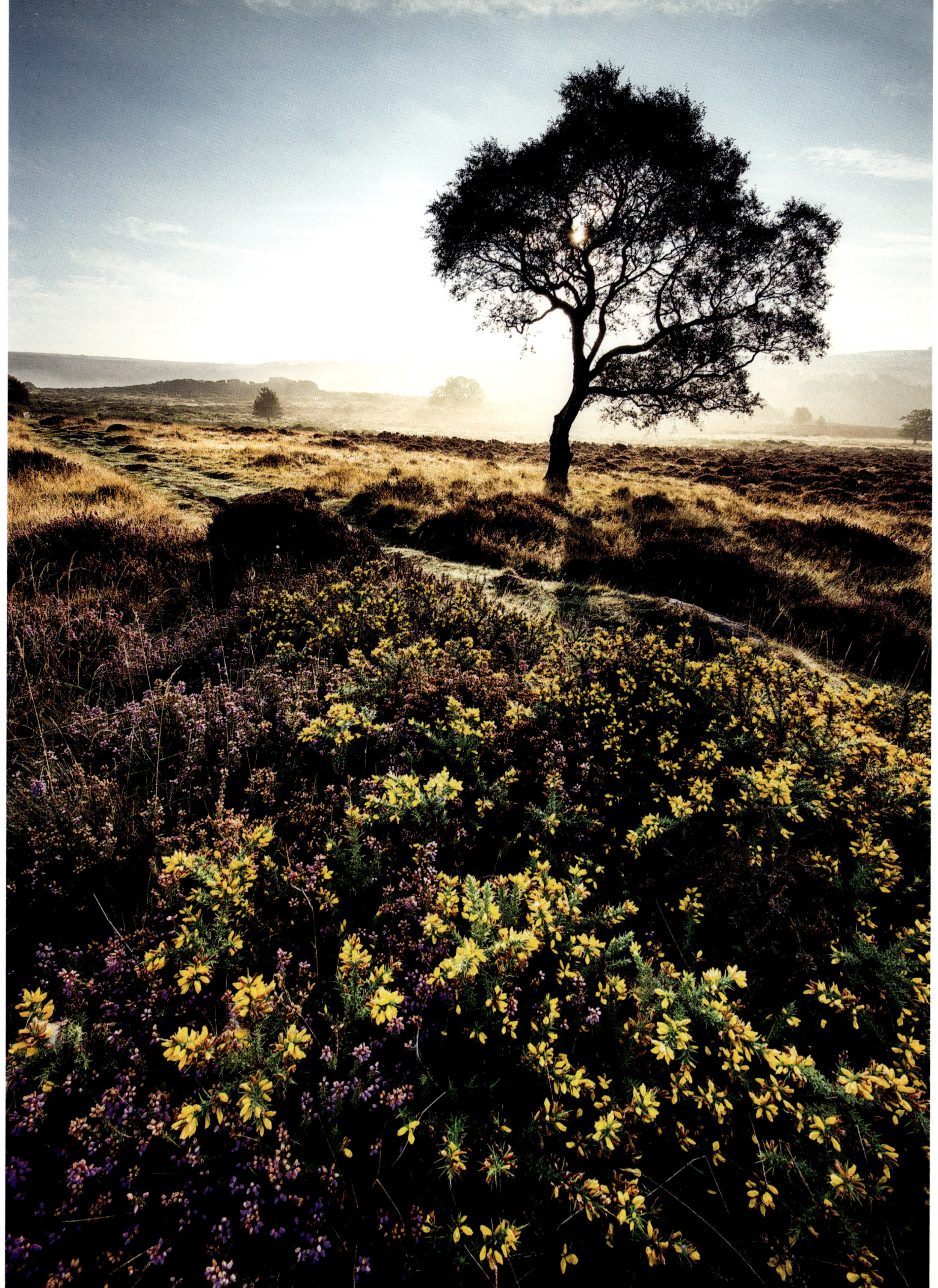

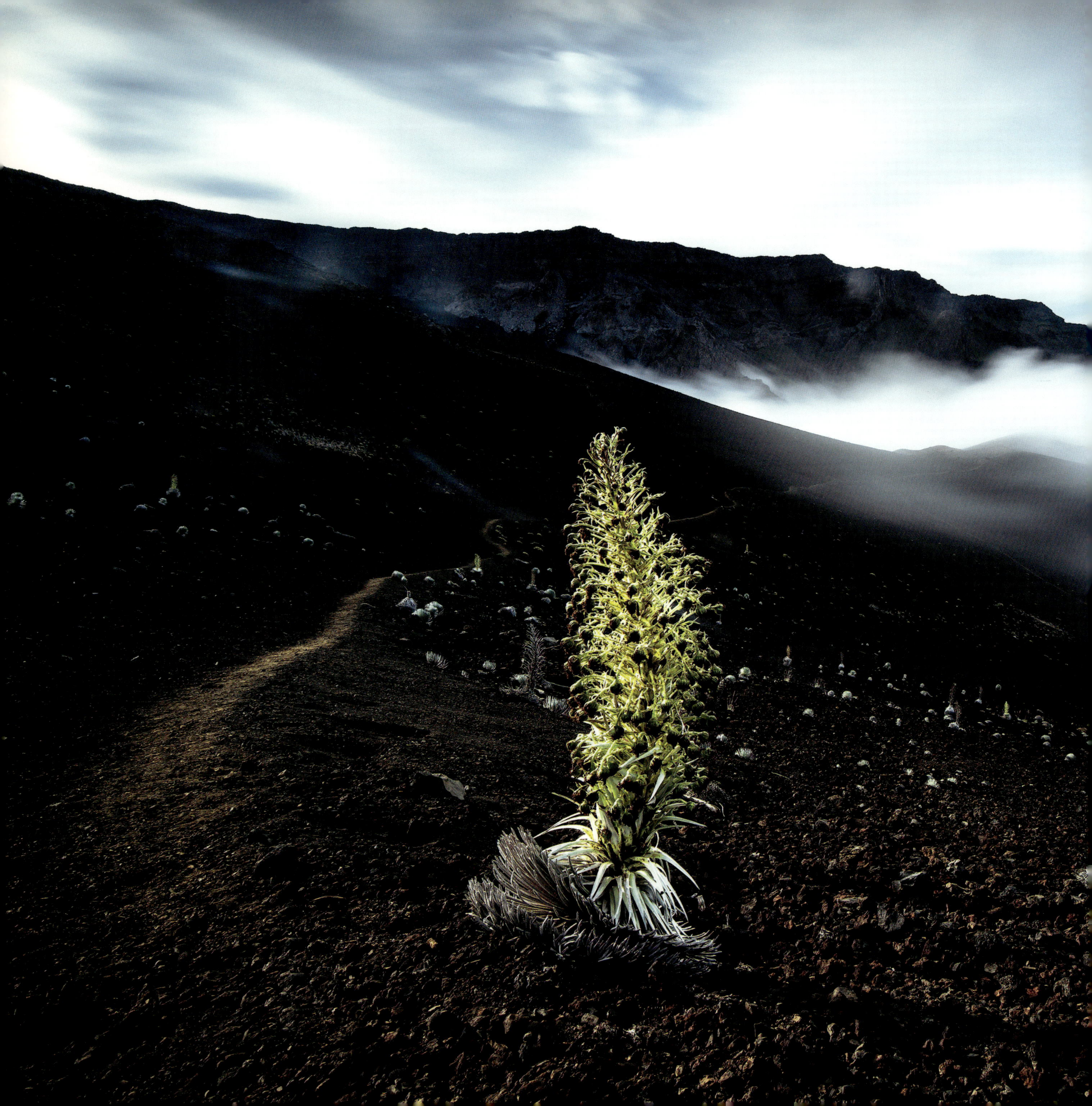

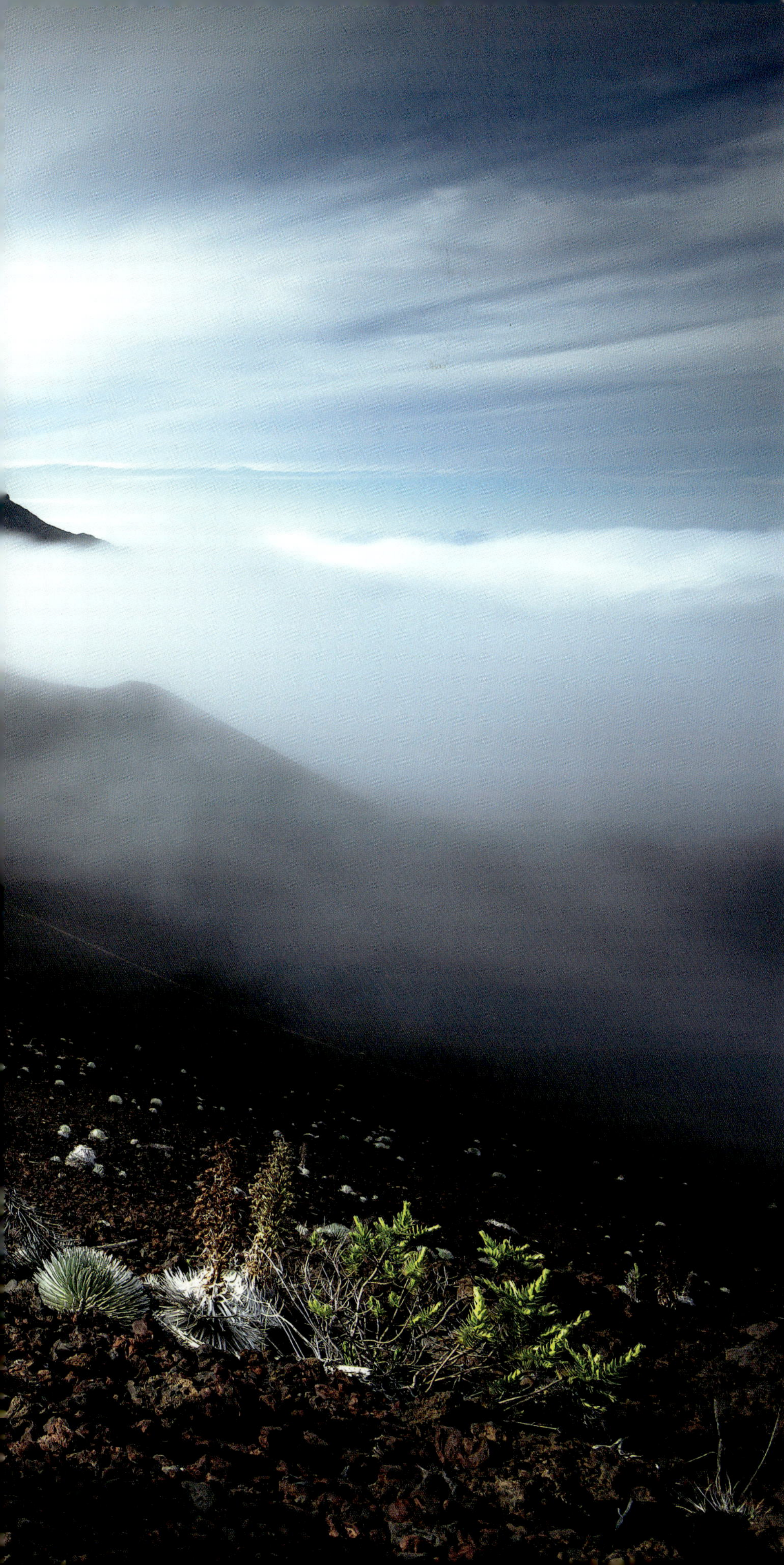

Off the Beaten Track
Haleakalā National Park, Maui, Hawaii

The silversword can live between three and ninety years and is one of Hawaii's most endangered plants. It can only be found in this crater at 10,000 feet above sea level; its rarity and uniqueness has made it the symbol of the Haleakalā National Park.

Nikon D800, Nikkor 16-35mm lens, 20sec at f/16, ISO 100. Tripod.

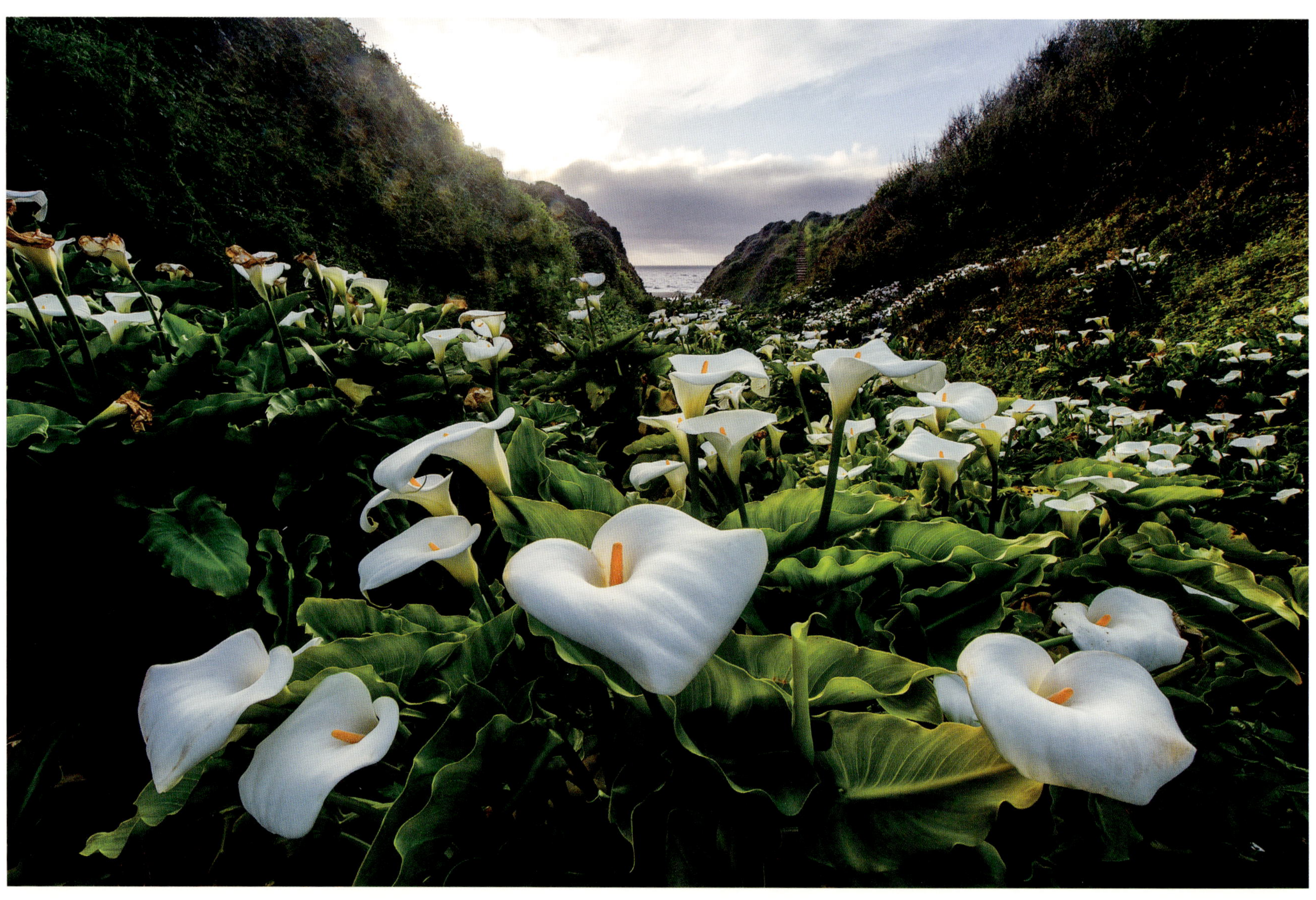

FINALIST

The Wild Cala Lily Valley
Highway One, California, USA

In Big Sur, California, there is a valley leading to the beach lined with naturalised calla lilies. It is so wonderful to smell the flowers, listen to the sound of waves and enjoy the breeze from the ocean. Photography is a kind of therapy when it becomes so relaxing and enjoyable.

Nikon D3S, Nikkor 14-24mm lens, 1/50sec at f/22. Tripod, circular polarising filter.

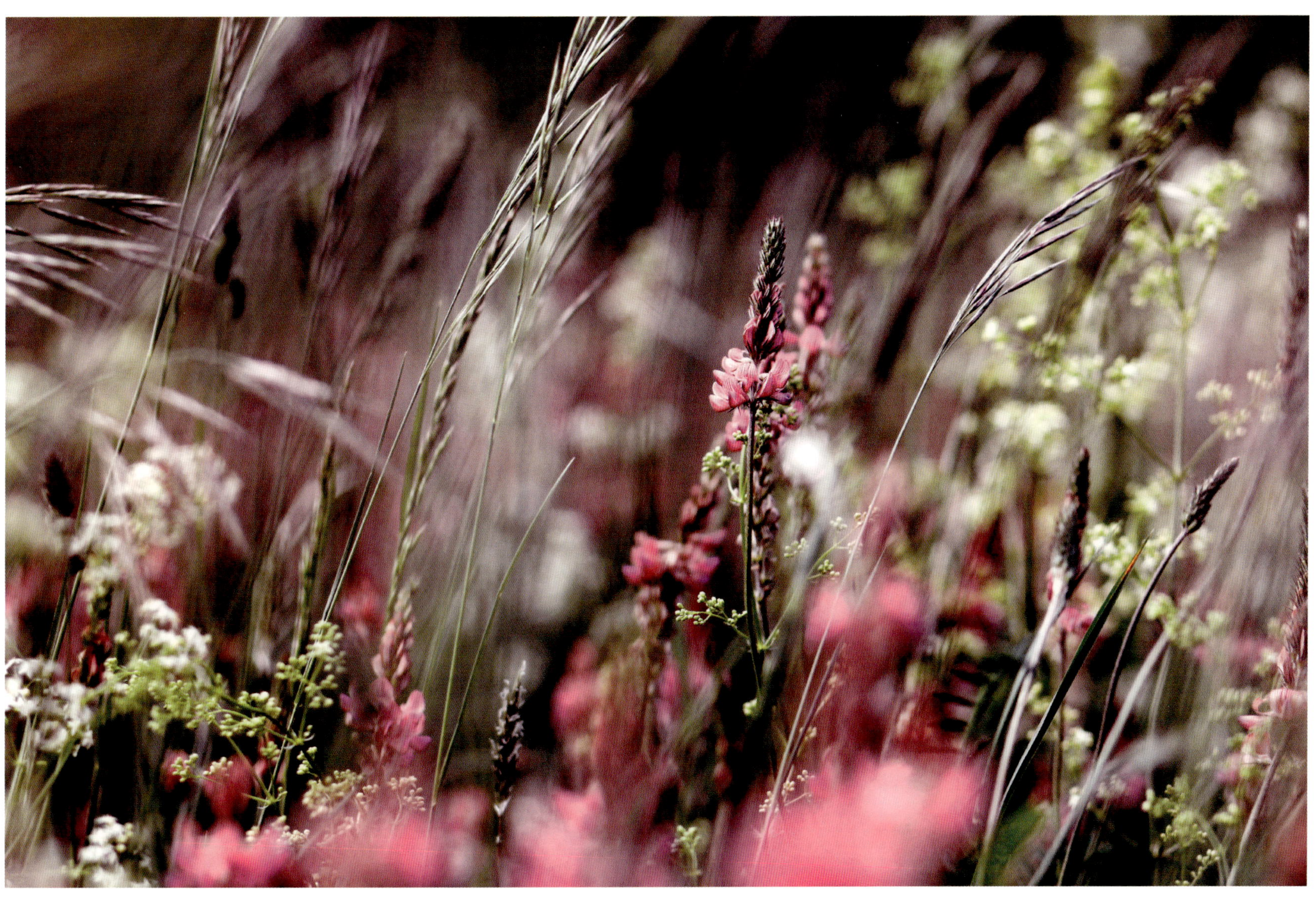

Wildflower Wilderness
Sougraigne, Midi-Pyrénées, France

This photograph was taken in a stunning wildflower meadow in south-west France. This field (along with many others) has been lovingly restored over the course of 25 years as part of a regenerative agriculture project called 'Le Paysage Comestible'.

Canon EOS 5D Mark II, Canon 85mm lens, 1/1250sec at f/2.8, ISO 100.

LESLEY CHALMERS ►

1ST PLACE

Yucca at Dusk
White Sands National Monument, New Mexico, USA

I was intrigued by the rarity and beauty of the white sand dunes, and by the challenges they pose to flora and fauna. At sunset it was quiet and there was a glow from the dunes as they reflected the changing light and colour. The shot was taken at 8.15pm local time – the light had almost completely gone and the park was closing. This single plant had come to the end of the day standing tall and in good condition, its seeds having been distributed by the 90mph hot winds of the season. A triumphant achievement, I thought.

Canon EOS 5D Mark III, Canon 24-10mm lens, 1/25sec at f/8, ISO 2000. Post-capture: basic image management.

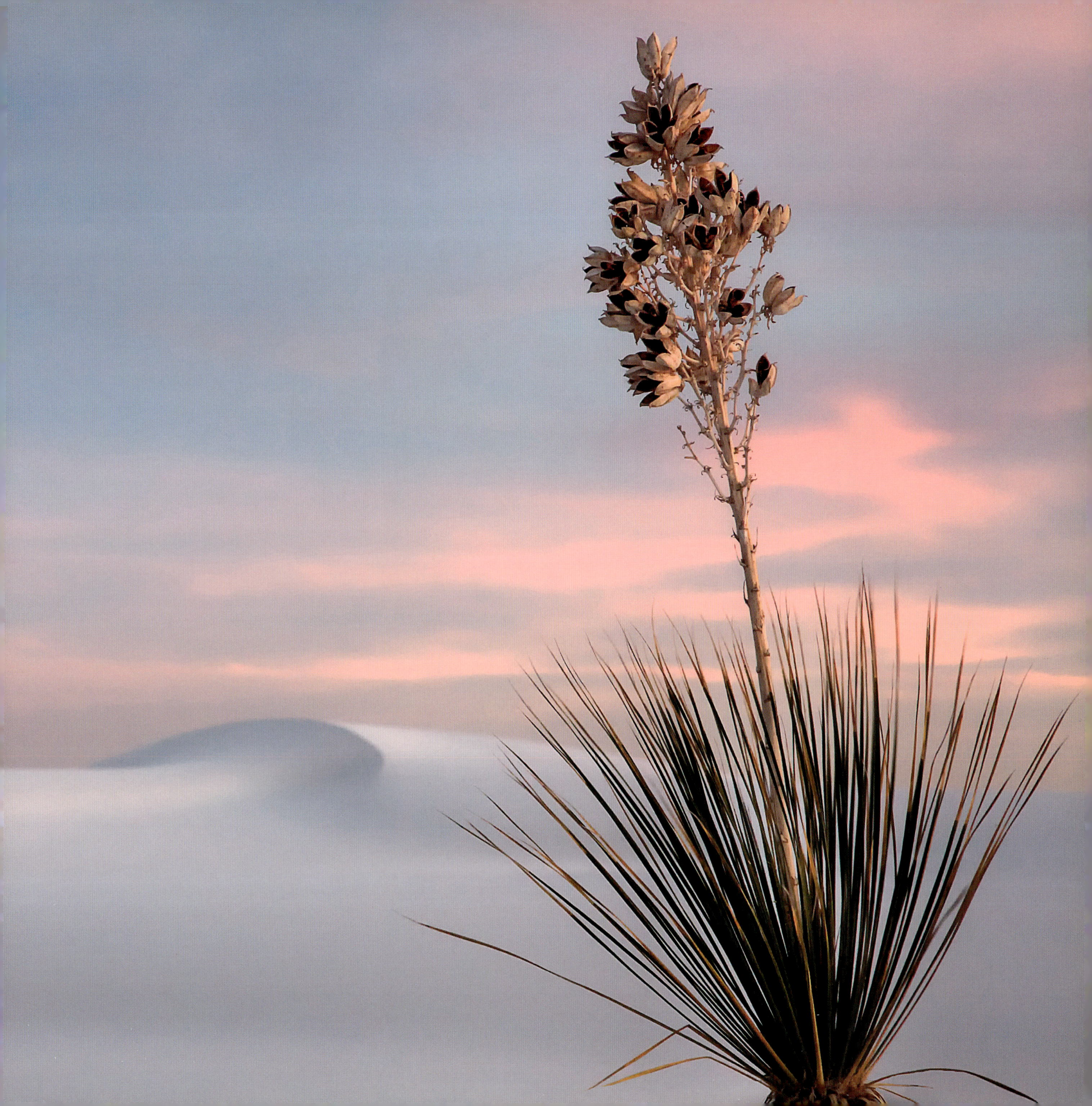

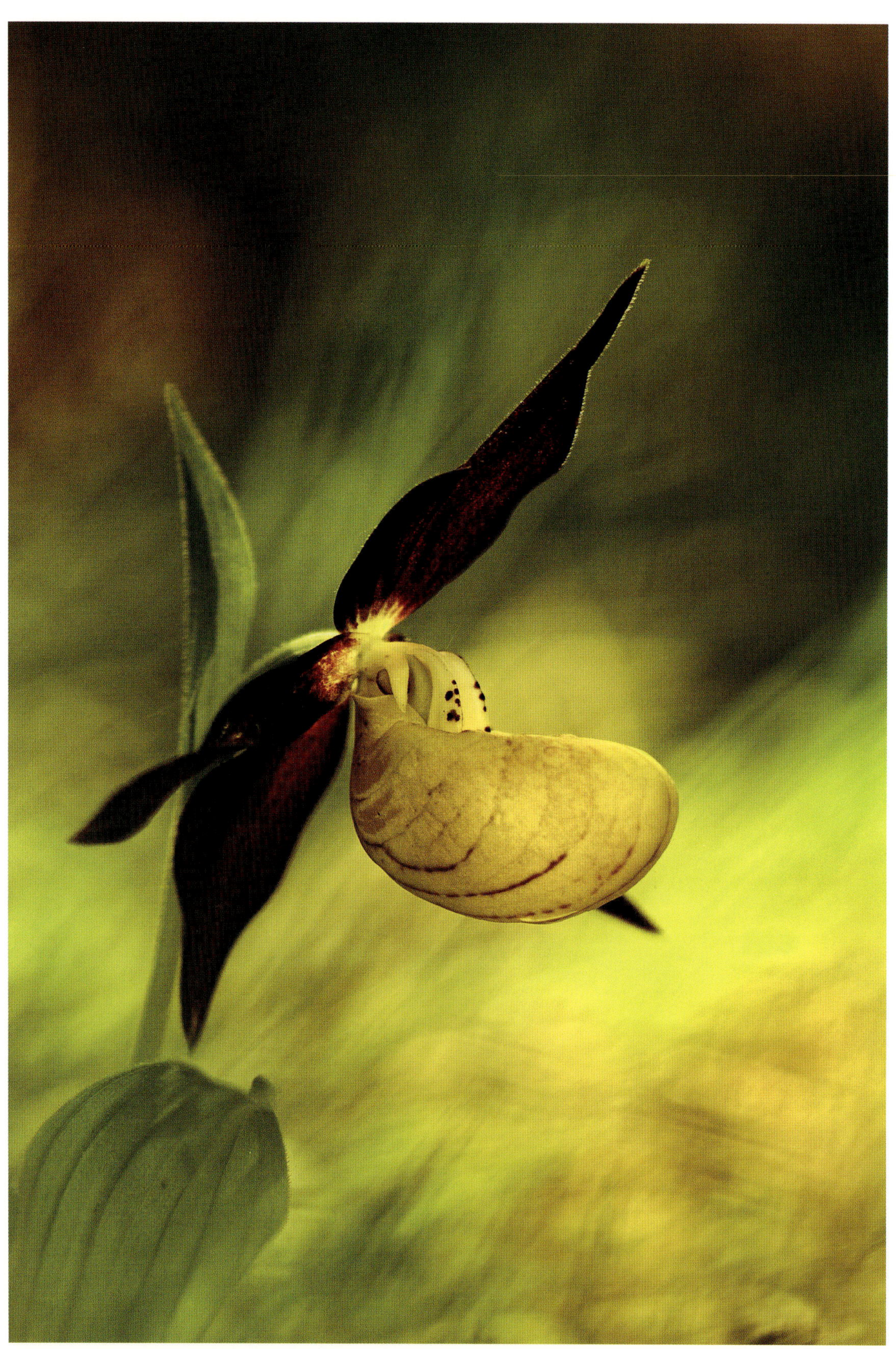

The Queen
Friulian Dolomites Natural Park, Italy

Lady's slipper is a protected species of orchid which grows in clusters. I wanted to capture a single plant portrait of this amazing orchid in order to enhance and isolate its beauty and colour.

Canon EOS 550D, Canon 300mm lens, 1/80sec at f/4, ISO 100. Tripod. Post-capture: basic image management.

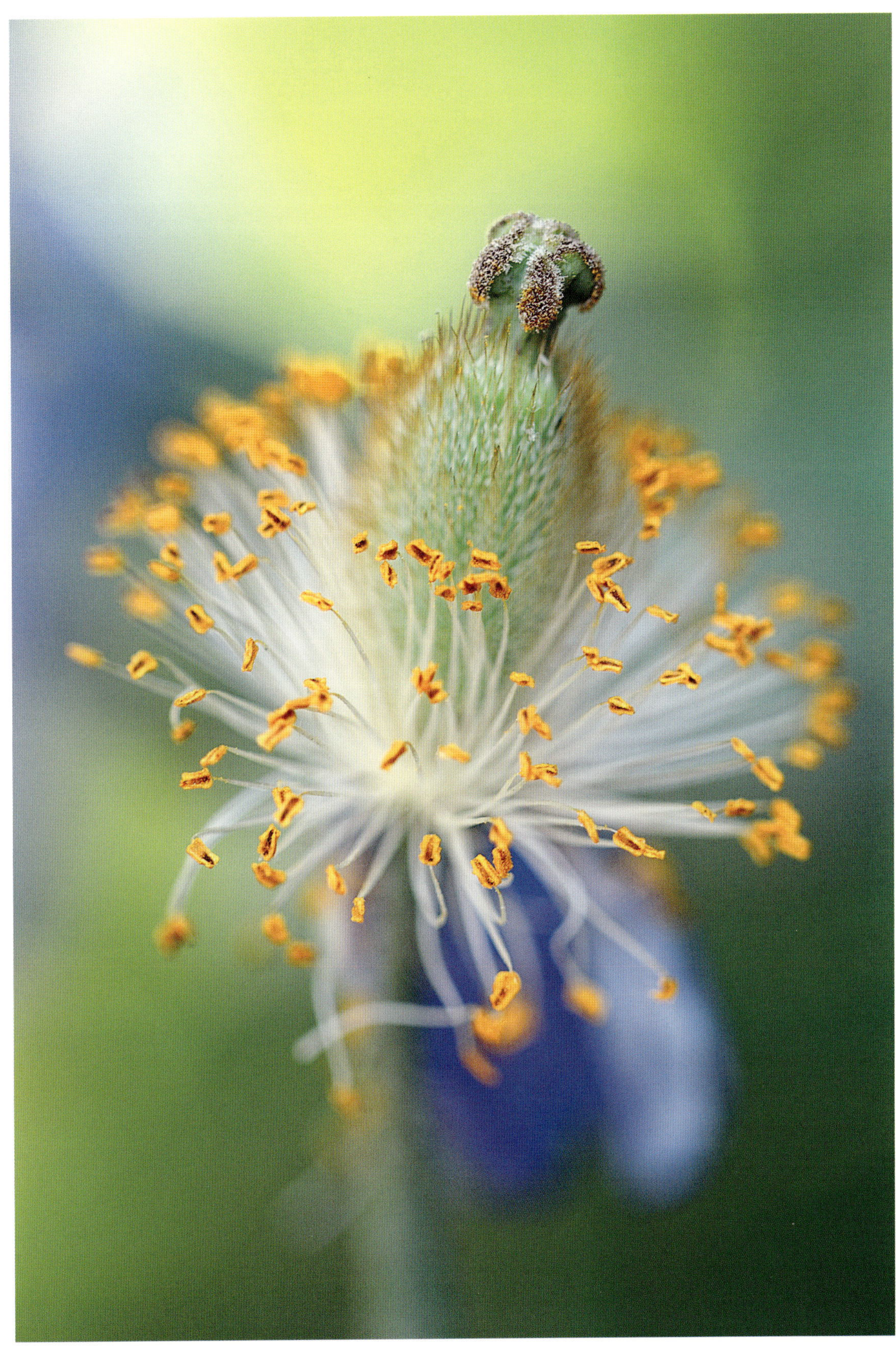

MANUELA ZINE ▶   3RD PLACE

Blue Poppy
Innsbruck Botanic Garden, Tyrol, Austria

I was attracted to this blue poppy because only one of the
blue petals remained. Besides the contrast of the different
colours - yellow, blue and green - the soft morning light made
a perfect background to emphasise the beauty of this flower.

📷 Canon EOS 6oD, Canon 100mm macro lens, 1/100sec at
f/2.8, ISO 100. Post-capture: basic image management.

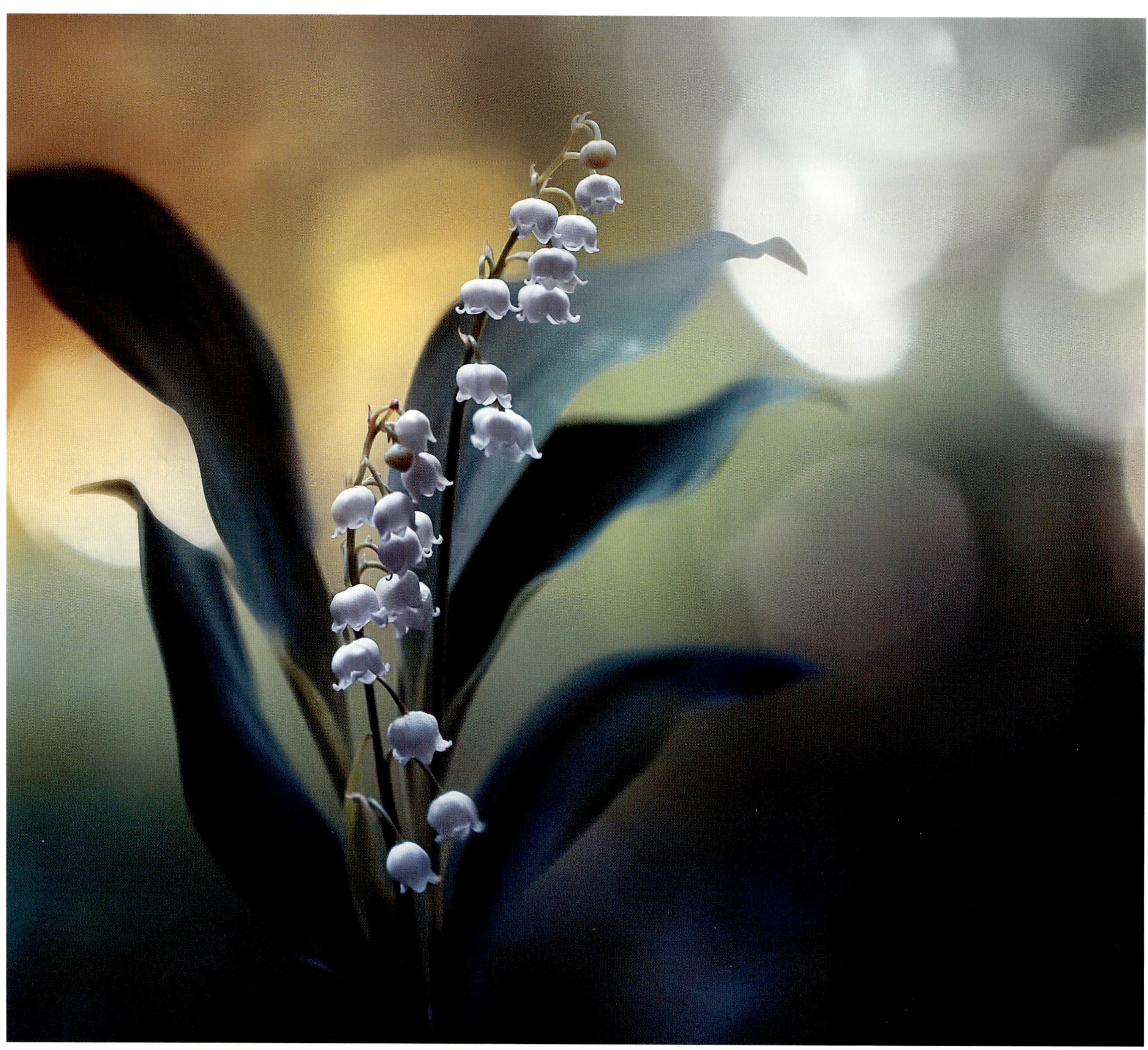

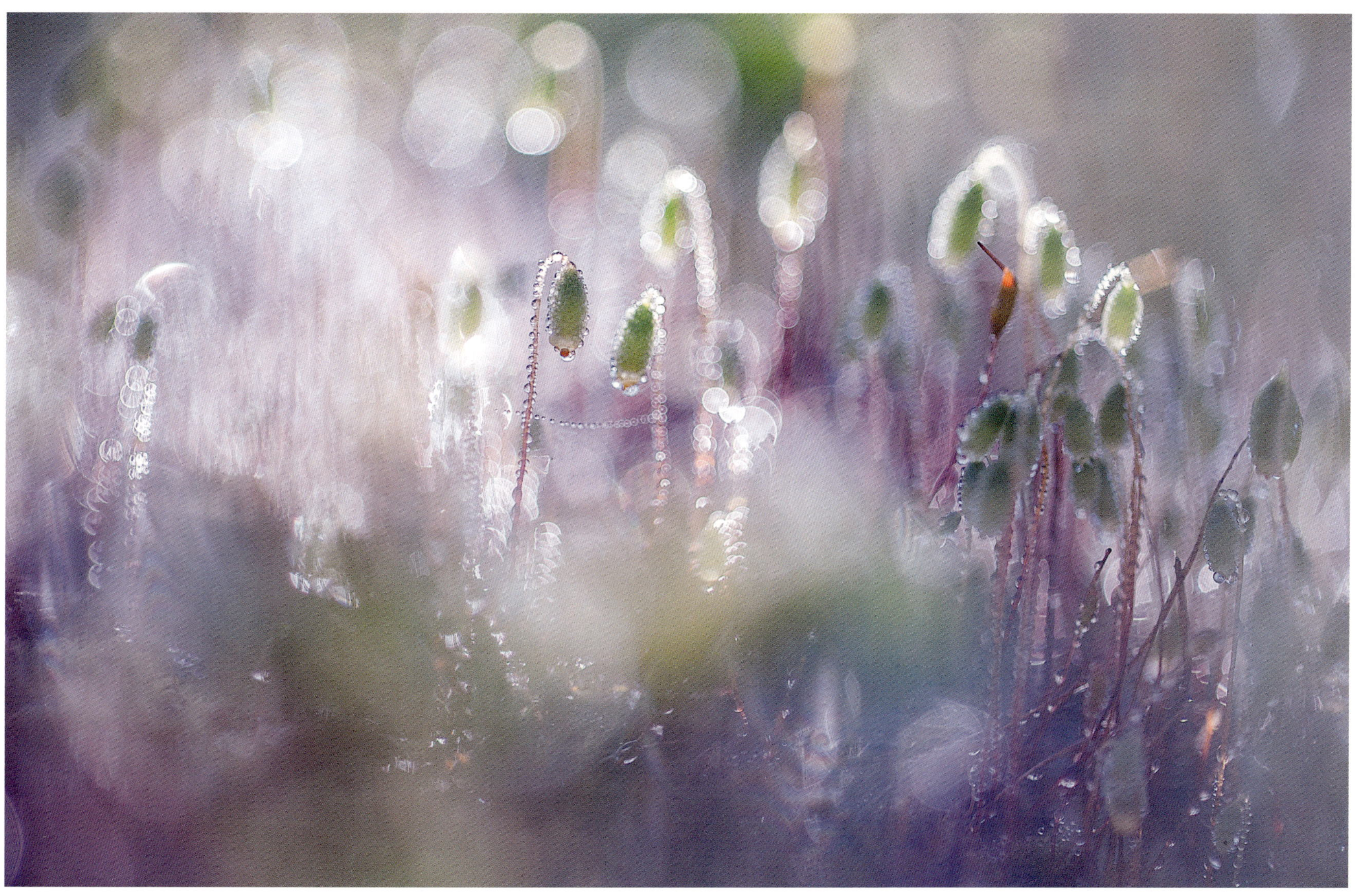

White Pearls
Waterloo, Ontario, Canada

I am fortunate to live in a city with many natural green areas. I love woods near my house and completely lose track of time when I am there. Springtime is especially amazing with the abundance of wild flowers. In the case of this photo, the evening sun cast its last rays of light through the trees and beautifully highlighted the wild lily-of-the-valley which appeared in the dark woods like little white pearls.

Canon EOS 60D, Canon 100mm macro lens, 1/100sec at f/2.8. Post-capture: basic image management.

Chained
Moscow, Russia

I take my camera with me almost everywhere I go (except the office where I work). Every weekend during the warmer period of the year I try to go out of the city to get closer to nature. On the day this was shot I woke up before sunrise hoping to enjoy a day of macro photography. I started with insects but then I knelt down to the moss which was covered in dew, giving it a delicate, crystalline appearance.

Nikon D700, Nikon 105mm lens, 1/800sec at f/4.5, ISO 200. Post-capture: adjusted the white balance.

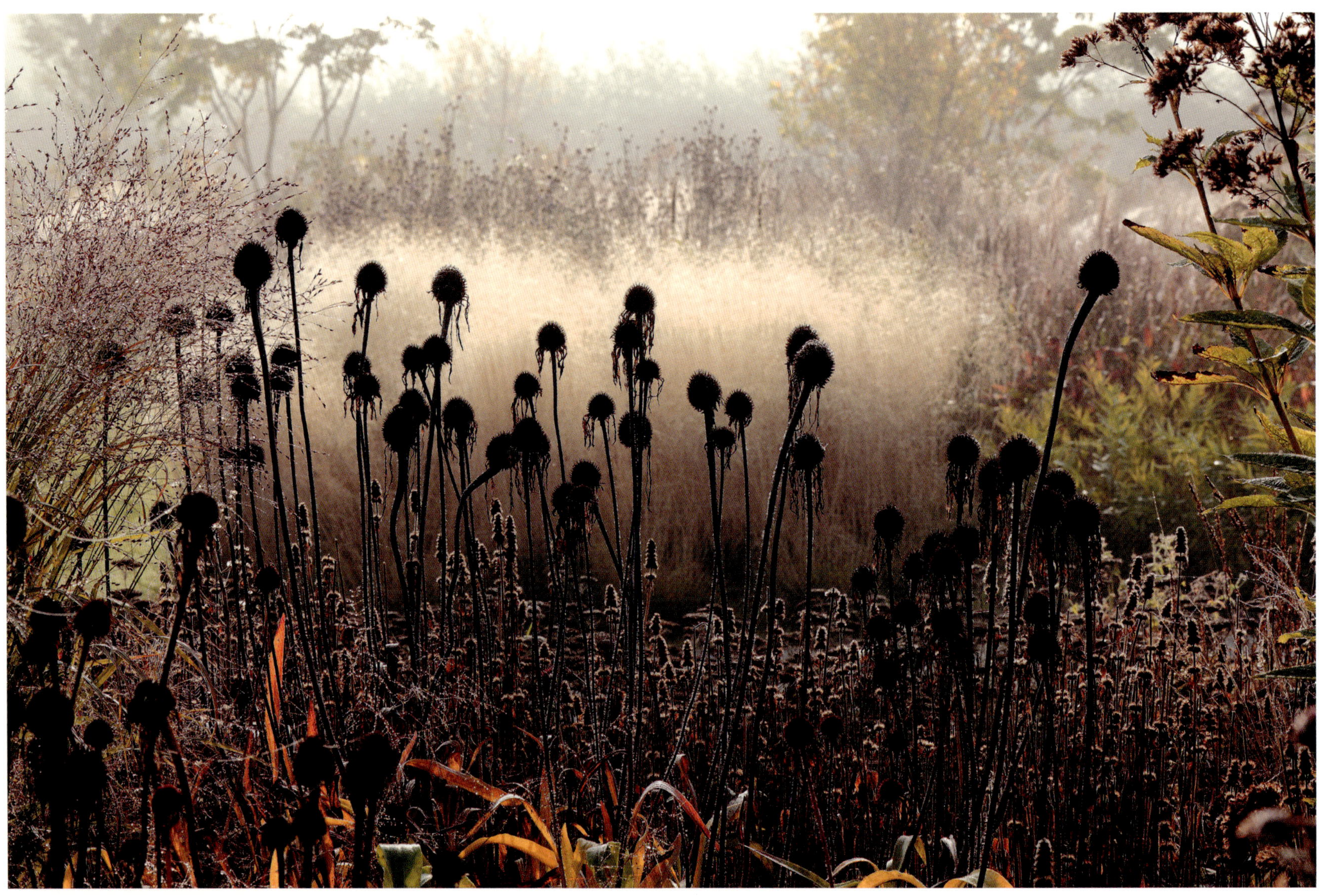

▲ HANS VAN HORSSEN FINALIST

Sound of Silence
De Vlinderhof, Maximapark, Utrecht, Netherlands

I was inspired by the beauty of decay, the extraordinary autumn colours and the peaceful atmosphere of the foggy weather. The faded flowers (*Echinacea pallida*) look like musical notation in the air. These to me are the notes which make the 'Sound of Silence'.

Canon EOS 6D, Canon 100mm lens, 1/200sec at f/16, ISO 640. Post-capture: basic image management.

GABOR KOVACS ▶ HIGHLY COMMENDED

Orange Dusk
Lake Velence, Hungary

This *Pulsatilla* plant has a very short, specific period of the year when it flowers. It was a very interesting subject to photograph, especially in the right light conditions which highlighted its layer of hairy trichomes.

Canon EOS 5D Mark II, Tamron 180mm macro lens, 1/80sec at f/3.5, ISO 200.

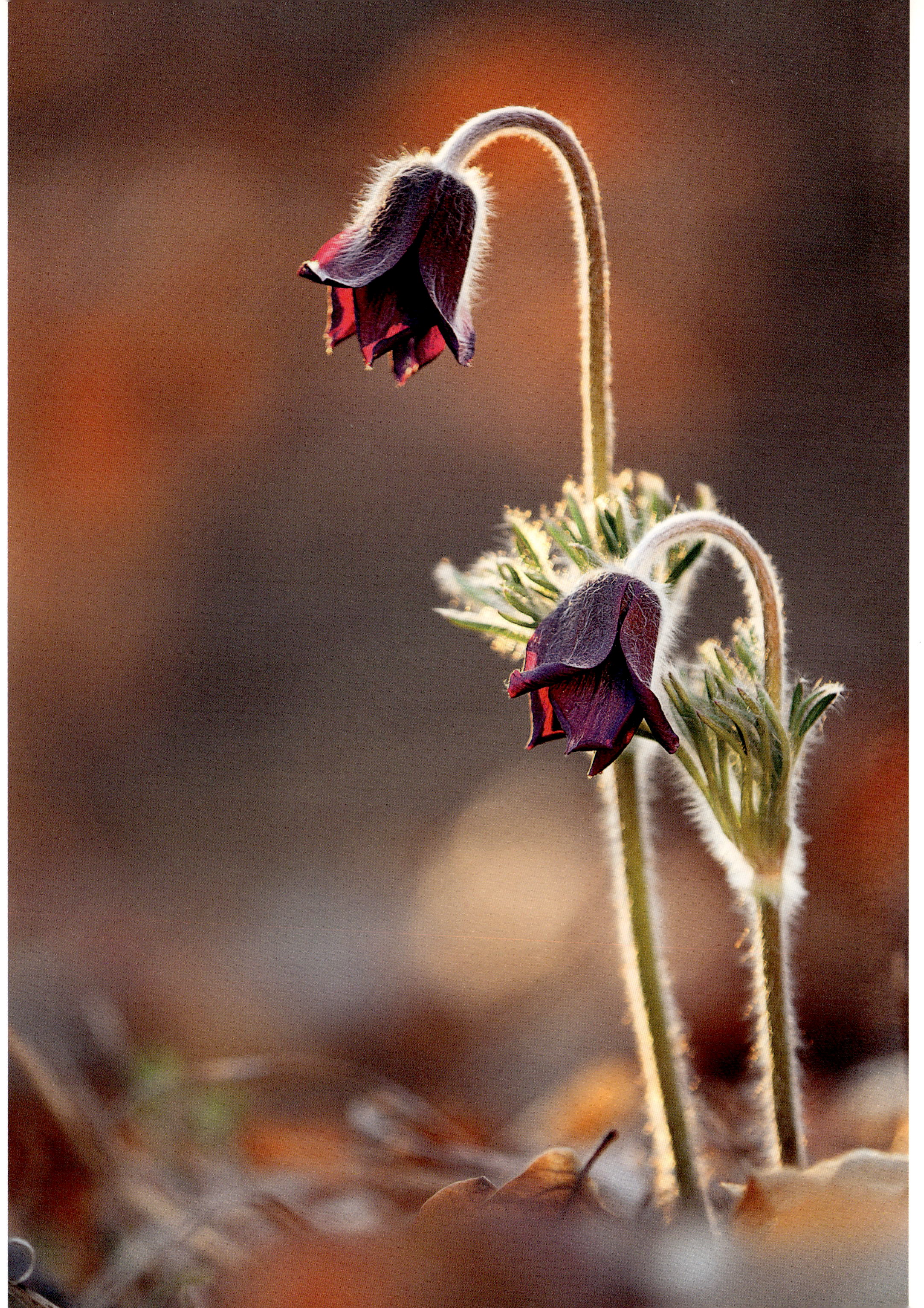

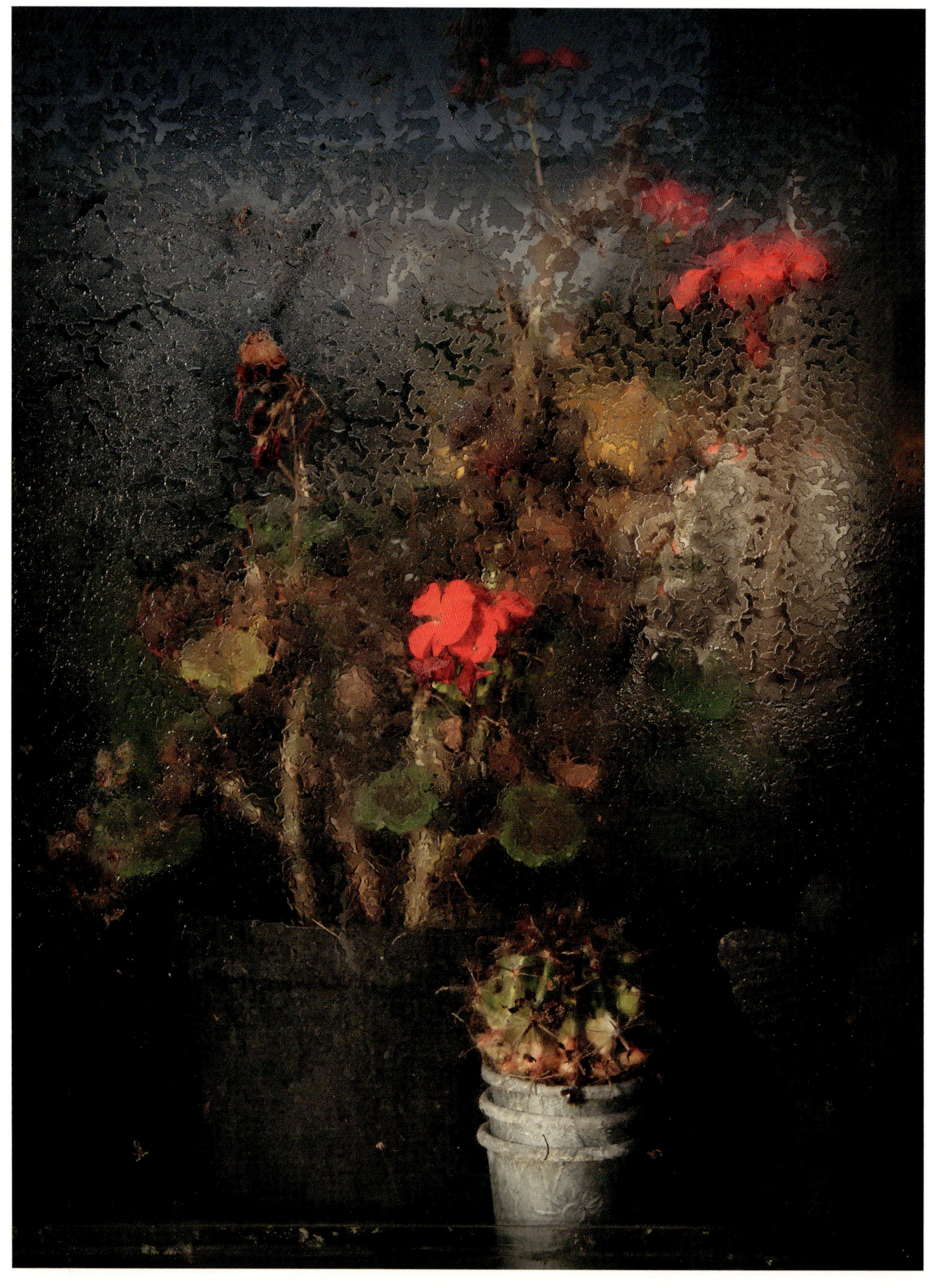

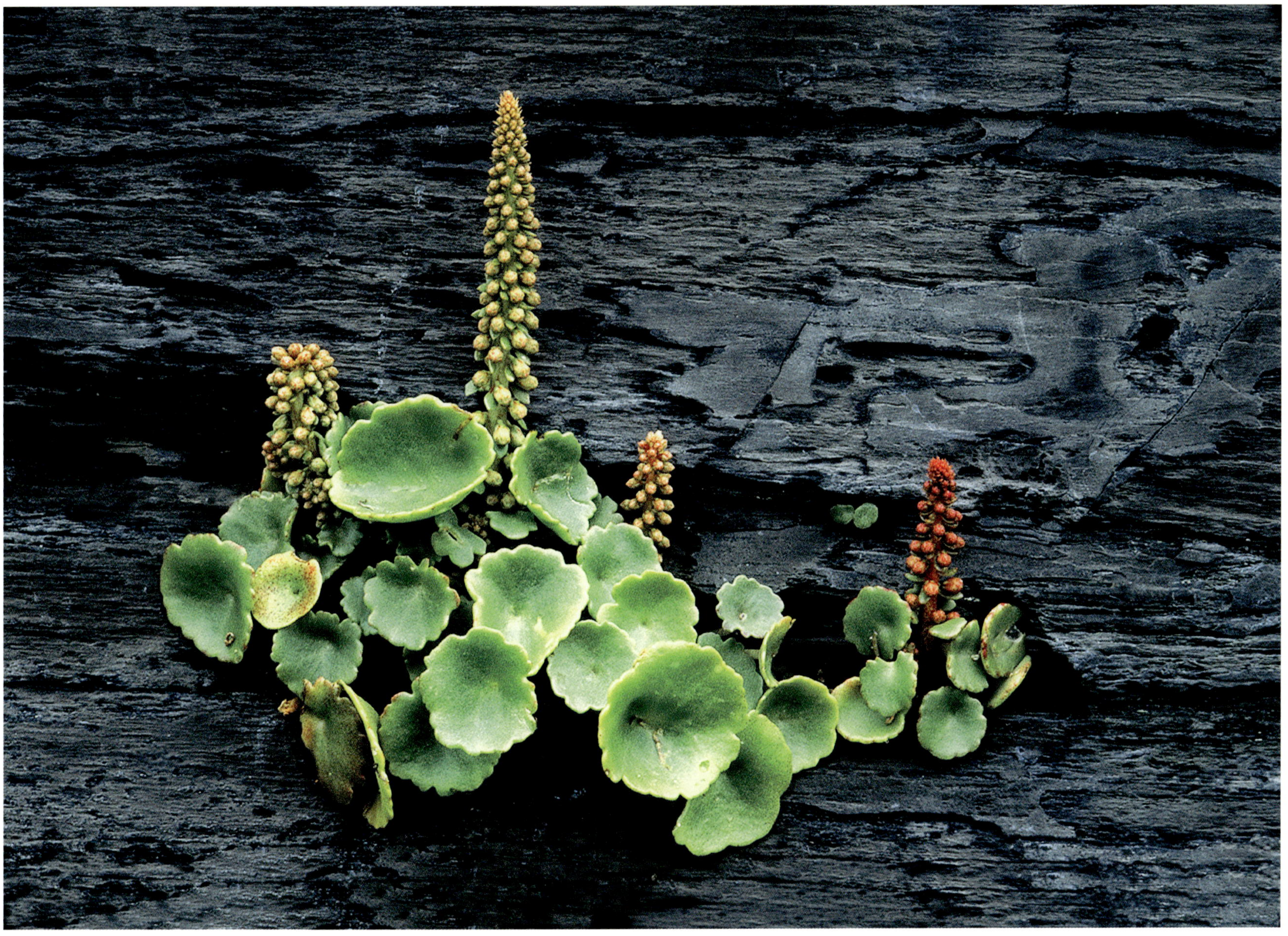

◀ **REBECCA NEX**   HIGHLY COMMENDED

The Frosted Greenhouse
Colchester, Essex, England, UK

This photograph is one of a series of images taken in winter of the greenhouse in my parents' garden. This particular day there was a frost pattern all over the window and a lovely early morning winter sun. The *Pelargonium* had been left in the greenhouse from the summer, and the petals were pressed up against the window, with the warm sunlight enhancing their vibrant colour. I was drawn to the image of the *Pelargonium* and cactus, well past their prime but still adding beauty to the otherwise cold scene. The frost on the window and the dirt on the glass softened and diffused the whole image, giving an almost impressionist, painterly feel to the picture.

Canon EOS 30D, Canon 17-85mm lens, 1/500sec at f/5.6, ISO 400. Post-capture: the edges were darkened with a vignette.

▲ **GILLIAN JONES**   HIGHLY COMMENDED

Wall Pennywort
Abereiddy, Pembrokeshire, Wales, UK

This wall pennywort was growing in the slate within a disused quarry. The flower bears candle-like spikes which rise to different heights amidst the fleshy, round, succulent leaves. This contrasted nicely with the dark slate background.

Canon EOS 3, Canon 28-200mm lens, 1/50sec at f/16. Tripod. Post-capture: slide scanned with a Nikon 5 digital scanner.

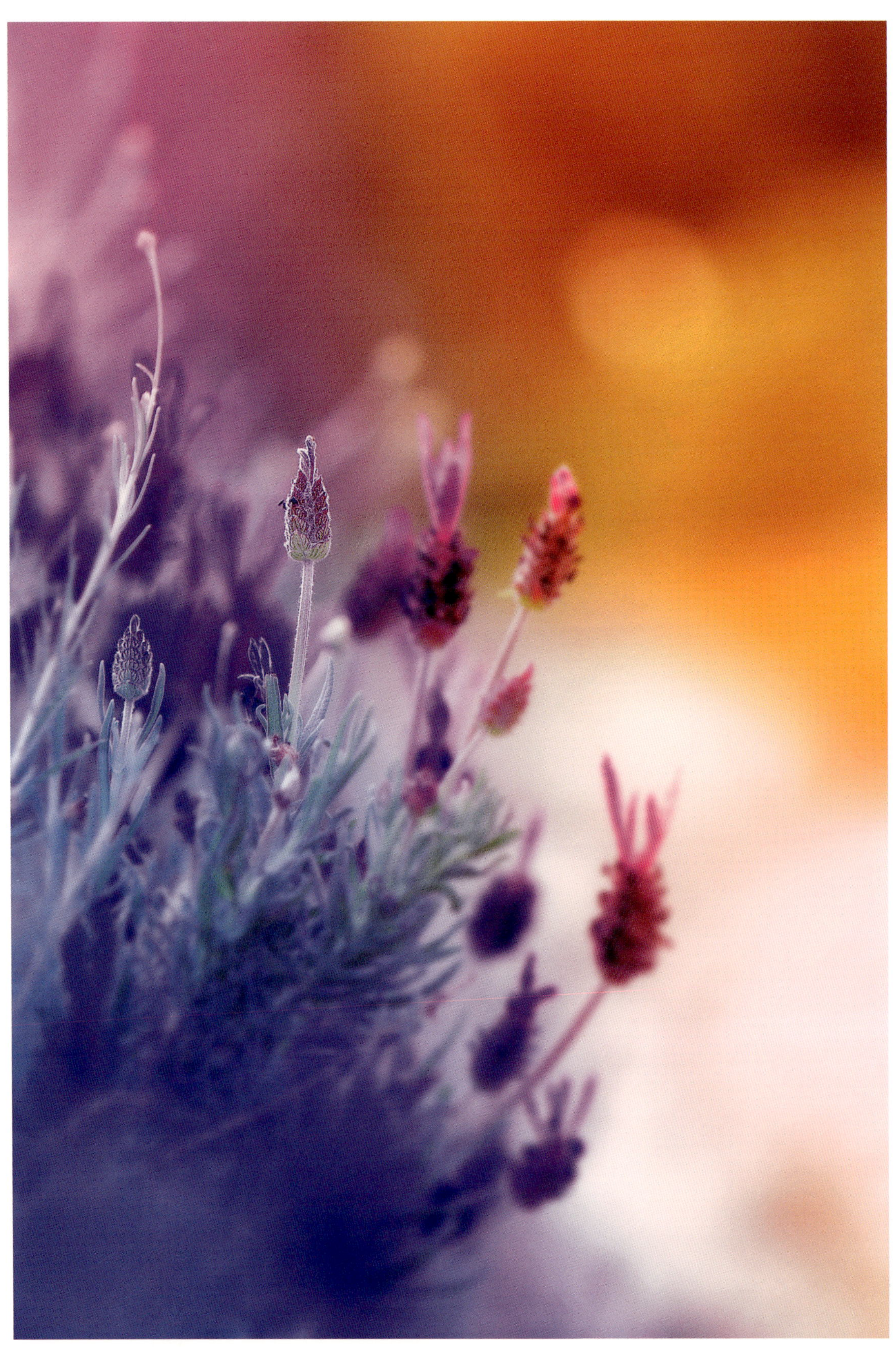

Newborns
Tróia, Grândola, Portugal

The flowers of this *Lavandula stoechas* were bursting with perfume and colour. I loved the shape of them and searched for the perfect cluster to photograph; I chose those which were just coming into bloom.

Canon EOS 6oD, Canon 100mm macro lens, 1/18osec at f/2.8, ISO 100. Post-capture: adjusted temperature and curves gradient, added a blurred vignette and selective sharpening.

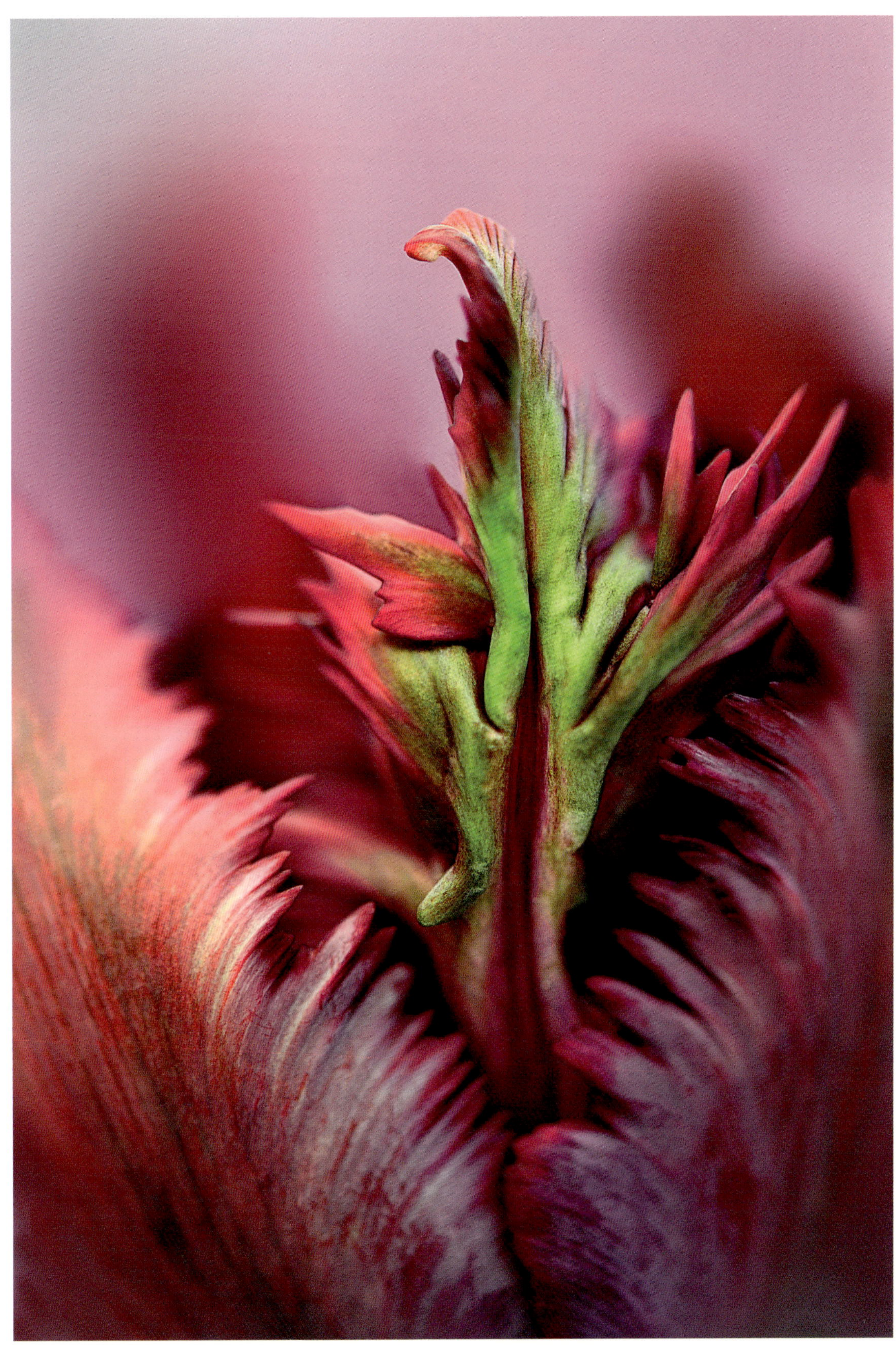

CHRISTIANE VANDROUX ▶   FINALIST

A Parade of Tulip
Chalon-sur-Saône, Burgundy, France

I like the outlines of parrot tulips, which remind me of
ephemeral sculptures. Every year, I observe them at length;
I particularly admired this new variety planted in my garden
last autumn. I was seduced by the contrast between the
central green petal and the warm shades of pink and purple
surrounding it.

Nikon D800E, Nikon 105mm lens, 1/320sec at f/3.5,
ISO 200. Post-capture: basic image management.

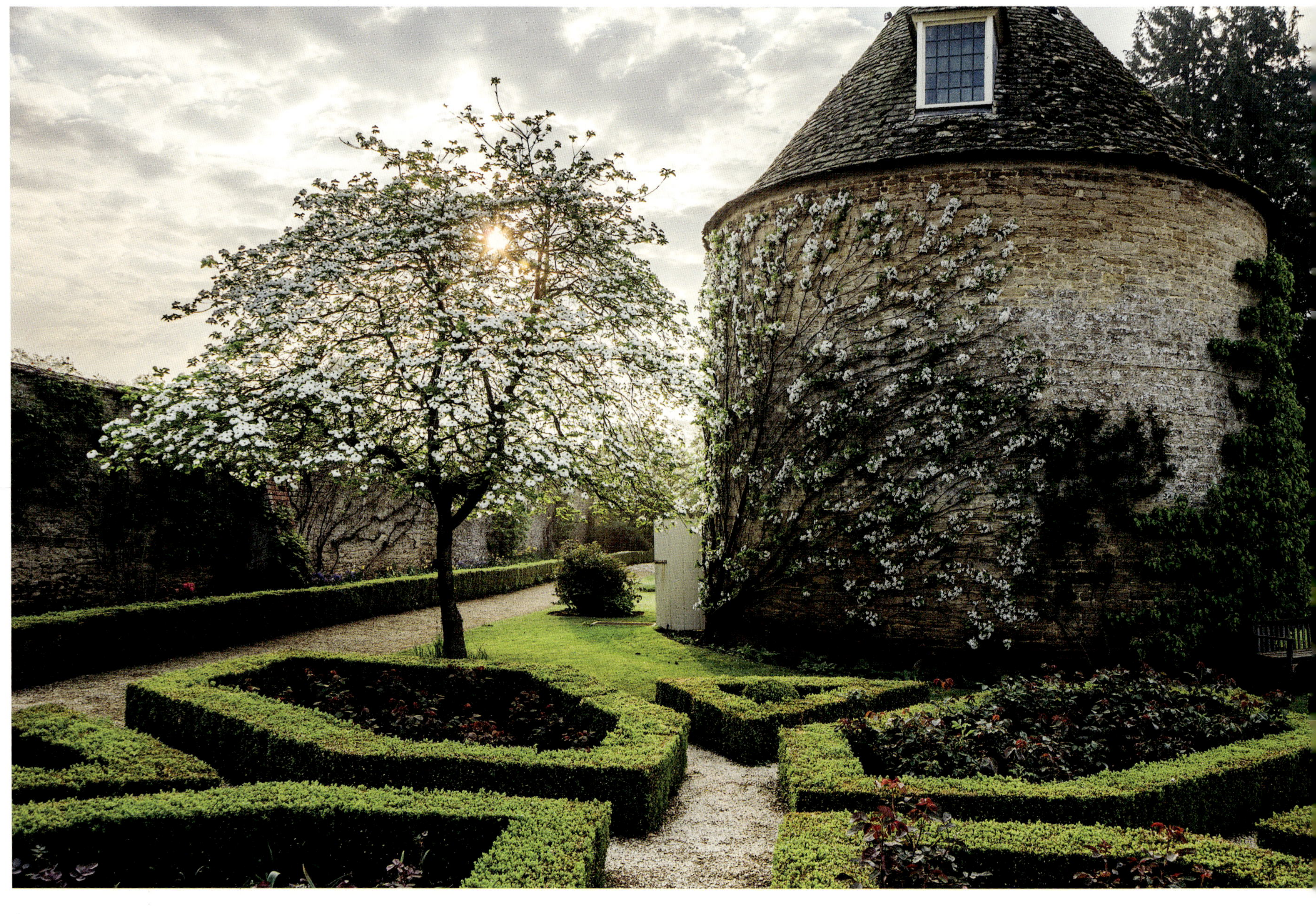

CAROLE DRAKE   1ST PLACE

Pigeon House at Dawn
Rousham House, Oxfordshire, England, UK

April is a special time in gardens, when everything is fresh and newly minted. The *Cornus*,
the blossom on the trained fruit tree and the crimson leaves on the rose bushes all signal the
beginning of the growing season. I was inspired by the balance of shapes in the garden, which
provided the perfect accompaniment to the breaking dawn and beautiful pearlescent light.

Nikon D700, Nikkor 24-85mm lens, 1/60sec at f/10, ISO 200. Tripod.

ROGER FOLEY   2ND PLACE

Sun Shower
Ruxton, Maryland, USA

I was photographing the garden on a gorgeous June morning when I felt a drop hit my hand.
At first I thought it was from an angry bird, but then I realised there was a tiny storm cloud up
in the bright blue sky. I went up to the house to keep the camera dry, then turned around in the
doorway to see fat raindrops hit the terrace as the sun poured through the maple. I rushed to set
up a tripod at a low angle and got off four shots before the rain stopped.

Canon EOS 5D Mark III, Canon 24-105mm lens, 1/15sec at f/11, ISO 400. Tripod.

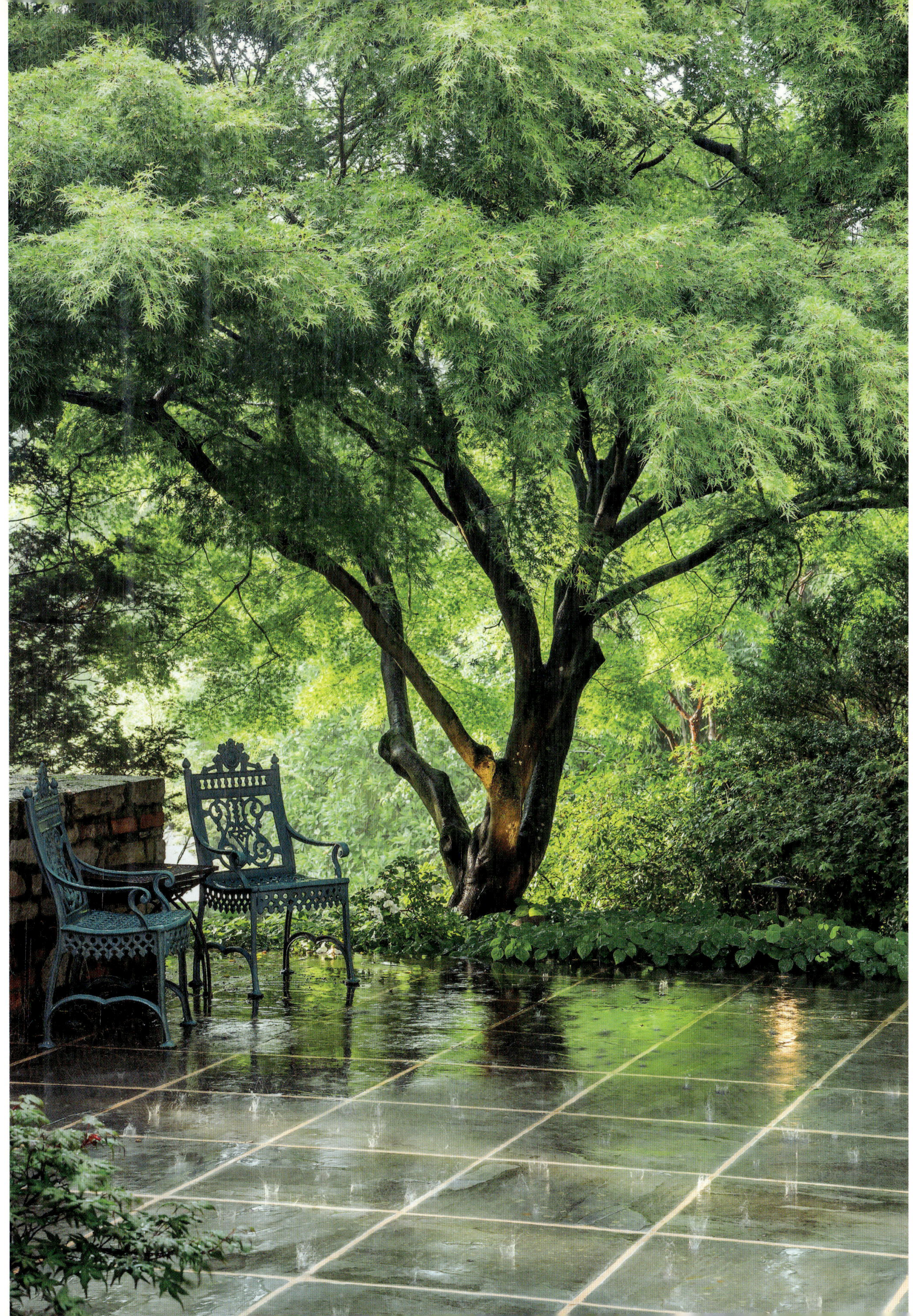

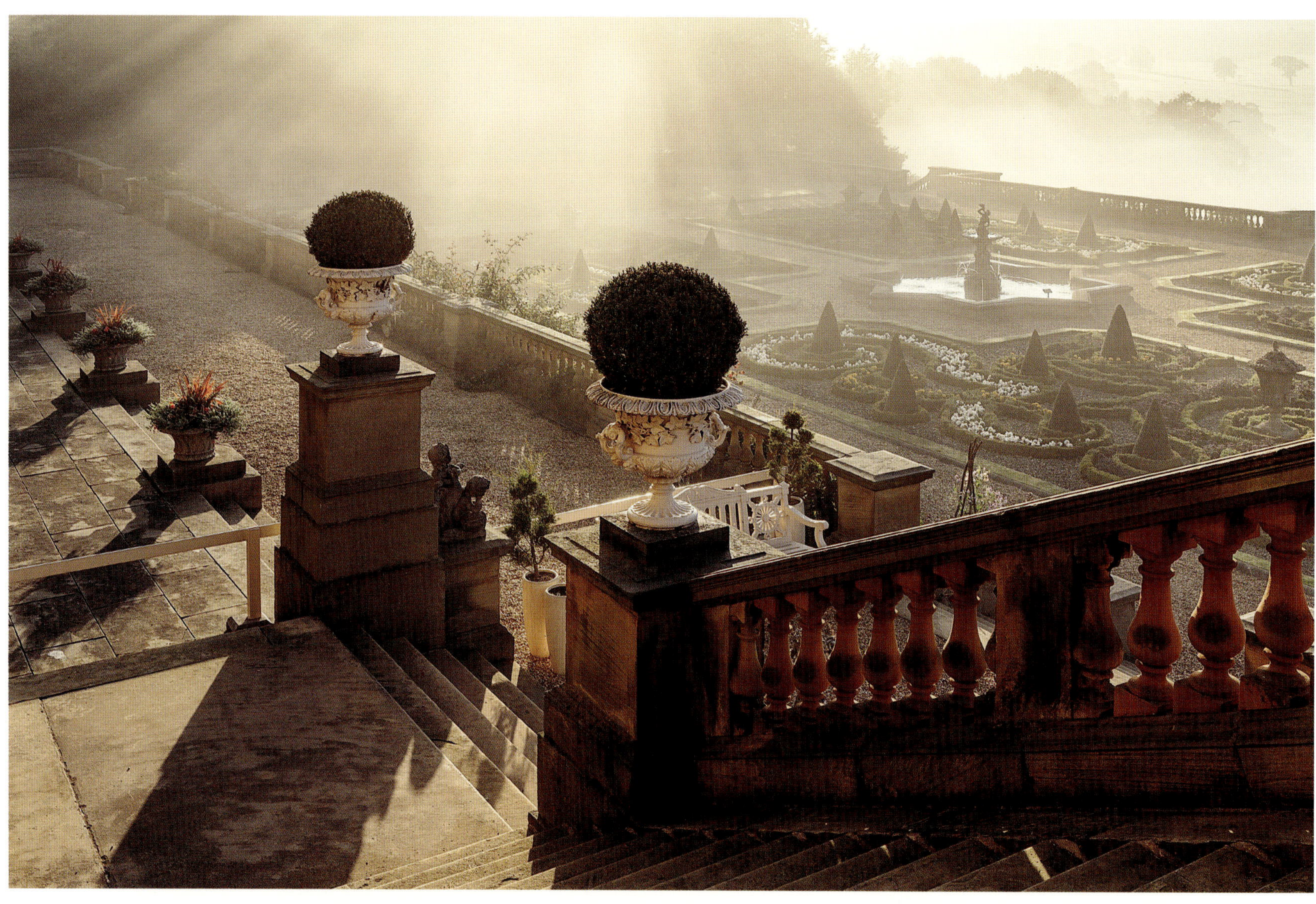

Misty Morning Magic
Yorkshire, England, UK

This is the Terrace Garden at Harewood House. It shows the view from the steps of the Terrace
Café over the parterre and on to the Capability Brown landscape beyond. The scene just got
better and better as the sun rose above the trees at the edge of the garden and burnt through the
early morning mist. I composed the shot to include the countryside in the distance so that I could
capture the mist-shrouded trees.

Canon EOS 5D Mark II, Canon 24-70mm lens, 1/40sec to 1/160sec at f/16, ISO 400. Tripod,
cable release. Post-capture: three different exposures were merged, basic image management.

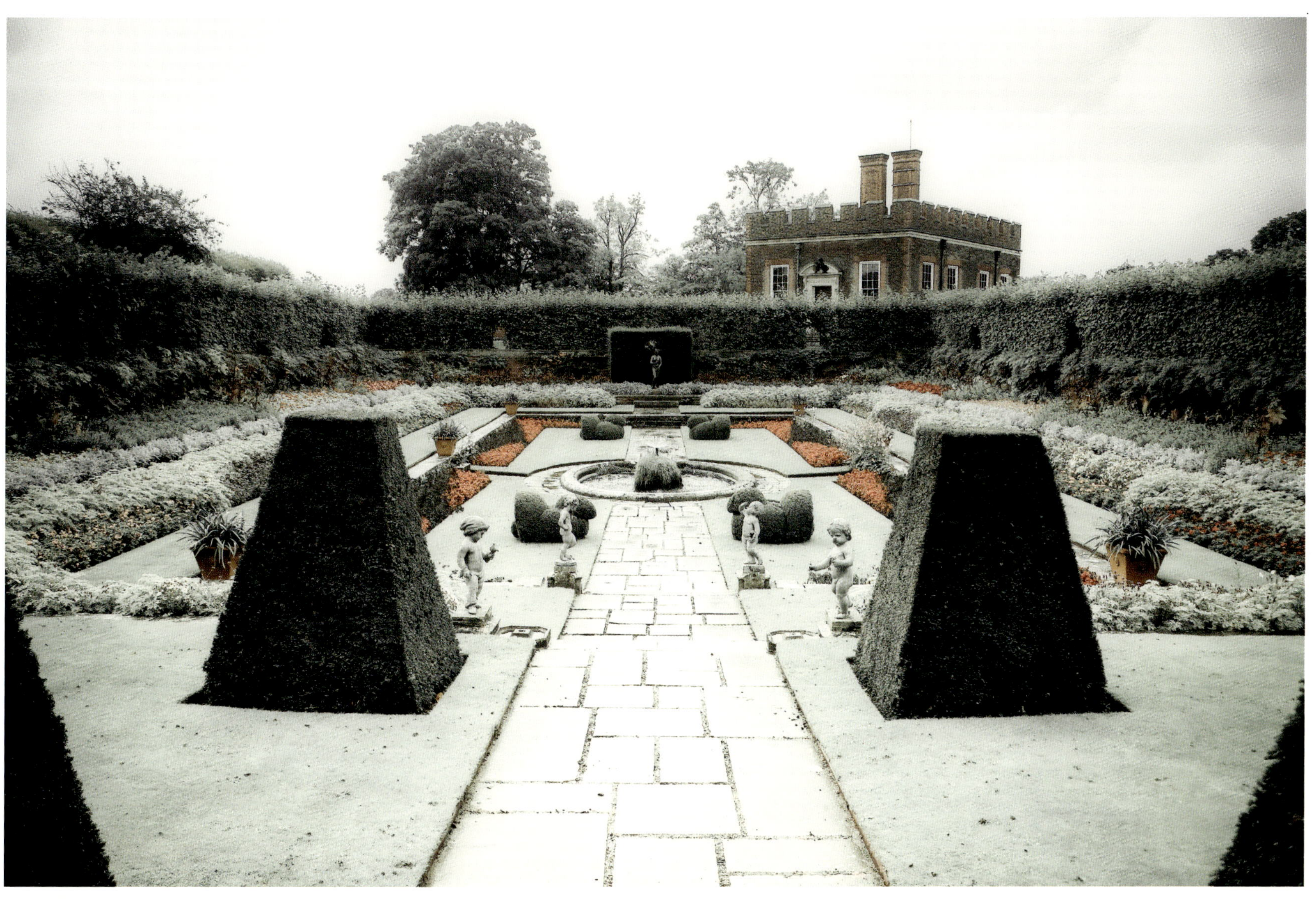

SIMON HADLEIGH-SPARKS FINALIST

The Pond Gardens
Hampton Court, Surrey, England, UK

This is the first of two sunken pond gardens, that were originally ornamental ponds for freshwater fish. Today they are planted with a glorious selection of spring and late summer flowers.

Canon EOS 5D Mark III, Canon 17-40mm lens, 1/200sec at f/9, ISO 200. Post-capture: basic image management, altered with a filter.

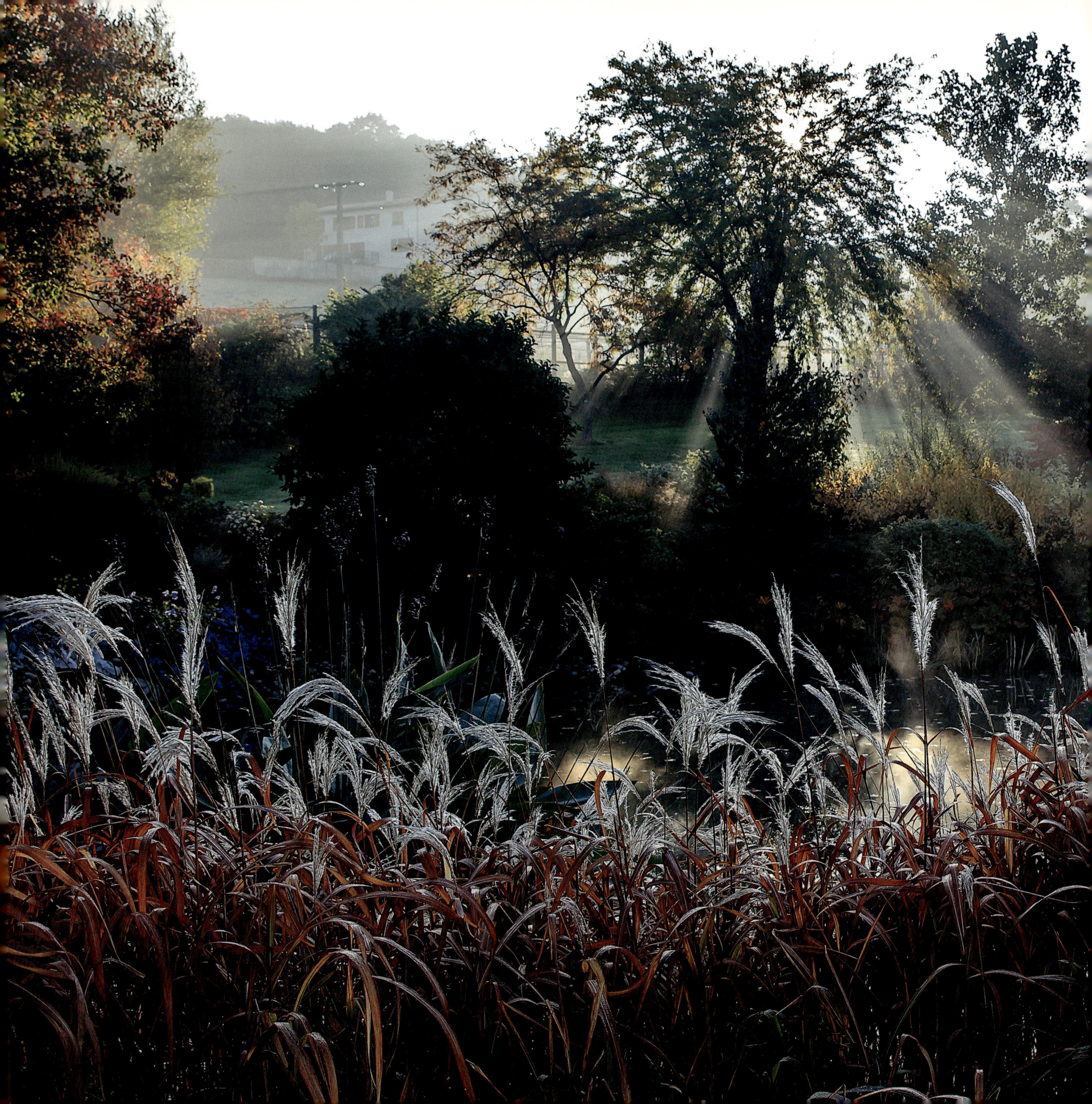

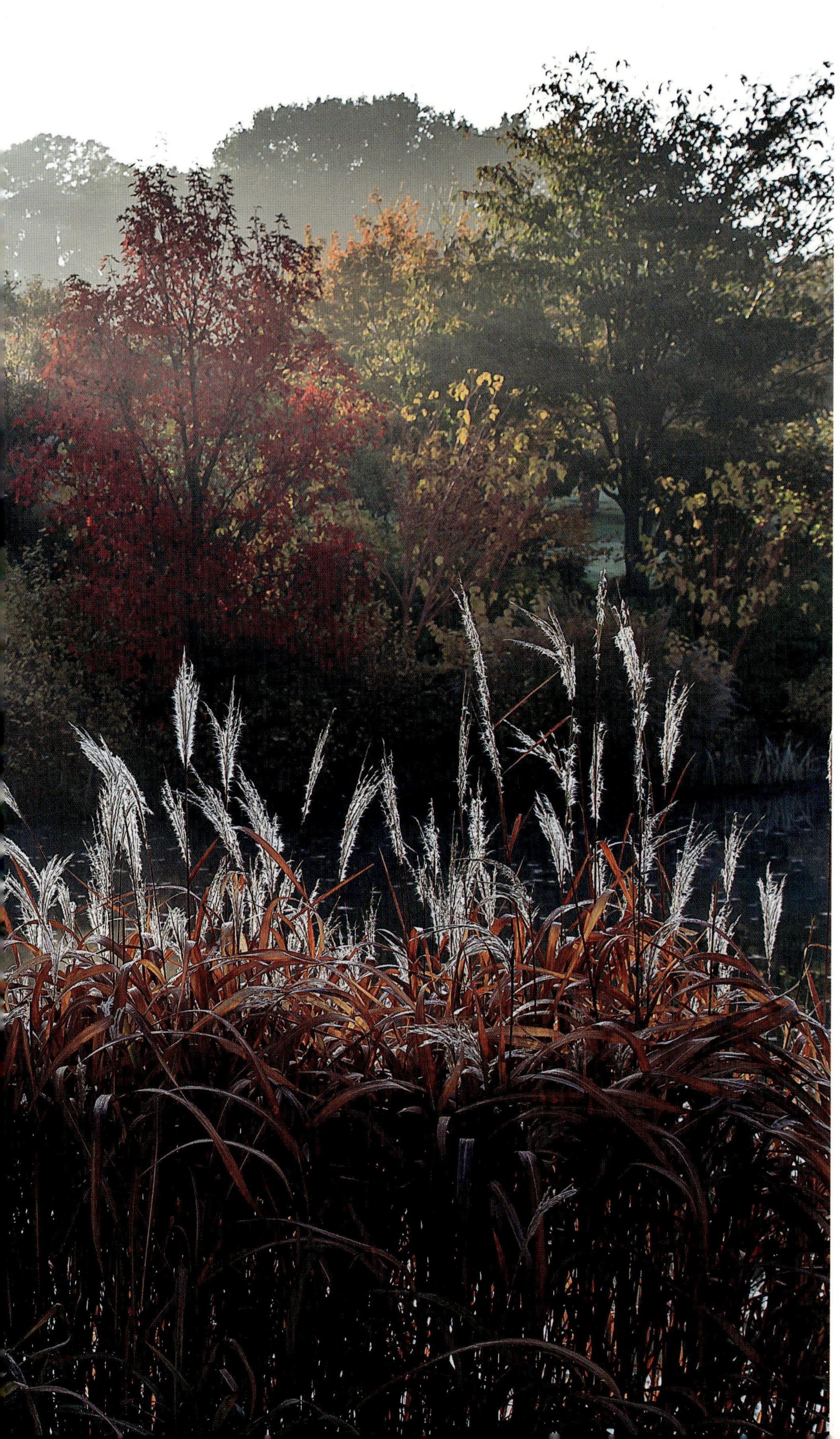

Magic Moment
Jardin du Bois Marquis, Isère, France

Bois Marquis is a large garden or arboretum in France, and I wanted to take romantic pictures in a place that is primarily a collection of trees. Composition wise, I knew the scenery would be hard to exploit, but this was part of the challenge. The opportunity came during a sunny morning in October, with the appearance of autumn colours.

Canon EOS 600D, 24-70mm lens, 1/160sec at f/7.1, ISO 200.

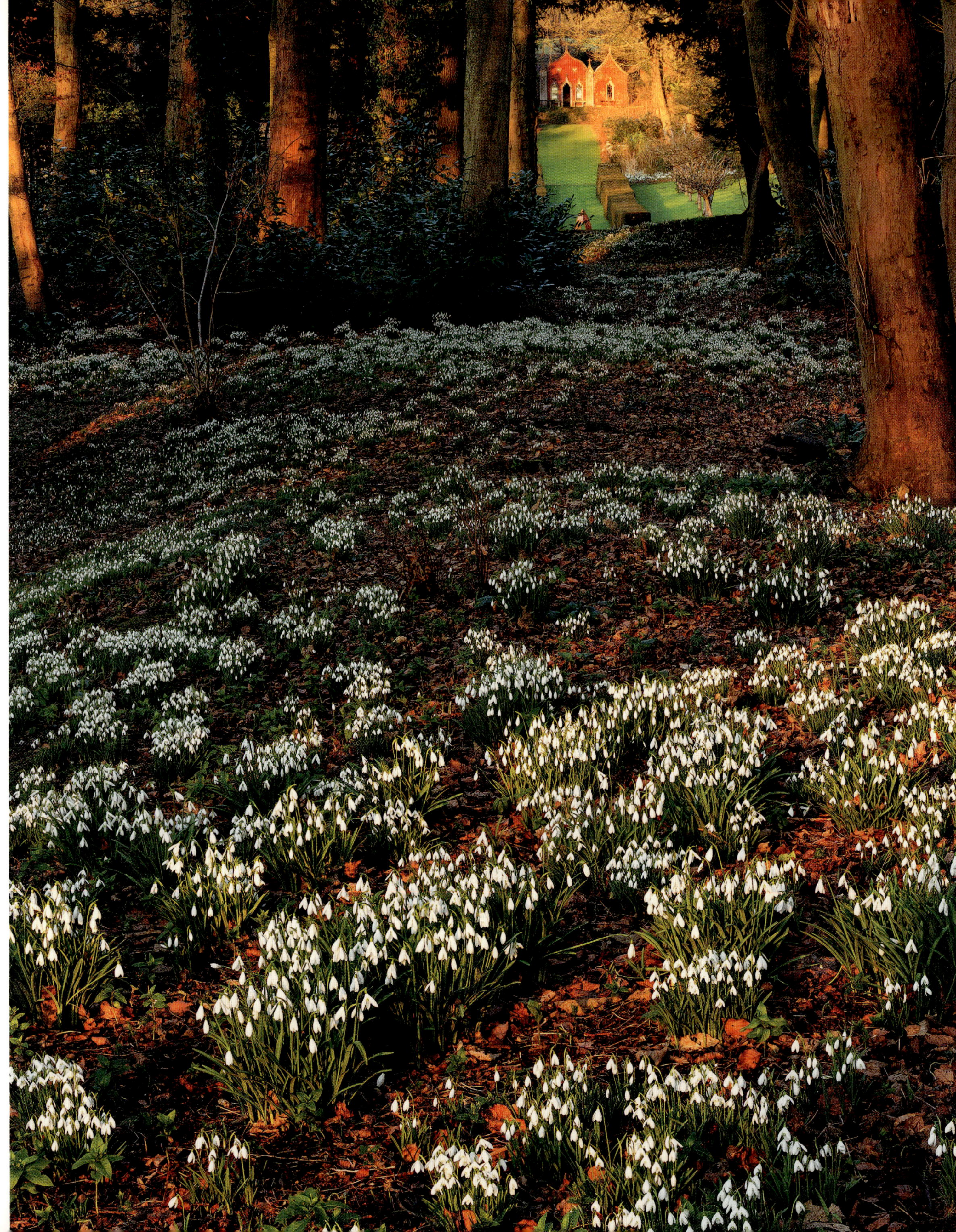

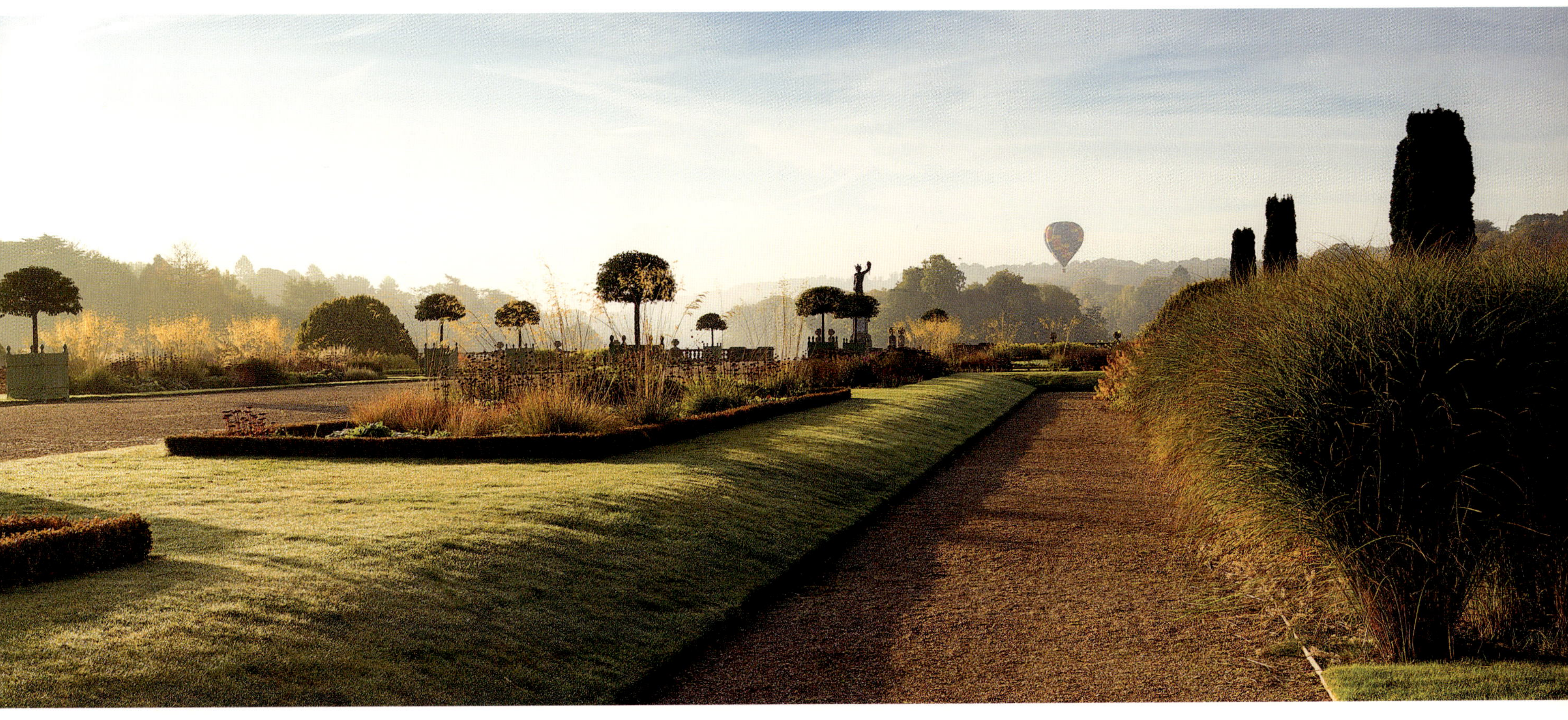

◀ **GEOFF KELL**   HIGHLY COMMENDED

Late Light
Painswick Rococo Garden, Gloucestershire, England, UK

The theatrical setting of Painswick Rococo Garden comes alive with its magnificent display of snowdrops in late winter. The last of the light on a clear winter day fell across the garden and I was attracted to this view through the trees, which drew my eye towards one of the garden's buildings, under a spotlight created by the late afternoon sun.

📷 Canon EOS 5D Mark III, Canon 70-200mm lens, 1/40sec at f/14, ISO 1600. Tripod. Post-capture: focus stacking, basic image management.

▲ **JOE WAINWRIGHT**   FINALIST

Hot Air Balloon over Trentham Gardens
Trentham Gardens, Staffordshire, England, UK

I wanted to photograph the garden early in the morning, shooting into the autumn sun if possible, to capture the vibrantly illuminated grasses and the silhouettes of seedheads, particularly of plants such as *Phlomis russeliana*. My aim was to illustrate how a garden, such as Trentham, which is brilliantly colourful in summer, has as much to offer in the autumn. I was photographing the borders when I noticed a hot air balloon rising from beyond the trees to the right of the picture. I felt that the balloon, hovering in the mists over the nearby lake, not only added interest to the sky but also a sense of narrative.

📷 Canon EOS 5D Mark II, Canon 24-70mm lens, 1/40sec at f/14, ISO 100. Tripod, soft graduated filter. Post-capture: basic image management.

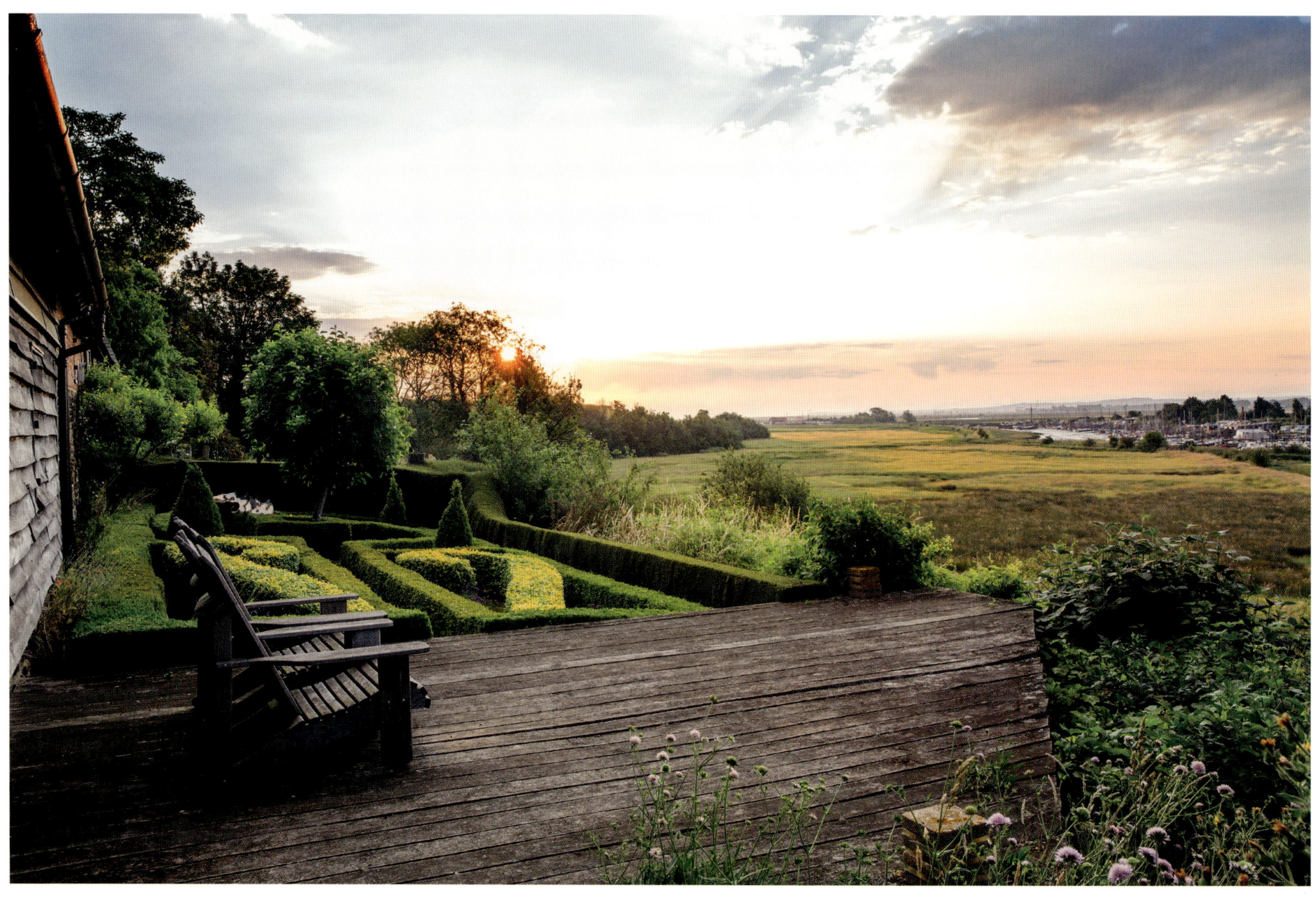

Dawn on the Deck
Kent, England, UK

A dawn view from a terrace and formal parterre across the meadows of the marshes of north Kent. The raised point of view gave a feeling of being on top of the world, surveying the marshes as if on the prow of a ship at sunrise.

Canon EOS 5D Mark III, Canon 24-70mm lens, 1/13sec at f/16, ISO 200. Tripod.

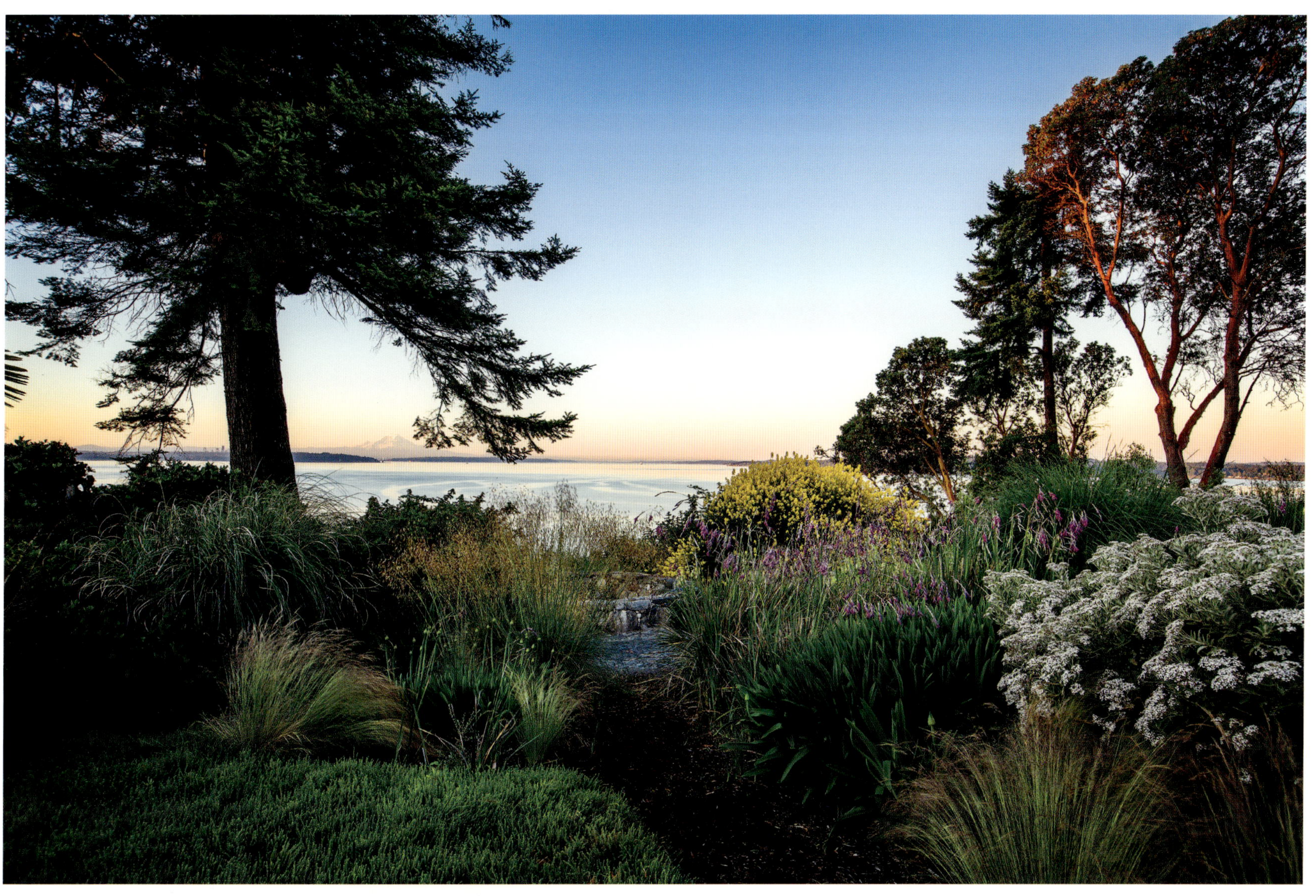

Windcliff, Dan Hinkley's Home Garden
Indianola, Washington, USA

It was such an incredible garden to photograph and I was so lucky that the weather was so calm and beautiful. Dan wanted the magnificent, but possibly dominating, Mount Rainier in the background, to blend into the vegetation and be found by visitors; I thought it was perfectly framed from this vantage point. The sunrise highlighted the manzanita tree to the right of the frame, showing off Hinkley's amazing plants and unique location.

Canon EOS 5D Mark III, Canon 16-35mm lens, 1/10sec at f/6.3, ISO 100. Tripod, cable release. Post-capture: combined two exposures.

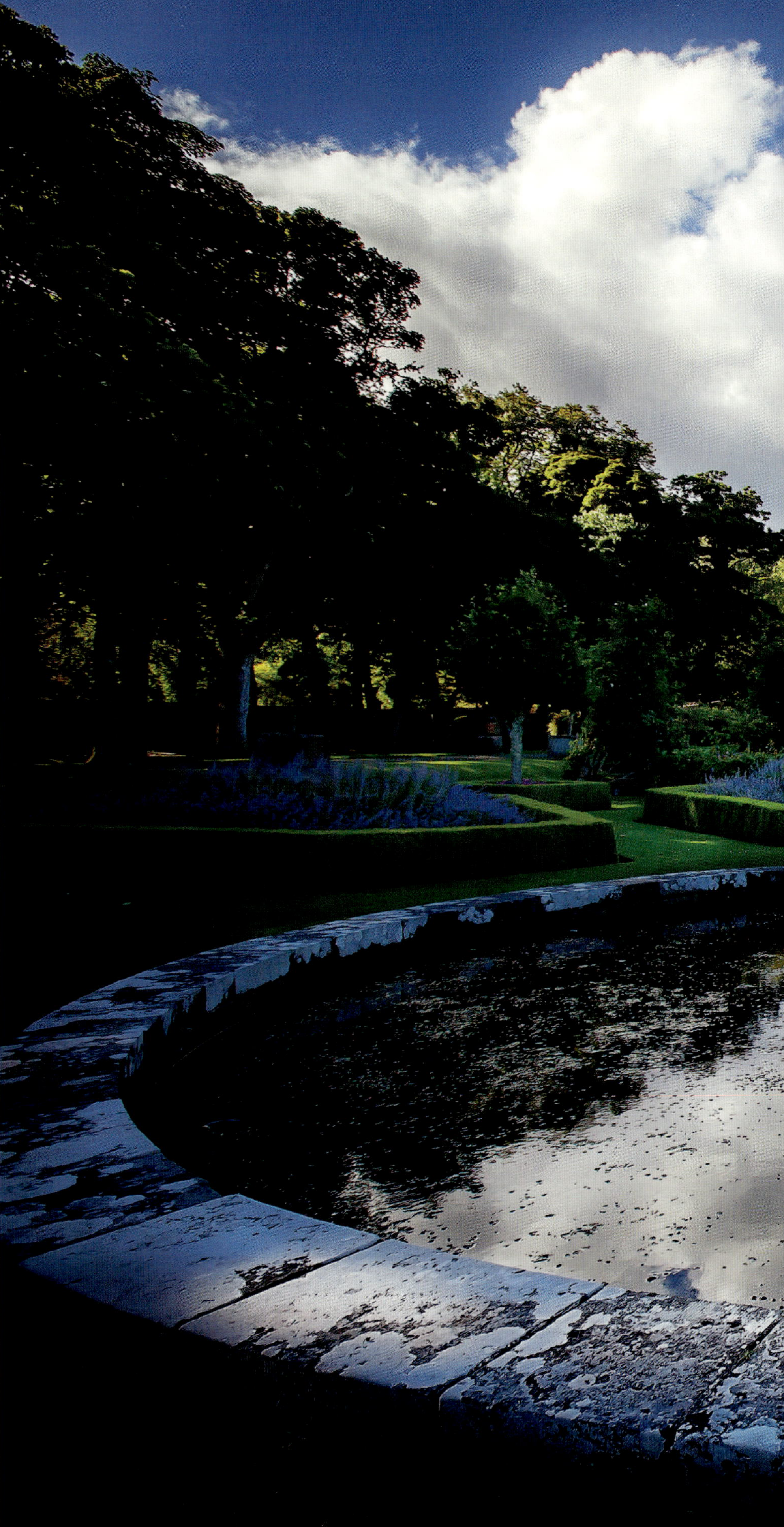

NICOLA MUNRO ▶   FINALIST

Reflections of the Past
Golspie, Sutherland, Scotland, UK

Taken on a beautiful sunny Sunday afternoon at Dunrobin Castle at the end of a North Coast 500 Tour. I did not have time to take a tour of the castle itself as the gardens were just too beautiful to leave.

📷 Canon EOS 5D Mark II, Canon 16-35mm lens, 1/1250sec at f/6.3, ISO 400.
Post-capture: basic image management.

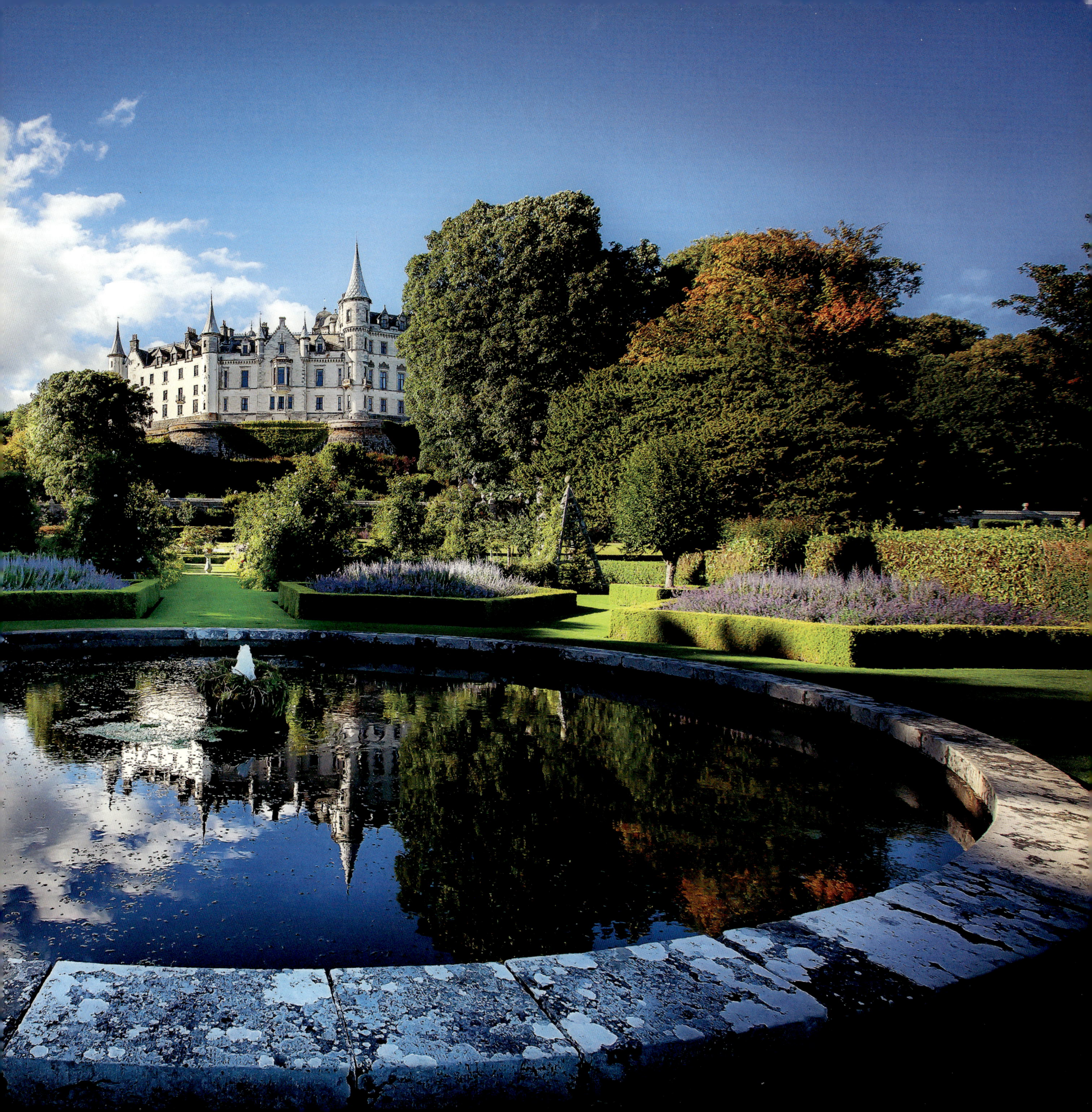

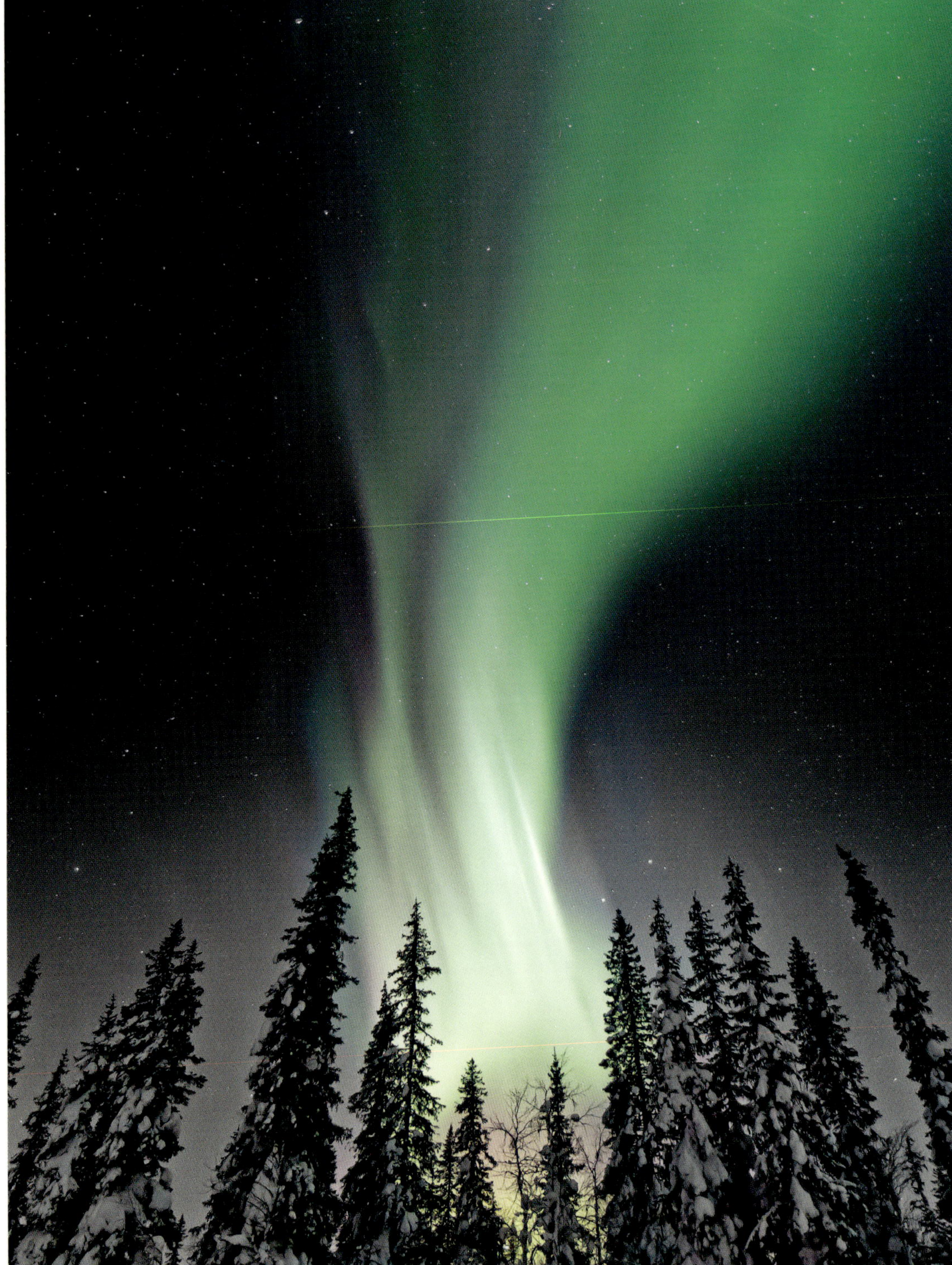

A Night to Remember
Kiruna, Swedish Arctic

I have visited this area of the world a number of times in winter, looking for suitable wildlife shots and of course to photograph the Northern Lights. The aurora borealis is such an incredible natural phenomenon and the boreal forest in the depth of winter is often covered in fluffy, powdery snow which provides a beautiful foreground to the amazing night-time displays. When I set up my equipment to take this picture the temperature was dipping below – 34°C. I continued to photograph the aurora for another seven hours.

Canon EOS 1D Mark IV, Canon 14mm lens, 15sec at f/2.8, ISO 1600. Tripod, cable release, head torch. Post-capture: basic image management.

Suwannee Valley Streaks
Suwannee River Valley, Florida, USA

In a backwater swamp of north Florida, fallen leaves drift toward the camera with a gentle current. A long exposure streaked the floating leaves while a polariser allowed the static sunken leaves to show through. At certain times of year this area is seven feet deep, although on this trip it was only two feet.

Sony α7R, Canon 24mm lens, 4sec to 30sec at f/13 to f/22, ISO 50. Post-capture: three landscape images stitched together using different exposures.

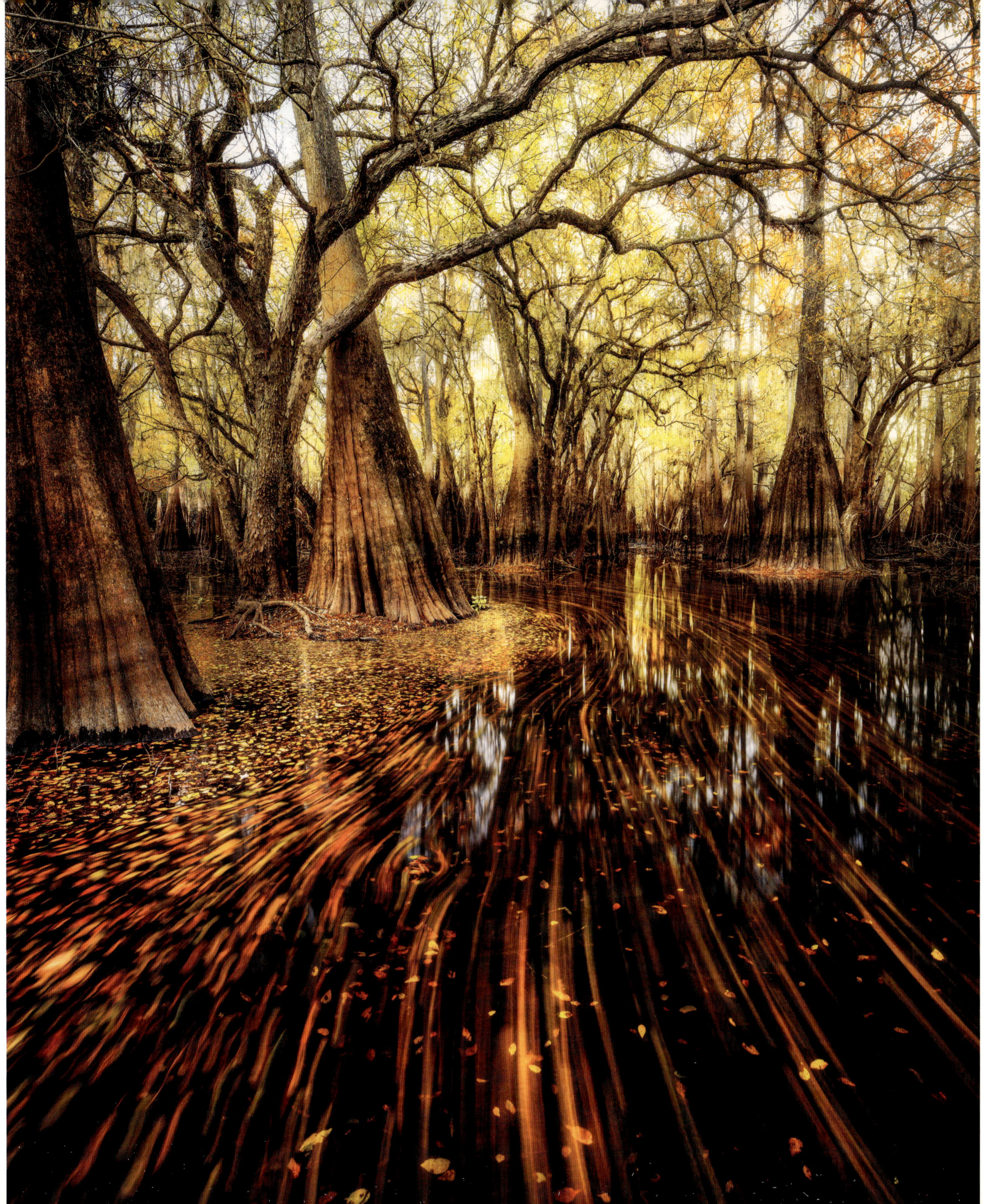

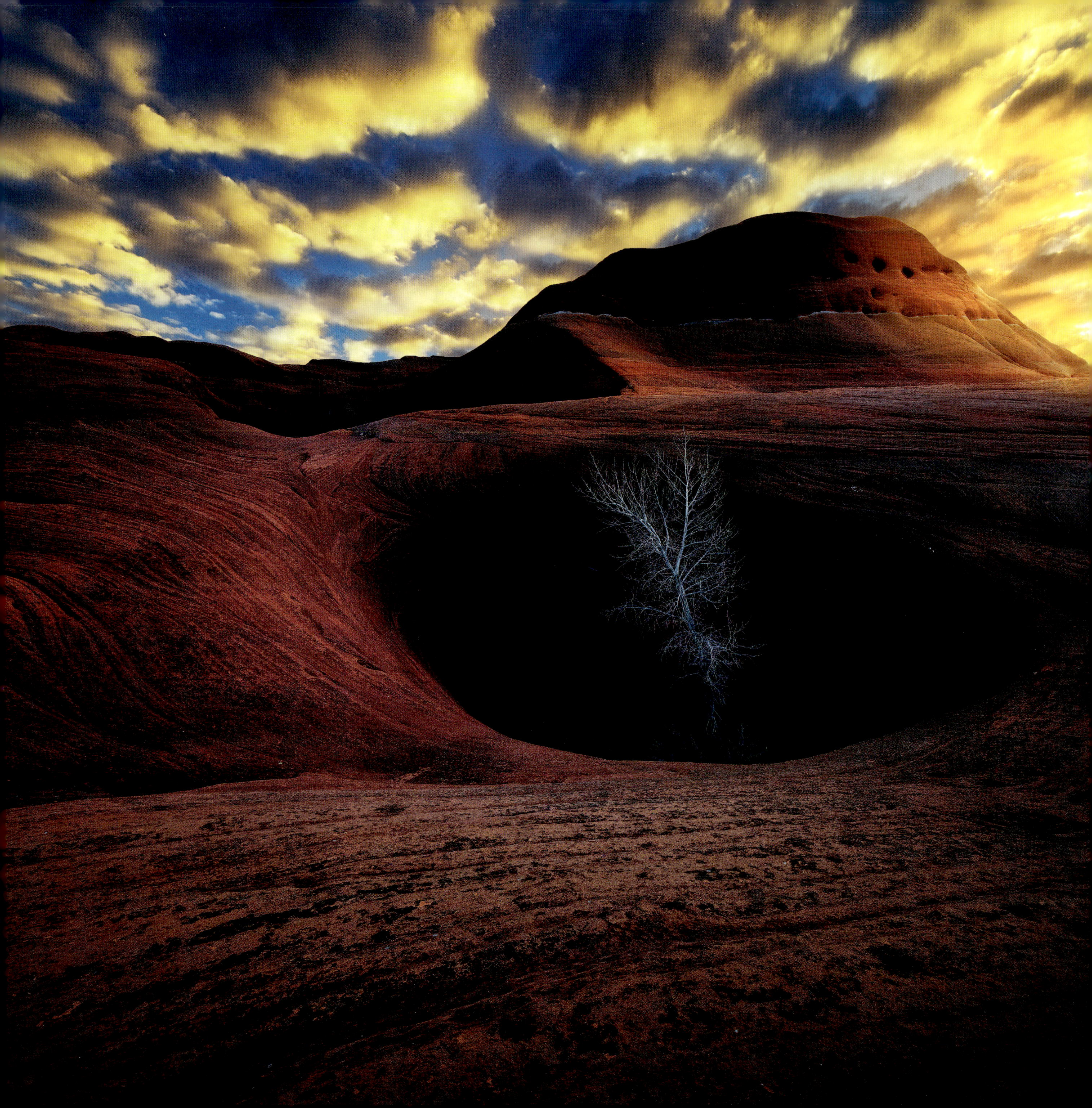

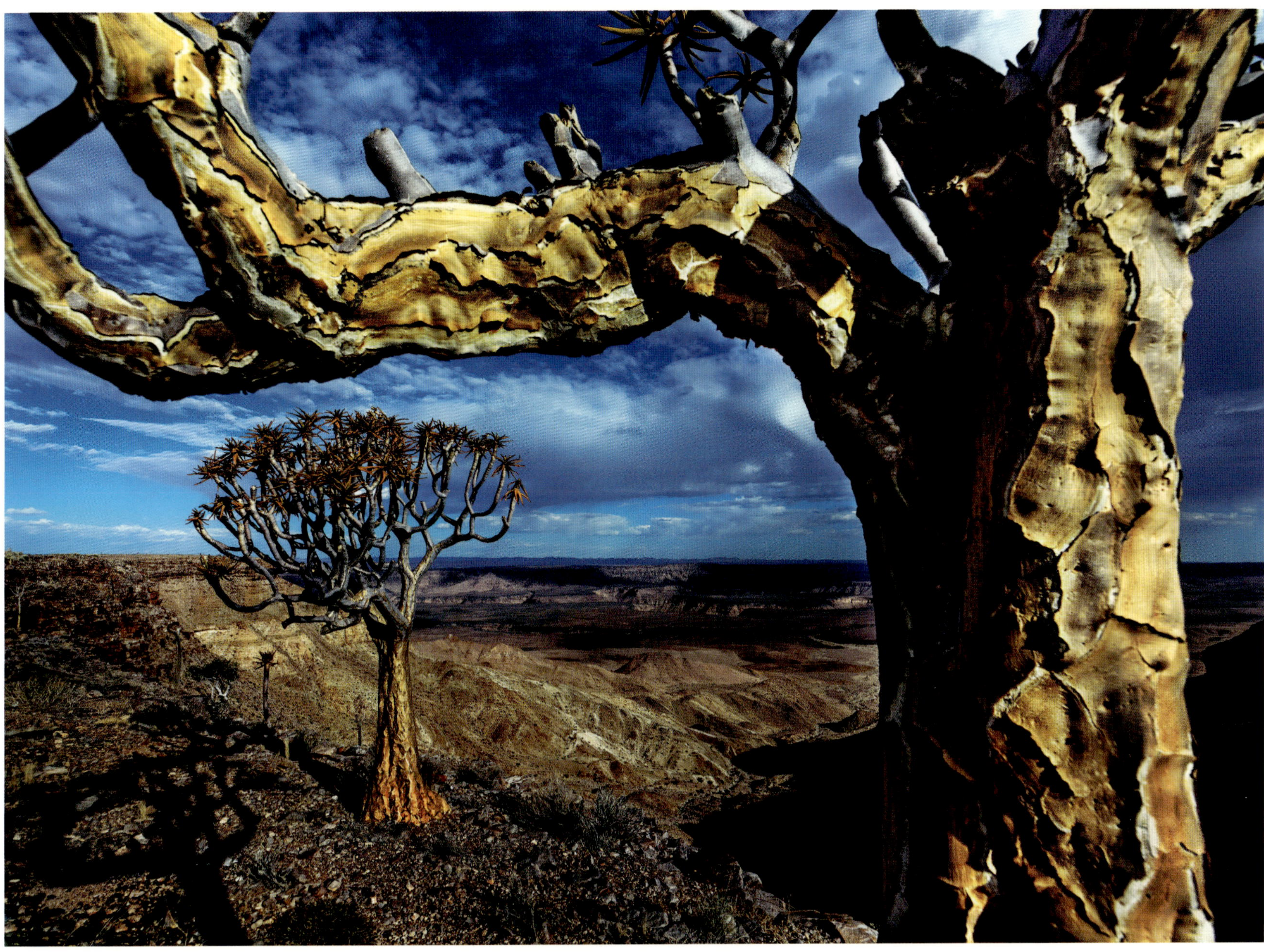

Shine on Life
Dance Hall Rock, Utah, USA

The first word that comes to mind when visiting Dance Hall Rock is 'surreal'. The line patterns in the sandstone and the trees that peek out of giant holes look simply out of this world. When I saw this composition whilst scouting I was impressed by the sheer fierceness of the lone cottonwood, a sign of life in an area where the struggle for survival is as real as it gets. Most of my work draws inspiration from other art mediums; in this particular case, the stark landscape reminded me of Salvador Dali's early work and of the sci-fi novel *Roadside Picnic* by the Strugatsky brothers.

📷 Sony α7R, Canon 17mm lens, 1/20sec at f/16. Tripod.

Quivertrees
Fish River Canyon, Rosh Pinah, Namibia

A quiver tree (*Aloe dichotoma*) on the edge of Fish River Canyon. I particularly liked the yellow resin on the tree trunks which reminded me of gold leaf.

📷 Phase One IQ180, Phase One 28mm lens, 1/400sec at f/14, ISO 100. Tripod, cable release.

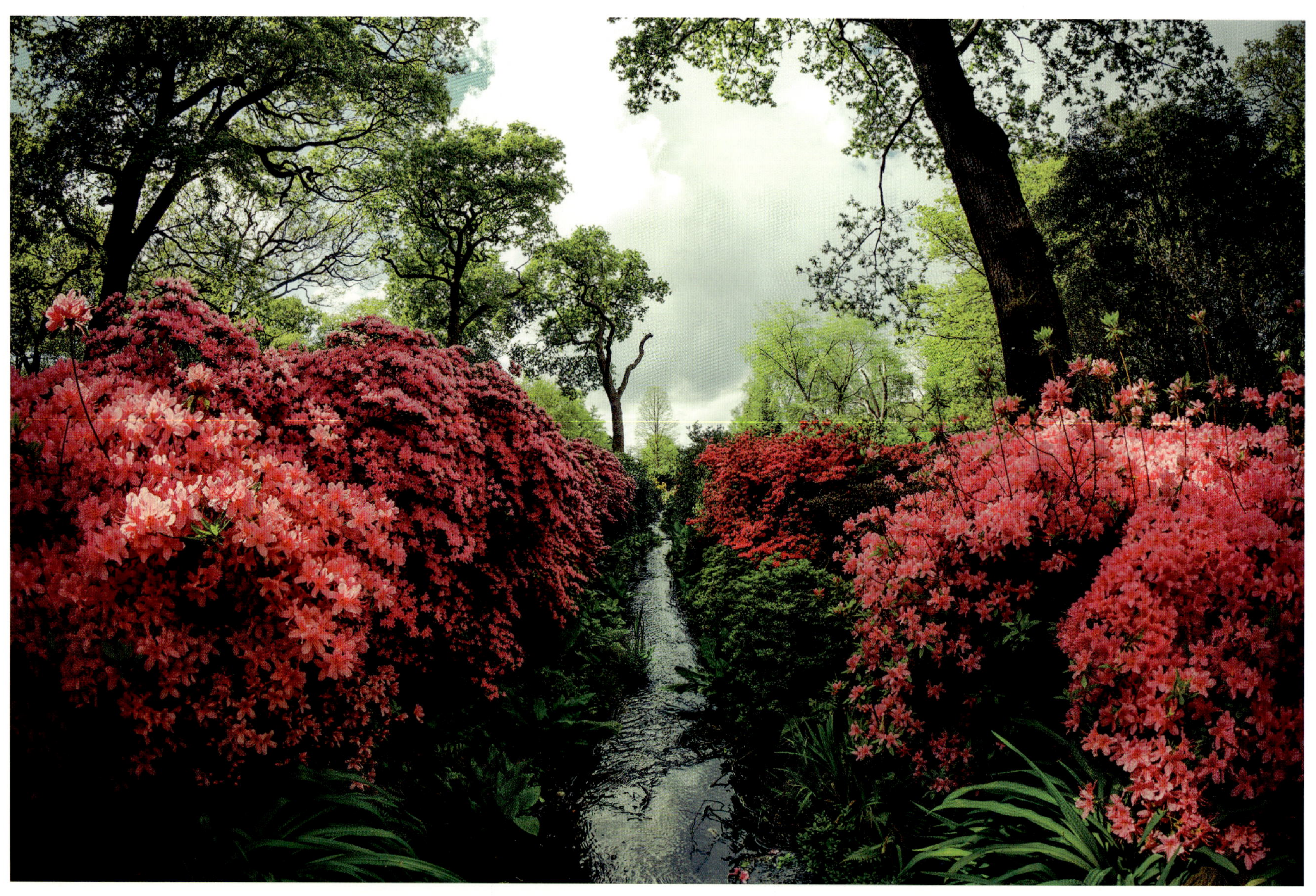

Isabella Plantation
Richmond Park, London, England, UK

Within the 40 acre woodland, evergreen *Azalea* line the ponds and streams. The sunlight and symmetry were just right.

📷 Sony α6000, Samyang 8mm lens, 1/200sec at f/2.8, ISO 160. Post-capture: basic image management.

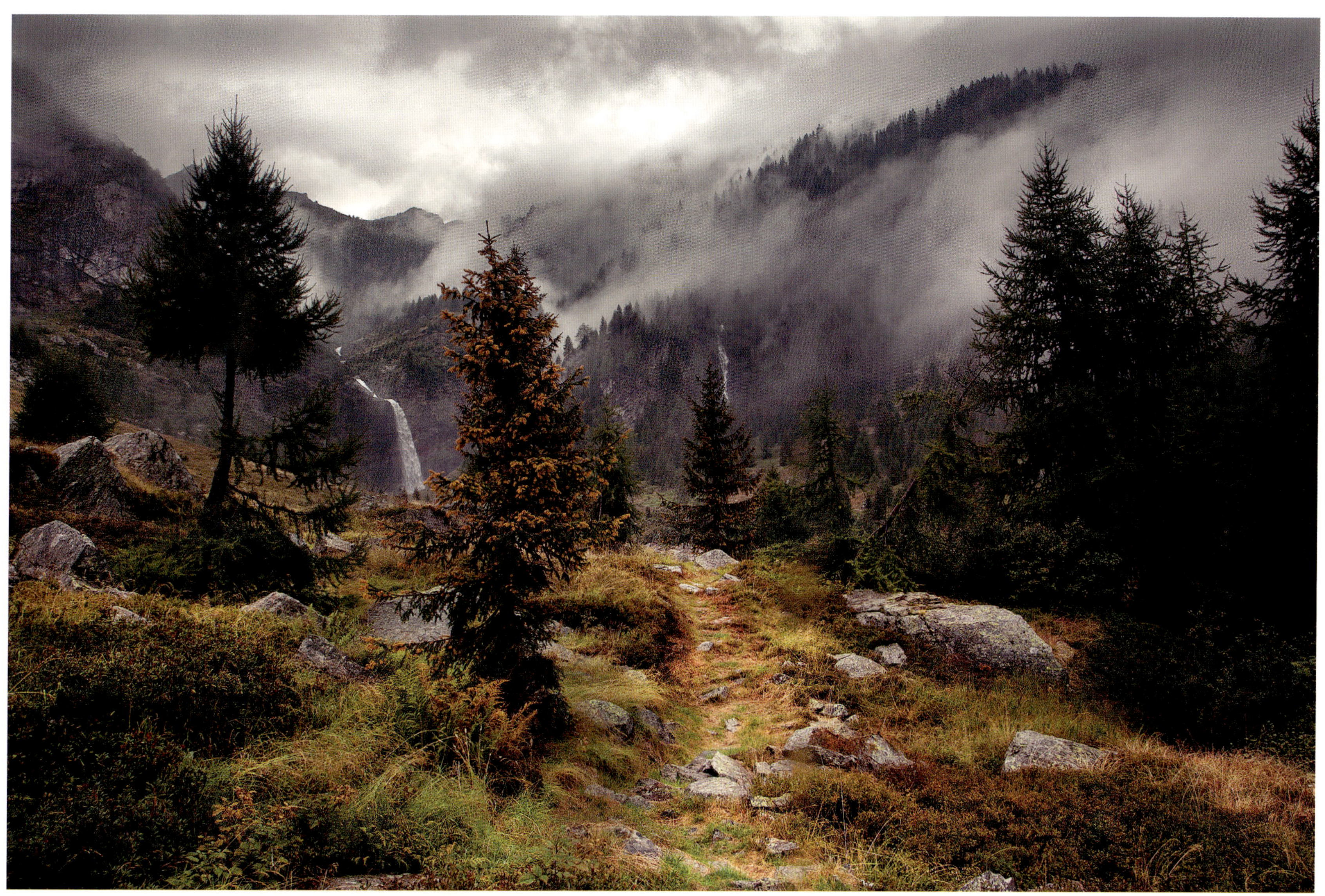

La Ragada del Ticinetto
La Ragada del Ticinetto, Ticino, Switzerland

This year Switzerland enjoyed record temperatures in July, although the weather changed dramatically in the second week of August. However, every cloud has a silver lining and the inclement weather presented, albeit briefly, this superb, painterly landscape.

📷 Canon EOS 5D, 24-105mm lens, 1/60sec at f/22, ISO 400.

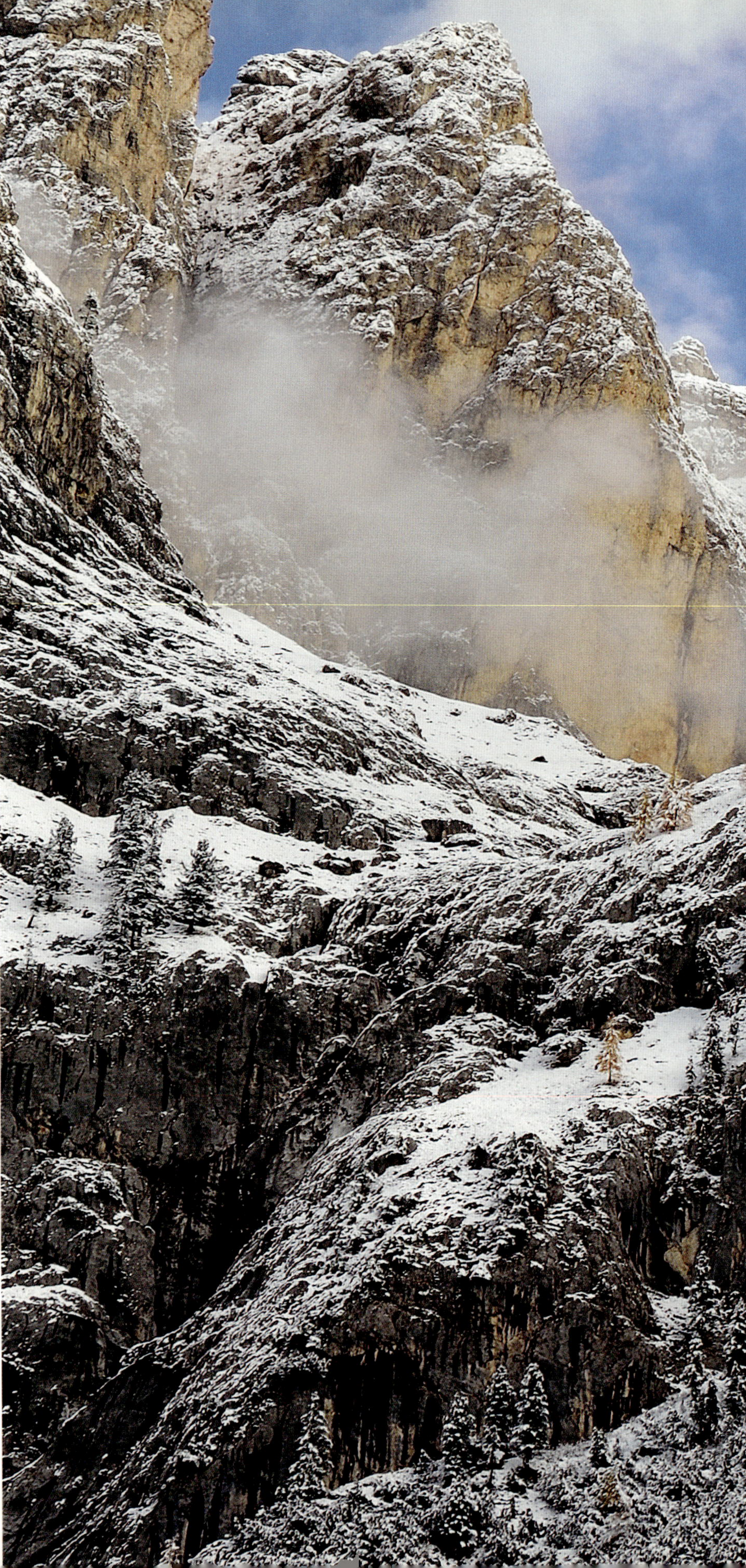

                                                FINALIST

Autumn Colours in the Forest
Dolomites, Sella Group, Trentino, Italy

The perfect combination of autumn and winter as the first snow settles on larch trees in the
Dolomites.

Nikon D4S, Nikkor 35-70mm lens, 1/160sec at f/16. Post-capture: basic image management.

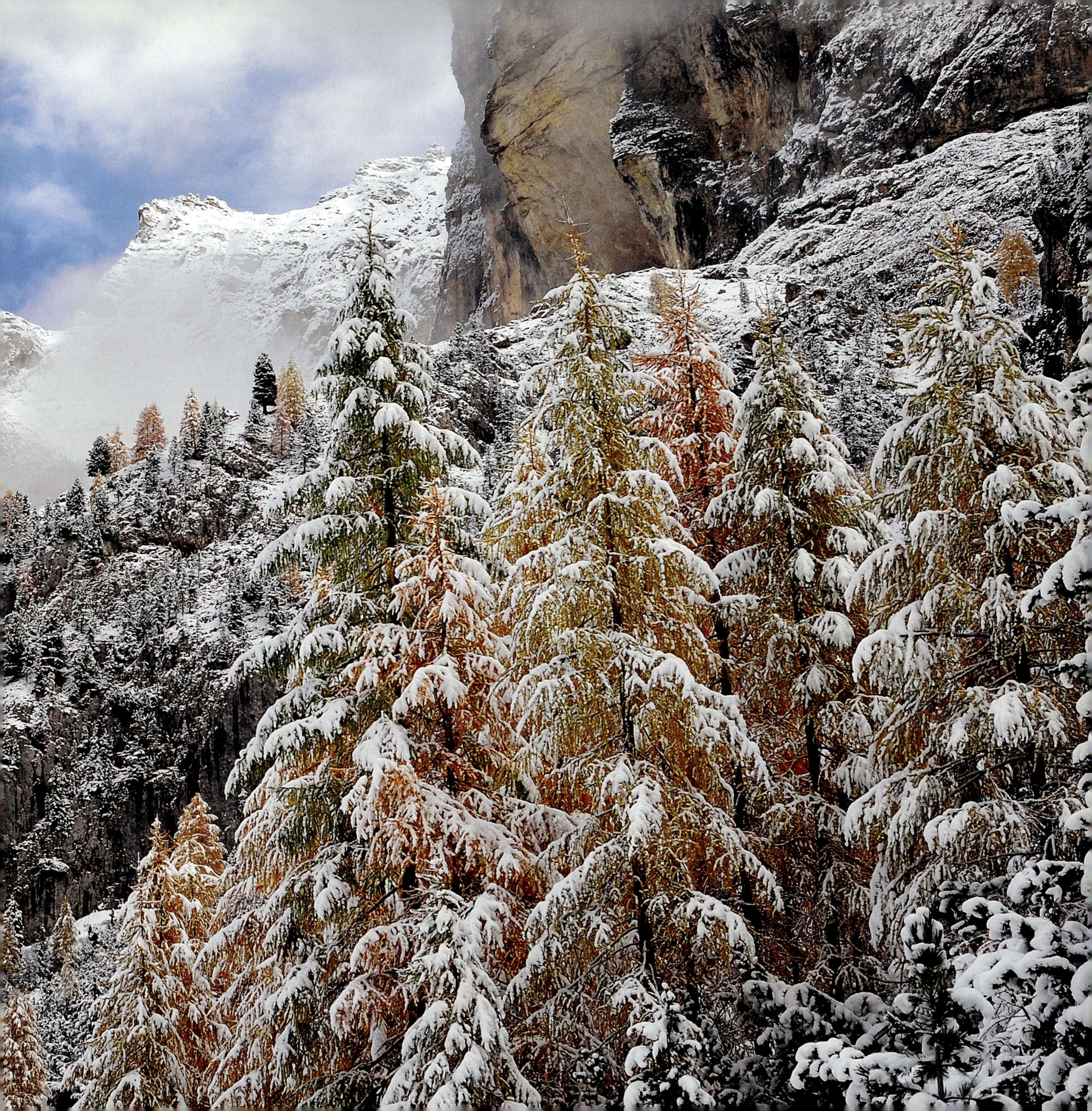

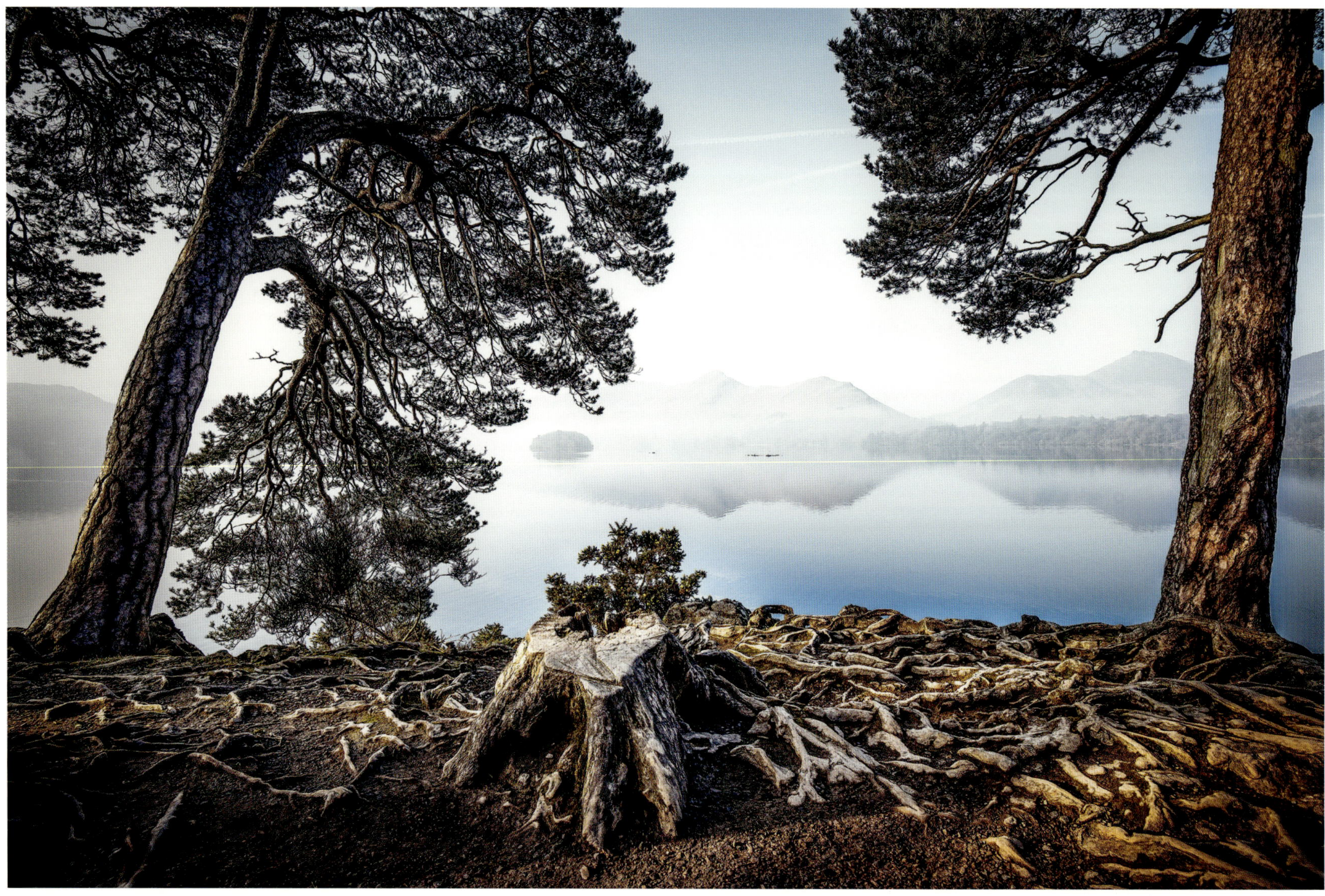

Catbells from Friars Crag
Derwentwater, Lake District, Cumbria, England, UK

I had visited this location many times, but on this occasion the conditions were perfect. The lighting was excellent, accentuating the shapes of the trees and roots, the water was mirror-like, and the distant Catbells was beautifully reflected in the lake.

Nikon D750, Nikkor 16-35mm, 1/90sec at f/8, ISO 100. Tripod. Post-capture: basic image management, minor cloning on the lake.

Waterfalls and Woodland
Yosemite National Park, California, USA

Yosemite Valley is mostly wooded, with towering pines framing gigantic walls of granite beyond. I had been concentrating on photographing a tighter crop of the lower falls, framed by the distinctive red barked pine trees. But while that made a strong composition I felt uneasy excluding the massive upper falls, so I opted for a second wider composition to show the full incredible scale of the valley and waterfalls. The enormous waterfall is awe inspiring, and yet the beautiful trees either side are not overwhelmed by it in this composition. In fact, without the trees the picture would not have anywhere near the same impact.

Nikon D800E, Nikon 24-70mm lens, 0.4sec at f/11, ISO 100. Post-capture: basic image management.

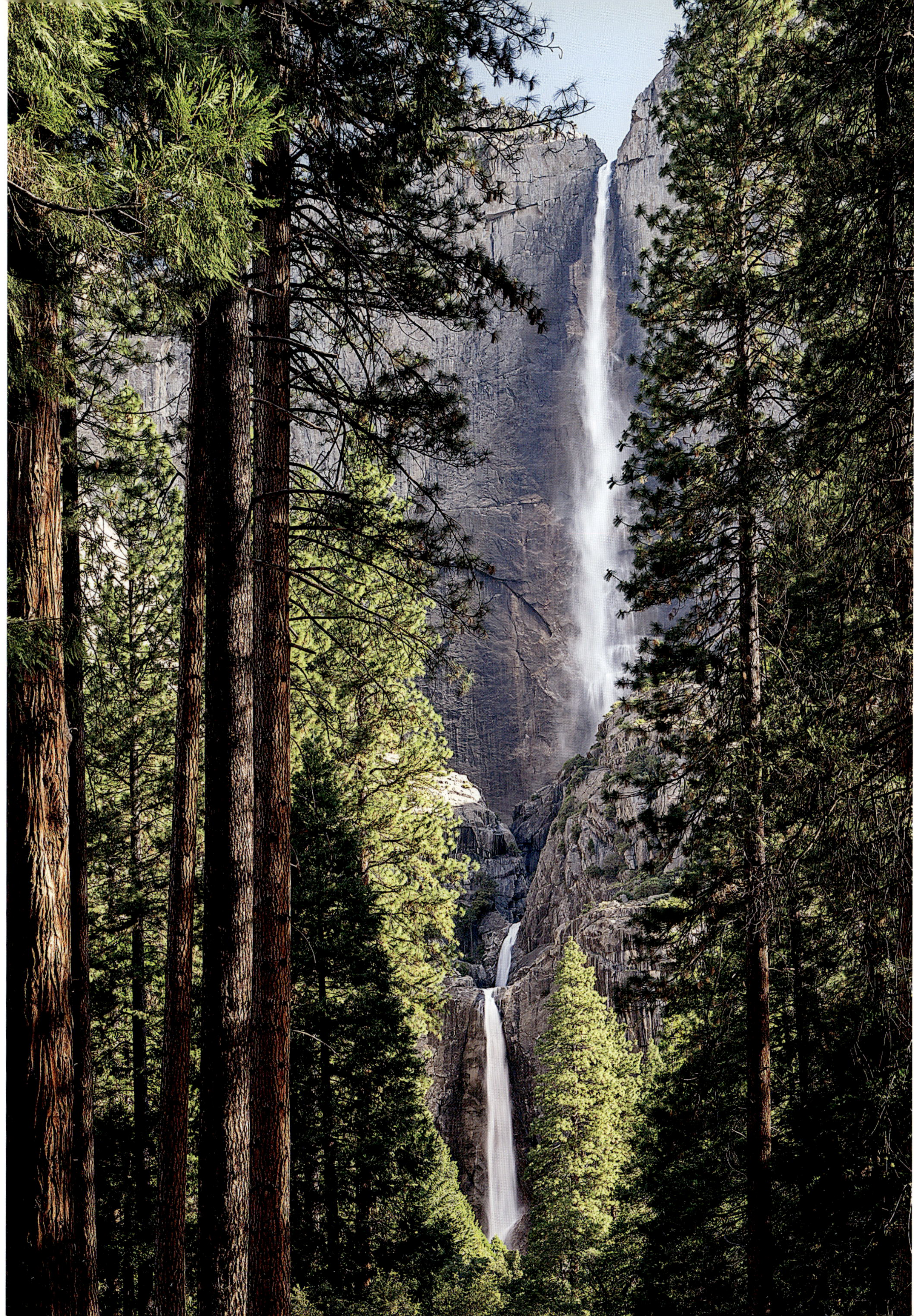

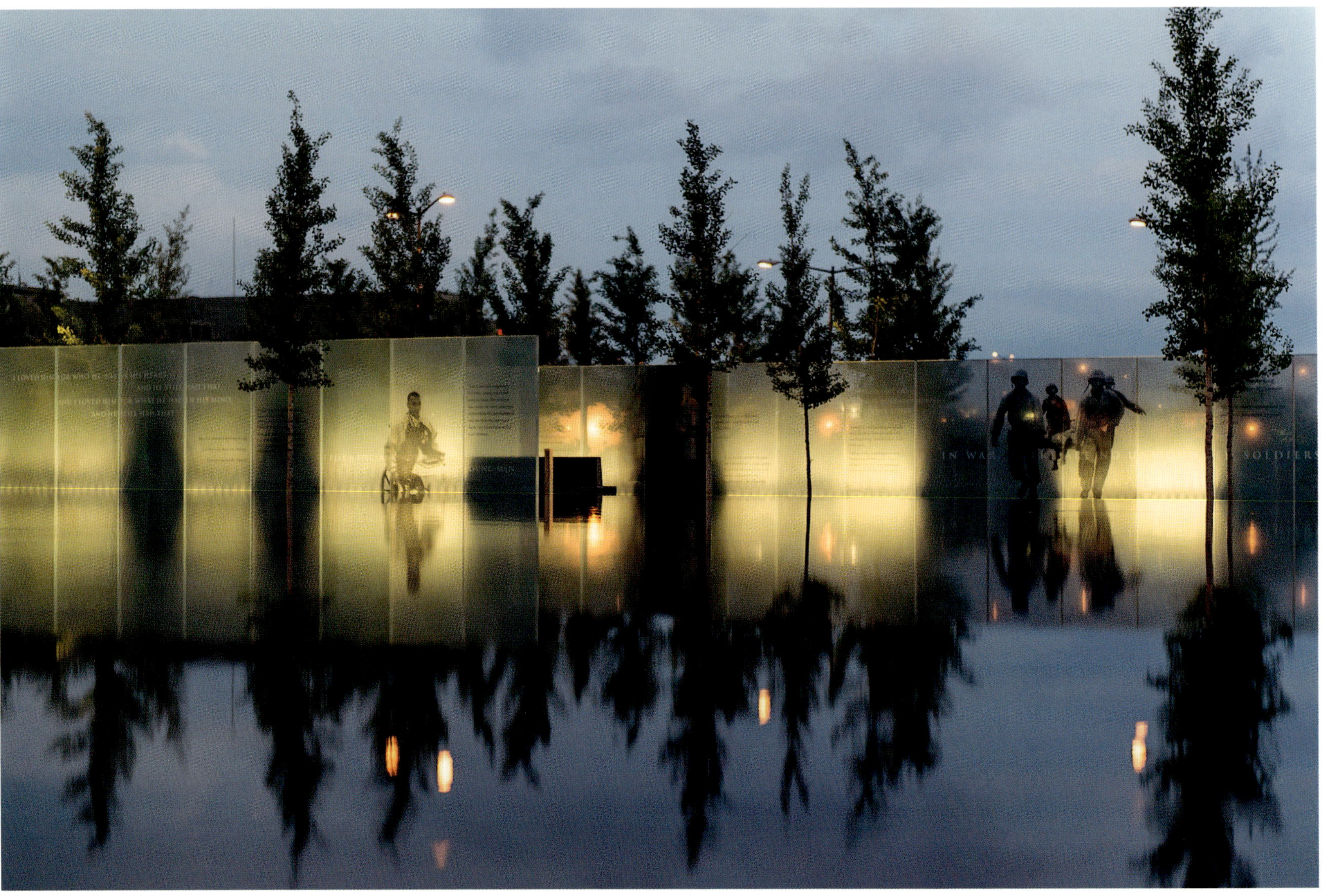

▲ **AMANDA KLEINMAN** 1ST PLACE

American Veterans Disabled for Life Memorial
Washington, D.C. USA

As a photographer, I enjoy visiting accessible public gardens and parks to capture snapshots during quiet moments. In this image I used a ground perspective to present a unified reflective pool and sky separated by *Ginkgo* trees and the backlit 'The Voices of Disabled Veterans' wall. To me, the visual elements of the memorial symbolise a human wholeness that does not change with the onset of physical disability. I believe that not many know of the existence of this memorial, and given its beauty and importance, I wanted to tell the story as intended by its designers and creators.

📷 Nikon D610, Nikkor 24-70mm lens, 1/40sec at f/2.8, ISO 400. Post-capture: basic image management.

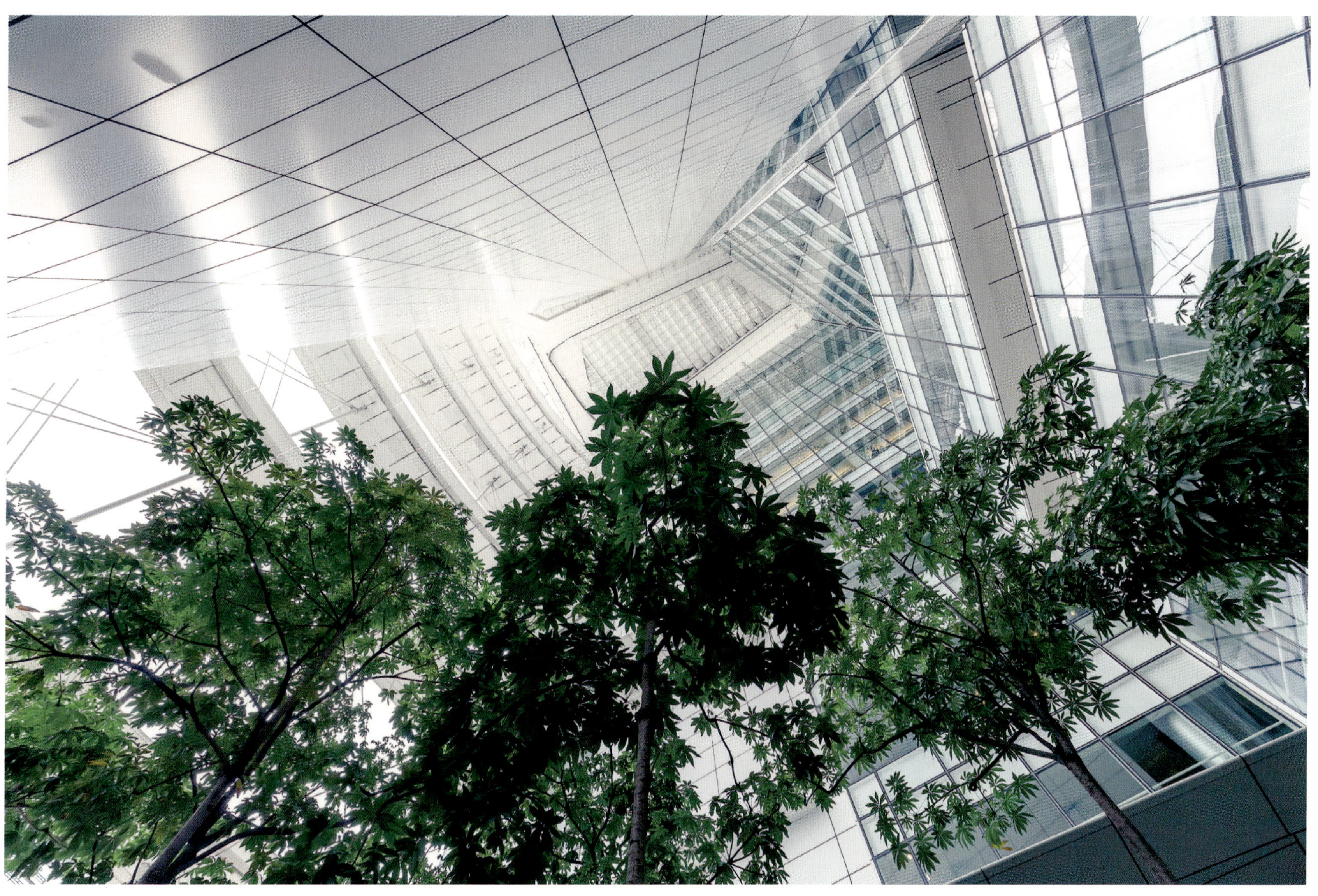

Synergy
Singapore

Despite being a highly urbanised city state, Singapore is also known worldwide as The City in a Garden. Having many green buildings is one of the key ways in which the city state achieves such a synergistic balance between nature and the built environment. This shot was taken at the National Library Building, a notable green building which I like not only because of its splendid architecture, but also because it incorporates greenery from within its own tropical landscape gardens.

Canon EOS 5D Mark II, Canon 16-35mm lens, 1/60sec at f/9.5, ISO 500. Post-capture: basic image management.

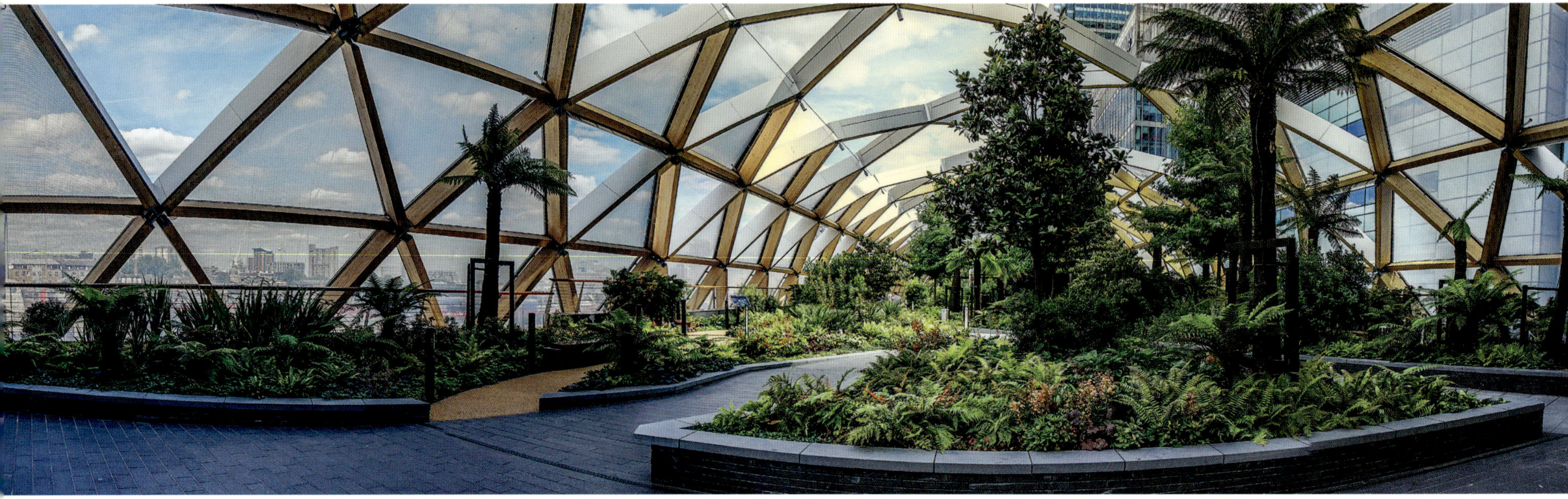

Crossrail Place Roof Garden
Canary Wharf, London, England, UK

Sitting above the new Crossrail station at Canary Wharf, the Crossrail Place Roof Garden designed by Foster + Partners, opened to the public in 2015. The planting selected for the gardens is intended to reference the area's maritime heritage. Many of the chosen species are indigenous to countries visited during the 19th century by trading ships that used the three docks built in the area by the West India Dock Company trading group.

Sony α6000, Sony 16-50mm lens, 1/125sec at f/8, ISO 100. Post-capture: several images stitched together to create the panorama, basic image management.

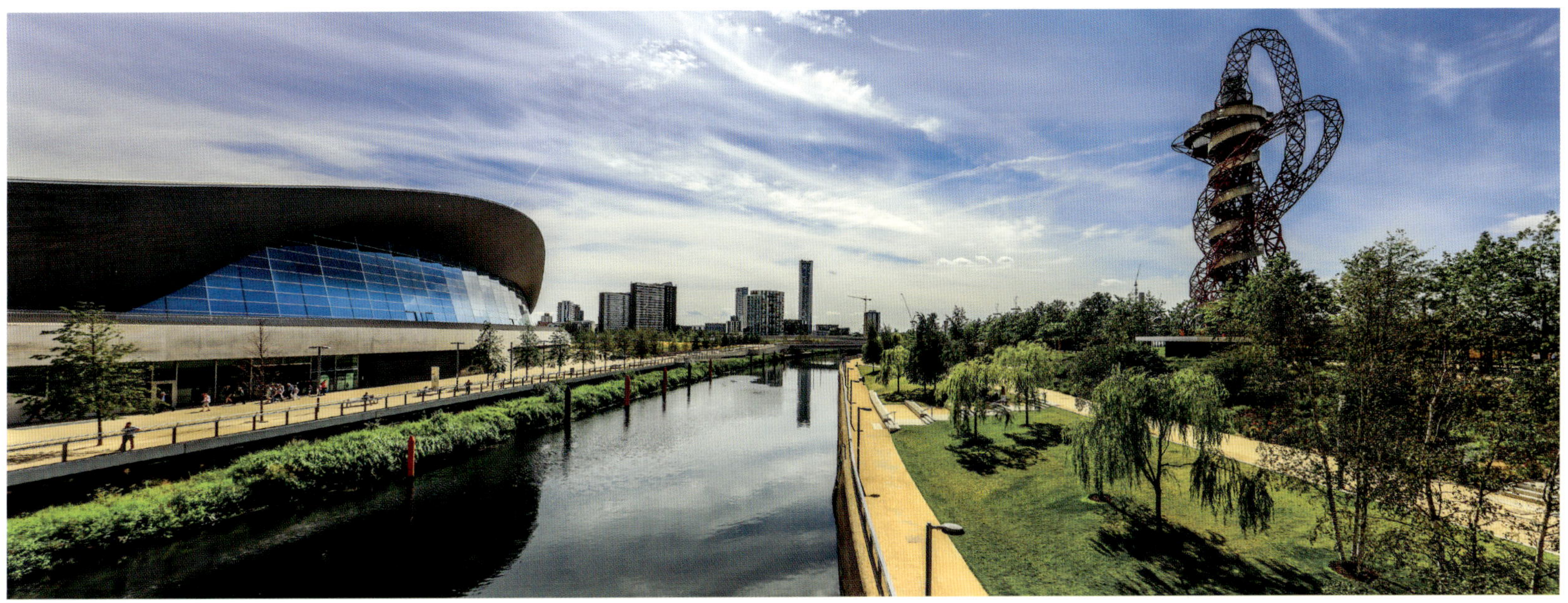

Queen Elizabeth Olympic Park
Stratford, London, England, UK

Once the games were over, the Olympic Park gardens were opened to the public to enjoy free of charge. On the right is the ArcelorMittal Orbit and on the left is the Aquatic Centre, with the River Lea running through the park.

Canon EOS 5D Mark III, Canon 17-40mm lens, 1/250sec at f11, ISO 100. Post-capture: stitched together three images to create the panorama, basic image management.

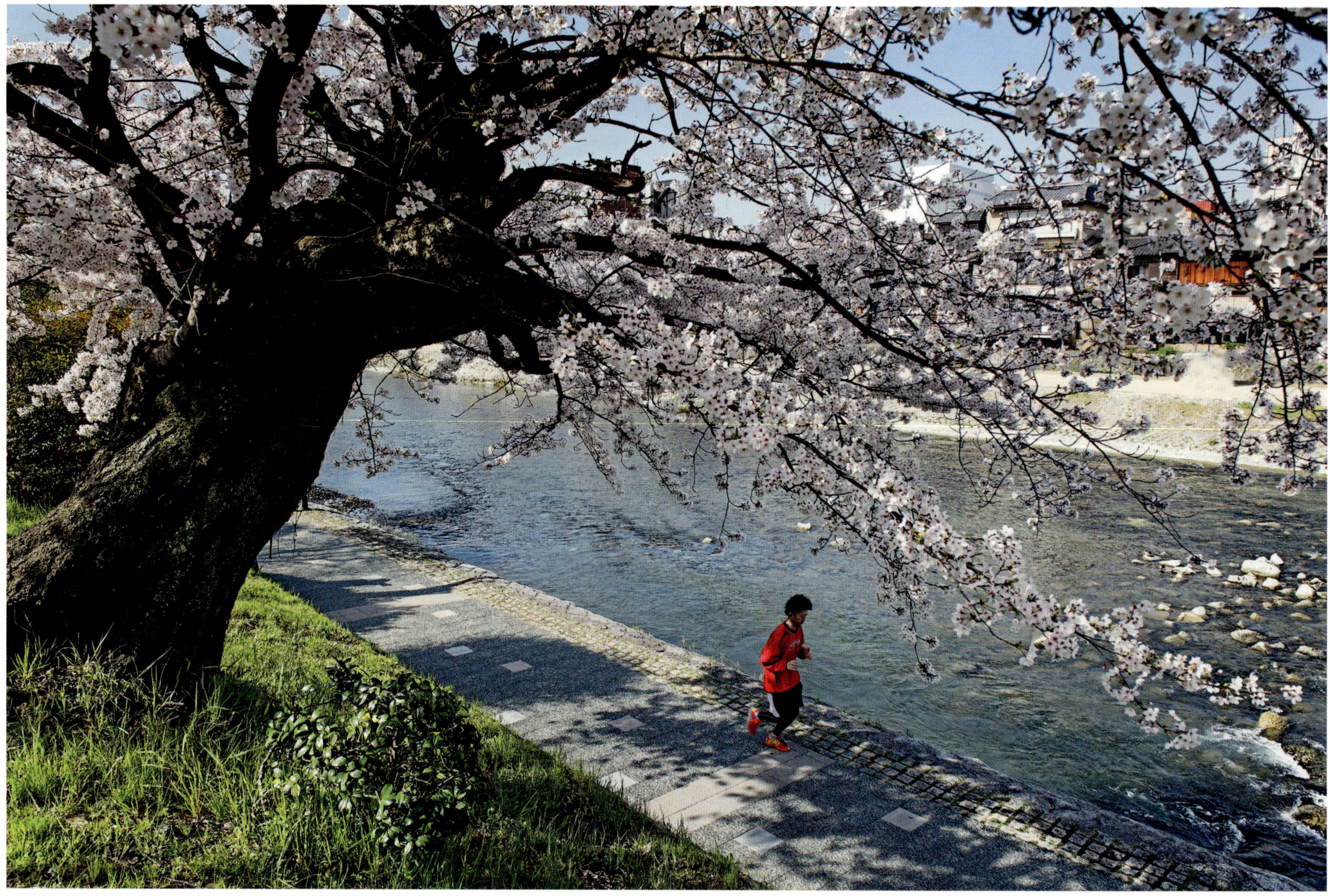

Morning Exercise
Kyoto, Japan

Kyoto is a historical city with a rich culture. In spring, cherry blossom embellishes the whole city, especially along the river banks where the trees are in full bloom. Locals exercise along the river in the morning whilst enjoying the surroundings, which form a beautiful picture.

Nikon D4, 24-70mm lens, 1/200sec at f/8, ISO 80.

High Line Purples
New York City, USA

This is one of my favourite locations for exploiting early morning light; I could feel summer fading away and autumn creeping into the city. I loved the complementary purple colours of the flowers and hazy background buildings.

Canon EOS 70D, Canon 100mm macro lens, 1/160sec at f/5, ISO 100. Post-capture: basic image management.

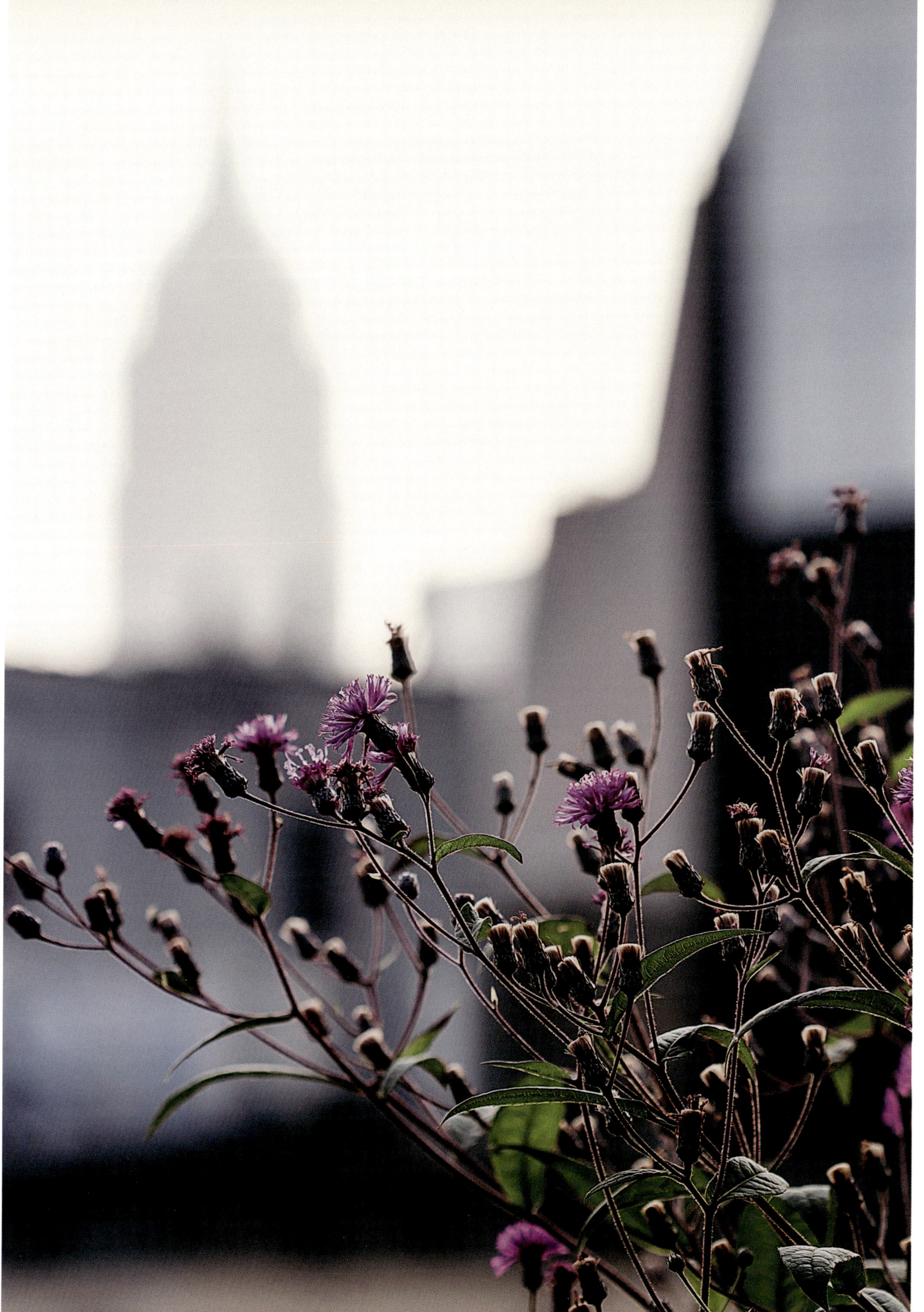

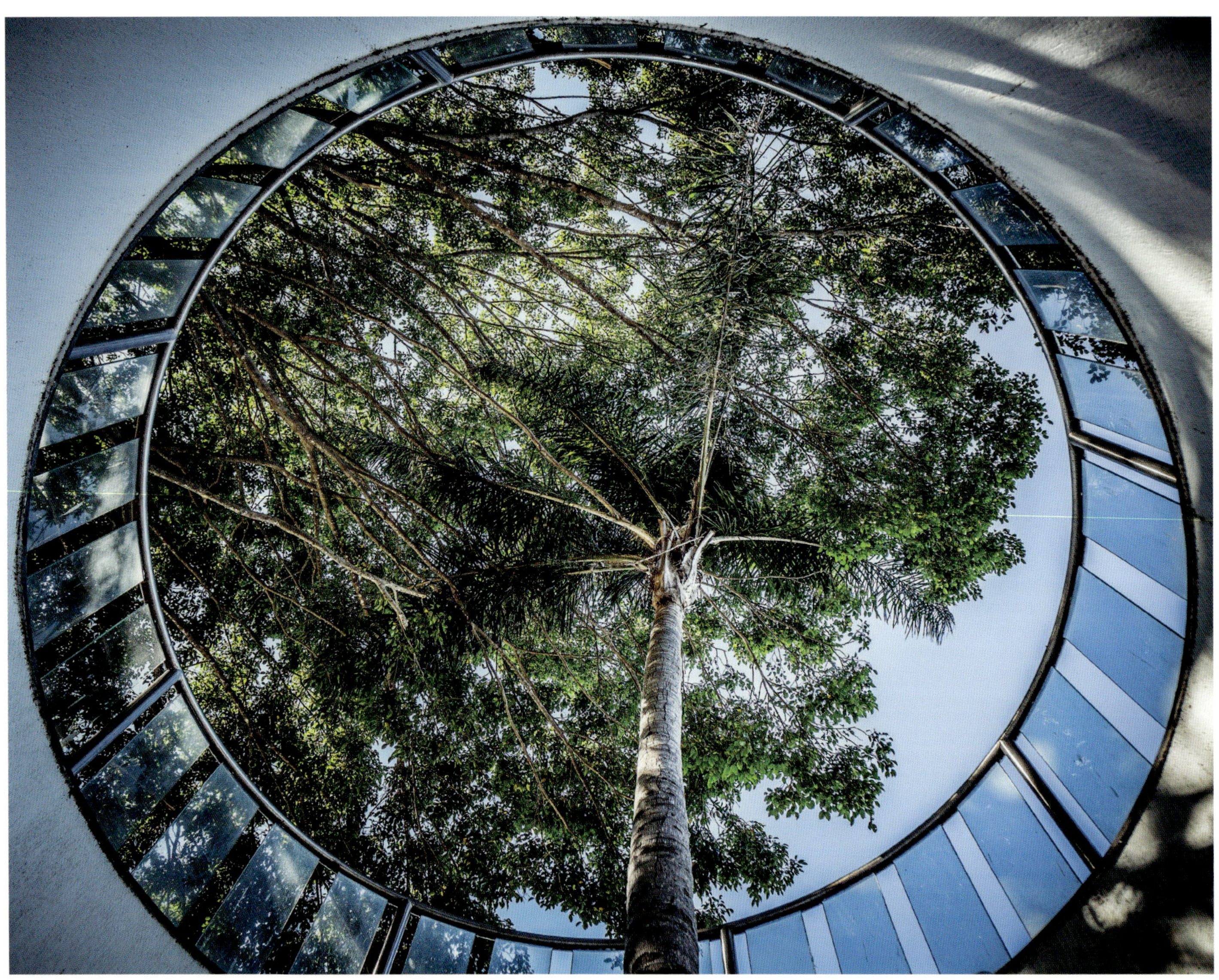

Reach for the Sky
Brisbane, Queensland, Australia

Whilst on holiday in Australia with my family, we walked along the City Reach Boardwalk on our way to Brisbane Botanical Gardens. I am always on the lookout for interesting trees to photograph and this was no exception. It was almost as if the boardwalk had been built around this particular tree, with the circular railing framing the composition.

Canon EOS 6D, Canon 24-105mm lens, 1/125sec at f/5.6, ISO 200.

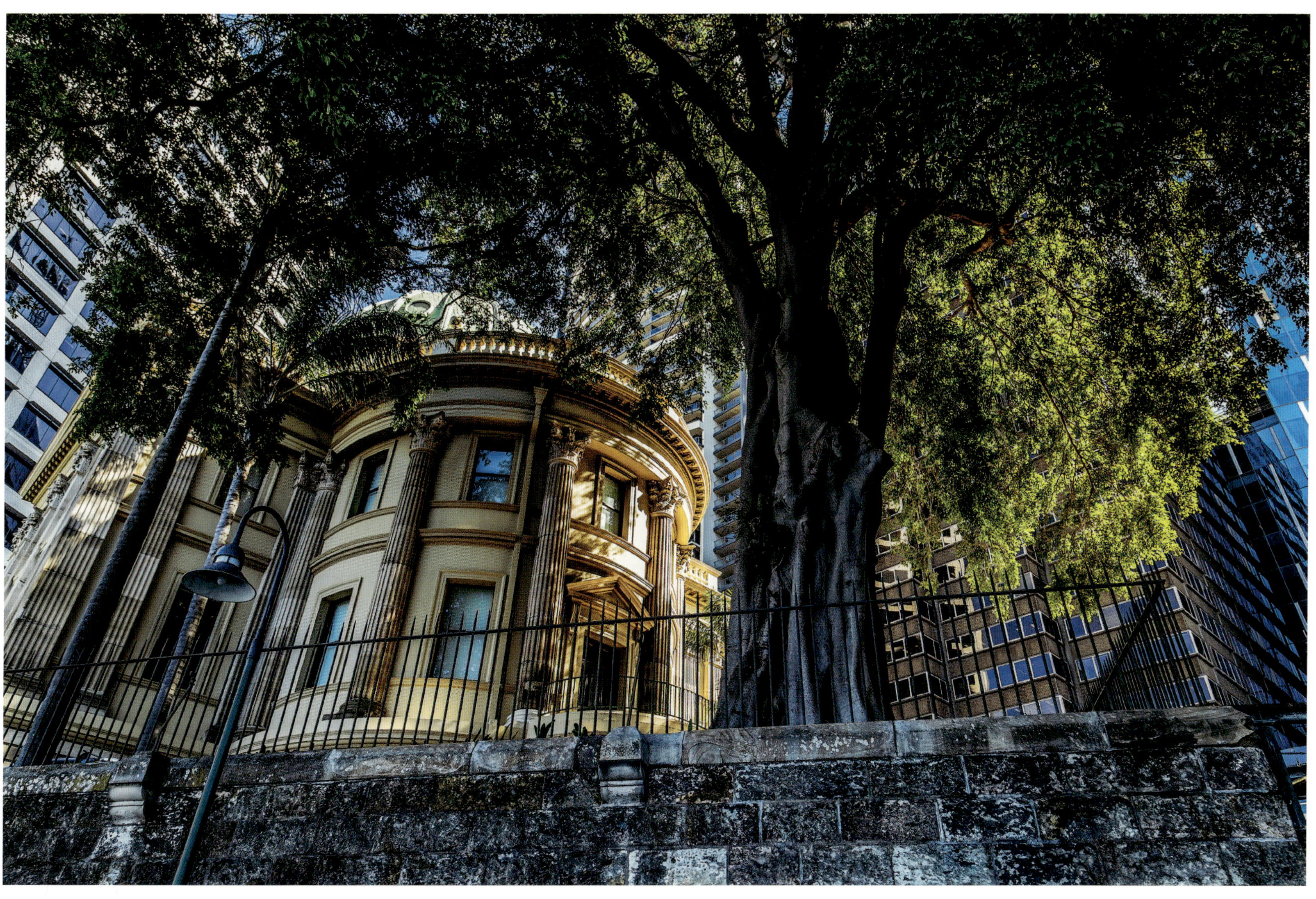

▲ **MARION SIDEBOTTOM** Finalist

Brisbane Street Tree
Brisbane, Queensland, Australia

On a visit to Australia I enjoyed looking at the street trees as they are so different to the ones
I see at home in the UK. Although Brisbane is a very modern city, the ultra-modern buildings are
interspersed with old ones. Many street trees have been planted which provide valuable shade to
city dwellers and important habitats for urban wildlife.

📷 Canon EOS 6D, Canon 24-105mm lens, 1/100sec at f/6.3, ISO 200. Post-capture: removed
item from wall to improve composition.

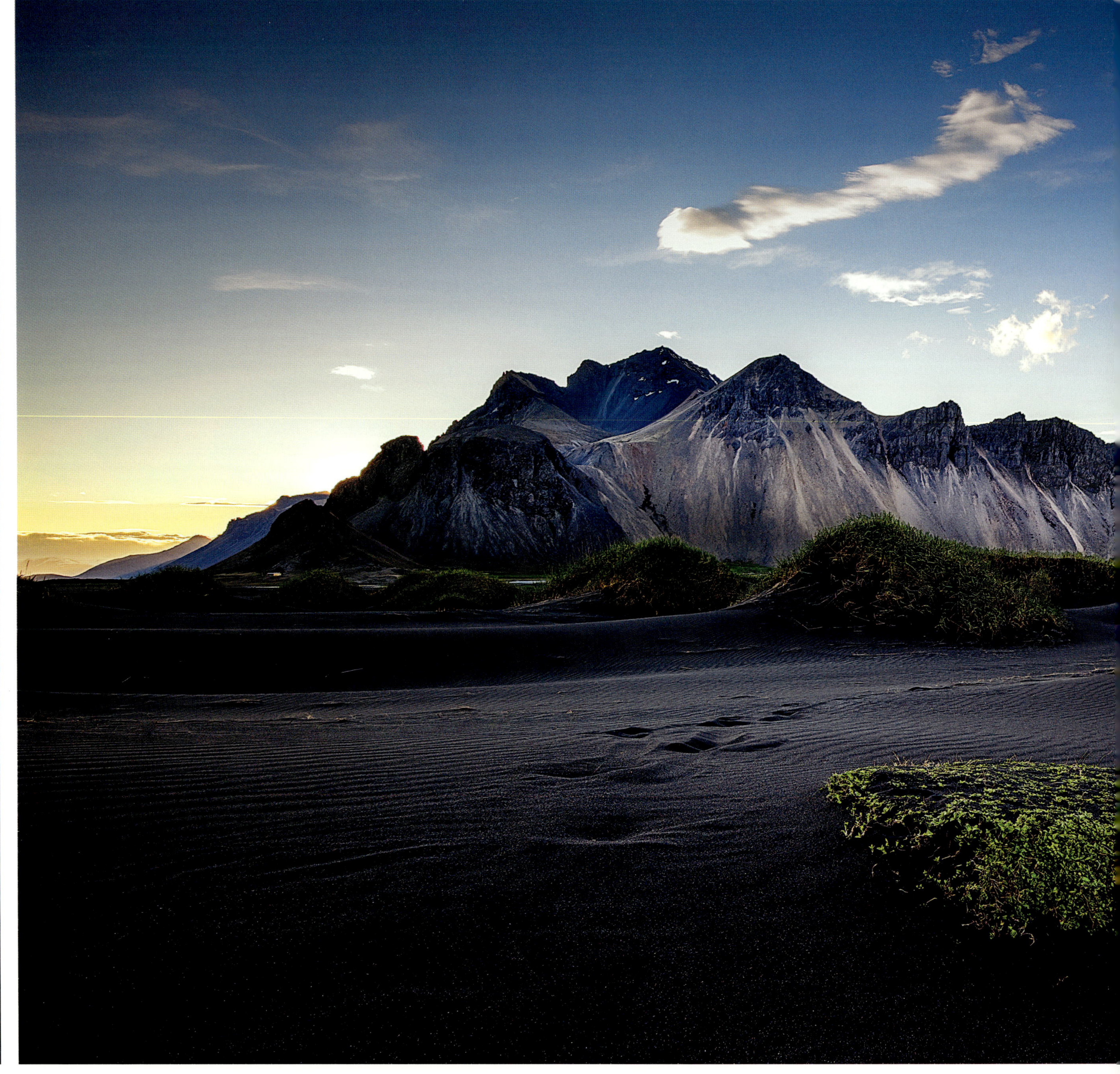

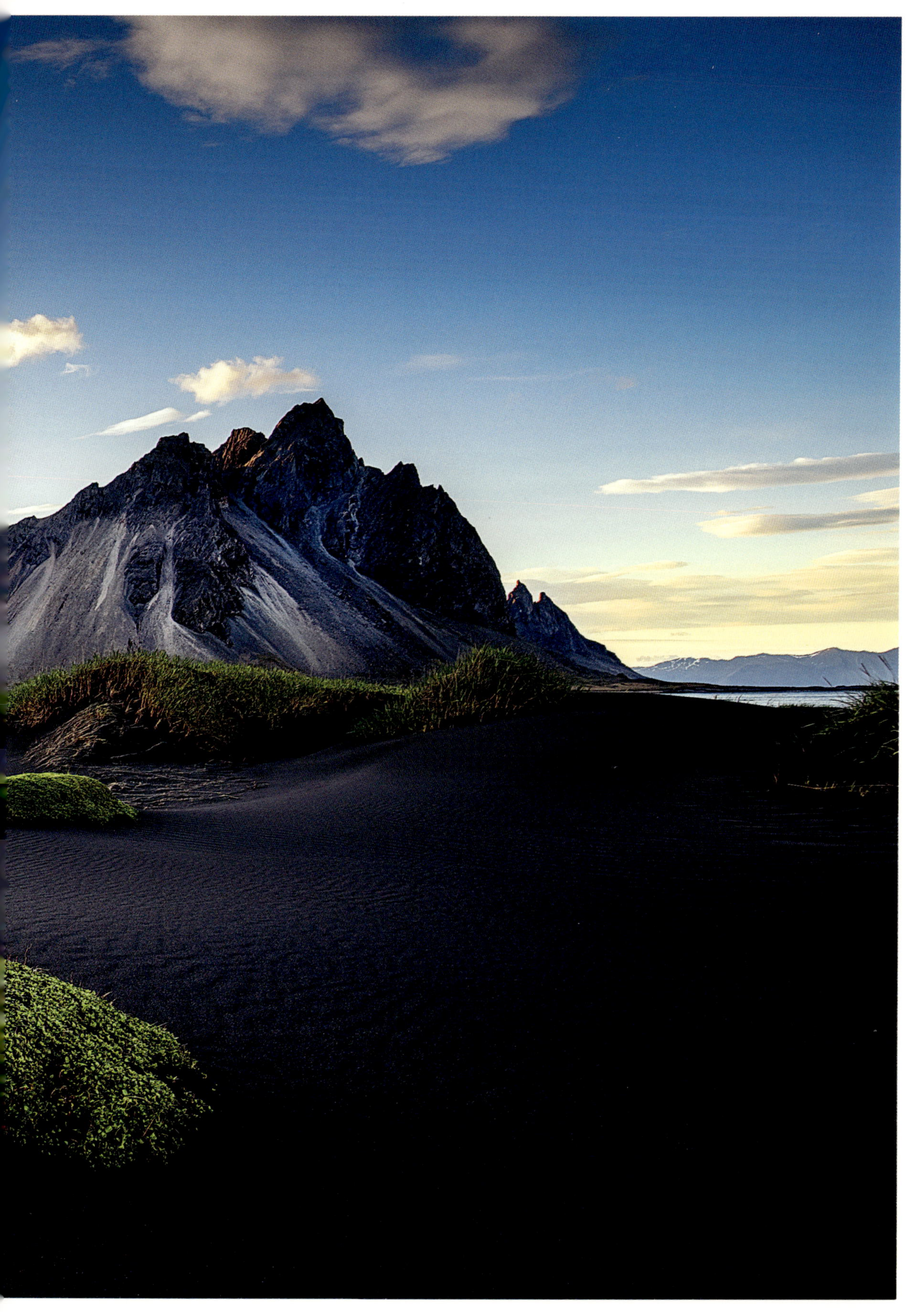

Mountain Views
Stokksnes, Iceland

The Vestrahorn is a stunning mountain situated just outside
Hofn on a headland known as Stokksnes in south-east Iceland.
I have seen many images of this location and have always been
drawn to it.

Nikon D810, Nikon 16-35mm lens, 1/80sec at f/11, ISO 100.
Tripod, cable release, graduated filter. Post-capture: basic image
management.

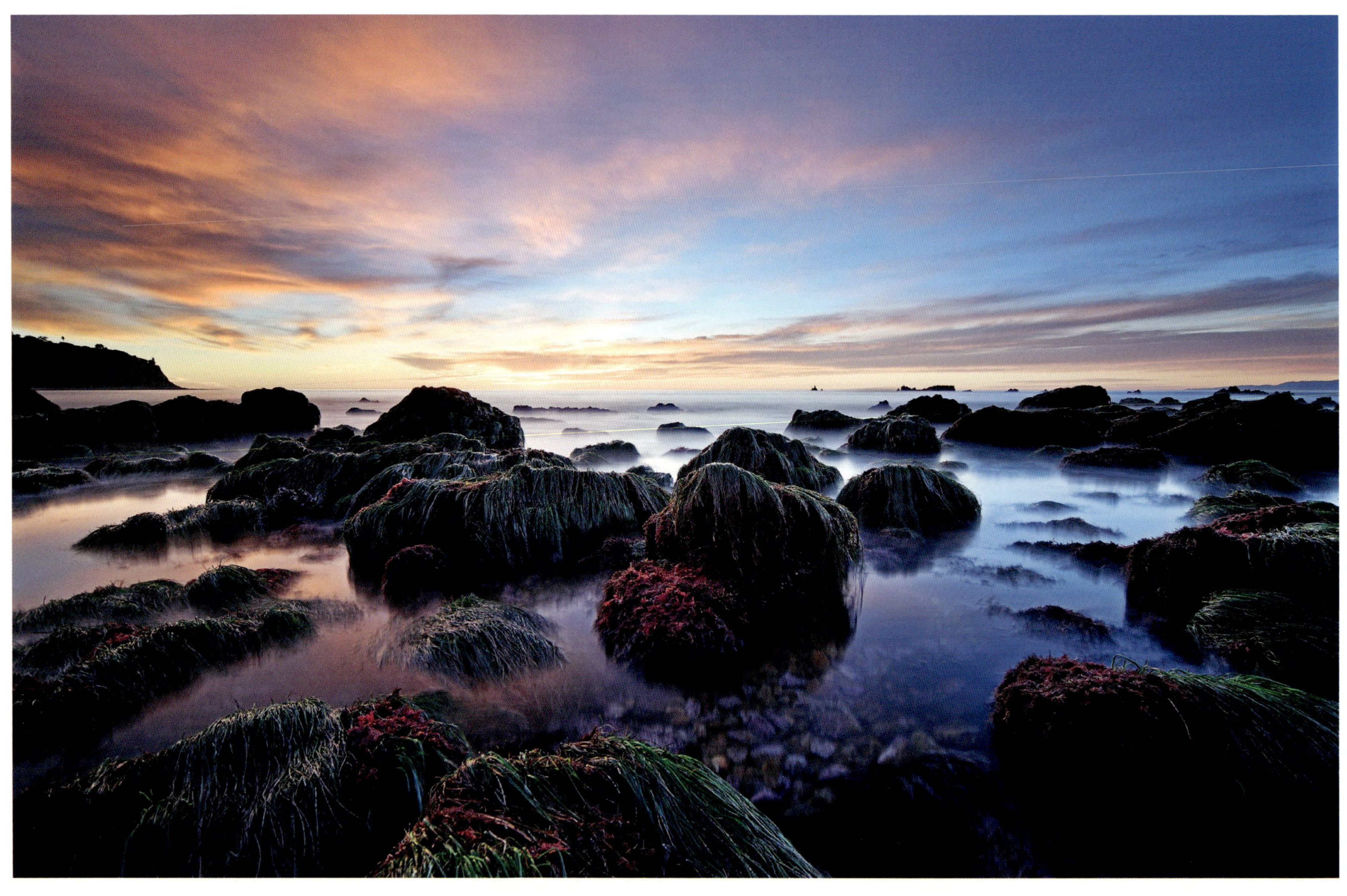

Mossy

Palos Verdes, California, USA

Checking tide charts for the week, I knew that low tide would line up with sunset on this day, so I made my way out to a local beach. Scrambling down the cliffs, I spotted a bunch of mossy rocks that are normally hidden by the tide. As I approached the rocks, there was an abundance of vibrant moss and sea grass scattered amongst them. I opted for a long exposure to smooth the water and focus attention on the plant life.

📷 Nikon D750, Tokina 11-16mm lens, 10sec + 108sec, ISO 100. Post-capture: two exposures of the foreground were blended with one of the sky.

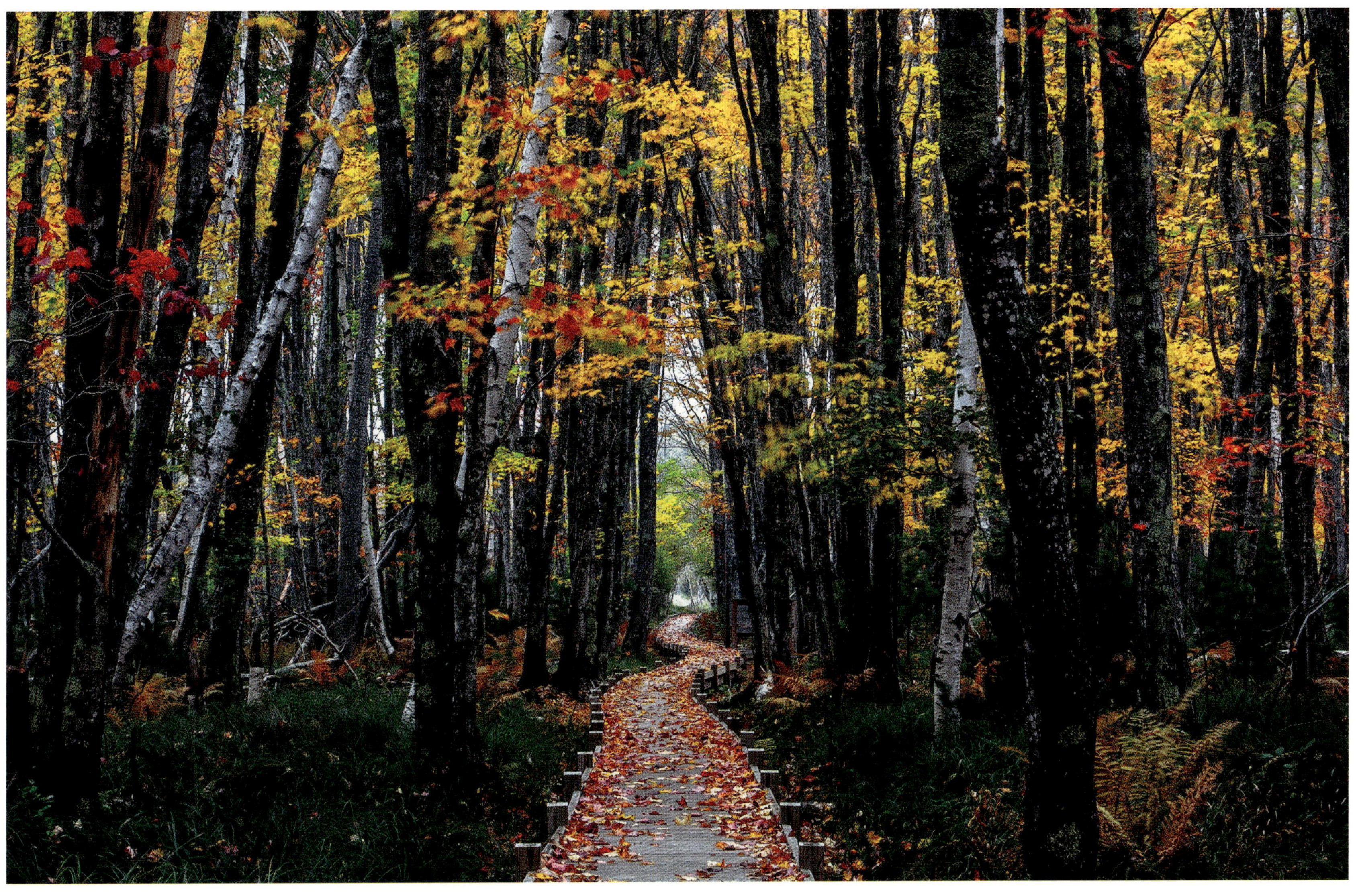

▲ J.K. PUTNAM 3RD PLACE

Jesup Path in Fall
Acadia National Park, Maine, USA

Fall is a very special time in Acadia National Park. I wanted to create a photograph that not only showed the beauty of this time of year but also gave the idea of people enjoying it. With my composition I am relying on the viewer's imagination, rather than posing a model in the scene, in the hopes that they will place themselves there.

Canon EOS 5DS, Canon 100-400mm lens, 1sec at f/32, ISO 100. Tripod.

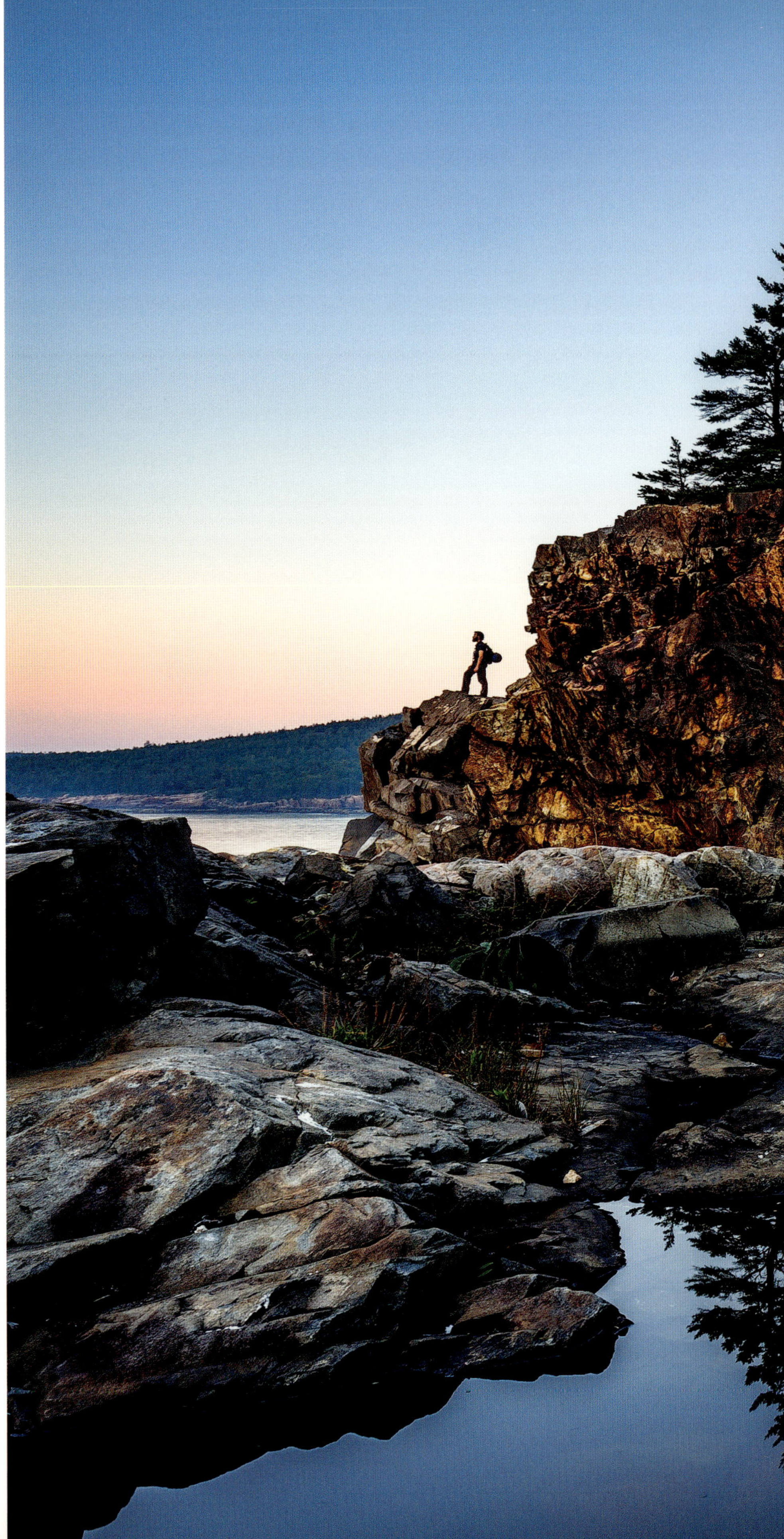

Hiker on Acadia's Coast
Acadia National Park, Maine, USA

This was an unplanned moment. The person in the photograph was a visitor to the area who I had been showing around for a couple of days. He had made his way out to the ledge in the photo to get a better look around. It is easy to lose yourself in the beauty of this landscape; I've experienced it many times as do most visitors to the area. I composed my image in a way that would represent this feeling of being lost in a landscape.

Canon EOS 6D, Canon 16-35mm lens, 4sec at f/22, ISO 100. Tripod, neutral density graduated filters.

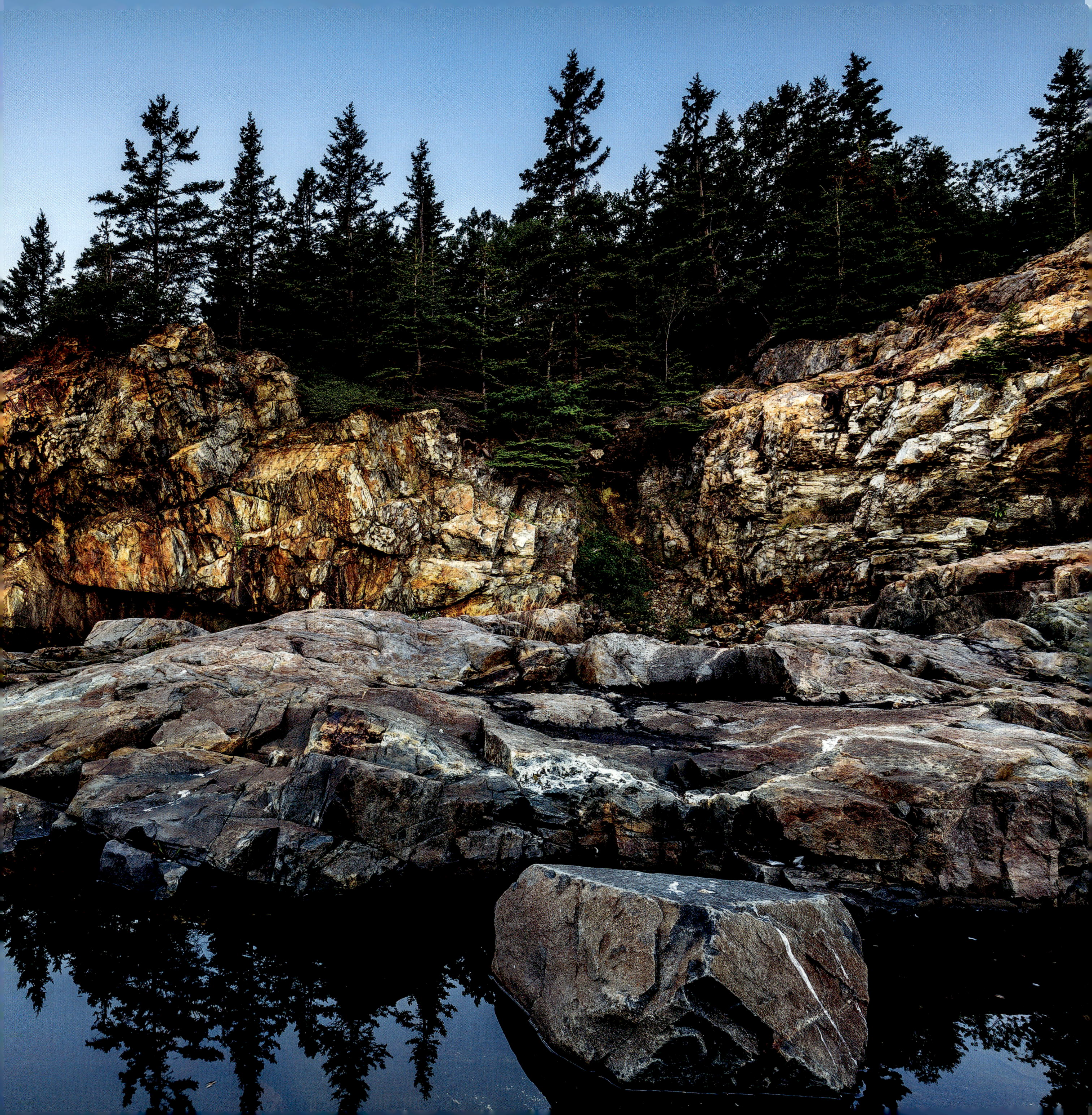

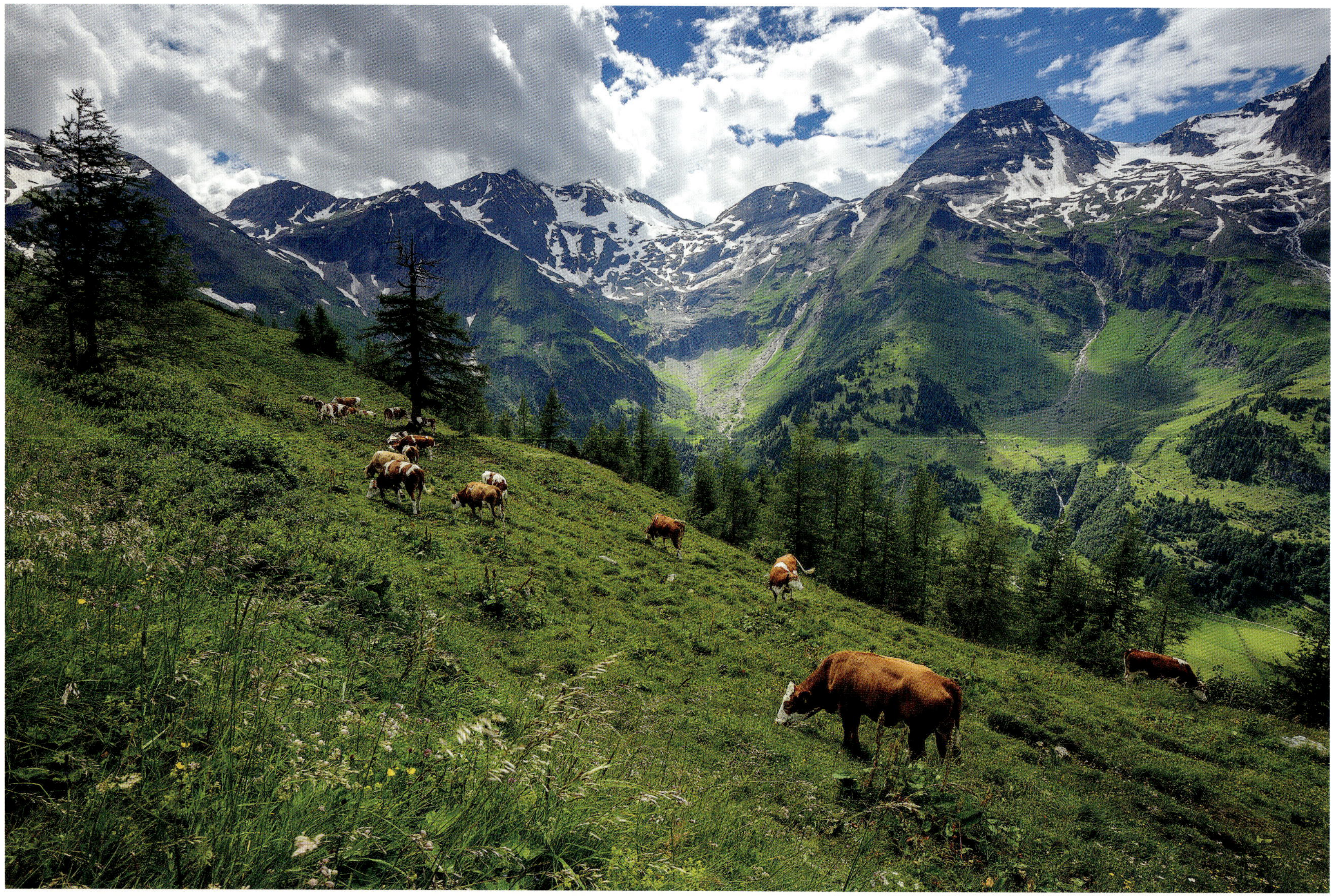

HIGHLY COMMENDED

Alpine Idyll
Austrian Alps, Austria

Every year I like to spend my summer vacation with my family in the Alps. On this particular day there was bright sunshine, clean air and a blue sky with spectacular clouds. I wanted to capture a moment of ultimate beauty and untouched nature; the peaceful cows and snow-capped mountains finished off the composition perfectly.

Nikon D600, Nikkor 16-35mm lens, 1/80sec at f/14, ISO 100. Post-capture: minor cloning, basic image management.

ADAM BURTON ▶

FINALIST

Yosemite Falls
Yosemite National Park, California, USA

At almost 1500 feet the immense Upper Yosemite Falls is one of North America's highest waterfalls. Yet, with the ongoing Californian drought, I was worried that the waterfall would be totally dry by the time I visited it in June. I shouldn't have been so concerned; although the waterfall was less powerful than during a typical spring, nevertheless it was flowing heavily enough to provide an awe inspiring backdrop to the breathtaking scenery of Yosemite Valley.

Nikon D800E, Nikon 17-35mm lens, 1/3sec at f/11, ISO 100. Post-capture: basic image management.

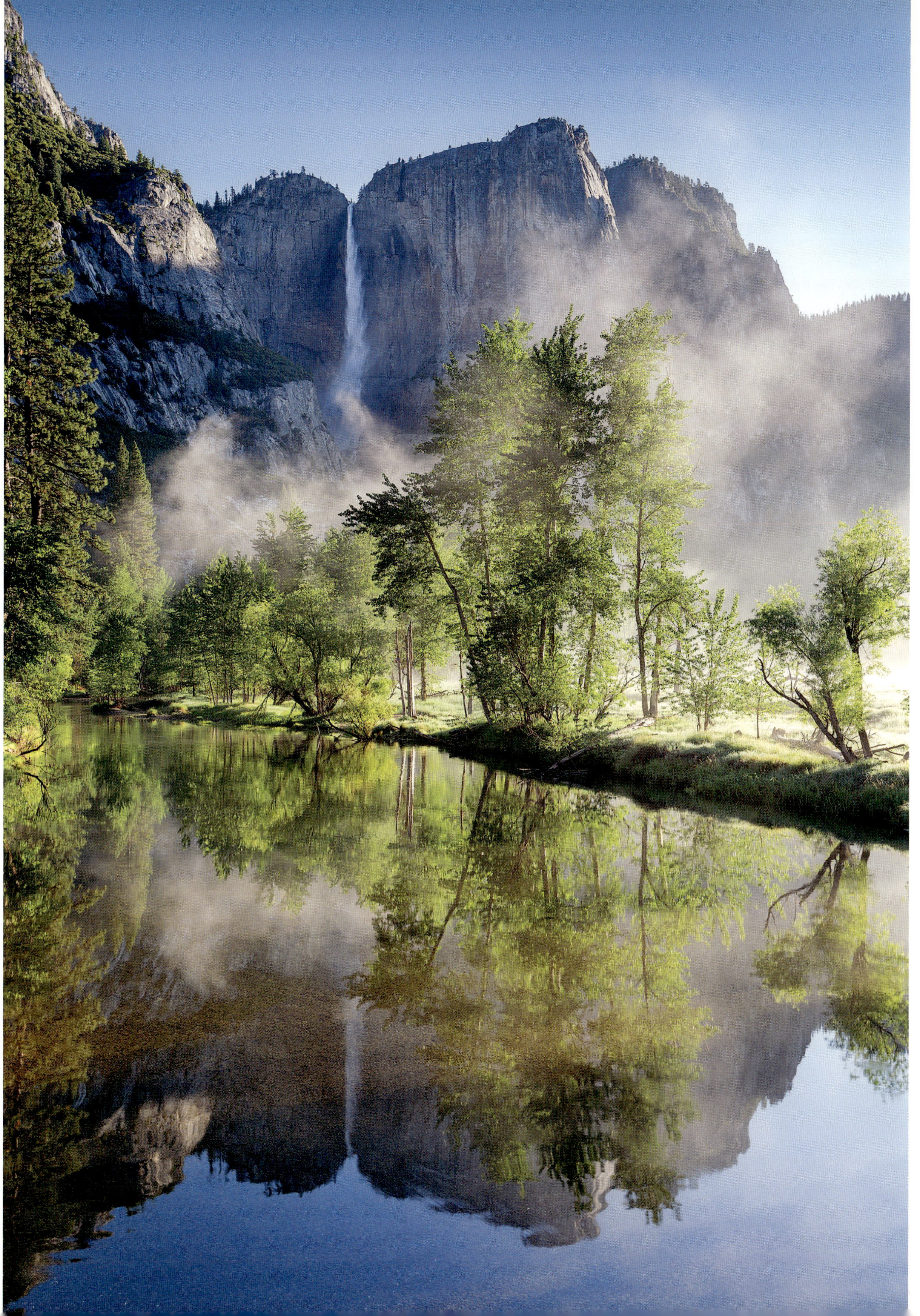

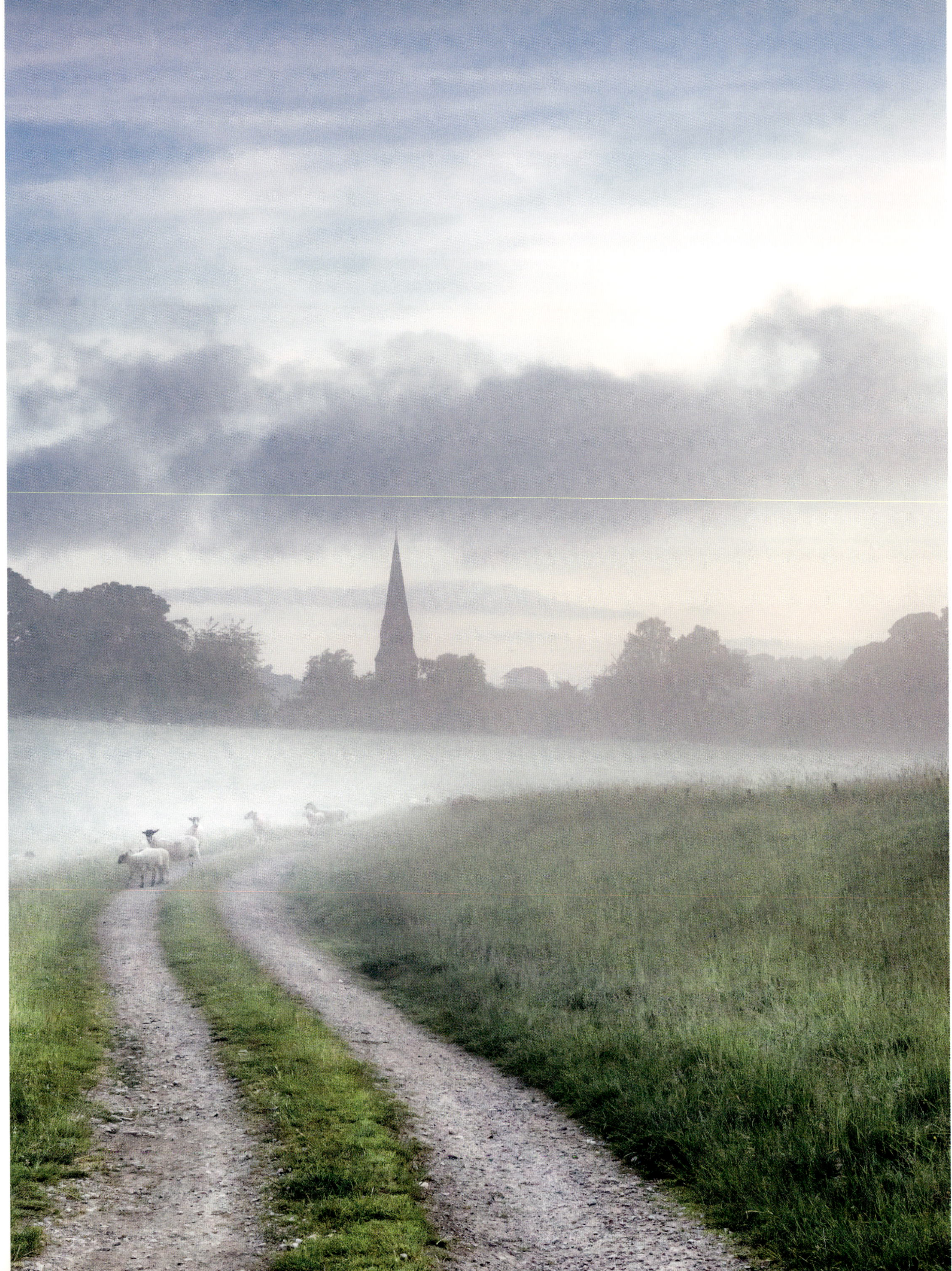

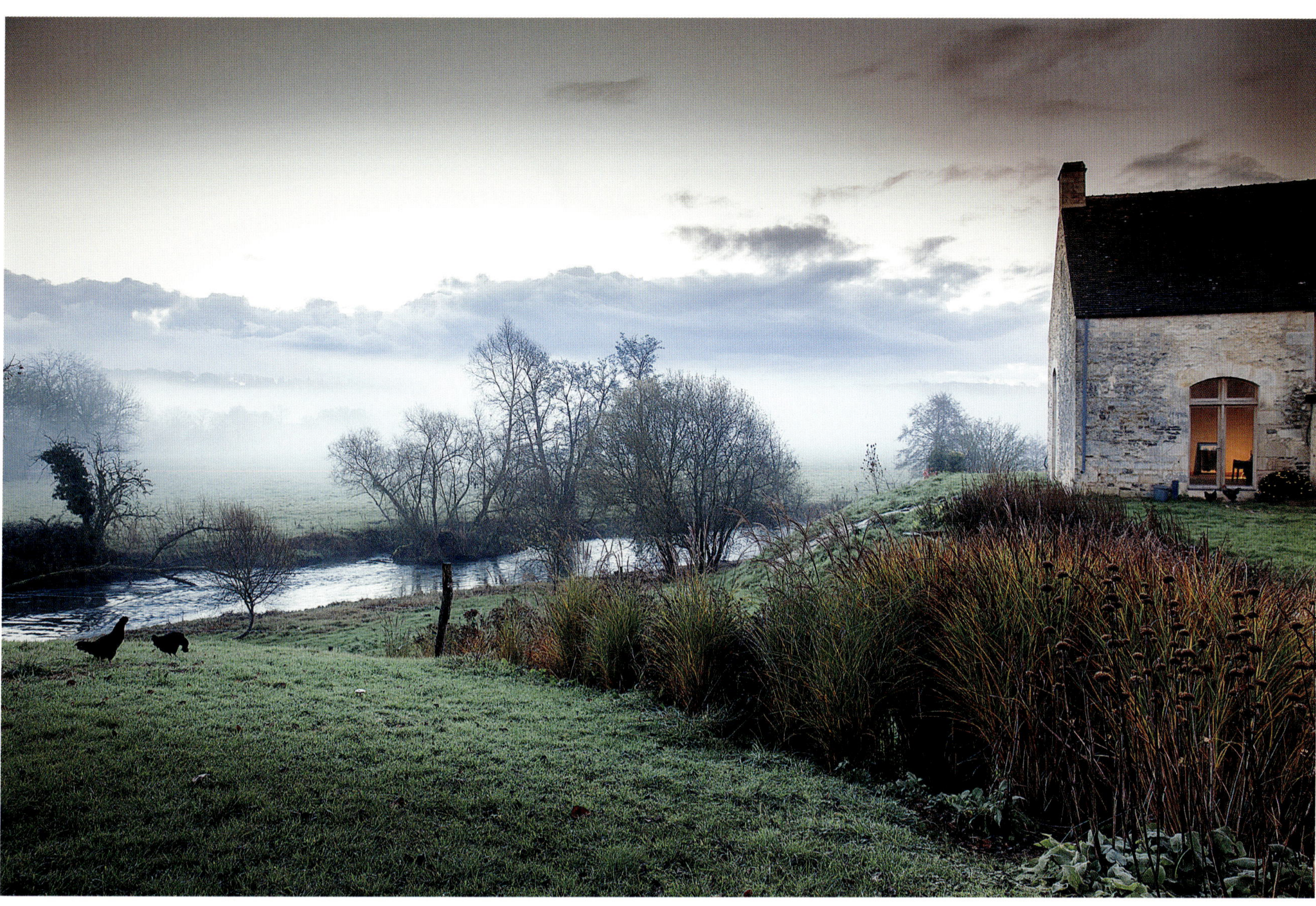

| ◀ **JUDE GADD** | HIGHLY COMMENDED | ▲ **SIBYLLE PIETREK** | HIGHLY COMMENDED |

Morning Mist
Chatsworth Park, Derbyshire, England, UK

I was on my way to photograph the sunrise down by the river in Chatsworth Park. The morning was very quiet and peaceful and as I walked along I saw before me this beautiful pastoral scene and just had to stop to photograph it. The sheep were so well positioned on the track and the mist and church were a perfect backdrop; there was even a tiny hint of colour creeping into the sky.

Sony α7, 28-70mm lens, 1/13sec at f/14. Post-capture: basic image management.

La Queurie
Normandy, France

This is a peaceful place in Normandy, with some beautifully renovated period houses belonging to my sister and her husband. I love staying there to work on my projects, as I am inspired by nature whilst there.

Canon EOS 5D Mark III, Canon 24-70mm lens, 1/13sec at f/5.6. Tripod. Post-capture: basic image management.

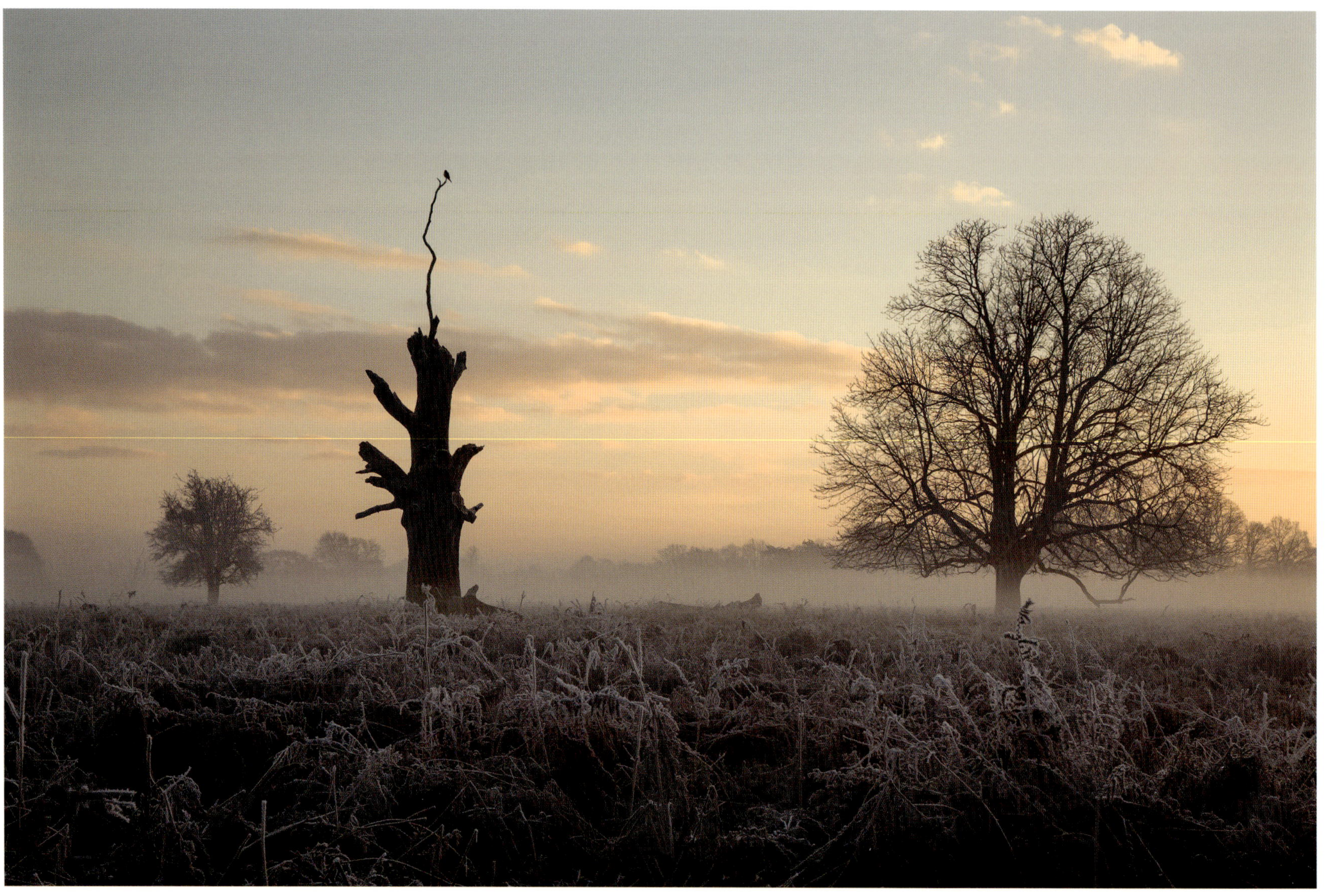

DUNCAN HERRING   HIGHLY COMMENDED

Winter's Morning
Bushy Park, London, England, UK

I took this image in Bushy Park on the perfect winter's morning. A thick hoar frost had formed overnight on withered bracken and a mist lingered in the still cold air. Dawn brought a gentle glow, illuminating the outline of my favourite tree. On that morning, a sparrowhawk, waiting for the sun's warming rays, topped its distinctive form.

Canon EOS 5D Mark III, Canon 24-105mm lens, 1/125sec at f/14, ISO 200. Tripod. Post-capture: basic image management.

MARK BOYD ▶   FINALIST

Poppies on Wheat II
Oxfordshire, England, UK

I was returning from a day on the River Cherwell in Oxfordshire when in the corner of my eye the bright sunlight illuminated a hidden corn field, capturing my attention. I stood watching the corn move slowly in the breeze, then it stopped; the corn stood still and two beautiful poppies gave all the contrast I needed. I set up my tripod and watched; I stood for half an hour, just waiting and watching for the perfect light conditions.

Canon EOS 5D Mark II, Canon 17-40mm lens, 1/6sec at f/16, ISO 100. Tripod.

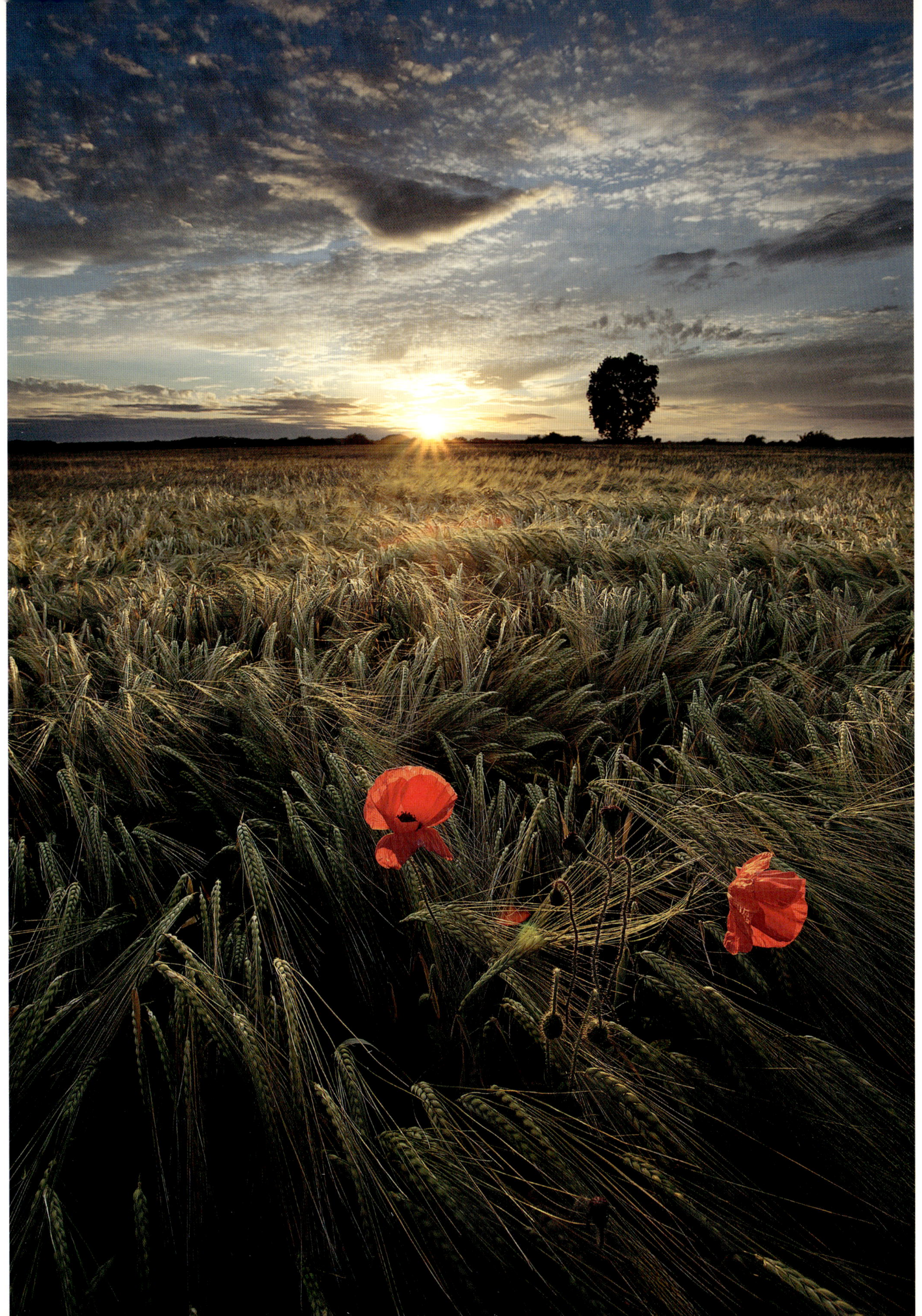

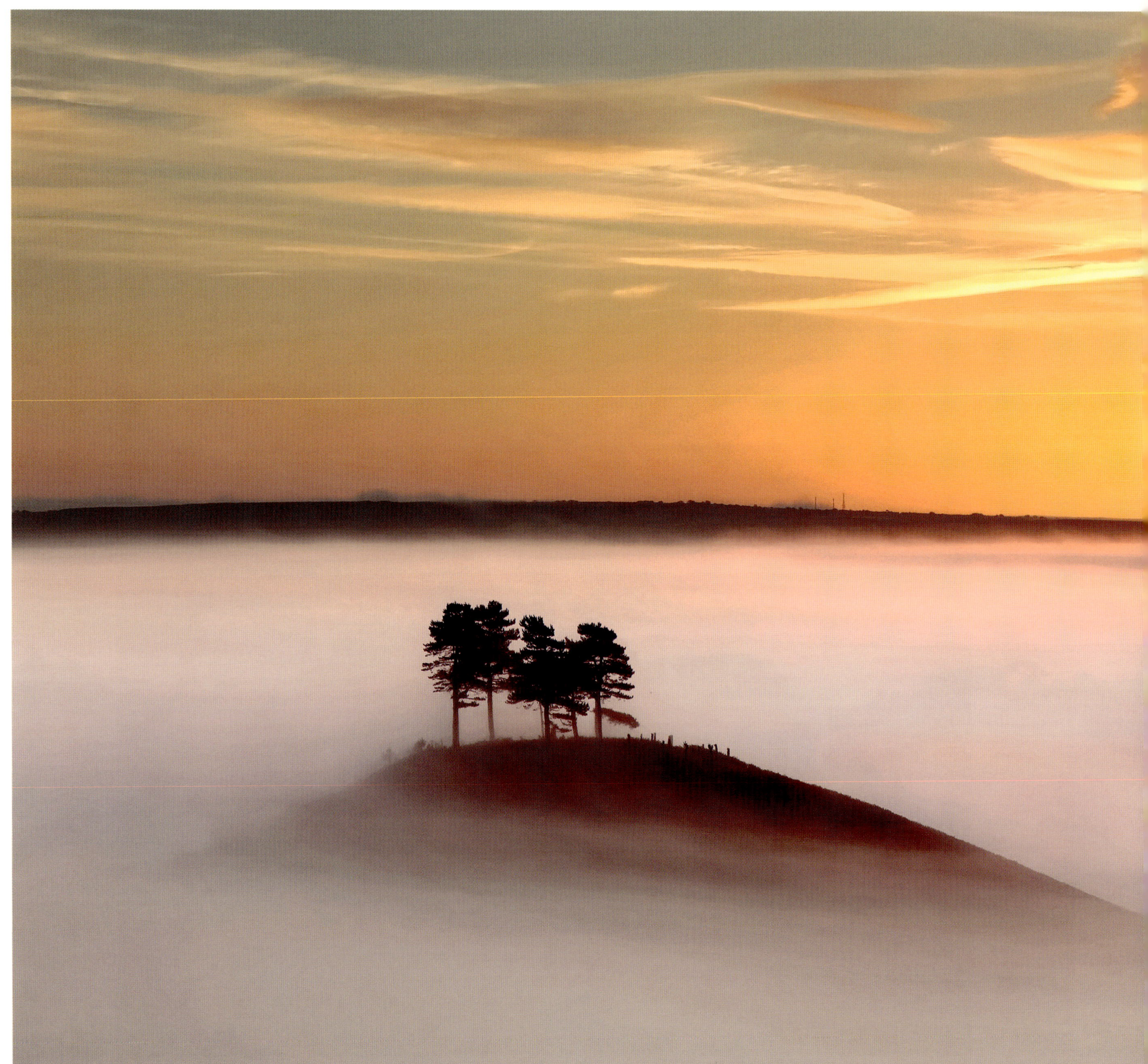

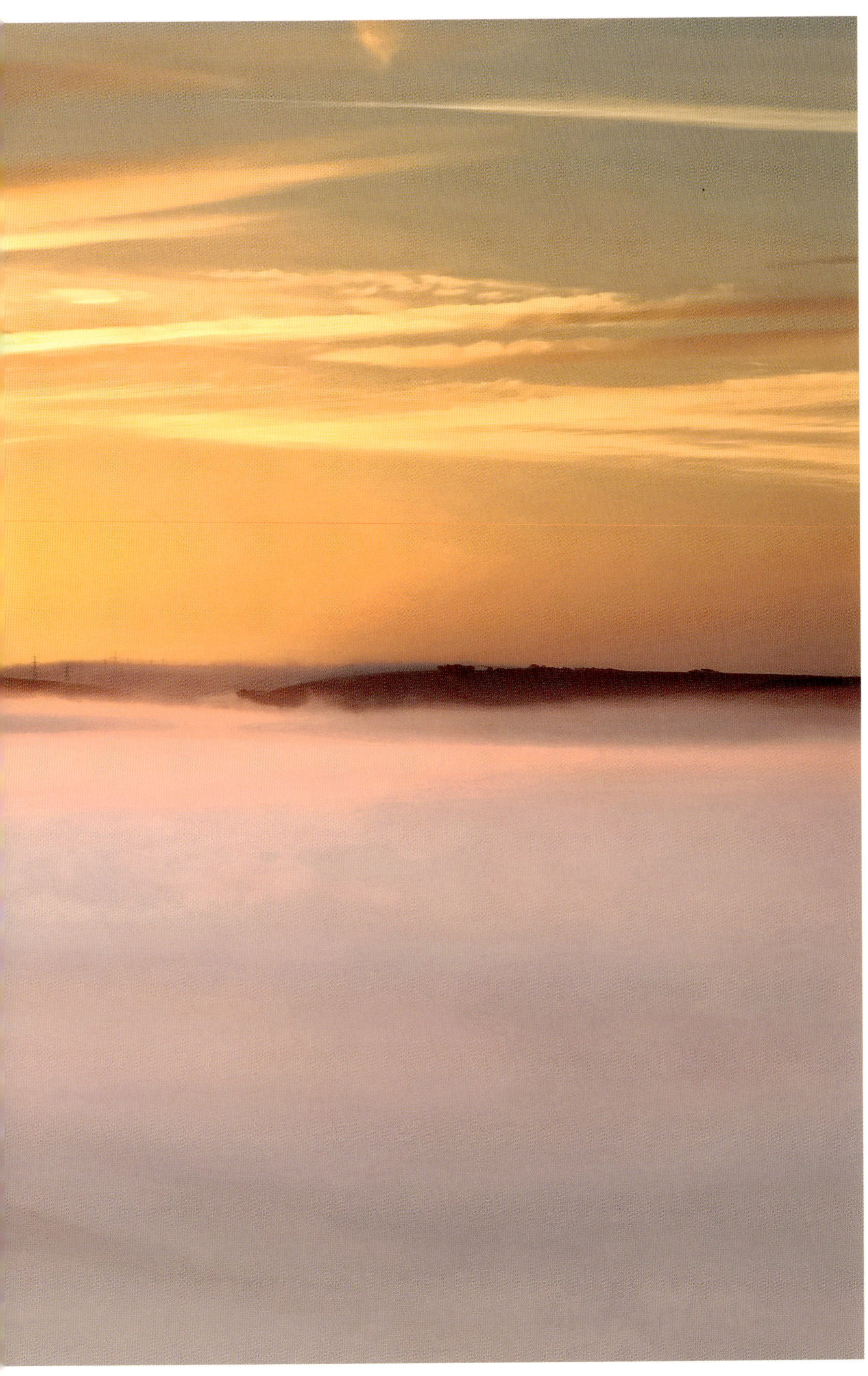

Breathe
Dorset, England, UK

This is Colmer's Hill, a well-known landmark in west Dorset. The location is particularly prone to mist and on this occasion it was thick enough to envelop the hill. A stand of Caledonian pine trees adorns the summit, planted by Major Colfox during the First World War.

Canon EOS 5D Mark II, Canon 24-105mm lens, 1/25sec at f/11, ISO 100. Neutral density graduated filter.

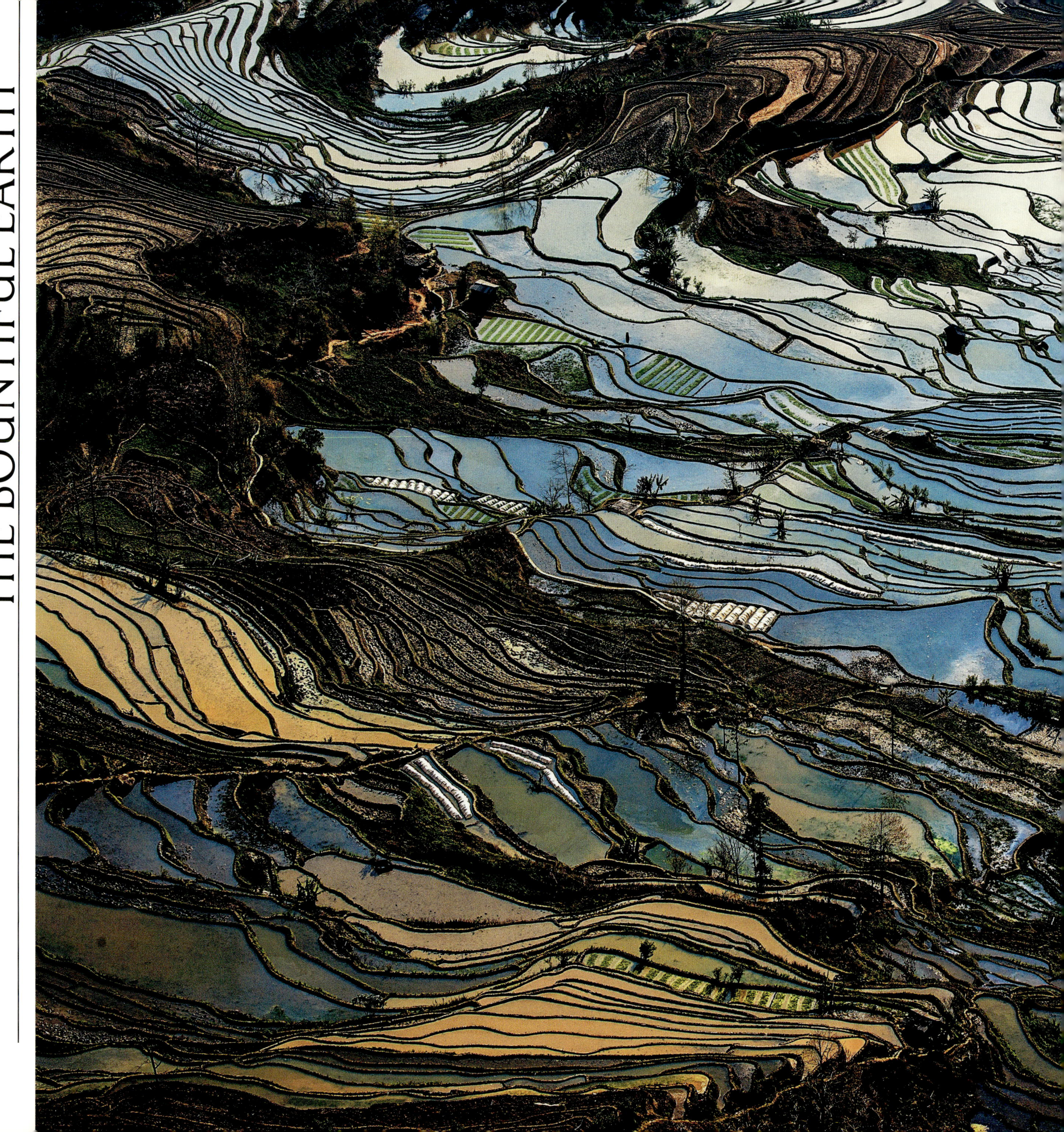
THE BOUNTIFUL EARTH

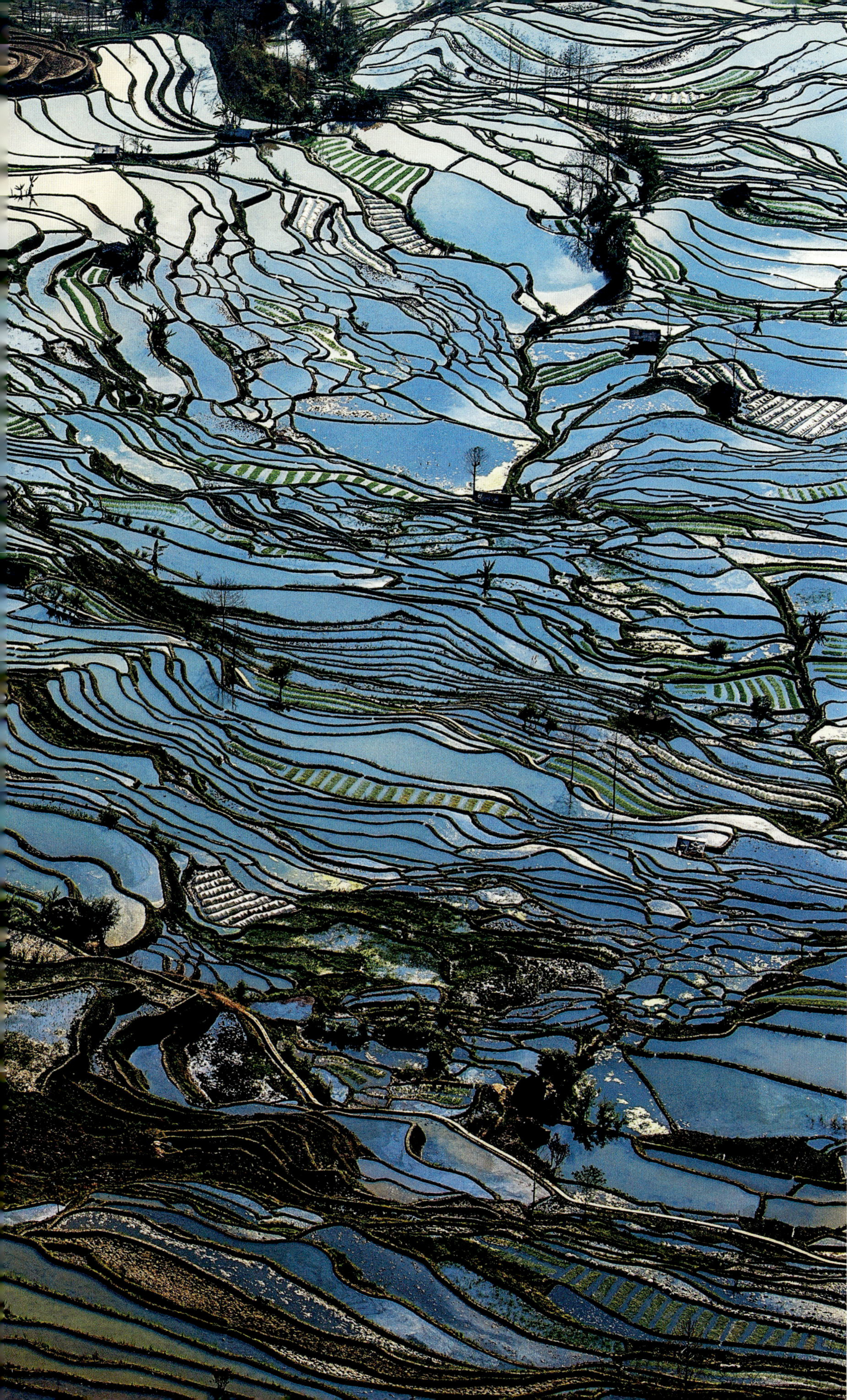

Picturesque Earth
Yuanyang, Yunnan, China

The Yuanyang Rice Terraces in Yunnan Province have over two thousand years of history. They are both widely recognised and greatly cherished. The colours have a deep artistic quality and take on myriad shapes and outlines; the lowest section of the terrace resembles a galloping horse.

Nikon D800E, 80-400mm lens, 1/160sec at f/16, ISO 100.

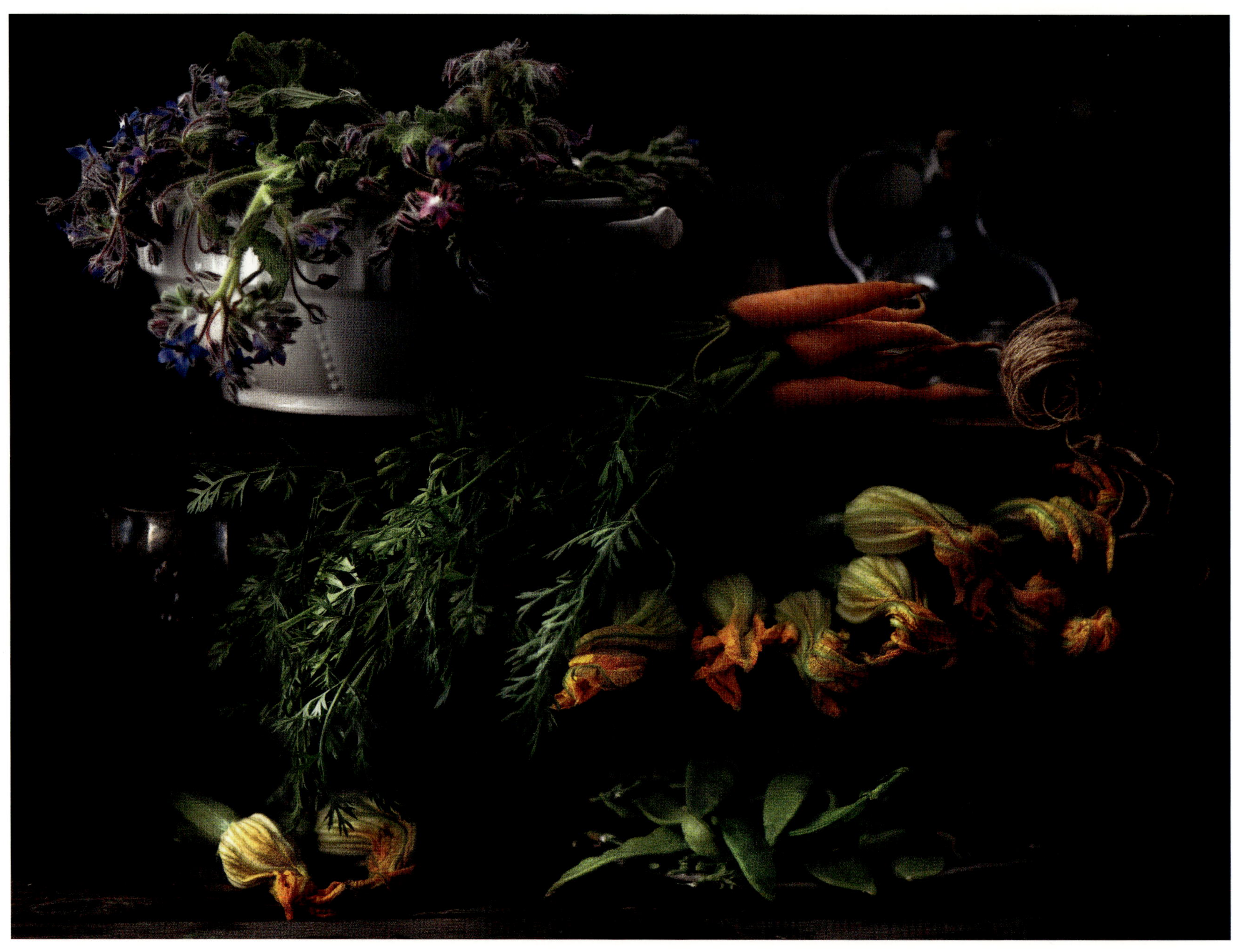

Summer Shelf
Torino, Piedmont, Italy

There is no better time than harvest time; for me, it's pure happiness. I also love the combination of antiques and the Dutch Master style of painting to create beautiful still life shots.

Nikon D700, Nikkor 105mm lens, 1/10sec at f/2.8, ISO 400. Post-capture: basic image management.

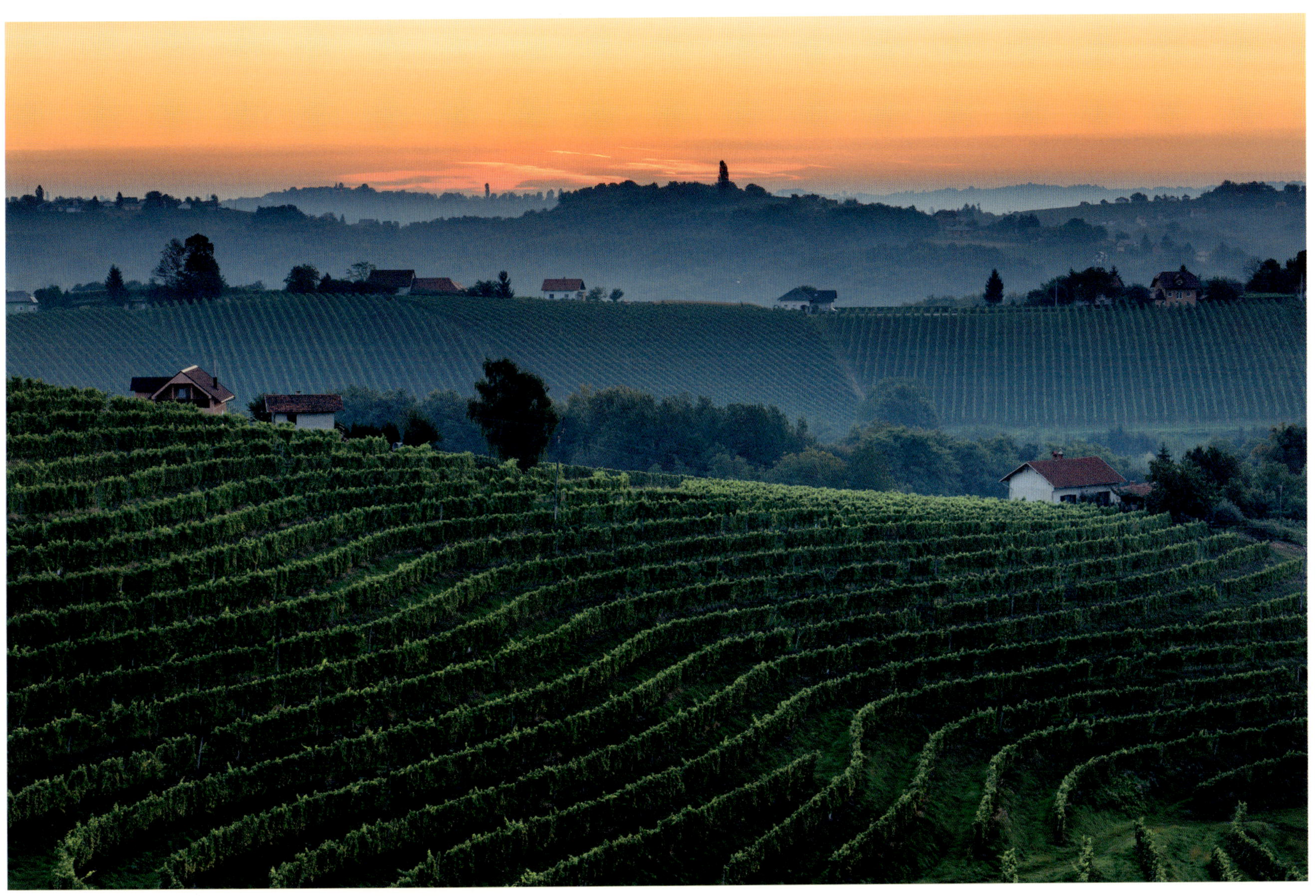

Endless Curves
Prlekija, Slovenia

Shot close to the Croatian border on a quiet morning, the gentle curves and layers of the vineyards disappear into the distance.

Nikon D800, Nikon 70-200mm lens, 1/5sec at f/16, ISO 200. Tripod, cable release.
Post-capture: basic image management.

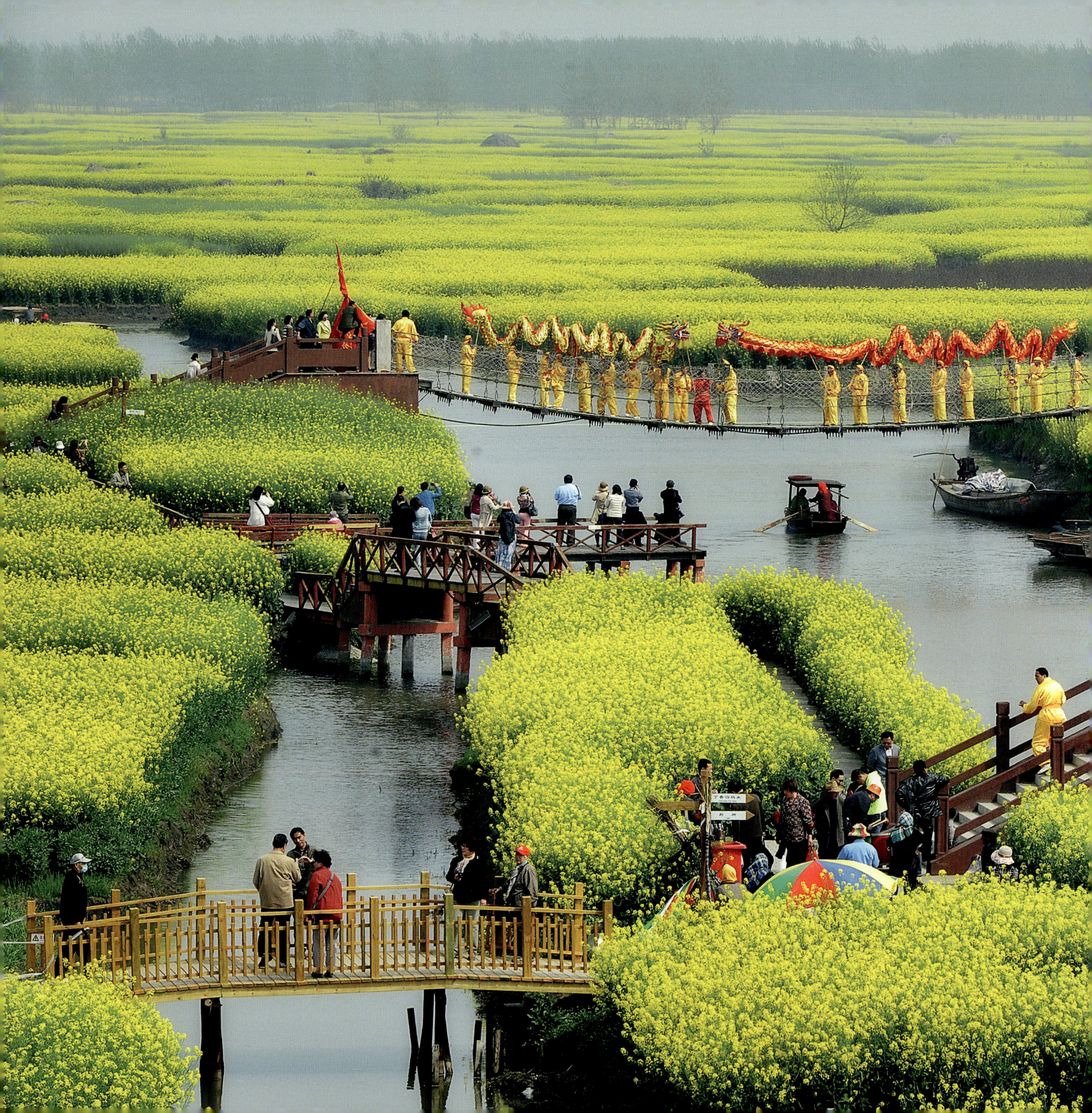

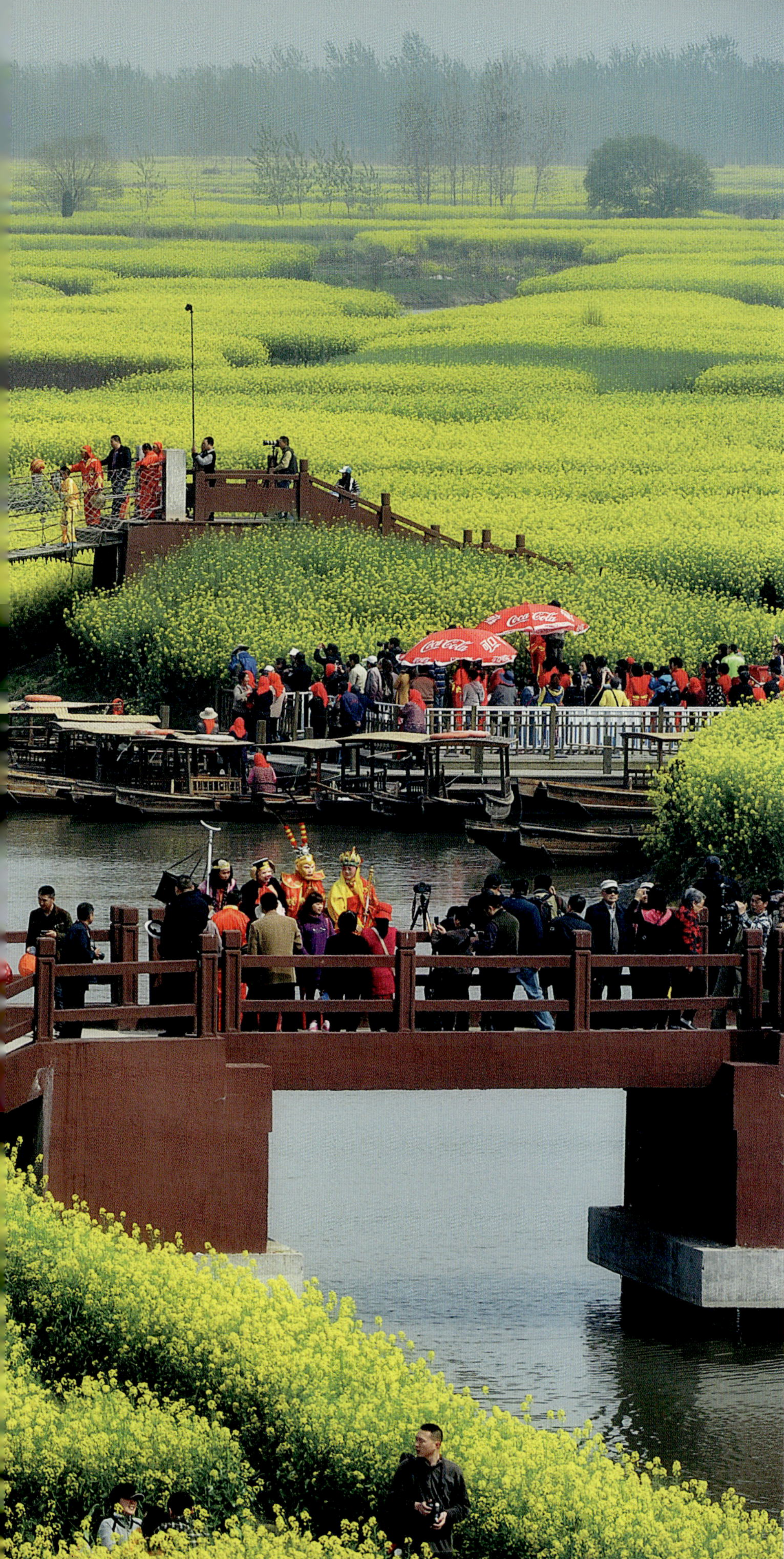

◄ **GUOMEI YANG**   FINALIST

Waterside
Xinghua, Jiangsu, China

In spring, visitors come to enjoy the beautiful view of blossoming rape flower. The colour of the flower indicates an auspicious and harmonious life for those who live in the countryside.

📷 Nikon D4, Nikon 80-400mm lens, 1/800 sec at f/11, ISO 1000.

81

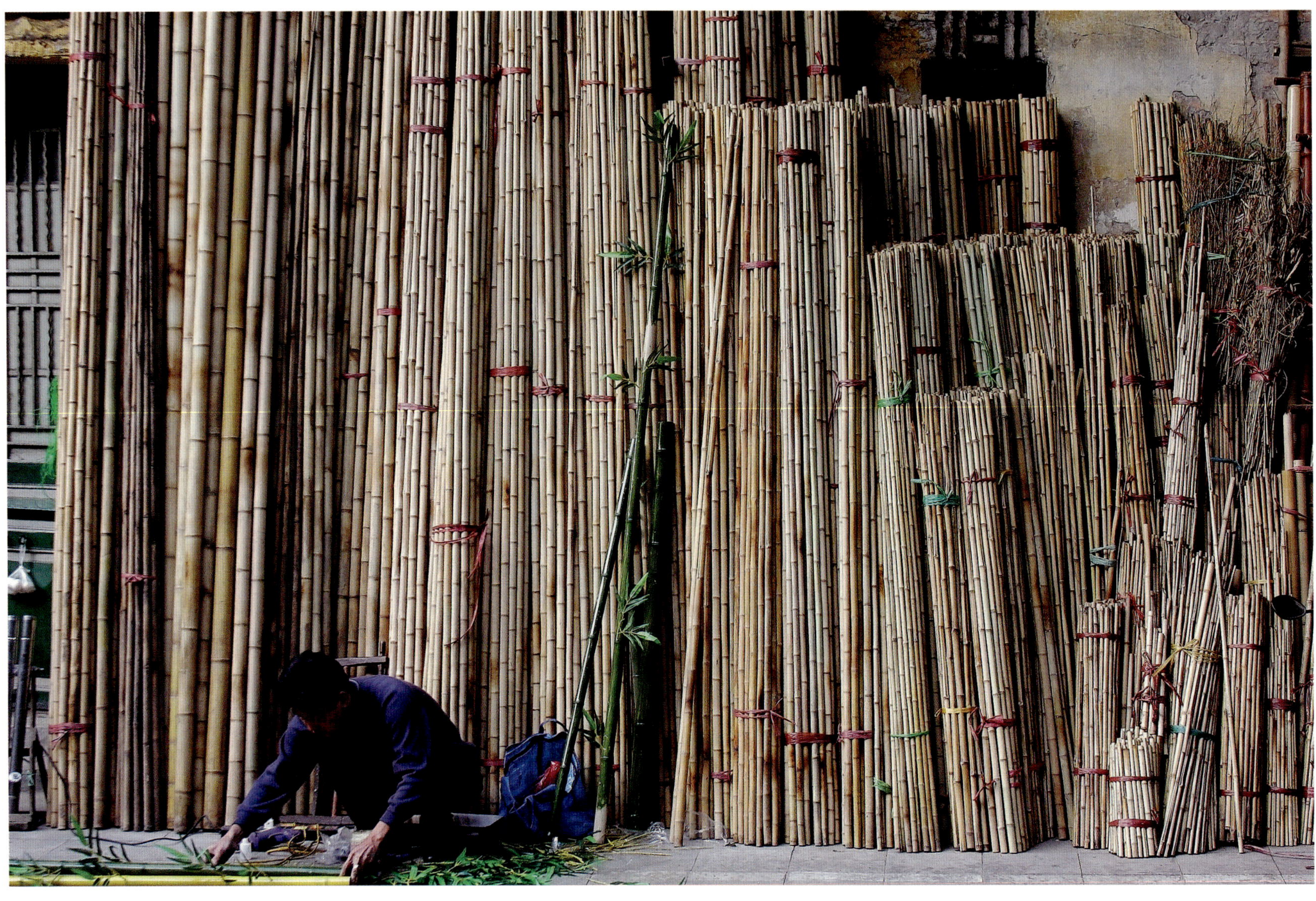

HIGHLY COMMENDED

Bamboo Seller
Hanoi, Vietnam

Hanoi is a frenetic city; the traffic, noise and dust are hard for a visitor to cope with, but this bamboo seller looked like he was a world away from the hectic streets. I waited for a break in the traffic to capture the scene.

Canon EOS 40D, Canon 28-135mm lens, 1/125sec at f/5.6, ISO 500.

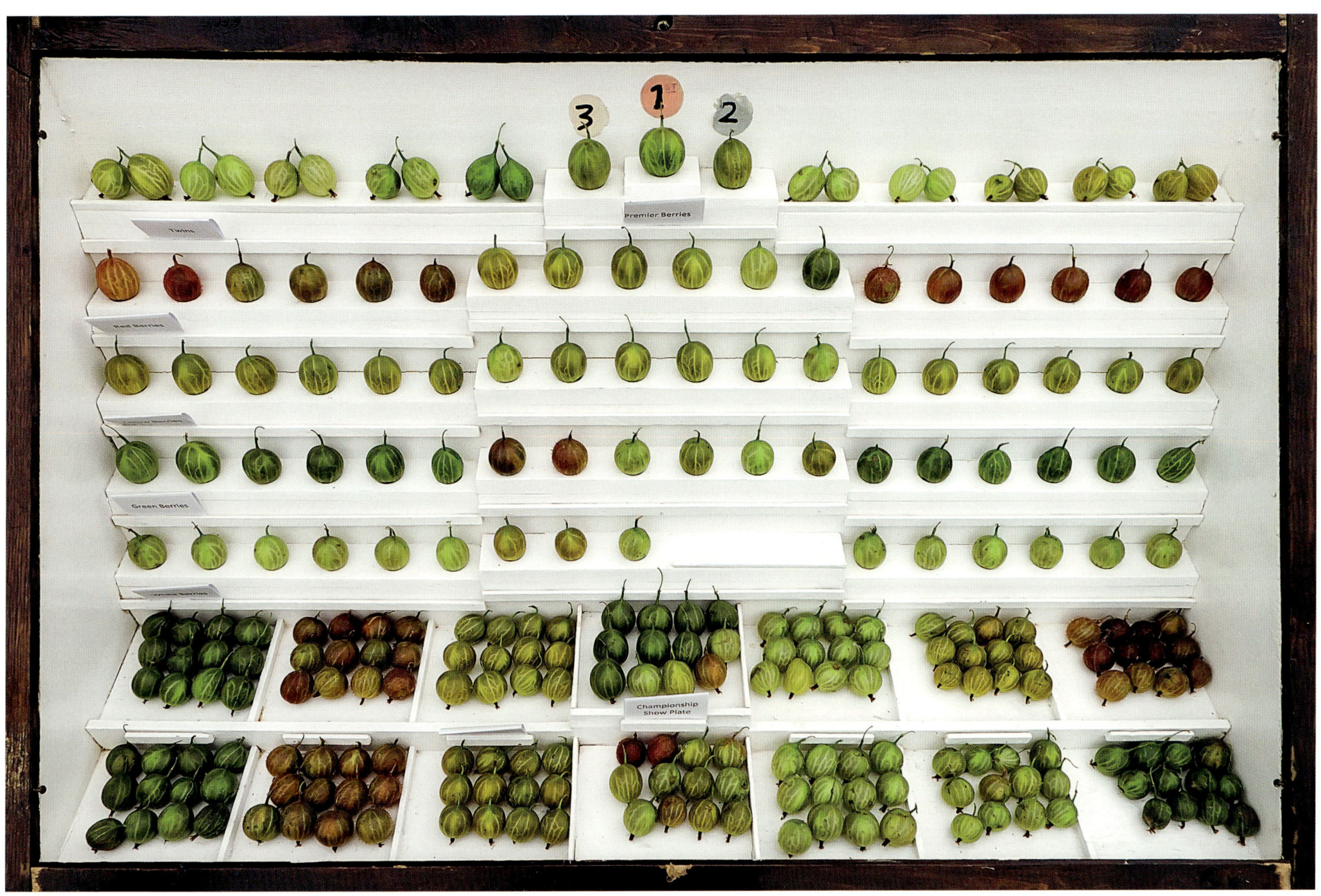

Gooseberry Display Case
Cheshire, England, UK

This image was taken on the stand of the Mid-Cheshire Gooseberry Association at the RHS Flower Show at Tatton Park in Cheshire. I found this display case and its contents so charming. The case looks to have been hand crafted and the fruits were so beautiful. I love the winners' podium; in my eyes, it is a total work of art.

📷 Panasonic DMC LX5, 1/250sec at f/2.8, ISO 125.

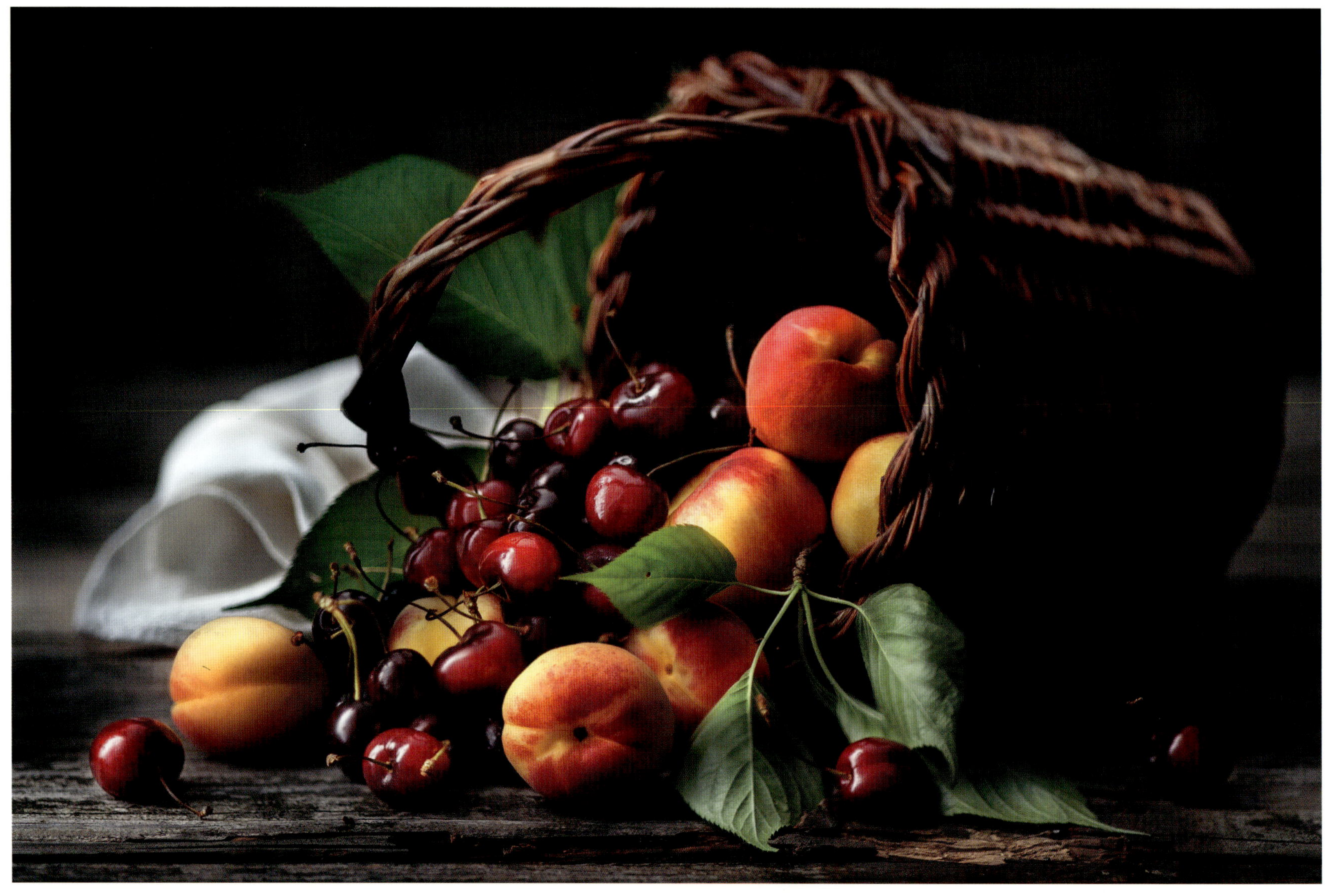

PATRIZIA PIGA HIGHLY COMMENDED

Summer Pouring
Torino, Piedmont, Italy

'Cavagnin' is the name used in the north of Italy for this particular basket. It is handmade by farmers from the branches of willow and used in the countryside to collect the products of the Earth. I couldn't find any better object to express the idea of a generous and plentiful summer.

Nikon D700, Nikkor 105mm lens, 1/2sec at f/2.8, ISO 200. Post-capture: basic image management.

FLAVIO CATALANO ▶ FINALIST

Nettles
Torino, Piedmont, Italy

Nettles I gathered by hand, in a wooden basket, ready to be made into a good soup with potatoes. The shot was inspired by the wild and severe aspect of the plant and produced with a look and feel reminiscent of Flemish painters.

Nikon D700, Nikkor 105mm lens, 1/6sec at f/2.8, ISO 400. Post-capture: basic image management.

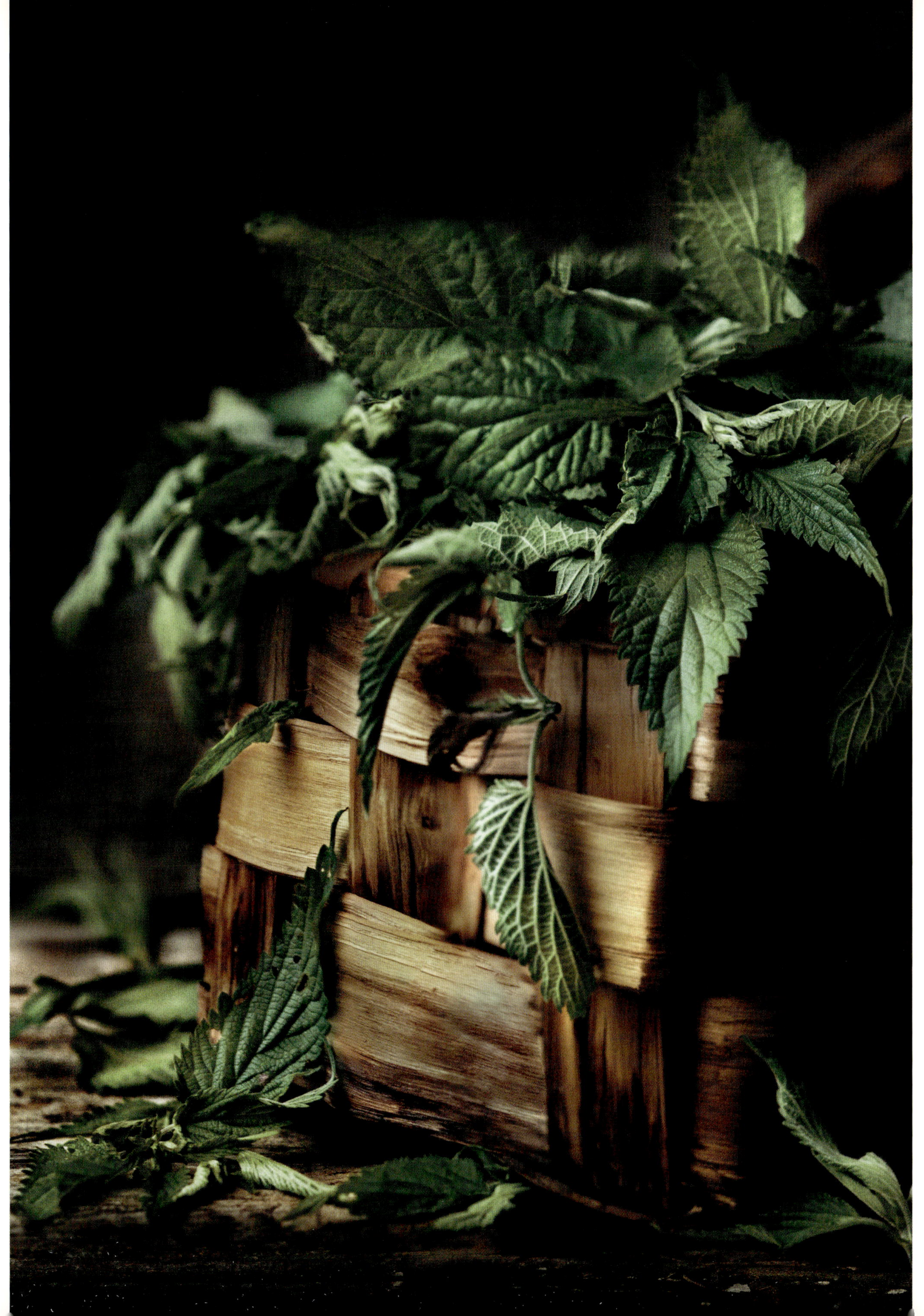

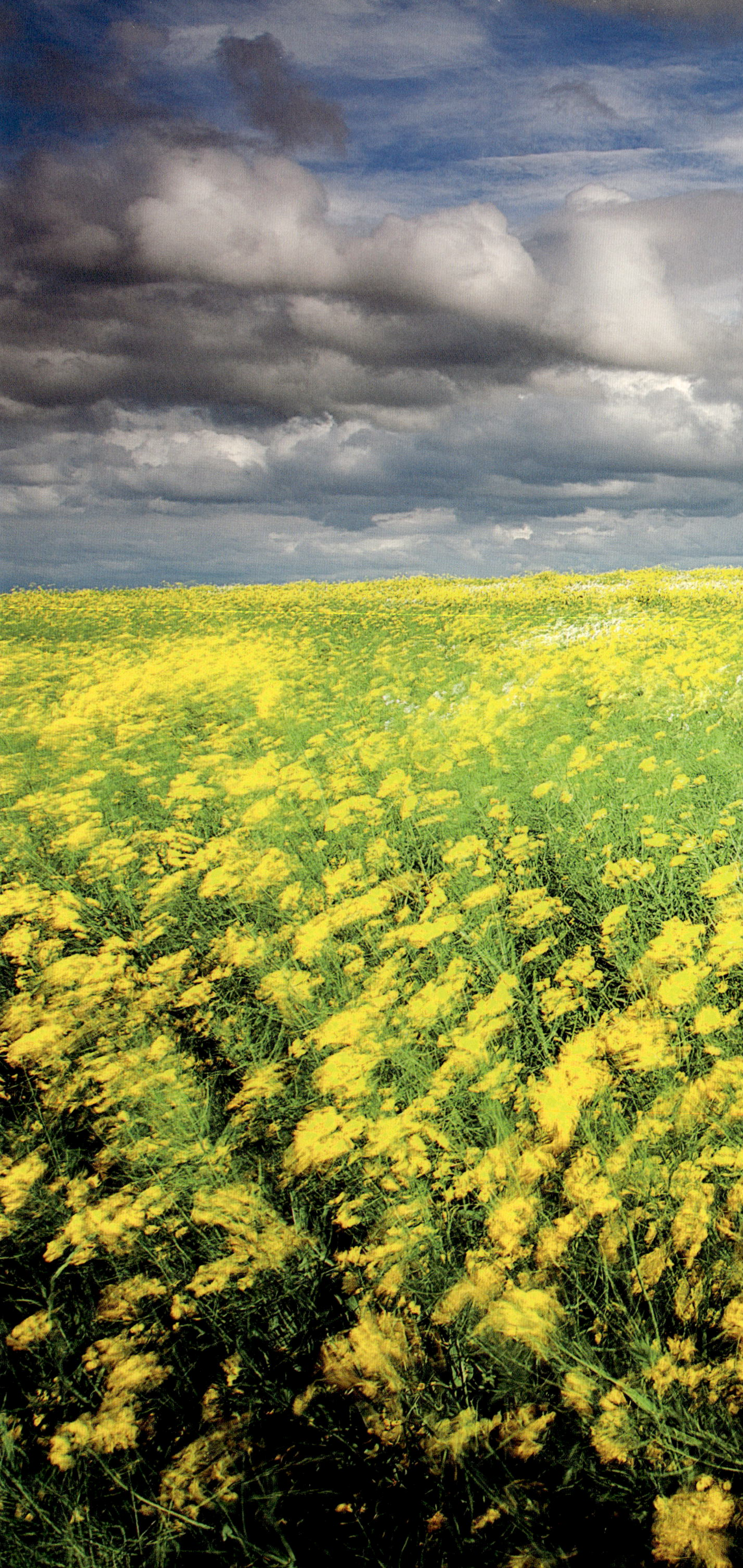

CHRIS HERRING ▶   FINALIST

Spring Breeze
Happisburgh, Norfolk, England, UK

Happisburgh Lighthouse in Happisburgh on the north Norfolk coast is the only independently operated lighthouse in Great Britain; It is also the oldest working lighthouse in East Anglia. The lighthouse sits at the highest point of the field, away from the cliff edge. A slow shutter speed was chosen to convey the sense of movement in the flowering oilseed rape.

Canon EOS 5D Mark II, Canon 17-40mm lens, 0.4sec at f/16, ISO 50. Neutral density graduated filters. Post-capture: basic image management.

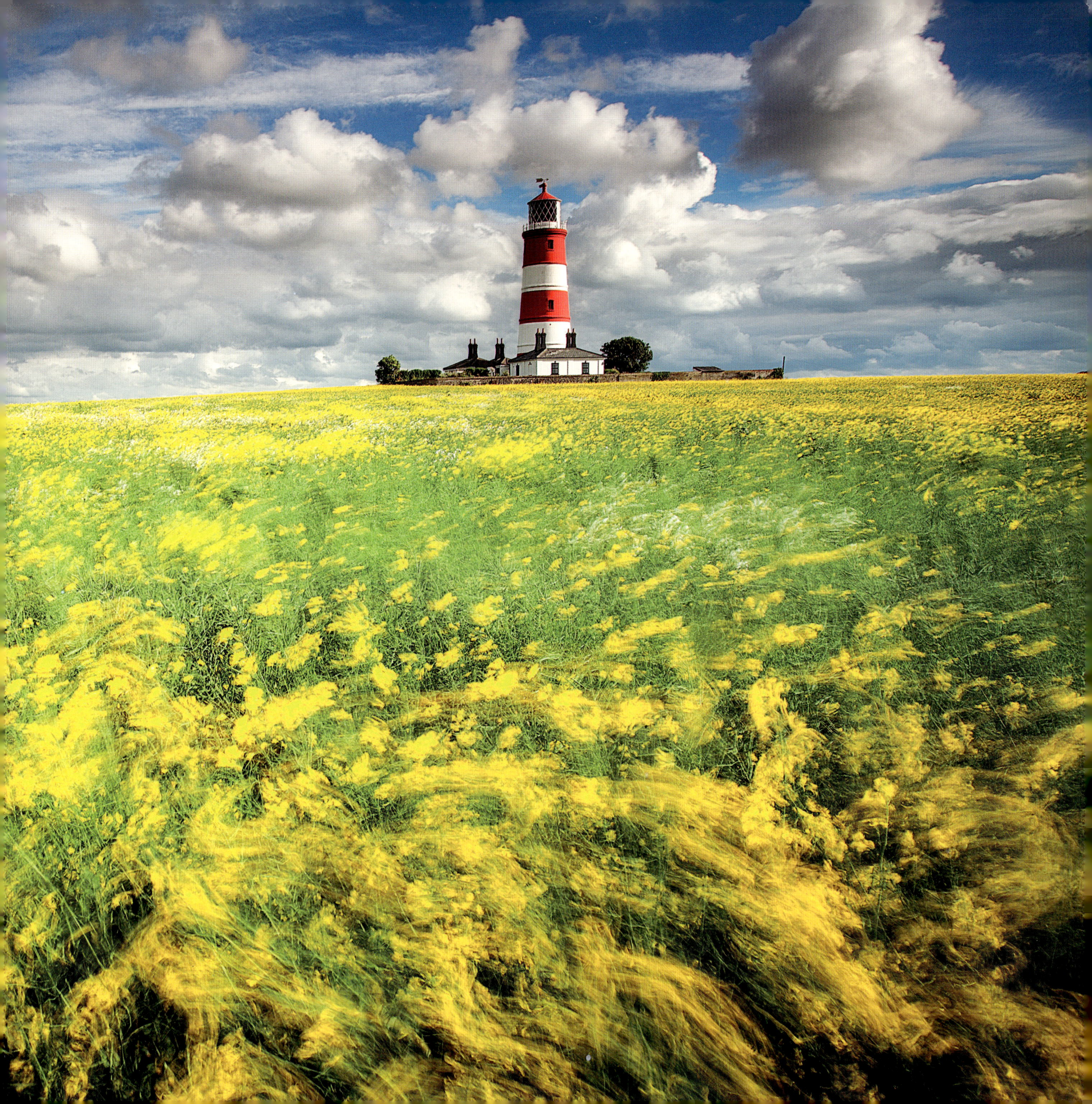

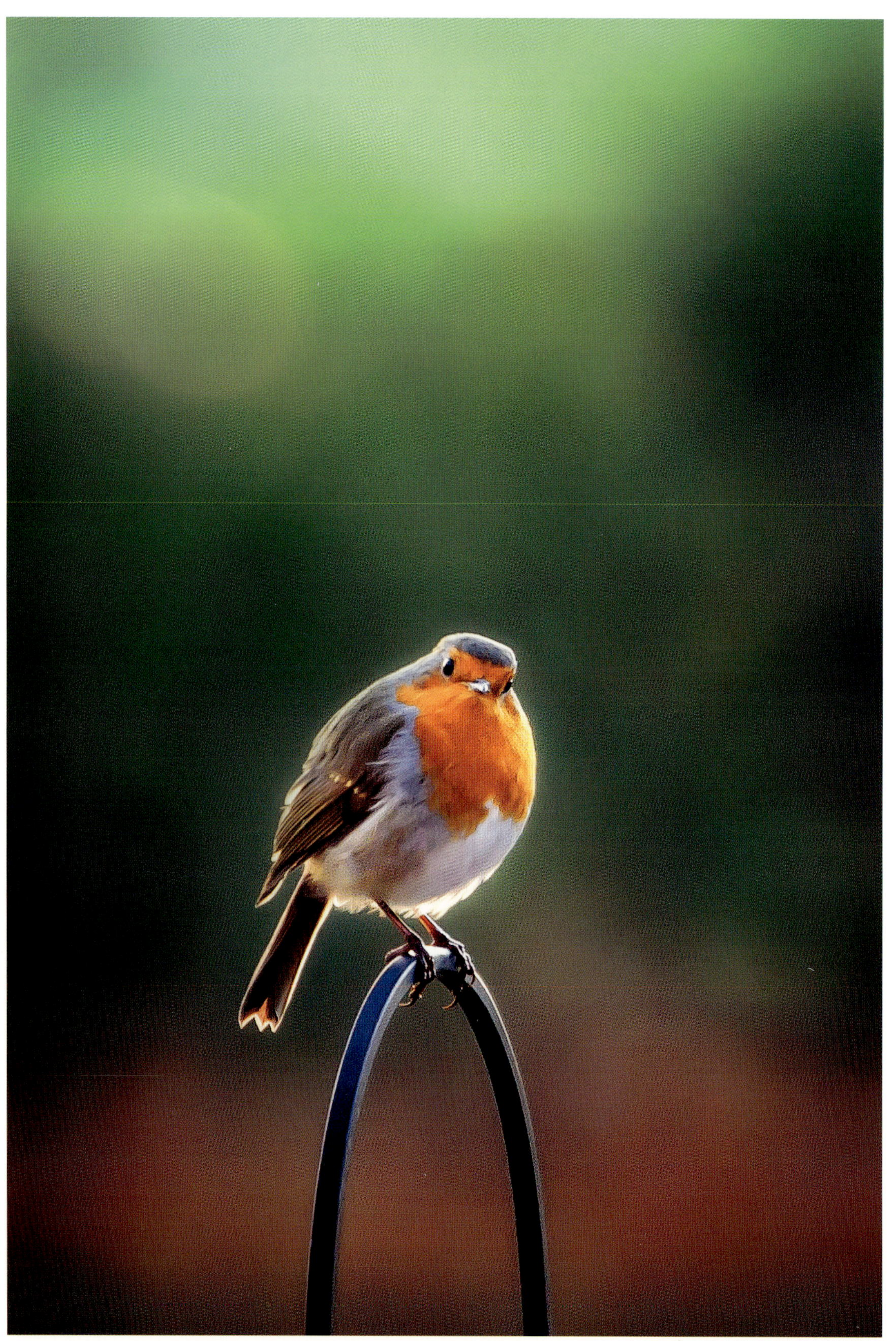

◄ **NICOLA MUNRO**   1ST PLACE

You Lookin' at Me?
Aberdeenshire, Scotland, UK

One of four robins I had as regular visitors in my garden during autumn and winter. Typically nosey and bold, it would come and sing its heart out whilst I went out to tidy up, out to the car and out to the bins; it seemed to be there whenever I was.

📷 Canon EOS 5D Mark III, Canon 70-300mm lens, 1/25sec at f/5.6, ISO 400. Post-capture: basic image management.

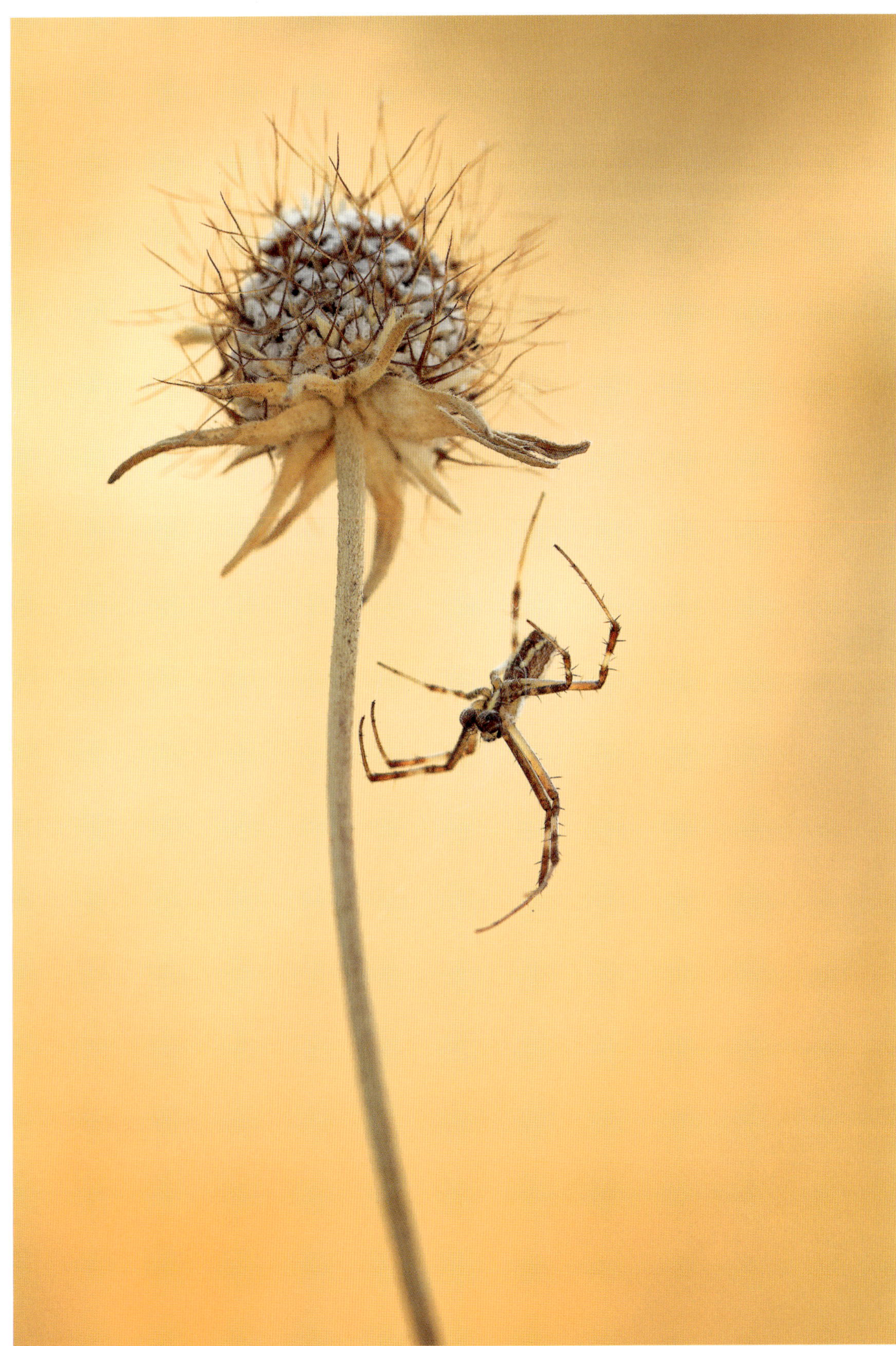

INÊS LEONARDO ▶   2ND PLACE

Aerial Dancer
Arrábida Natural Park, Setúbal, Portugal

Almost every weekend I go to the Arrábida Natural Park.
It's packed full of interesting wildlife, like this spider, which
was shot in the middle of the summer. The plants and fields
were beginning to show the effects of the long, dry days and
these colours and shapes mirrored that of the balletic spider,
dancing in the wind.

📷 Canon EOS 60D, Canon 100mm lens, 1/180sec at f/5.6,
ISO 800. Post-capture: basic image management.

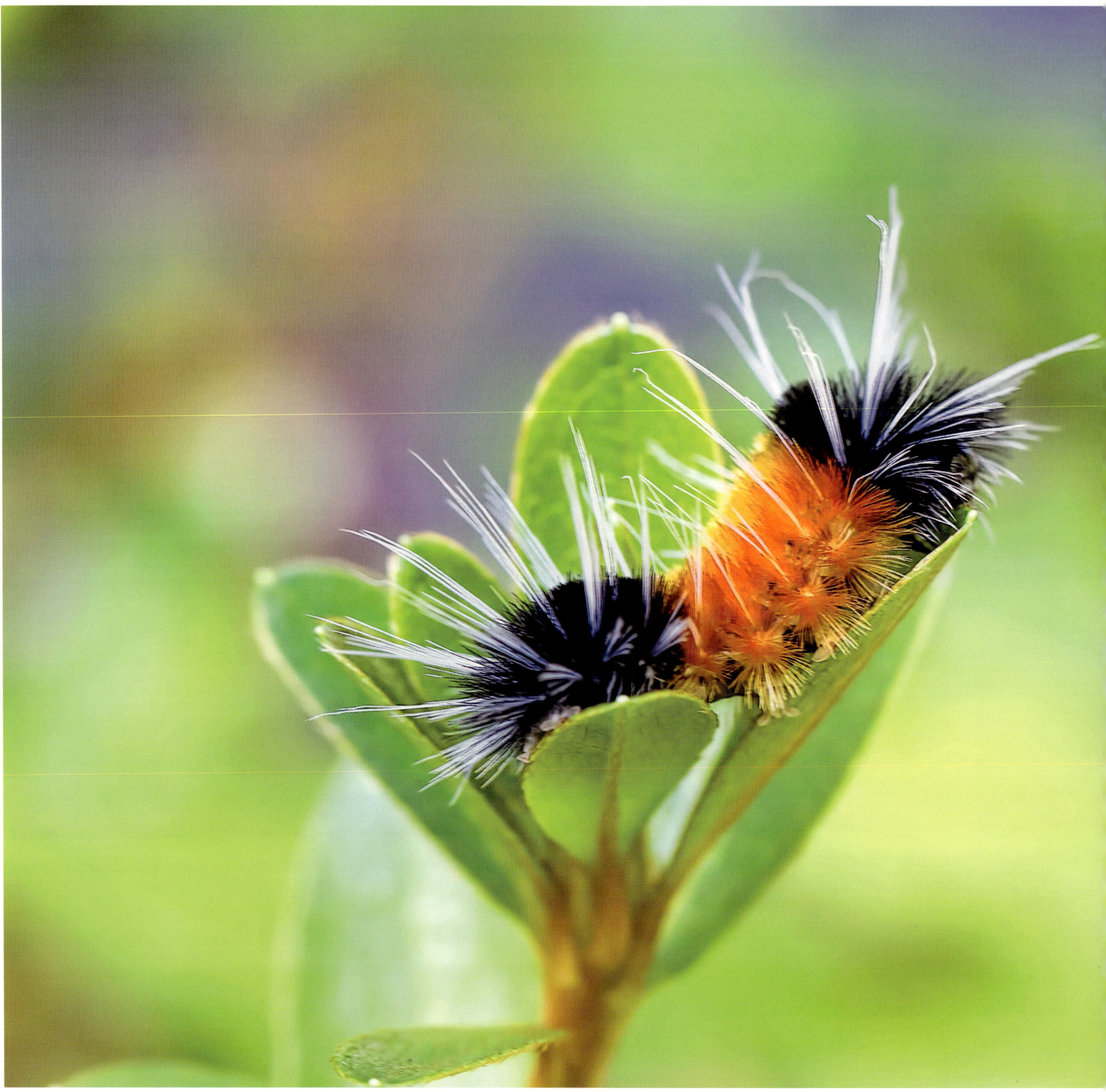

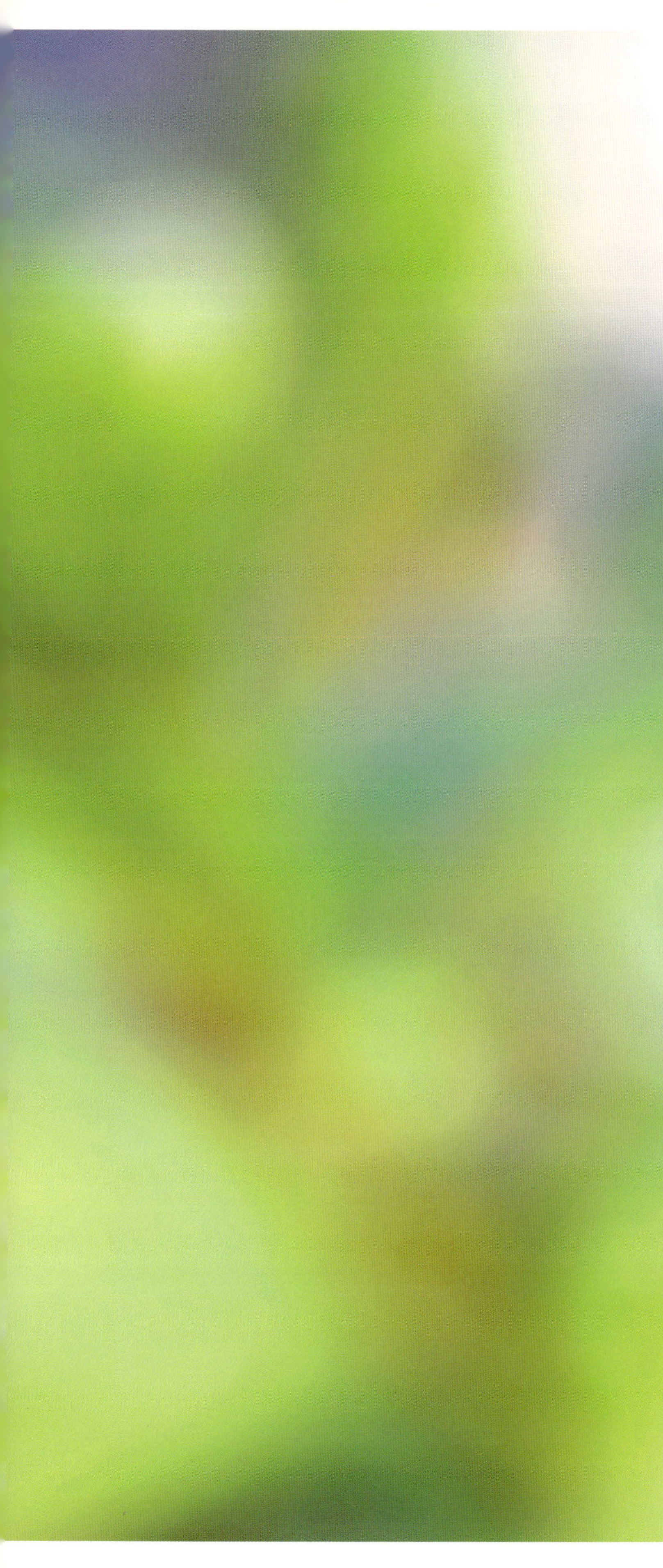

Woolly in a Teacup
Ridgefield National Wildlife Refuge, Ridgefield, Washington, USA

I headed out to the Ridgefield Wildlife Refuge with the hope of photographing eagles, nestling owls or even tree frogs. I didn't see anything until I spotted this little guy just waiting for a photographer to show up. It was still a challenge to get the shot, since it didn't stay still very long. I was smiling when I left with a photograph of what I told myself was the only living thing in the entire wildlife refuge.

Canon EOS 7D, Canon 100mm macro lens, 1/125sec at f/5, ISO 640. Post-capture: basic image management.

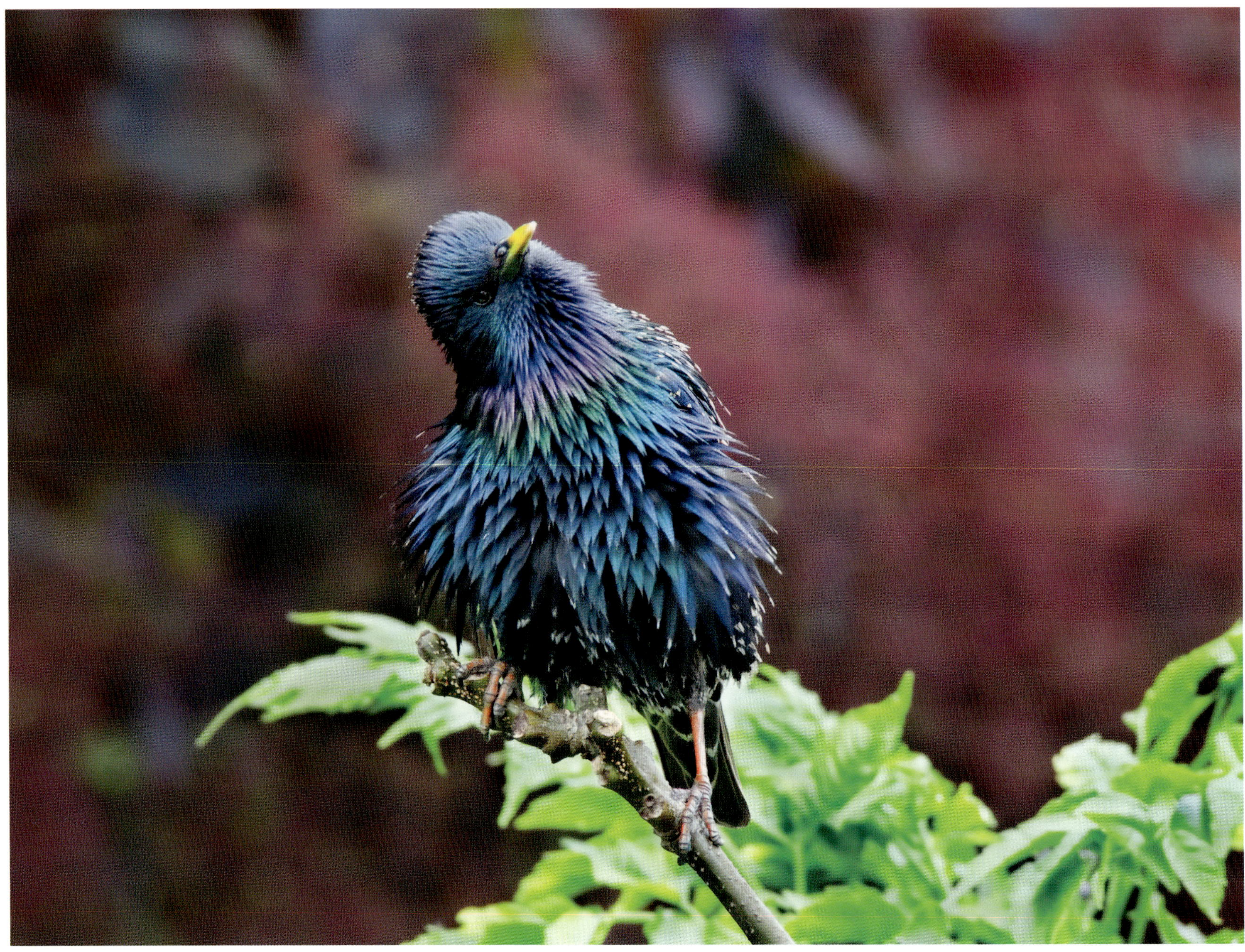

Iridescent Starling
Surrey, England, UK

Starlings are one of my favourite birds and I have always been looking for a good shot that displays the iridescent quality of their feathers. This starling was perched on my Persian lilac tree and suddenly shook itself, allowing the glancing sunlight to produce a full spectrum of colours amongst its feathers.

Canon EOS 7D, Canon 200mm lens, 1/180sec at f/9.5, ISO 800. Tripod. Post-capture: basic image management.

Frozen
Zwolle, Netherlands

The green-veined white is a remarkably early species of butterfly which takes flight from the start of April. With a bit of luck, it's possible to photograph this butterfly in combination with hoar frost, and that's exactly what I managed to achieve. Amazingly, they are able to survive this frost and after about an hour the sunlight sufficiently thaws them out, allowing them to fly away.

Canon EOS 70D, Sigma 150mm macro lens, 1/25sec at f/4. Tripod. Post-capture: basic image management.

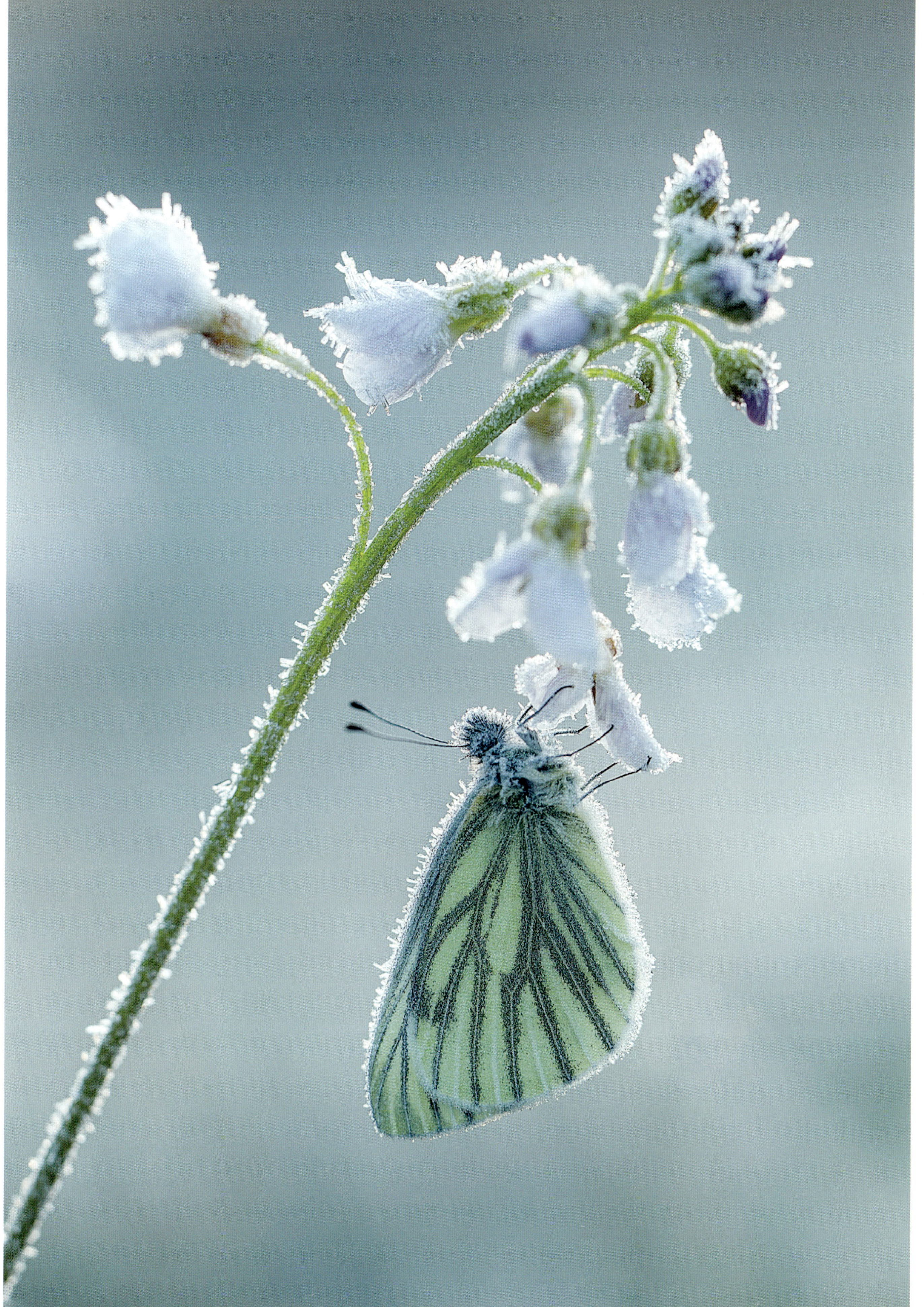

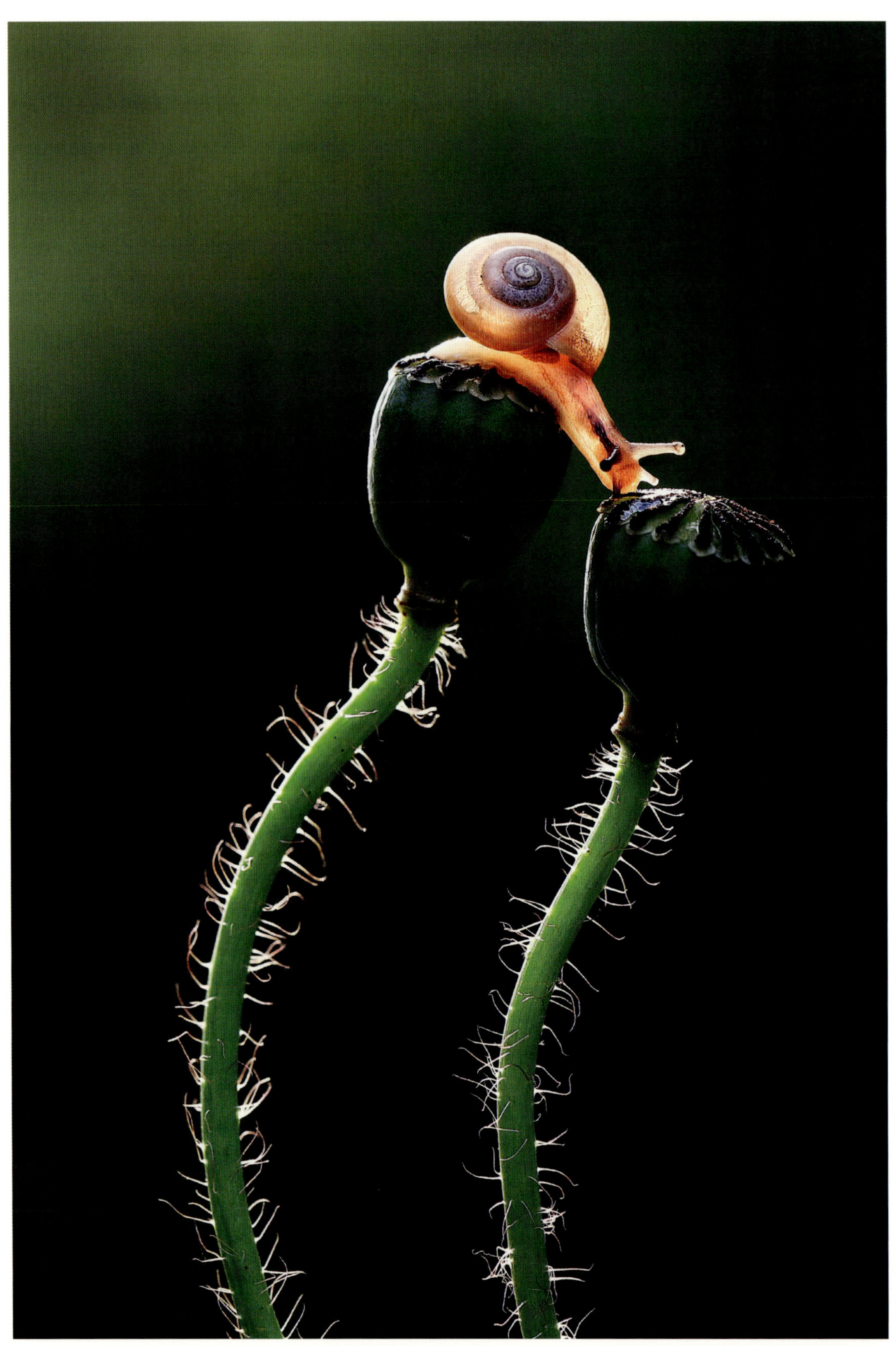

HIGHLY COMMENDED

Find the Steps Down
Wuhan City, China

After the rain, a snail ventures out to climb to the top of a poppy. It reminds us that when we reach certain high points in life, it's important to stop and look back at the landscape behind us, not just in front.

Canon EOS 70D, Tamron 90mm macro lens, 1/125sec at f/8, ISO 250. Post-capture: basic image management.

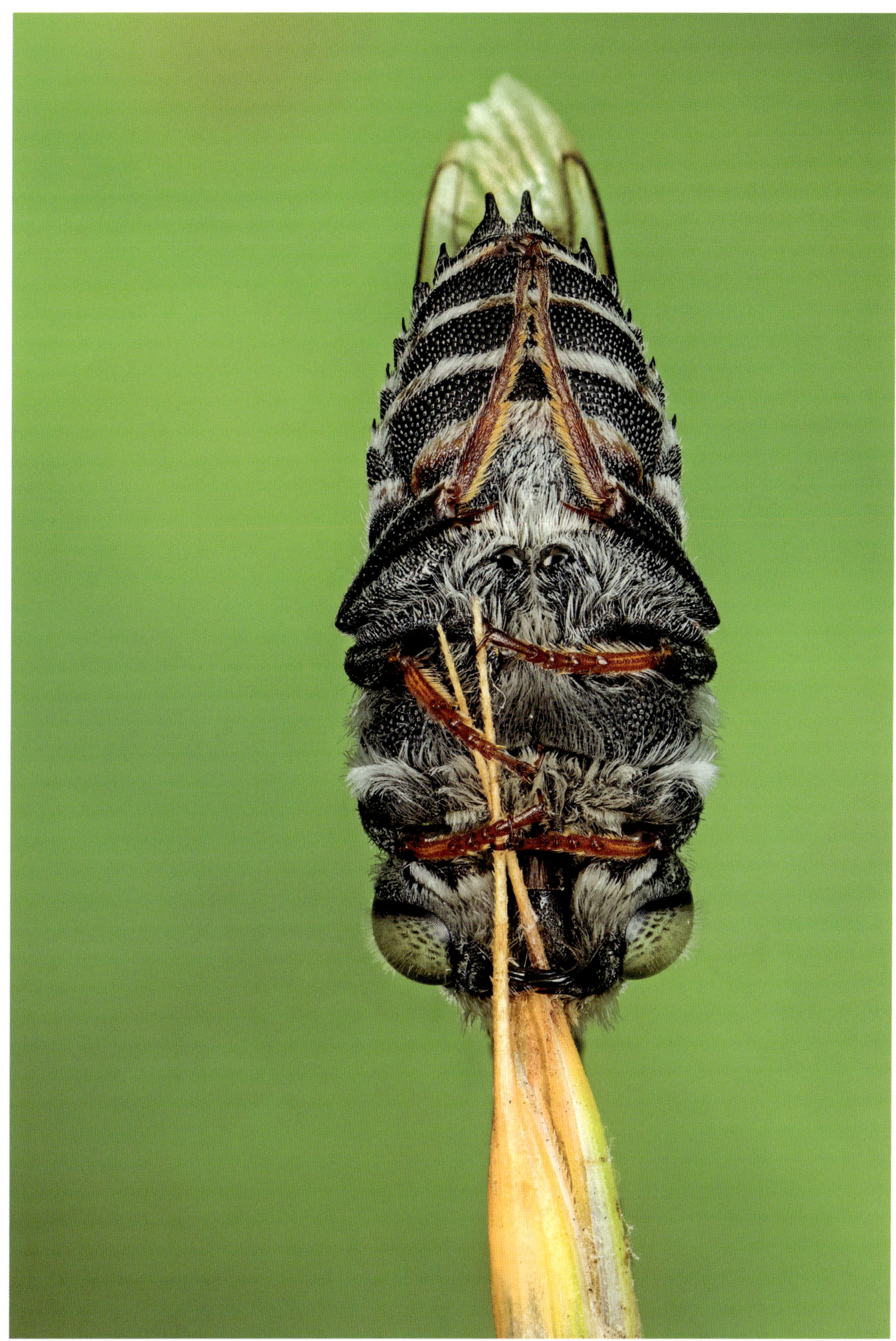

Sleeping Acrobat
Oshawa, Ontario, Canada

The common name – cuckoo bee – is used for a species of bee that lays its eggs in the nests of other bees. Known as kleptoparasites, these bee larvae kill the host larvae and feed on the pollen and nectar provided by the host bee. They do not take shelter in a hive or nest, but use their mandibles to lock onto a sturdy plant - usually upside-down - and settle for the night. This particular bee was photographed early in the morning before it had time to warm up and fly off.

📷 Canon EOS 7D Mark II, Canon 65mm macro lens, 1/200sec at f/7.1, ISO 160. Post-capture: focus stacking.

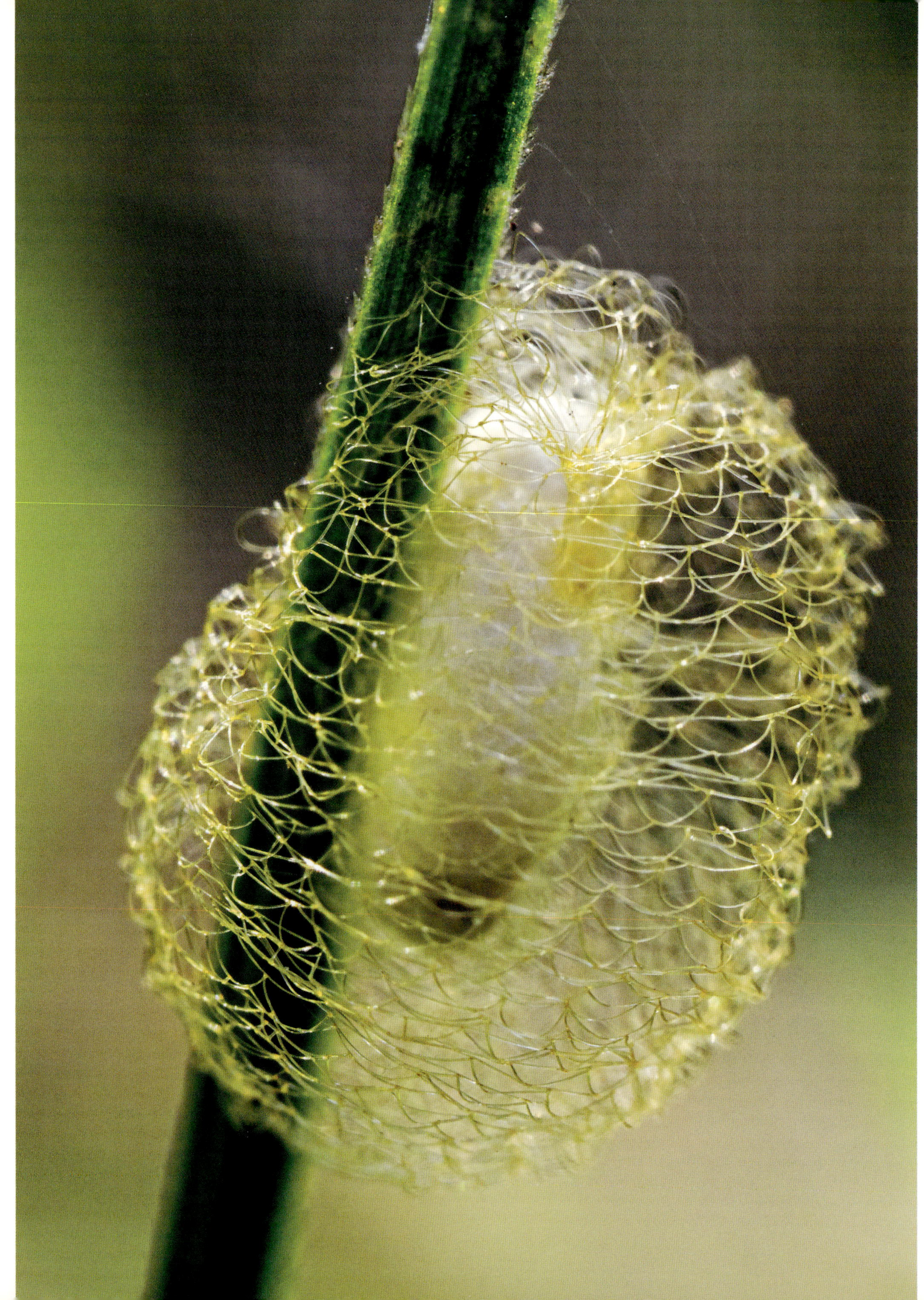

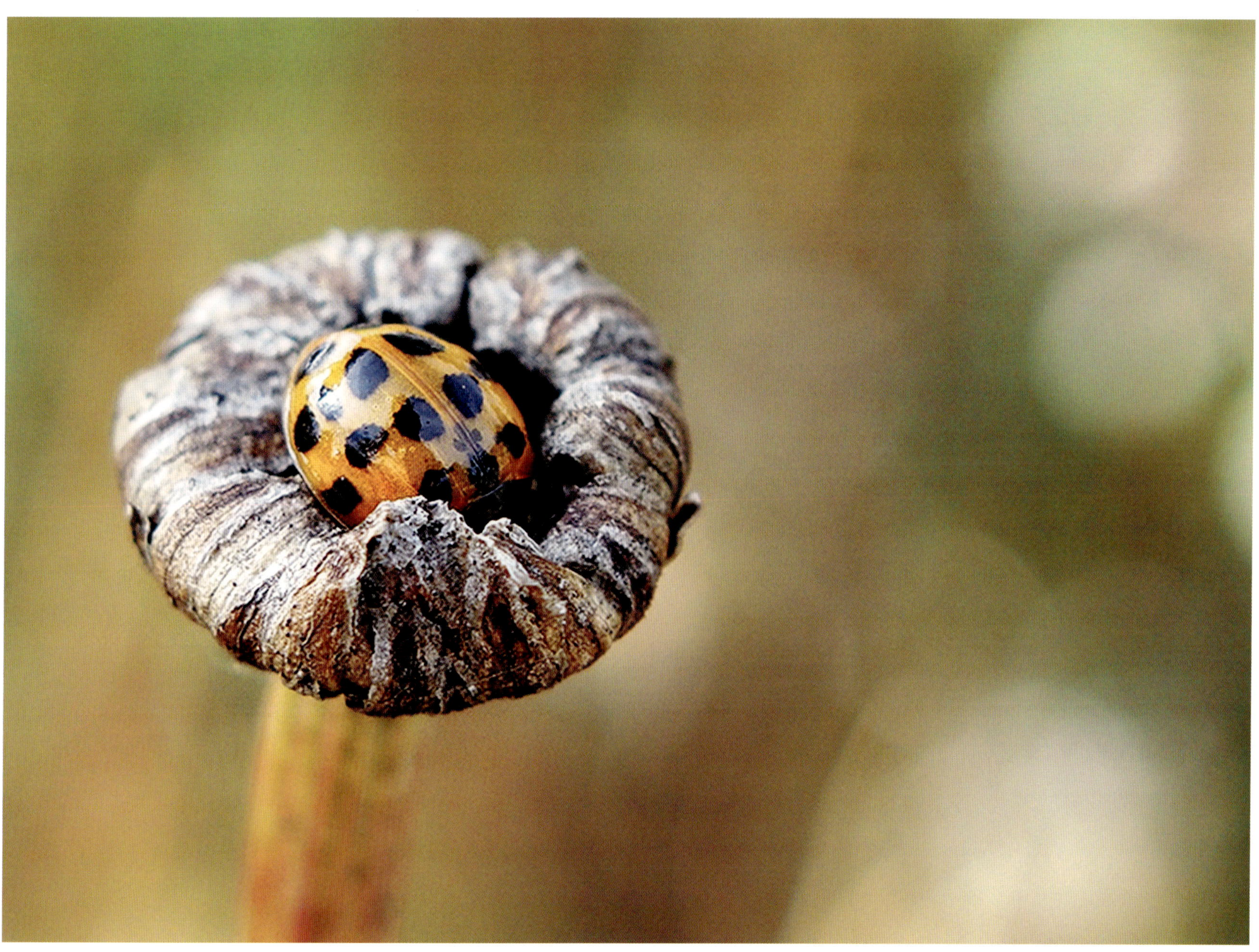

Cocoon
Walter Sisulu National Botanical Gardens, Gauteng, South Africa

It is often difficult to tell the difference between moths and butterflies, but it is known that a moth makes a cocoon, which is wrapped in a silk covering and a butterfly makes a chrysalis, which is hard, smooth and has no silk covering. The botanical gardens and this particular river forest habitat provide great opportunities to discover, observe and capture the insect world in the garden. It was only when looking through my macro lens that the true beauty of the cocoon became apparent.

Canon EOS 6D, Canon 65mm lens, 1/25sec at f/11, ISO 2000. Tripod. Post-capture: basic image management.

Snug as a Bug
York, England, UK

It was a warm sunny afternoon and I cycled up the hill to the university to try and photograph poppies and wild flowers which cover the very beautiful wildflower roundabout. I was just about to leave when this ladybird caught my eye, nestled into the seed head of a wild flower.

Olympus PEN E-PL5, Olympus 14-42mm lens, 1/500sec at f/5.6, ISO 500.

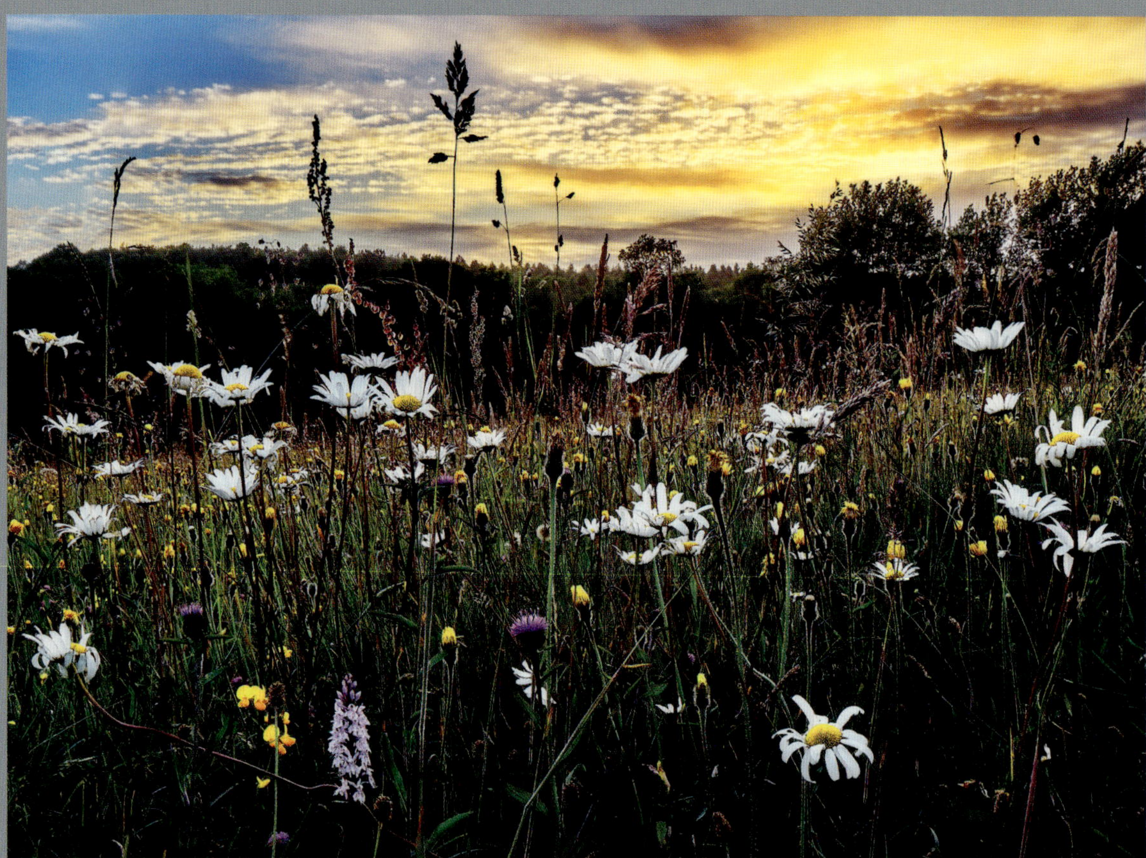

ROCKS FARM MEADOWS

MATTHEW THOMAS

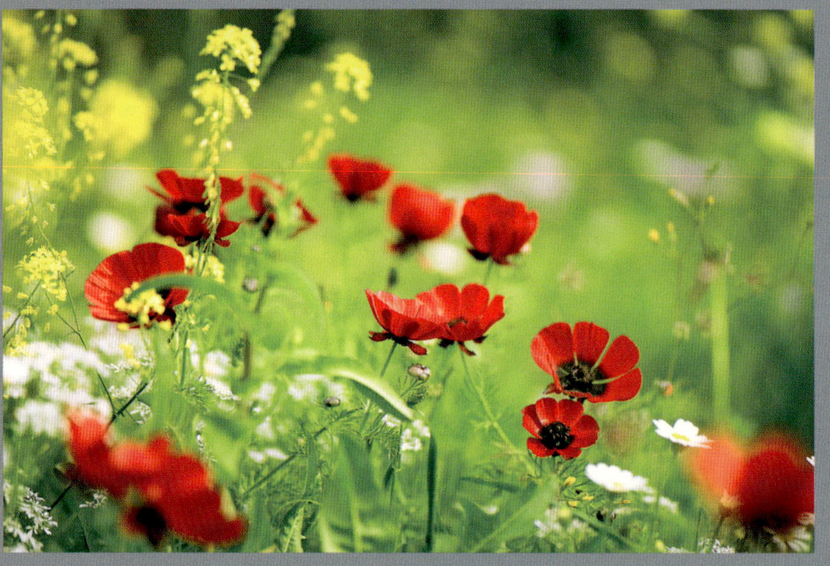

RED BLOOM

OLGA SWIFT

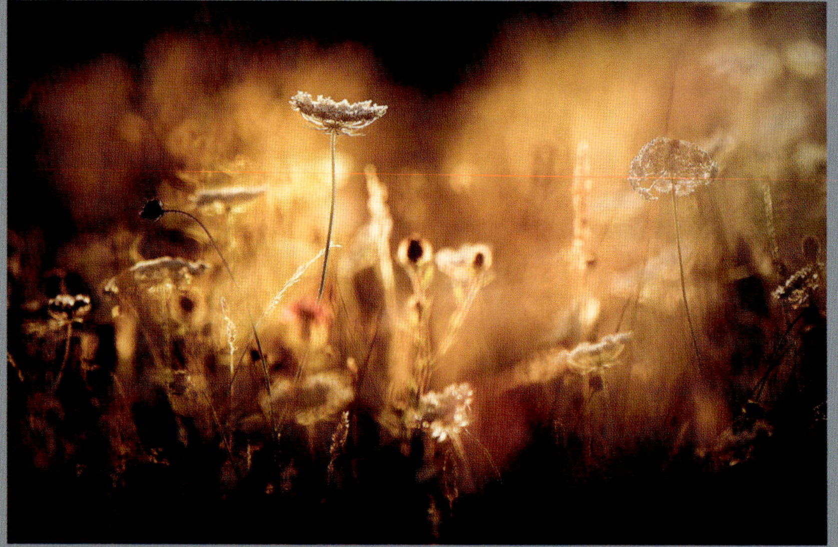

MEADOW SUNSET

NEIL DAVIES

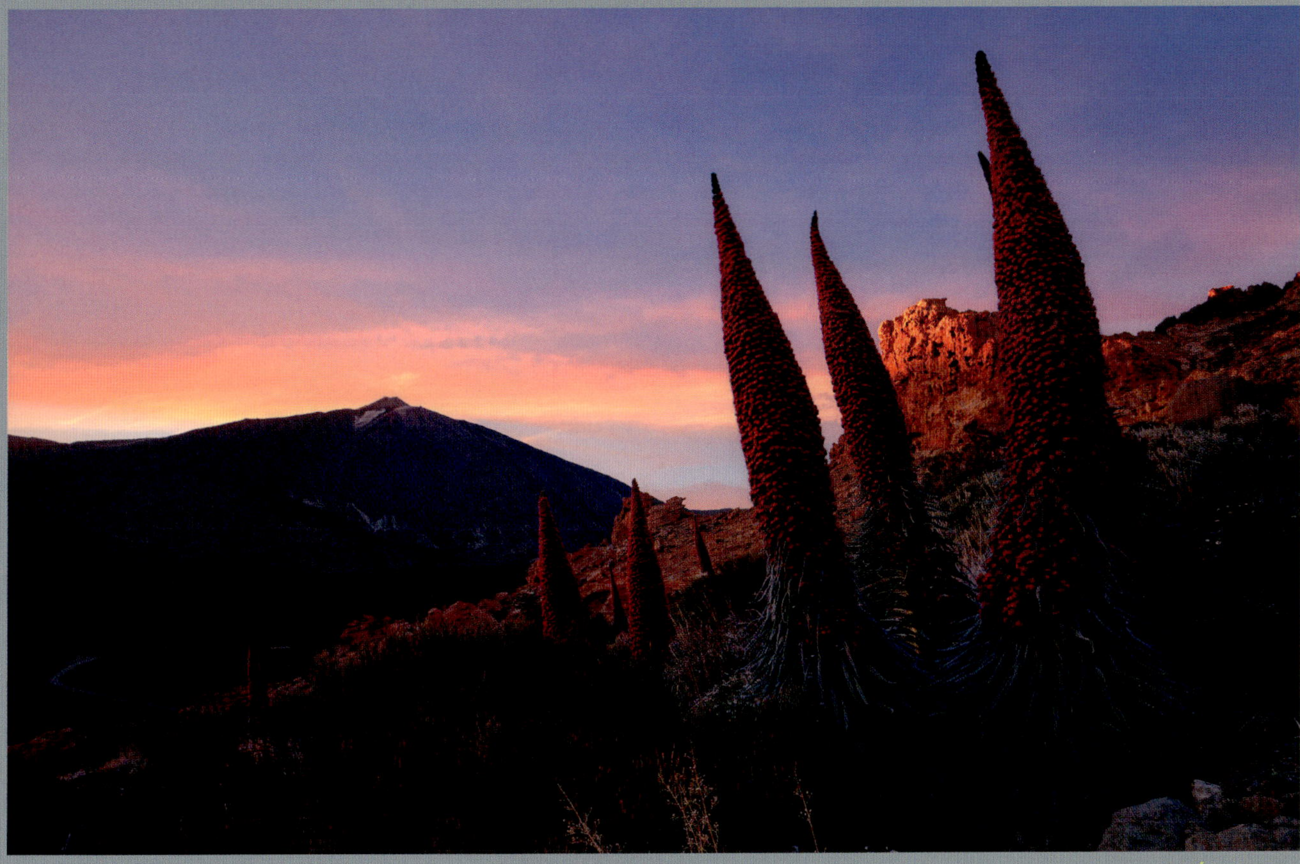

MOUNT TEIDE BUGLOSS — SENÉN MEDINA

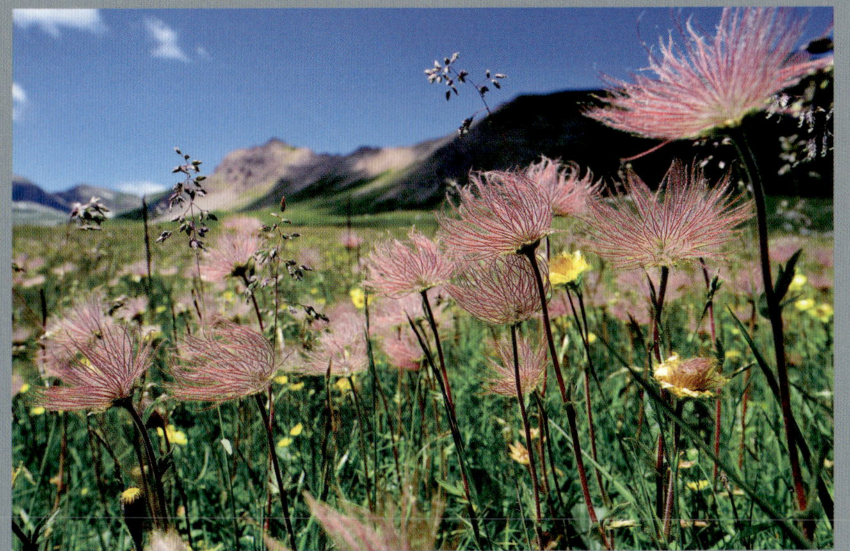

BRENTA MOUNTAINS — ALBERT CEOLAN

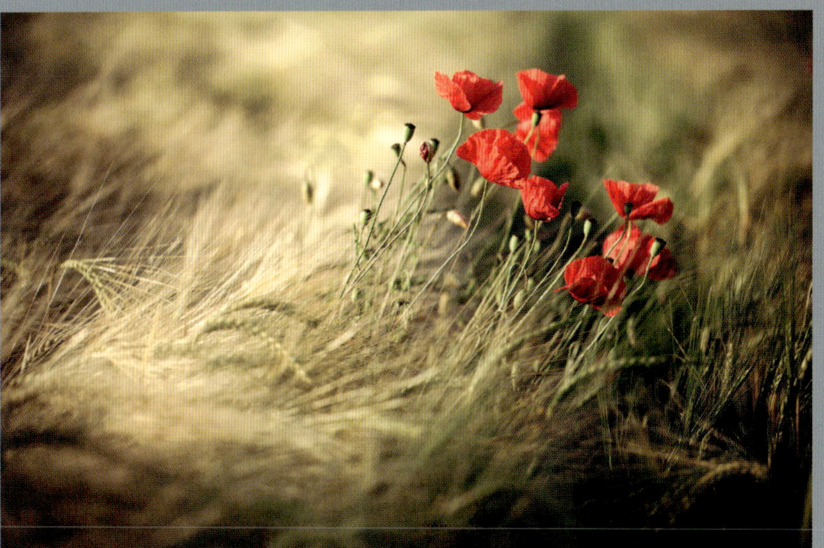

SOFT TOUCH — JUSTIN MINNS

WILDFLOWER LANDSCAPES

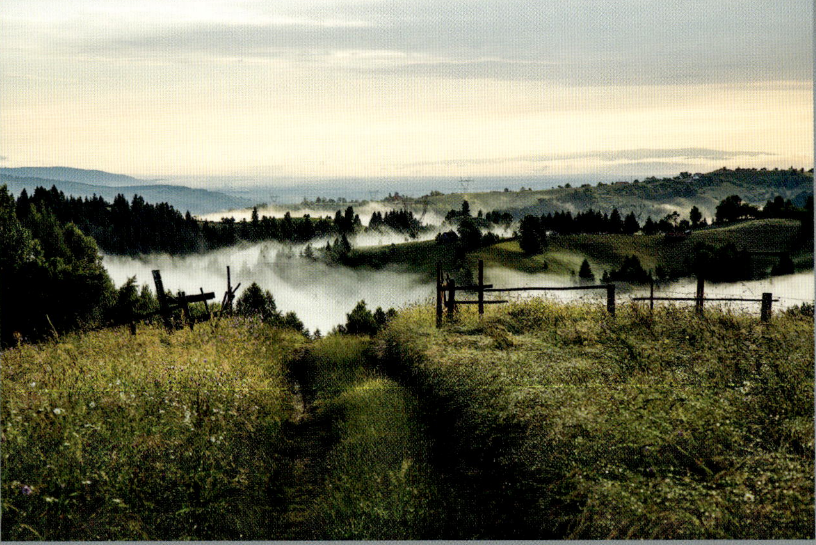

CARPATHIAN MEADOWS

CATHY COOPER

THE BEAUTY OF PLANTS

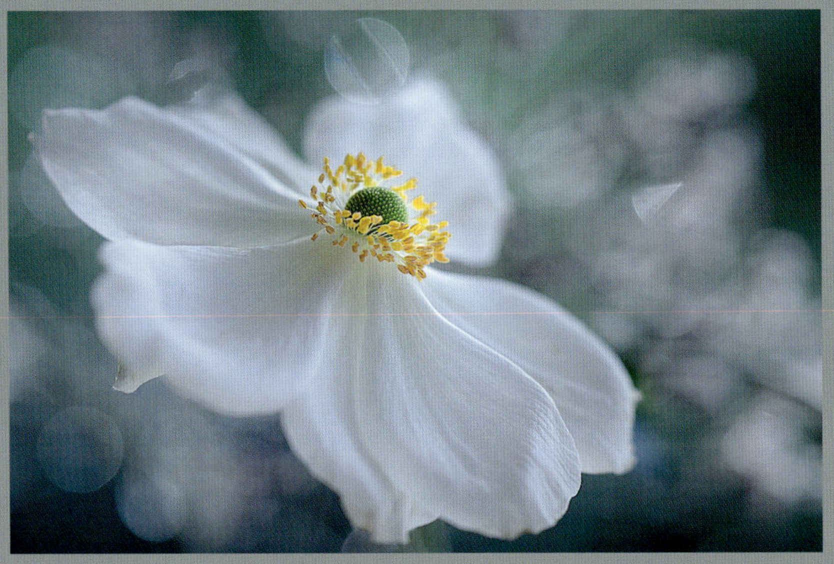

JOY

CHRISTL DECKX

THE BEAUTY OF PLANTS

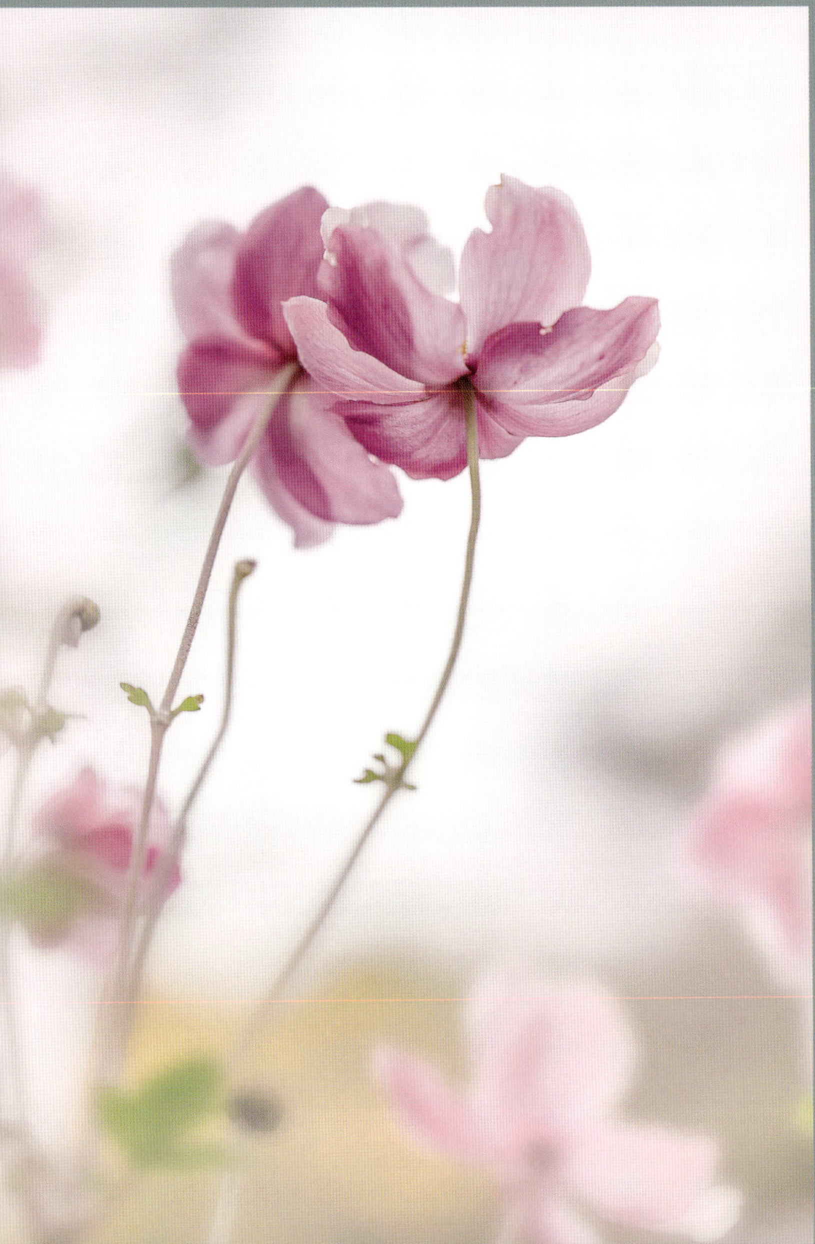

PINK ANEMONES

RAYMOND JONES

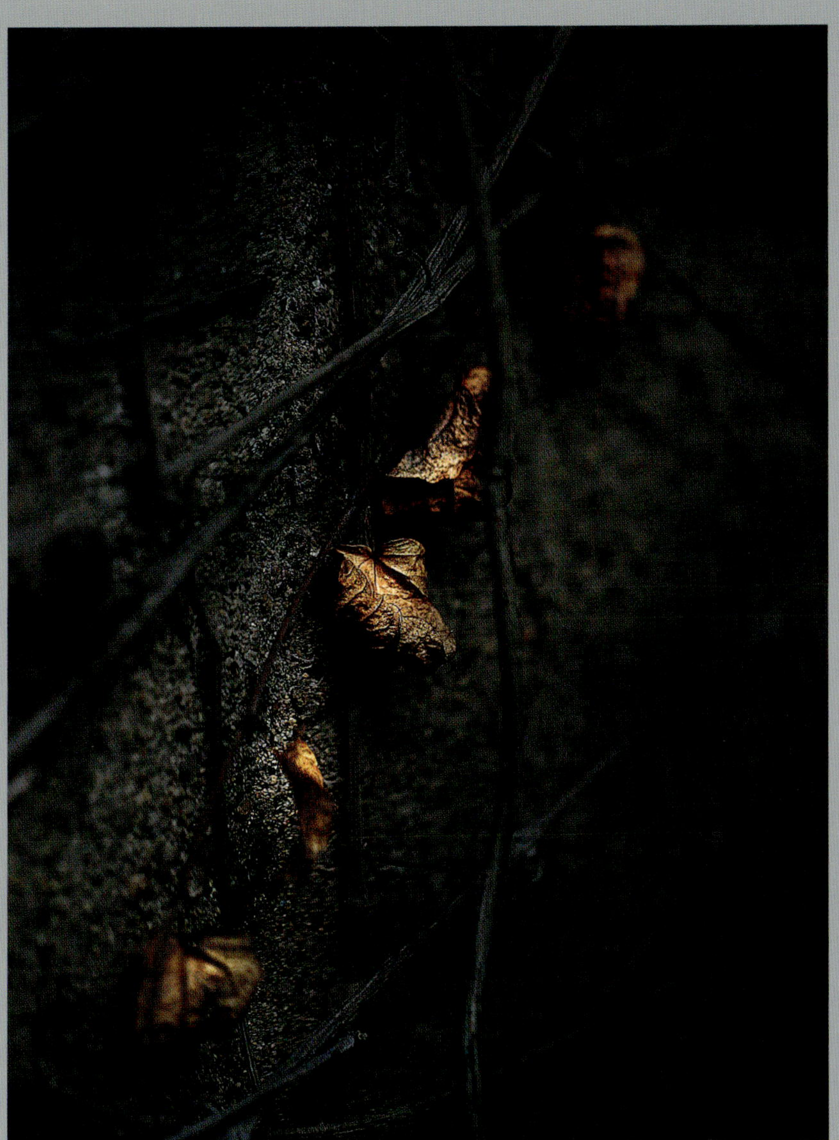

WAITING FOR WINTER   JIE LV

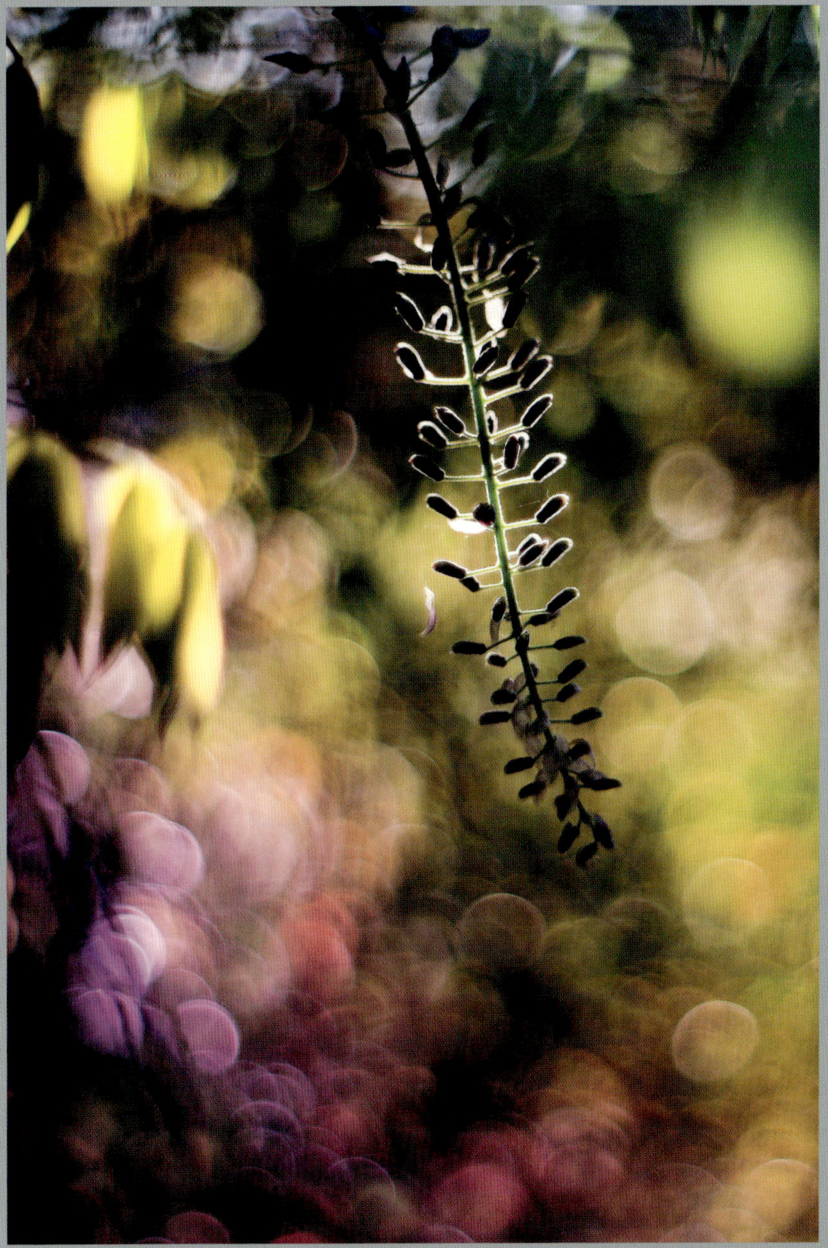

IN THE RAYS OF THE MORNING SUN   KARINA KOWALKA-KNYSPEL

BEAUTIFUL GARDENS

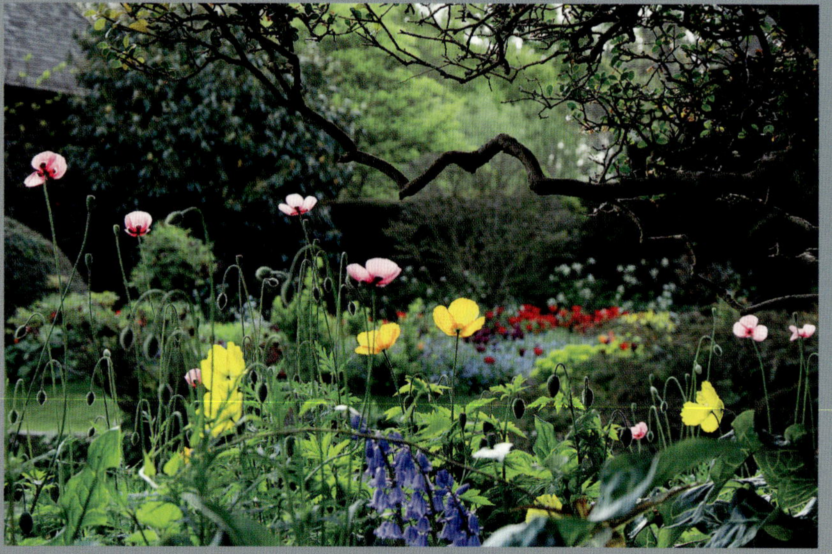

BACKLIT POPPIES CAROL CASSELDEN

BEAUTIFUL GARDENS

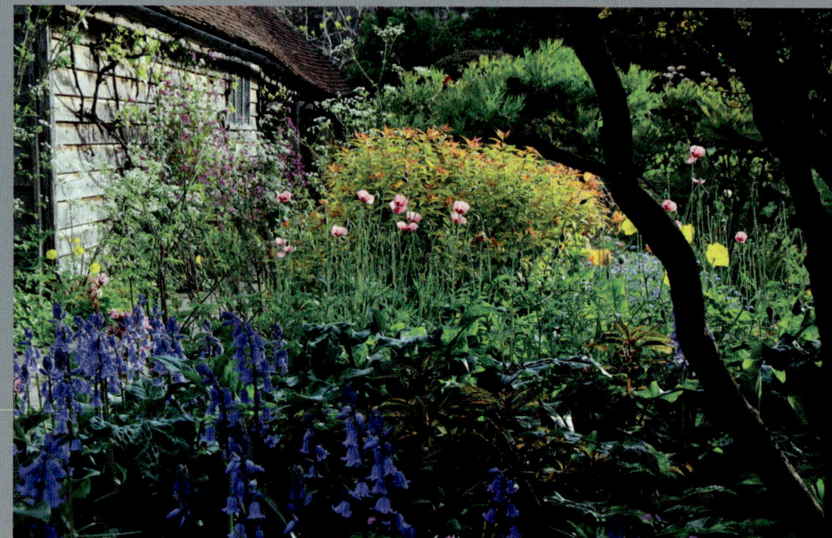

THE BARN GARDEN CAROL CASSELDEN

BEAUTIFUL GARDENS

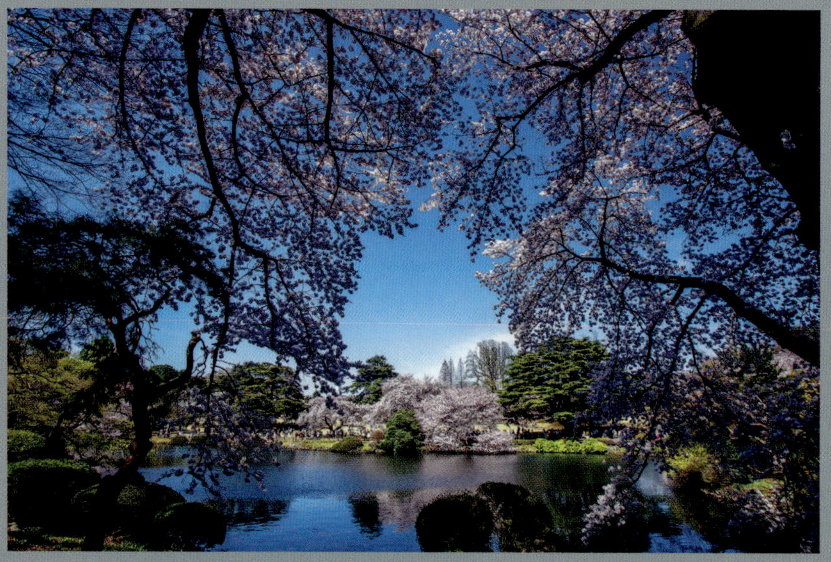

CHERRY BLOSSOM ARTEM LALIN

BEAUTIFUL GARDENS

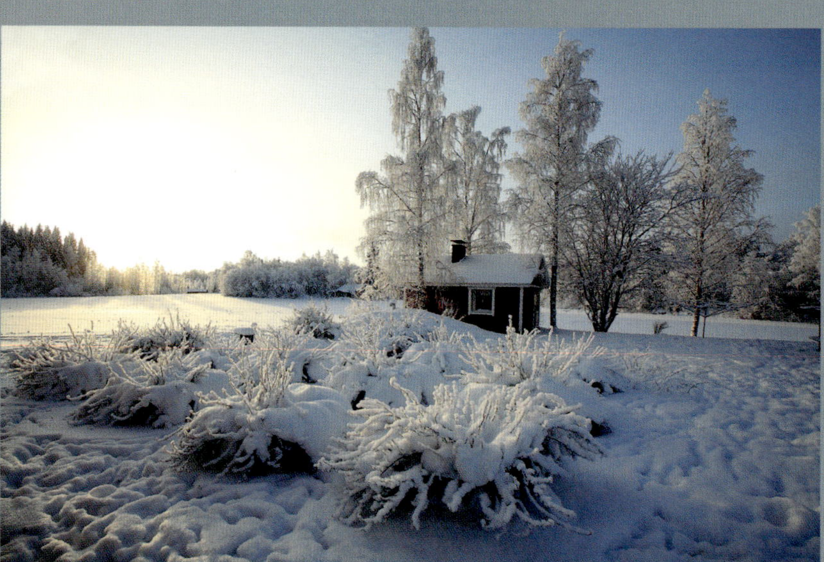

SUNRISE IN NORTHERN COUNTRY GARDEN SERGEY KAREPANOV

BEAUTIFUL GARDENS

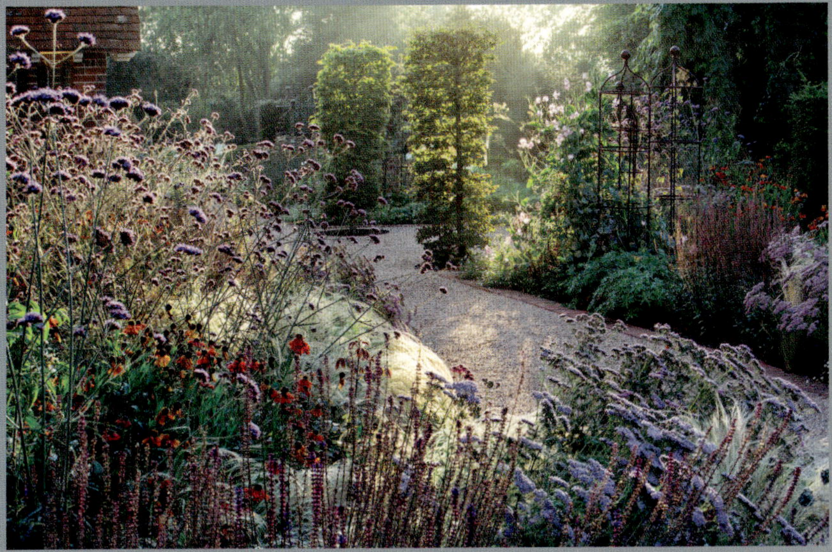

A GENTLE AWAKENING **MARIANNE MAJERUS**

BEAUTIFUL GARDENS

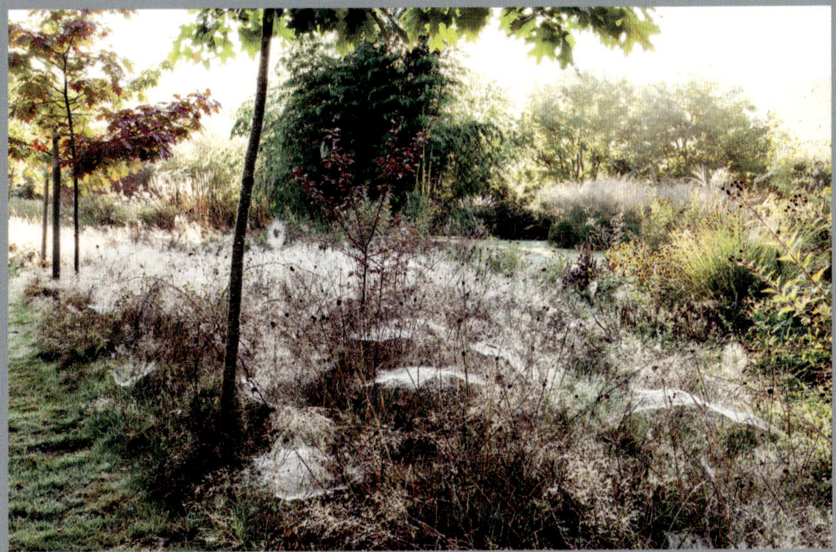

A HINT OF AUTUMN **ANNETTE LEPPLE**

TREES, WOODS & FORESTS

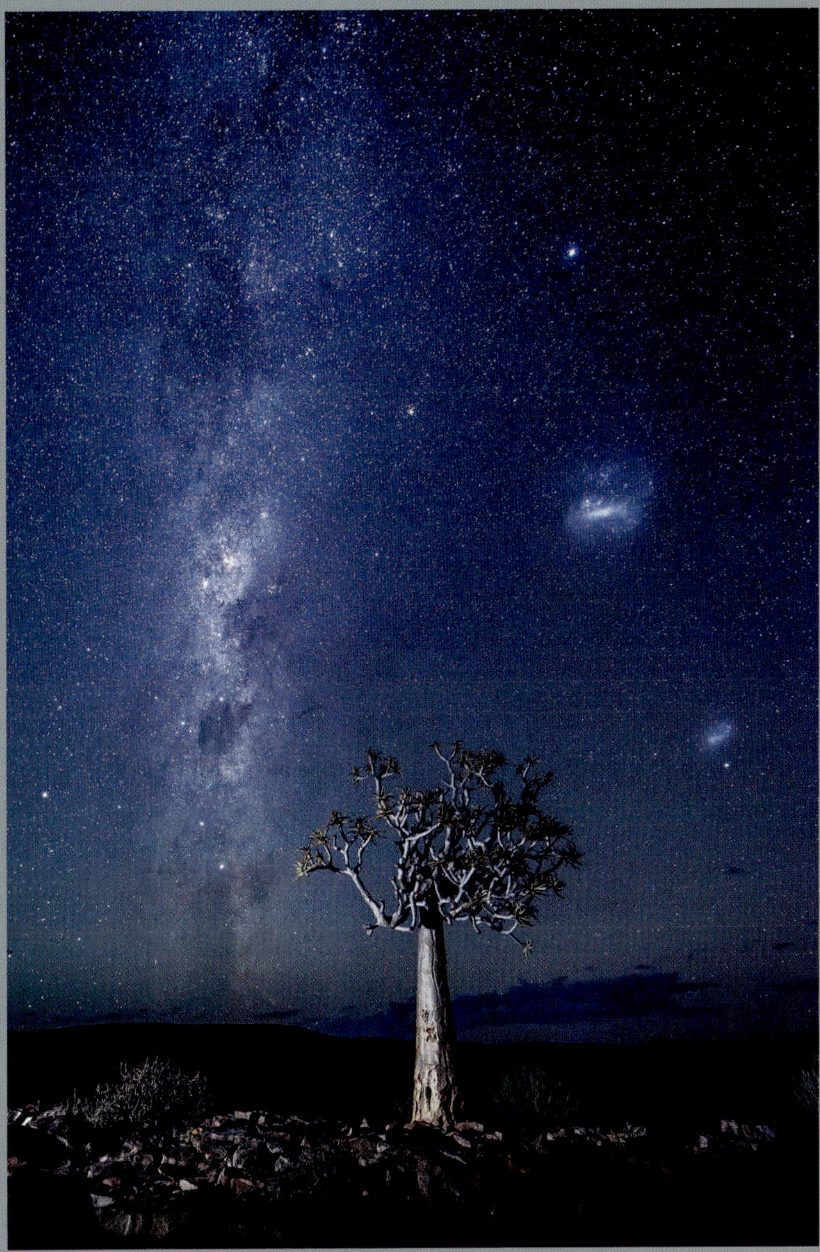

THE QUIVER AMONGST THE GALAXIES **KATHY McINROY**

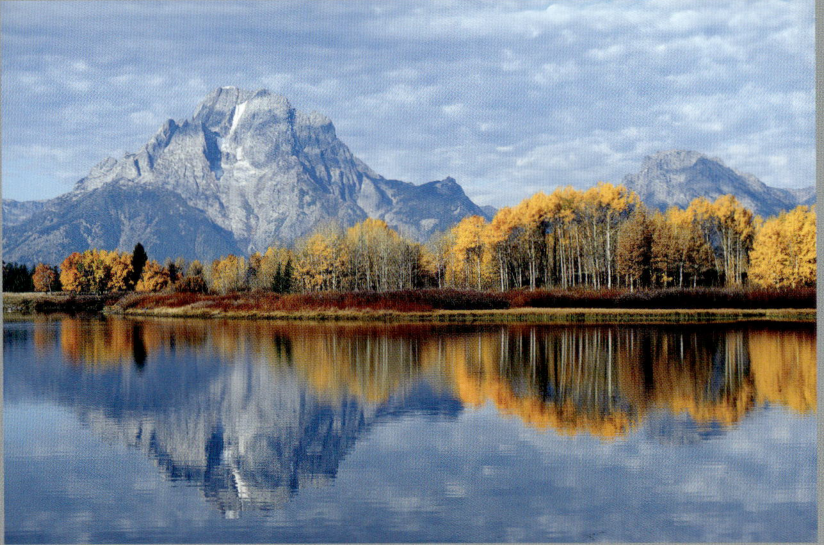

AUTUMN IN YELLOWSTONE — VICTOR KANUNNIKOV

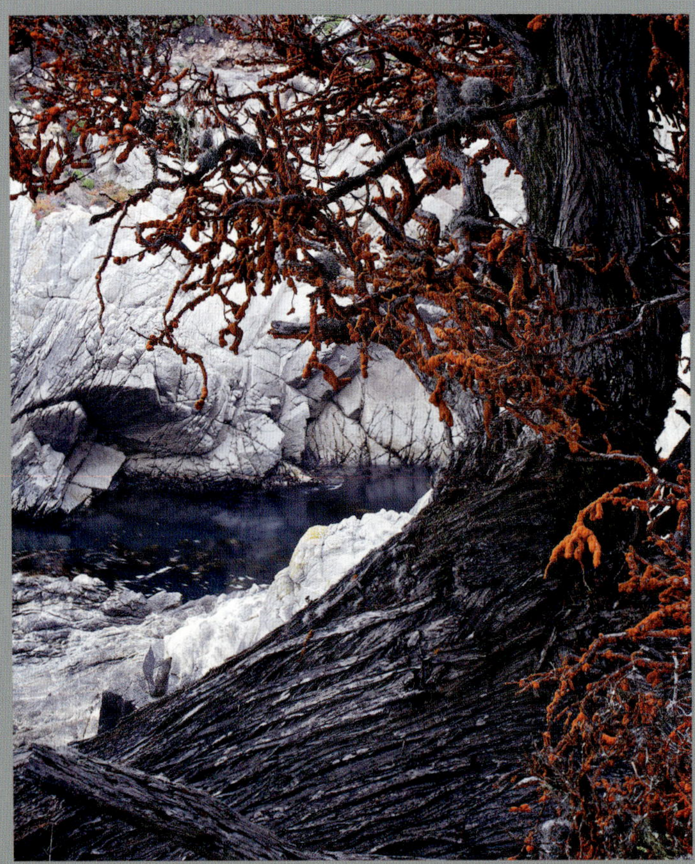

MONTEREY CYPRESS — PETER HYDE

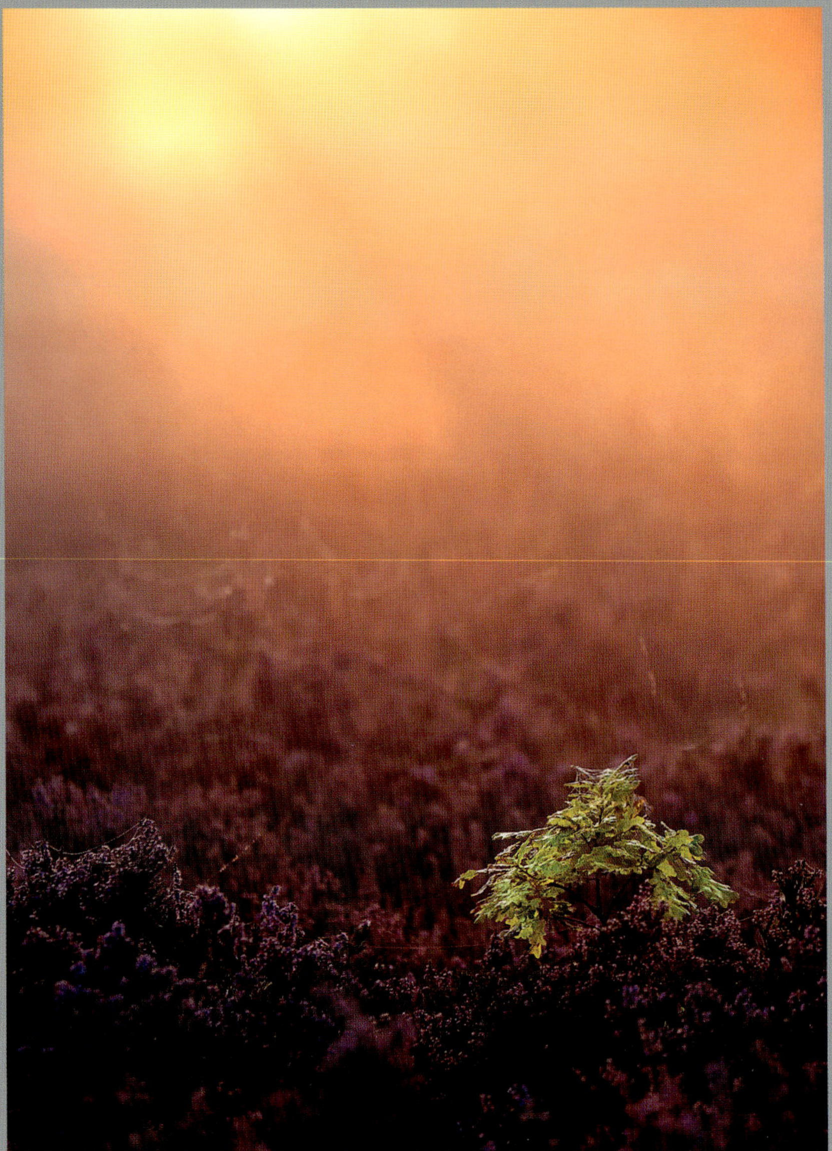

LITTLE OAK — STEVE PALMER

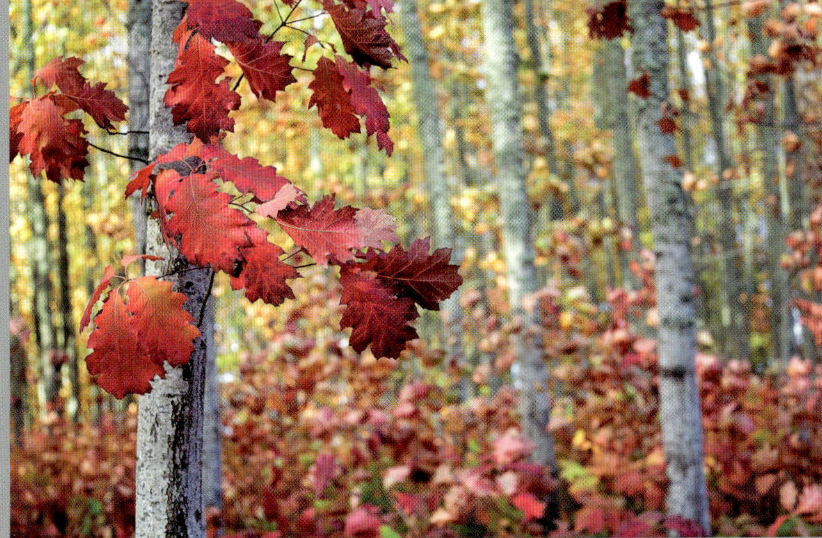

AUTUMN'S FIRE

RENAE SMITH

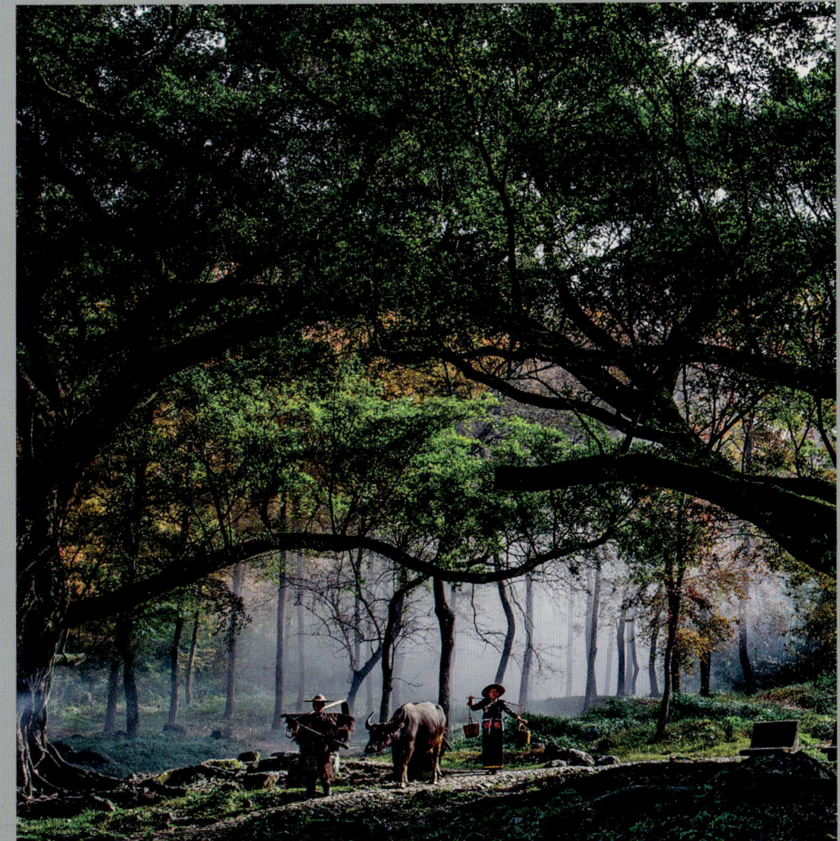

THE FOREST TRACK LEADS ME HOME

JING LAI

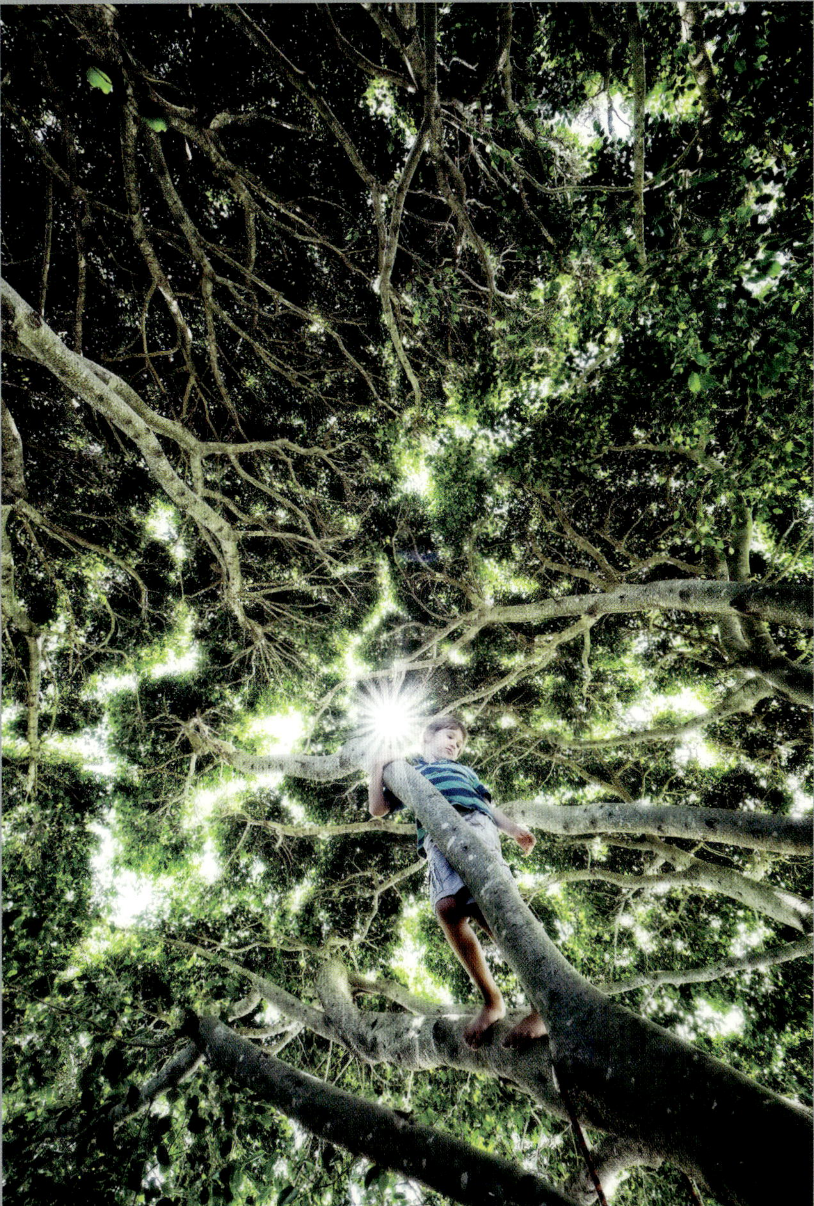

THE LEAFY WAY

DAVID MALIKOFF

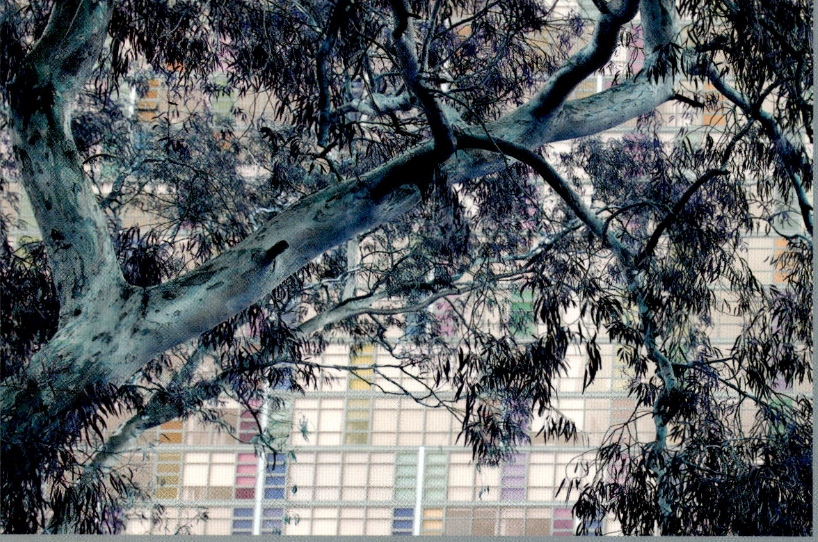

BLUE GUM EQUALISER — ANNE POREMSKIS

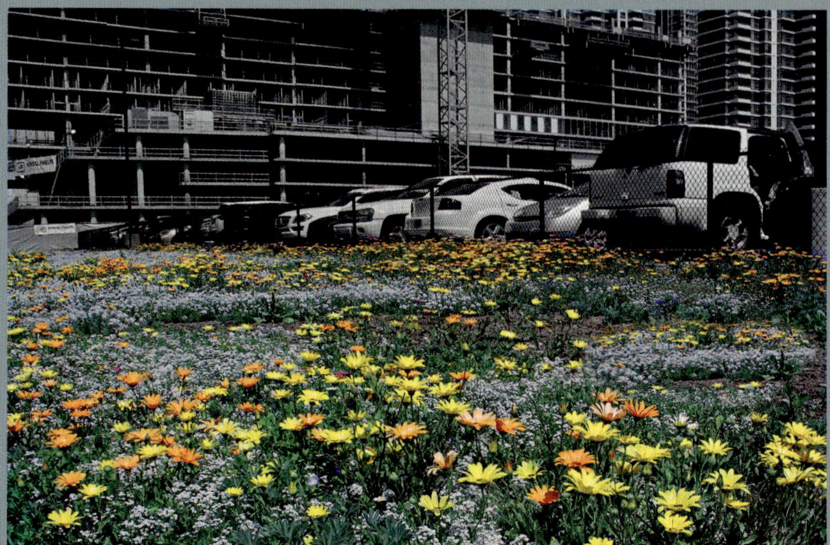

LIFTING THE GREY — SALLY BEVINGTON

GREENING THE CITY

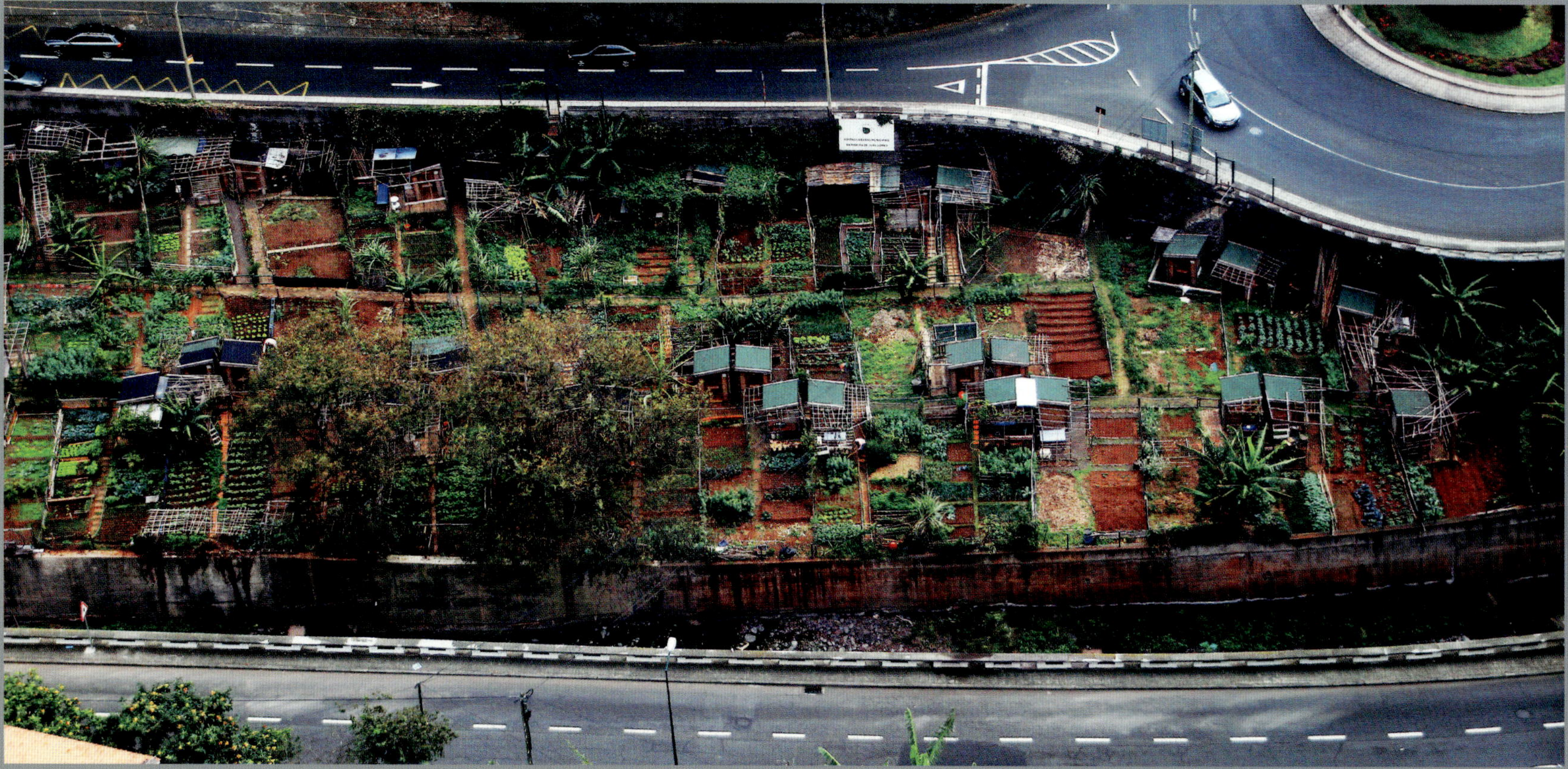

ALLOTMENTS IN FUNCHAL — SALLY BEVINGTON

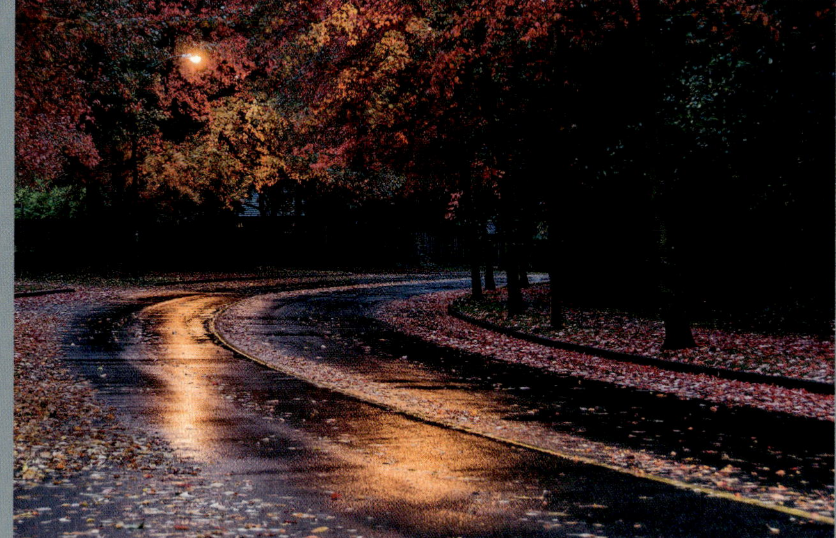

AUTUMN REFLECTIONS   **EVELYN NODWELL**

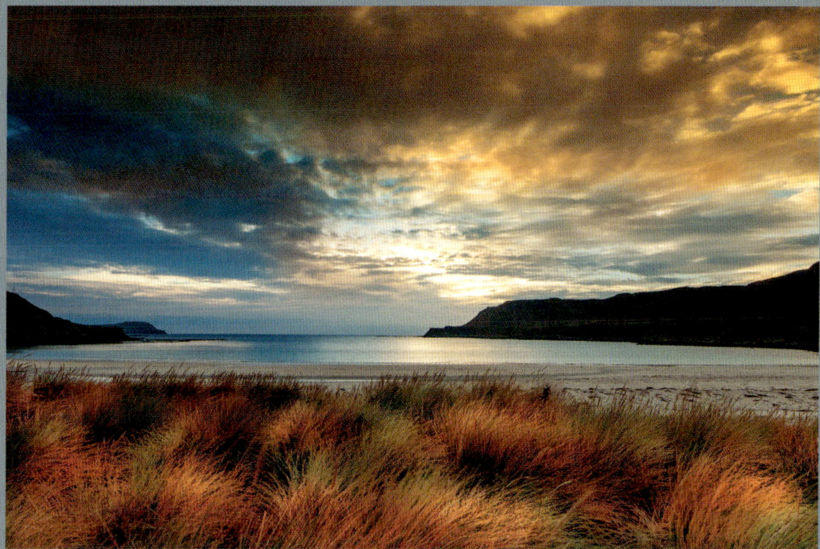

CALGARY SUNSET   **LINDSEY BUCKNOR**

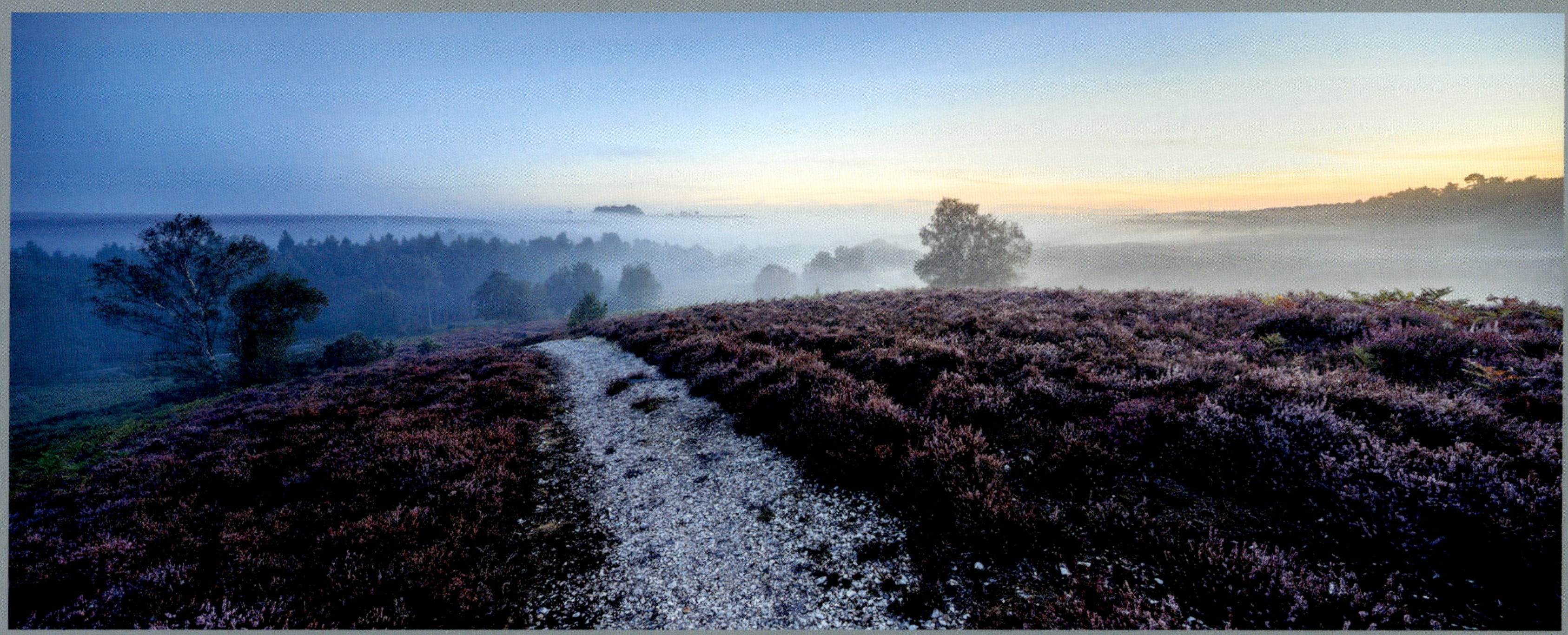

HEATHER AND MIST   **MARK BAUER**

BREATHING SPACES

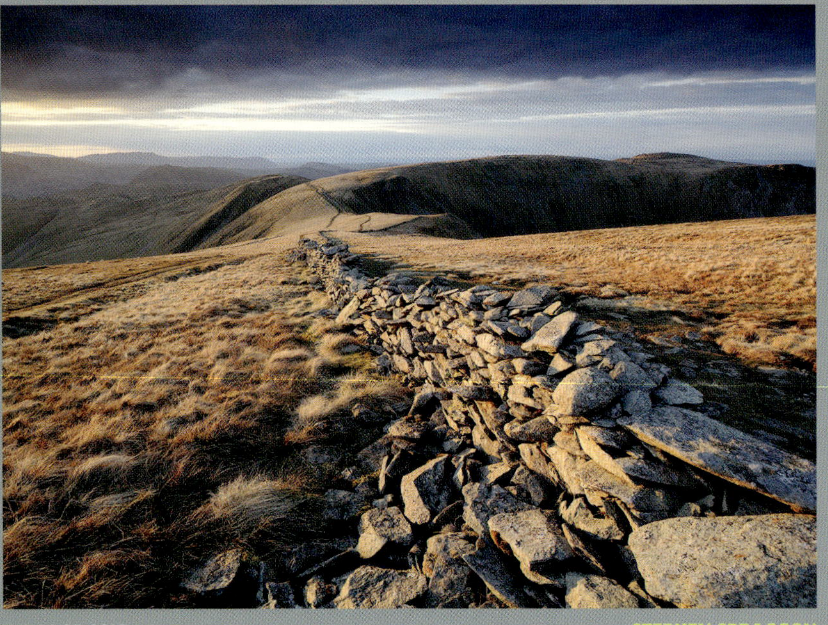

WINGS OF GOLD — STEPHEN SPRAGGON

BREATHING SPACES

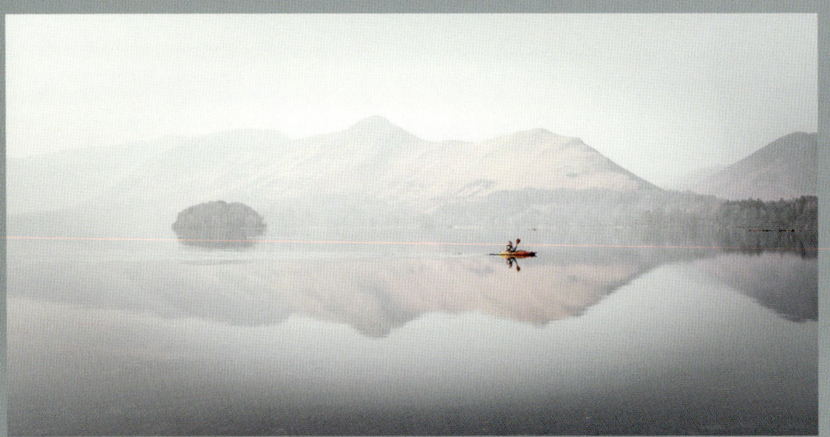

TRANQUILLITY — PETER STEVENS

BREATHING SPACES

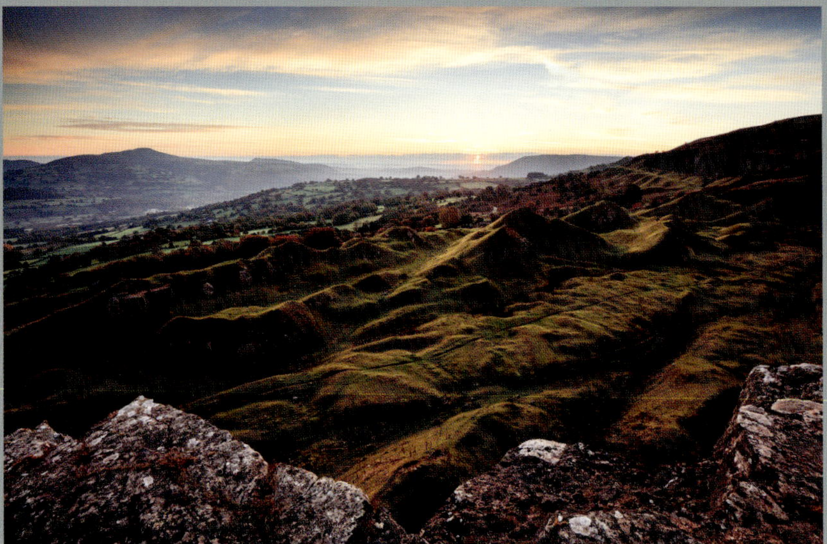

SUNRISE AT LLANGATTOCK ESCARPMENT — MARK BAUER

THE BOUNTIFUL EARTH

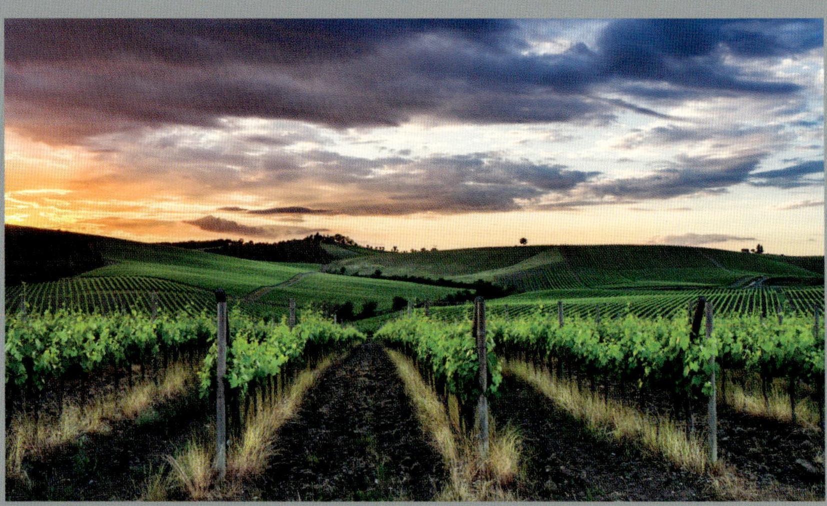

VINEYARD AT SUNSET — JUDE GADD

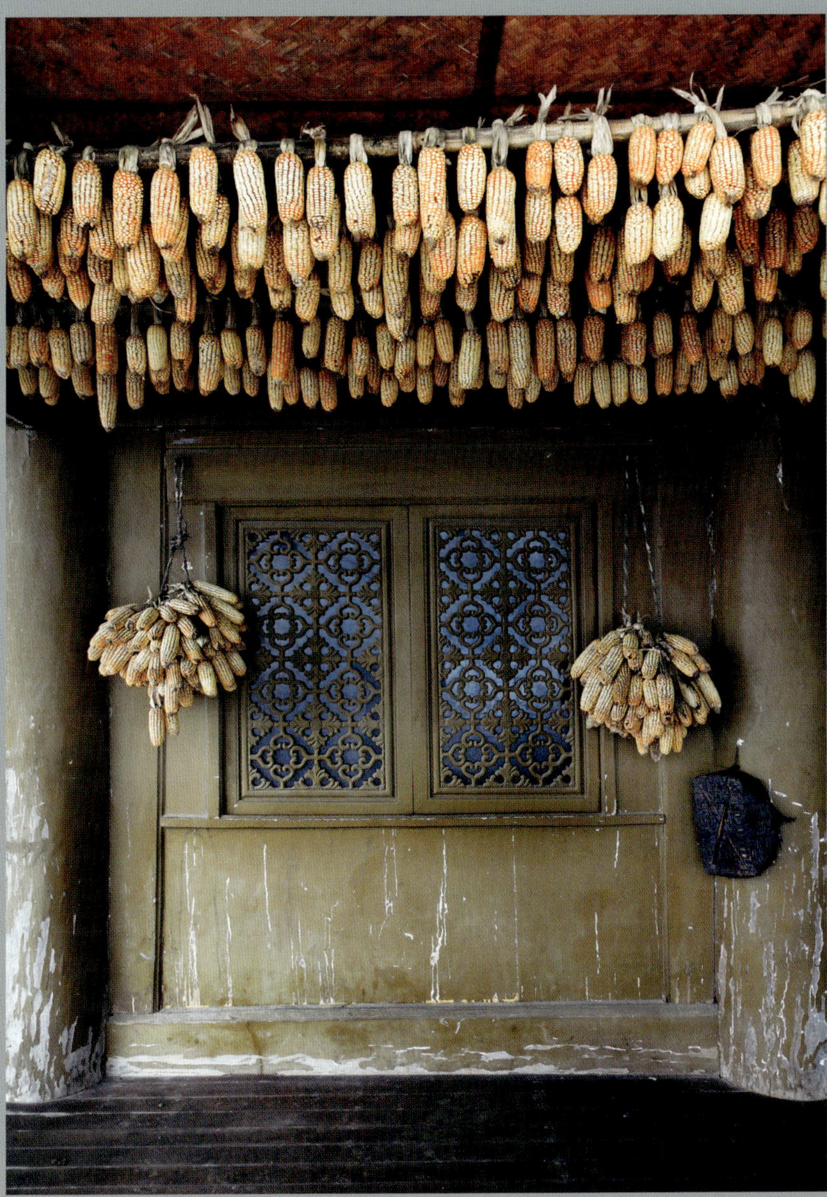

CORN COBS — **LIZ EVERY**

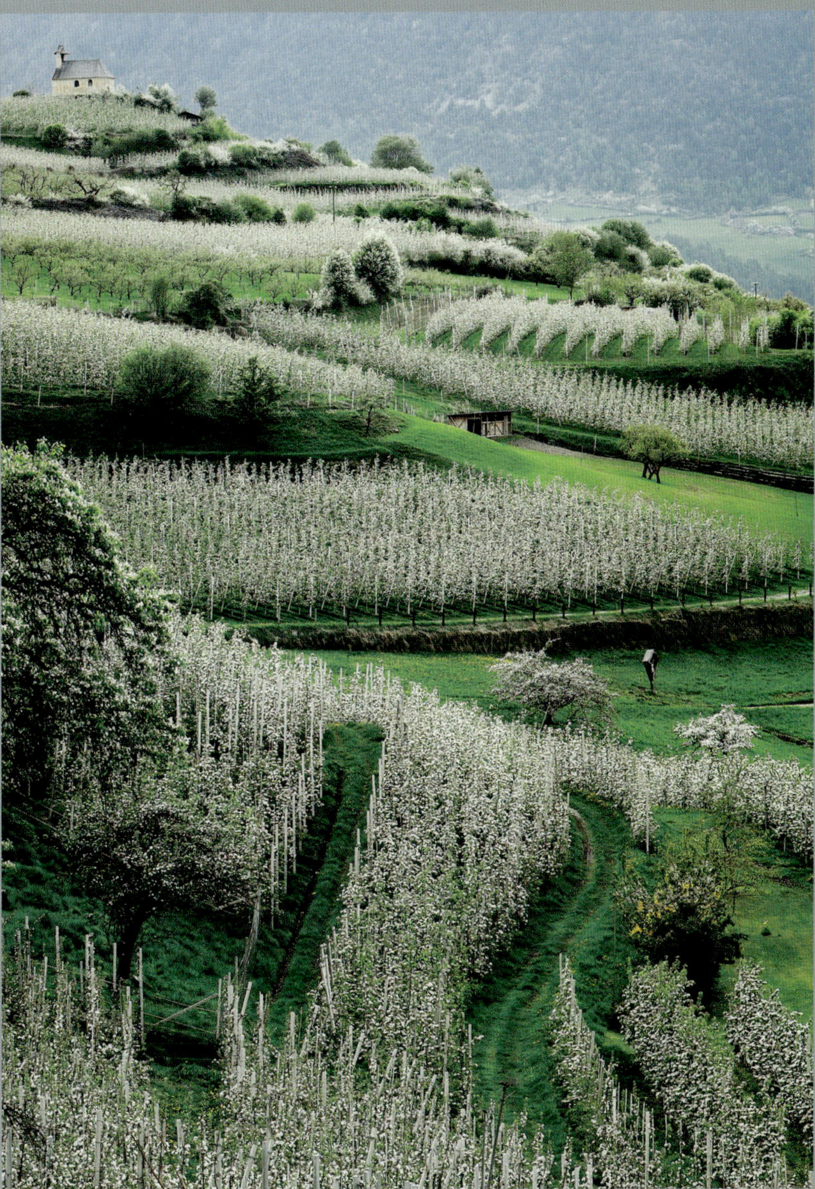

SPRING IN THE ORCHARD — **ALBERT CEOLAN**

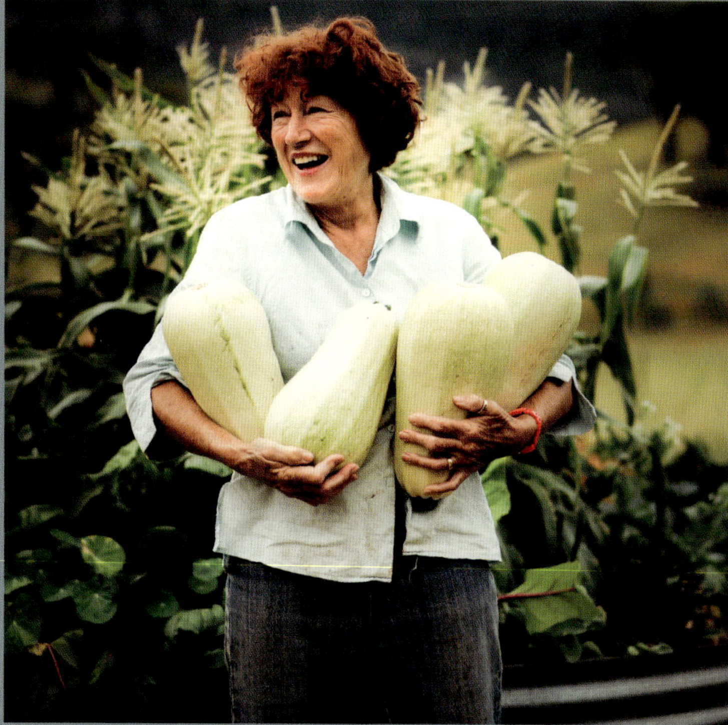

I CARRIED A ZUCCHINI   KATHERINE McINROY

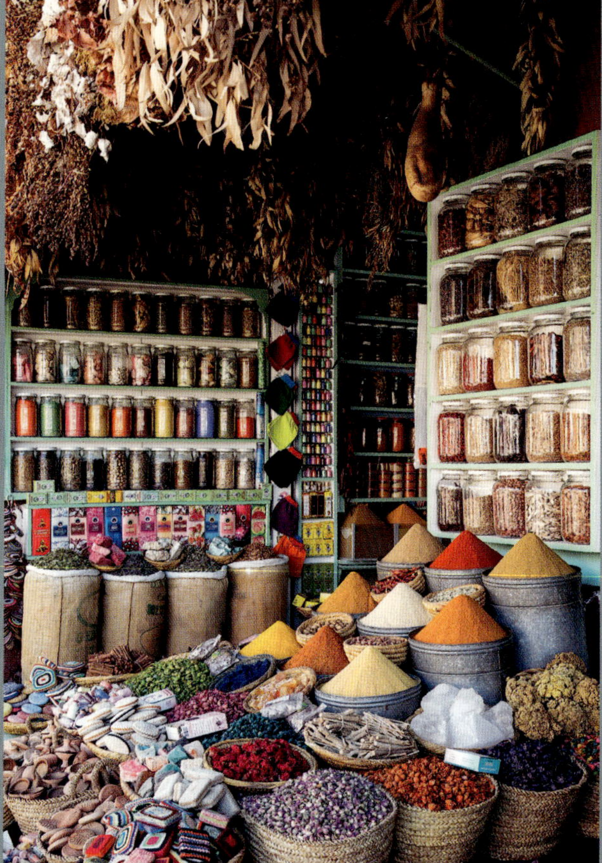

HERBS AND SPICES IN THE SOUK   STEPHEN STUDD

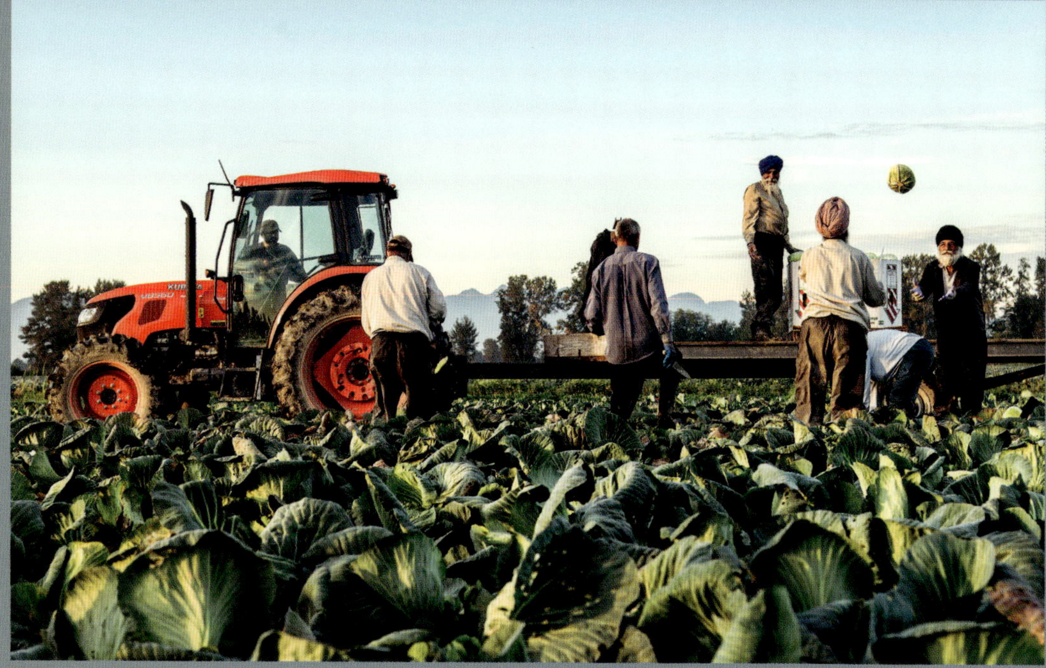

HARVESTING CABBAGE   EVELYN NODWELL

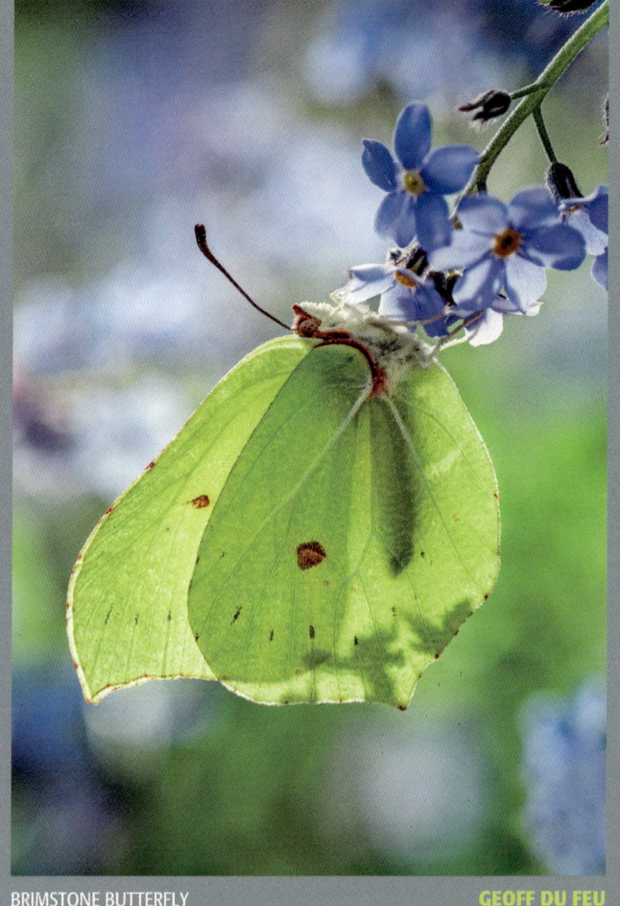

BRIMSTONE BUTTERFLY **GEOFF DU FEU**

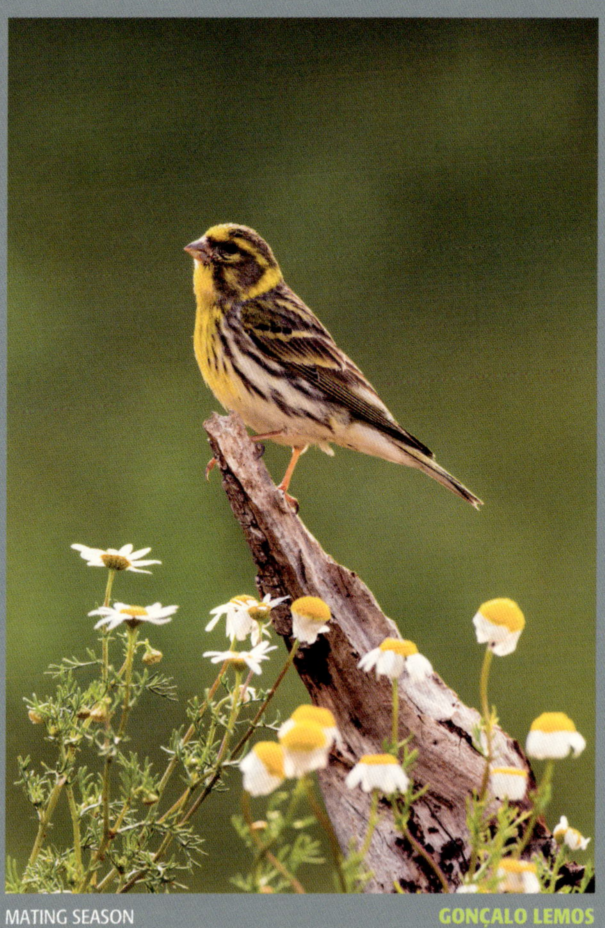

MATING SEASON **GONÇALO LEMOS**

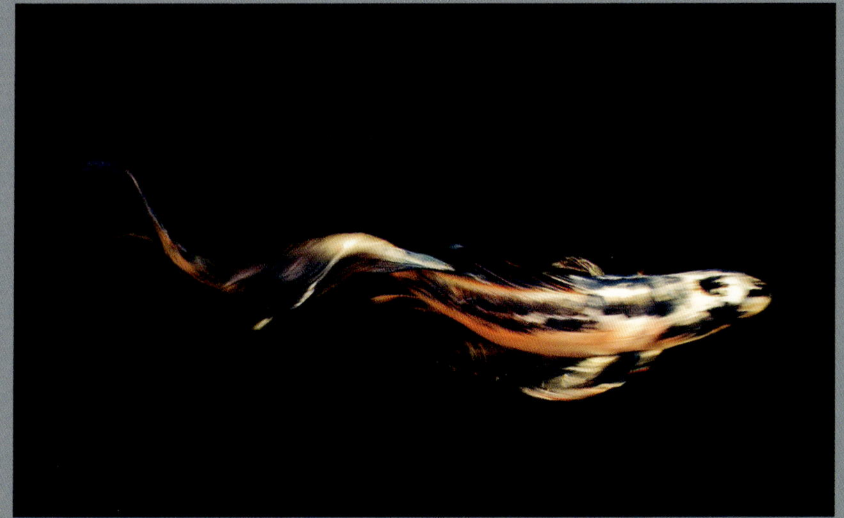

KOI ABSTRACT NUMBER ONE **MARC SHERIDAN**

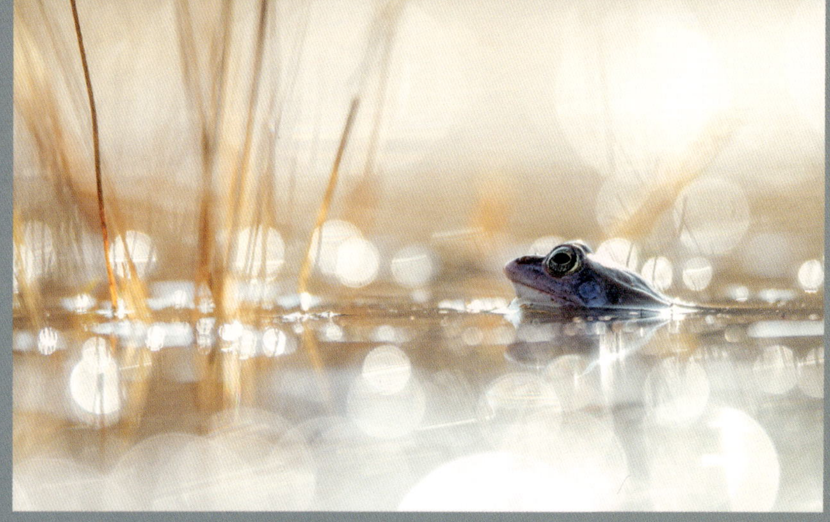

FROG PRINCE **JOHANNES KLAPWIJK**

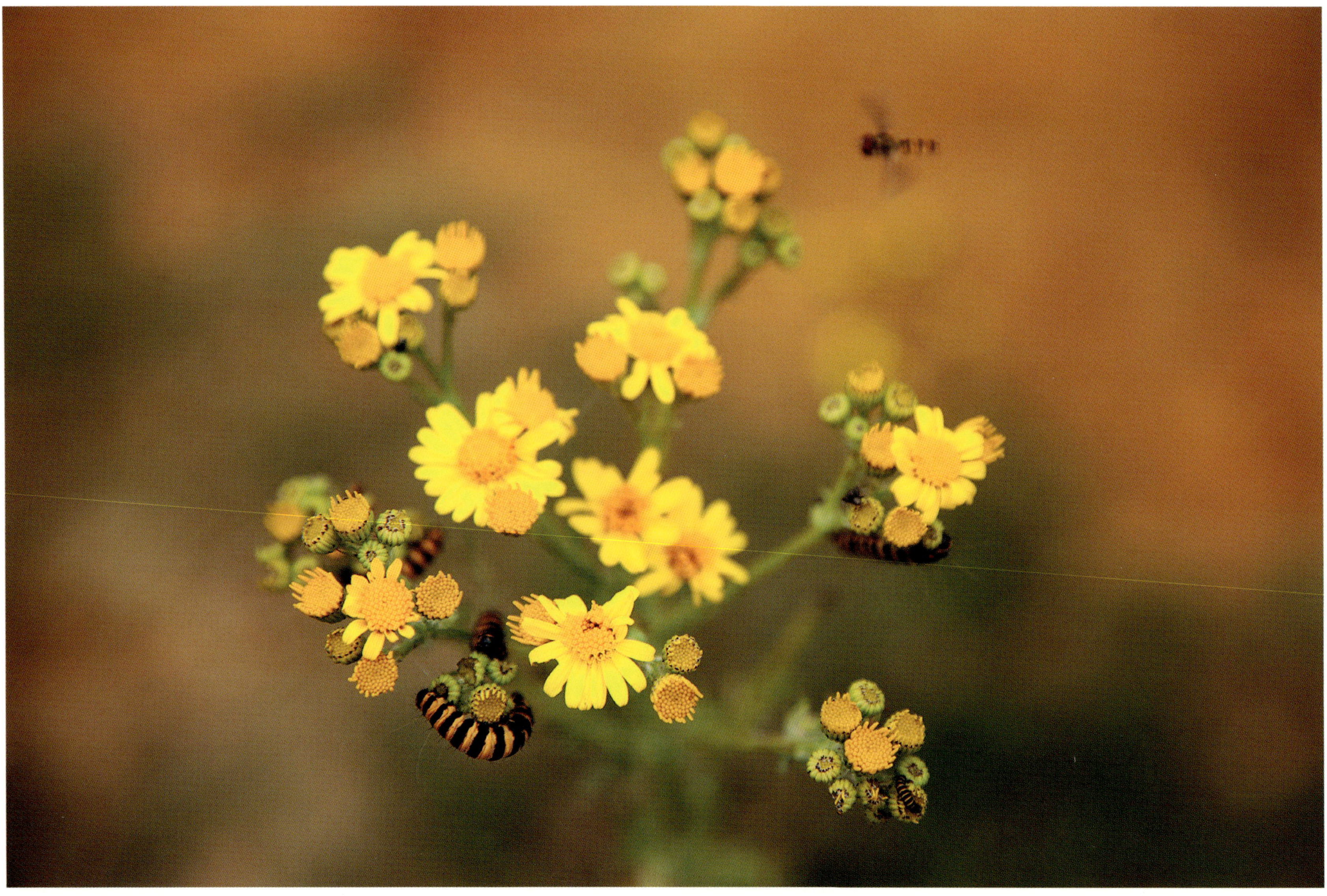

▲ WILL JENKINS – AGE 13   1ST PLACE, THE BEAUTY OF PLANTS

The Housing Estate
Suffolk, England, UK

We were walking my golden retriever and the air was just buzzing with insects. When I looked closer at the tall yellow plants in the hedgerow, I realised that they were crawling with hundreds of stripy caterpillars.

📷 Canon EOS 5D Mark II, Canon 24-105mm lens, 1/640sec at f/4.5, ISO 320.

YOUNG GARDEN PHOTOGRAPHER OF THE YEAR

WILL JENKINS

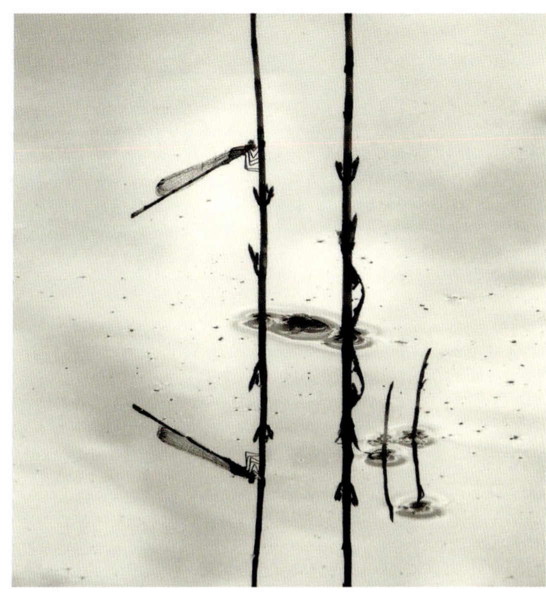

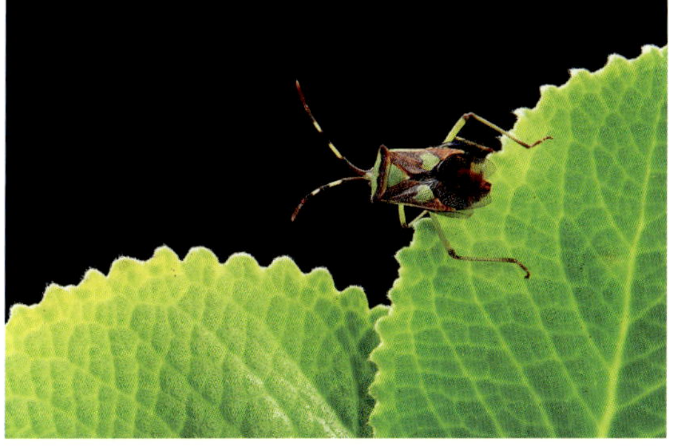

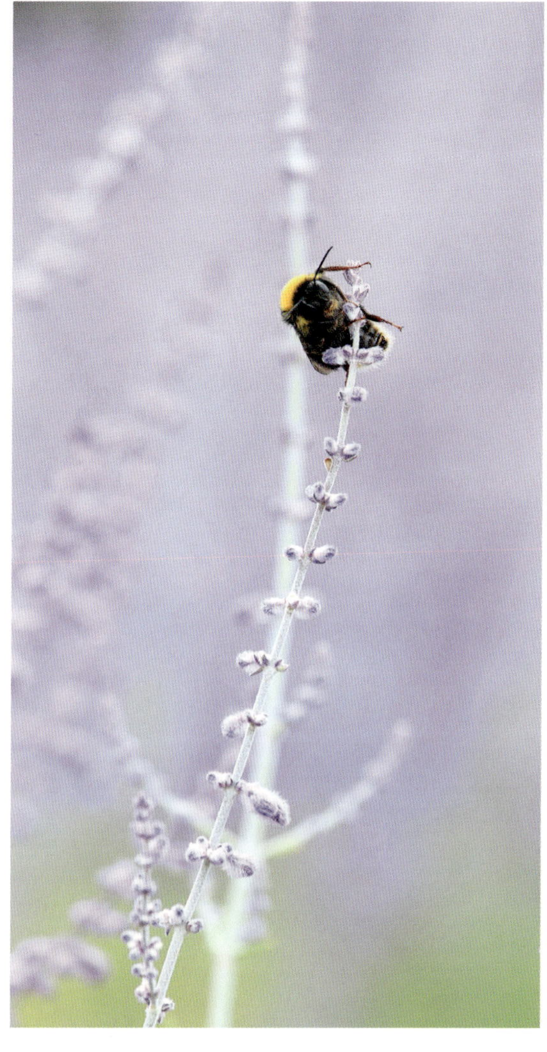

▲ JASMINE CLEGG – AGE 14
2ND PLACE, WILDLIFE IN THE GARDEN

▲ ANSHUL KHATRI – AGE 14
3RD PLACE, WILDLIFE IN THE GARDEN

▲ KASIA REES-JAUKE – AGE 14
FINALIST, WILDLIFE IN THE GARDEN

Damsel Reflected
Red River Valley Nature Reserve, Cornwall,
England, UK

The Red River Valley is a local nature reserve, managed by
a group called the Red River Rescuers, who work to restore
swathes of this once heavily industrialised area that is
becoming overgrown. It provides habitats that attract a number
of target insect species, including damselflies and dragonflies.

Fujifilm SL1000, 1/400sec at f/5.8, ISO 100. Post-capture:
conversion to black and white, minimal cloning.

Colours of Nature
Indore, India

I used a black cloth to take this photo of a very beautiful insect
in my back garden.

Nikon D80, Nikon 18-135mm lens, 1/160sec at f/20, ISO 100.

Bee Pollinating *Perovskia*
National Botanic Garden of Wales, Carmarthenshire,
Wales, UK

I was watching bees pollinating the *Perovskia* (Russian sage),
when this one bee caught my attention. It was clinging on to
the flower head, reminding me of their fragile state in this
changing world.

Canon EOS 70D, Canon 70-200mm lens, 1/320sec at f/6.3,
ISO 400.

MANDY DISHER 1ST PLACE, THE BEAUTY OF PLANTS
THE ROYAL PHOTOGRAPHIC SOCIETY GOLD MEDAL

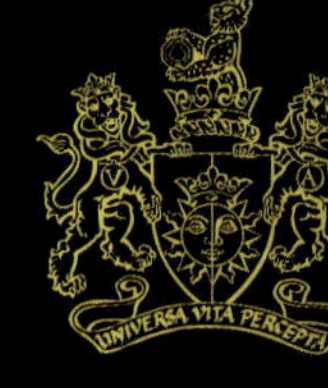

Full Circle
Cambridgeshire, England, UK

When the flowers have finished, seed cases and pods develop, bearing their valuable treasure inside, until the time is right for nature to set them free to grow and mature once again. I like the diversity of the interesting shapes and textures, from the papery *Lunaria* and the fragile *Physalis* and *Allium*, to the prickly *Dipsacus* and the sturdy *Papaver*.

📷 Canon EOS 6D, Canon 100mm macro lens, 1/4sec to 1/8sec at f/13 to f/18. Subjects arranged on a light pad. Post-capture: other leaves and grasses merged with the main subject at varying densities.

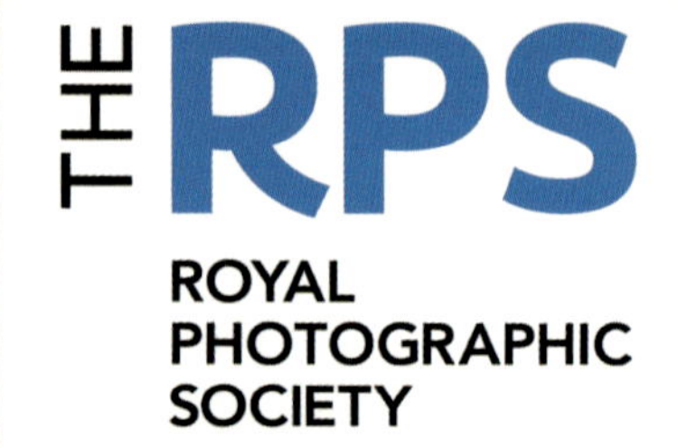

Gold, silver and bronze medals awarded by the Royal Photographic Society

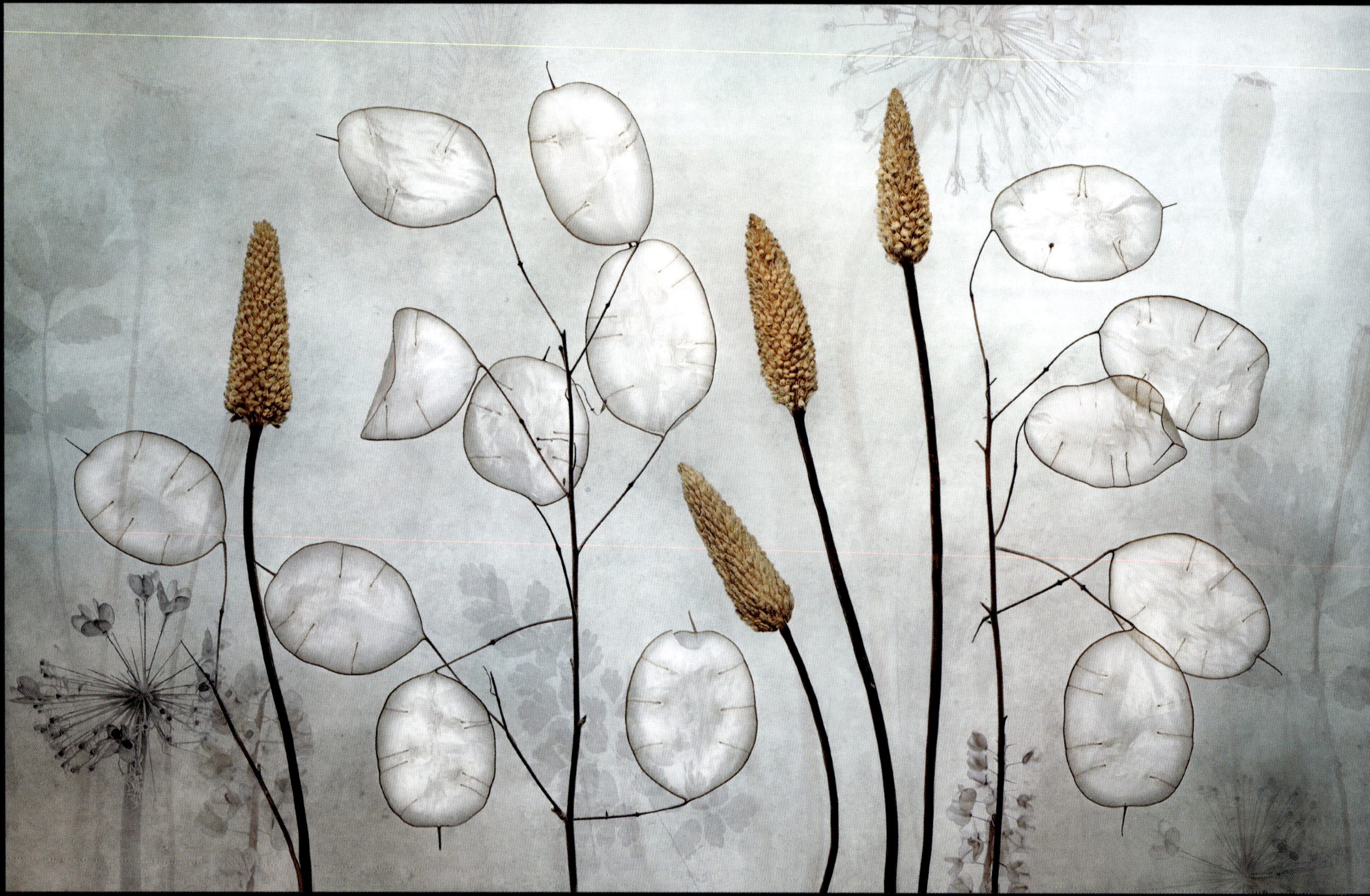

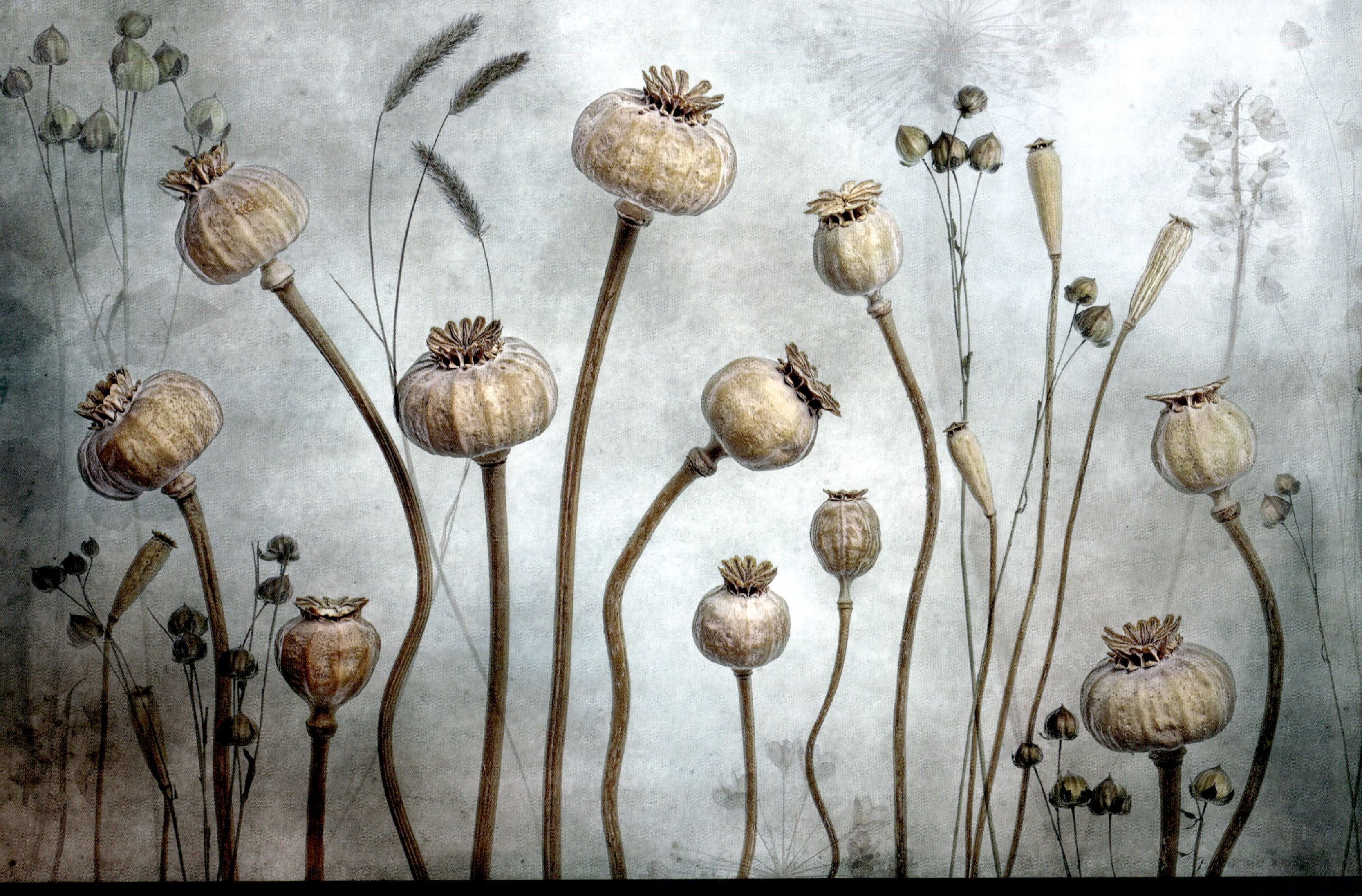

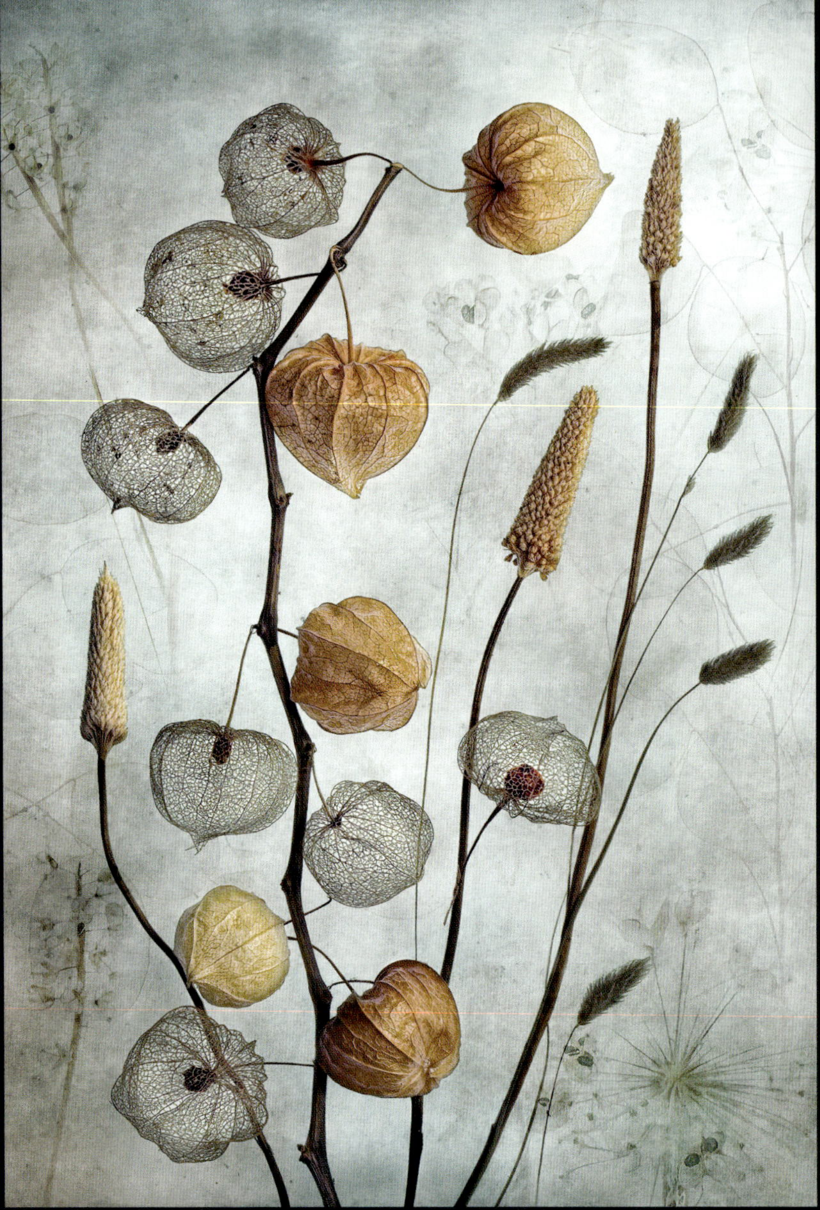

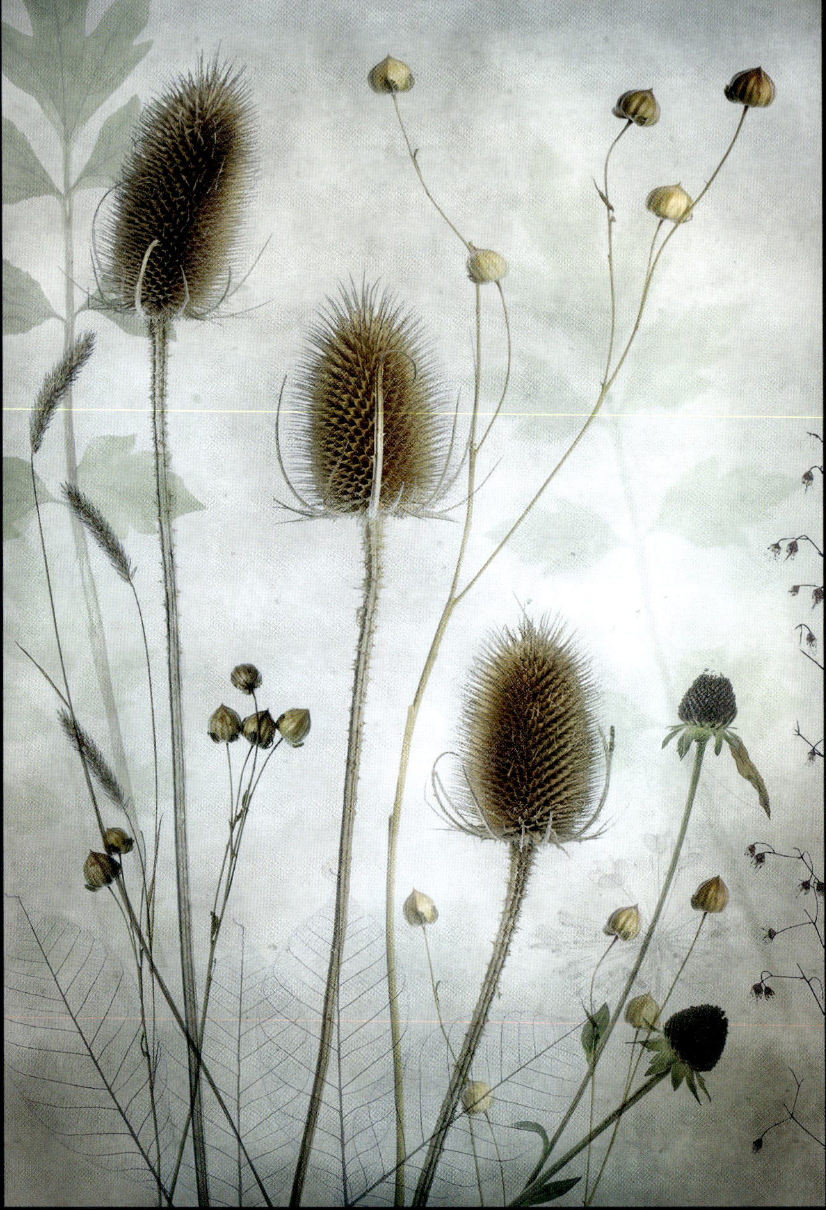

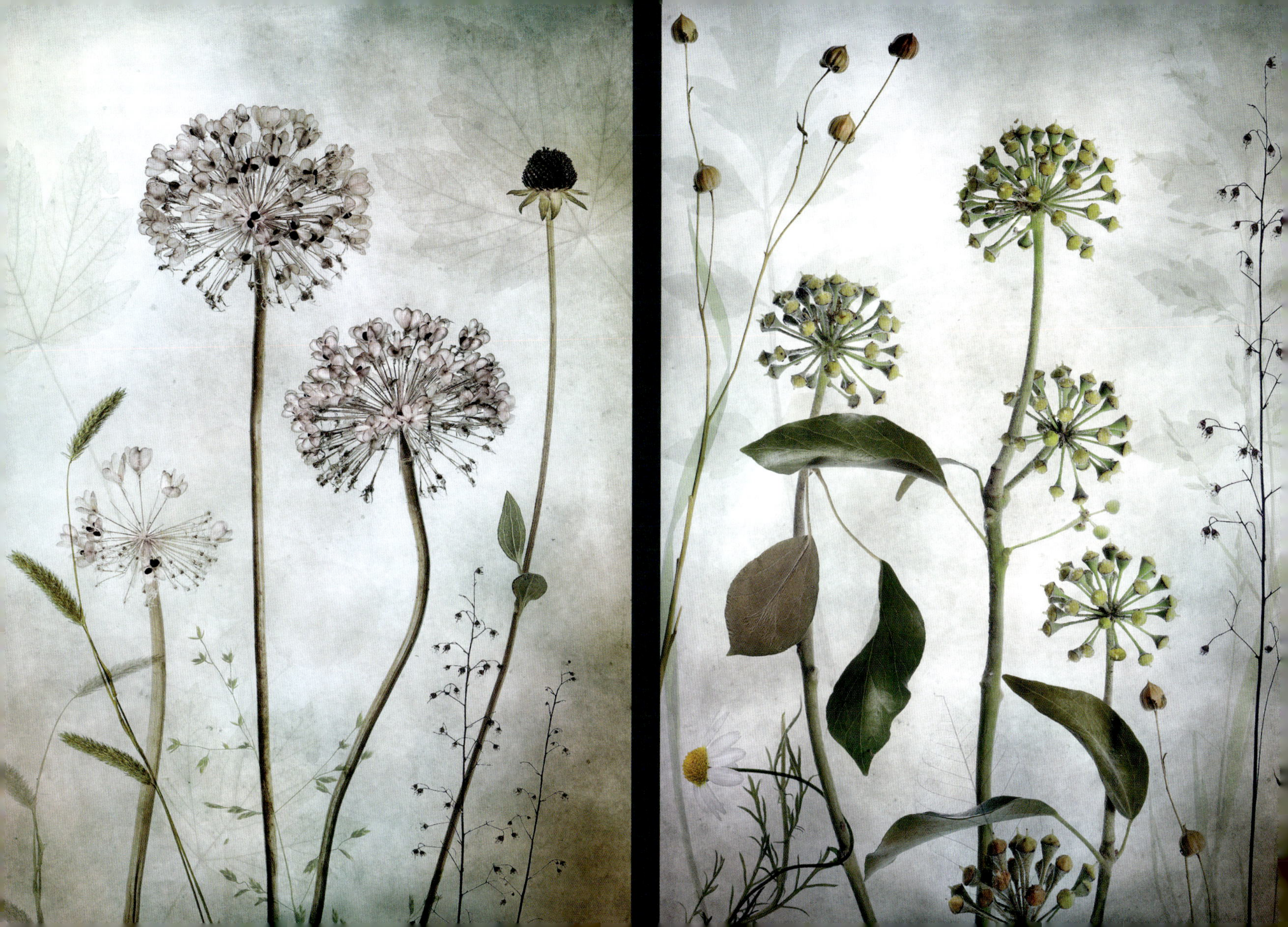

LEE ACASTER 2ND PLACE, TREES, WOODS & FORESTS
THE ROYAL PHOTOGRAPHIC SOCIETY SILVER MEDAL

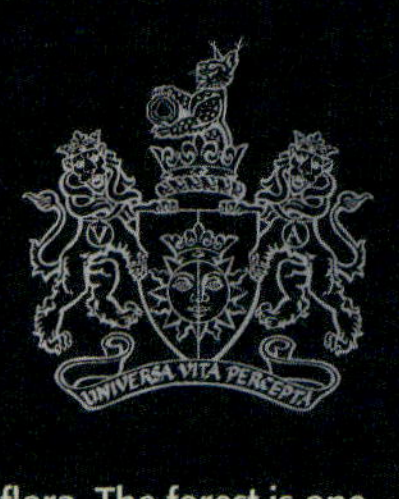

Phoenix
Thetford Forest, Norfolk, England, UK

Thetford Forest is looked after by the Forestry Commission and is a mix
of pines, heathland and broadleaf woodland with a rich variety of fauna and flora. The forest is one
of my favourite haunts for walking and taking images and I was dismayed to hear the news of a
large forest fire. I decided to survey the damage, and document the recovery.

Canon EOS 5D Mark II, Sigma 35mm lens + Canon 70-200mm lens, 0.3sec to 1/200sec at
f/2.8 to f/11. Tripod, polarising filter. Post-capture: basic image management.

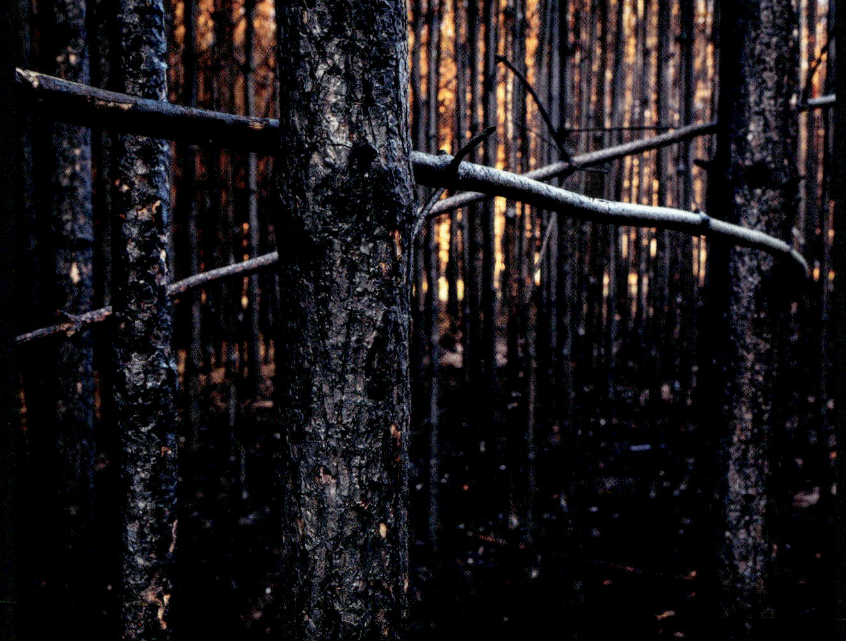

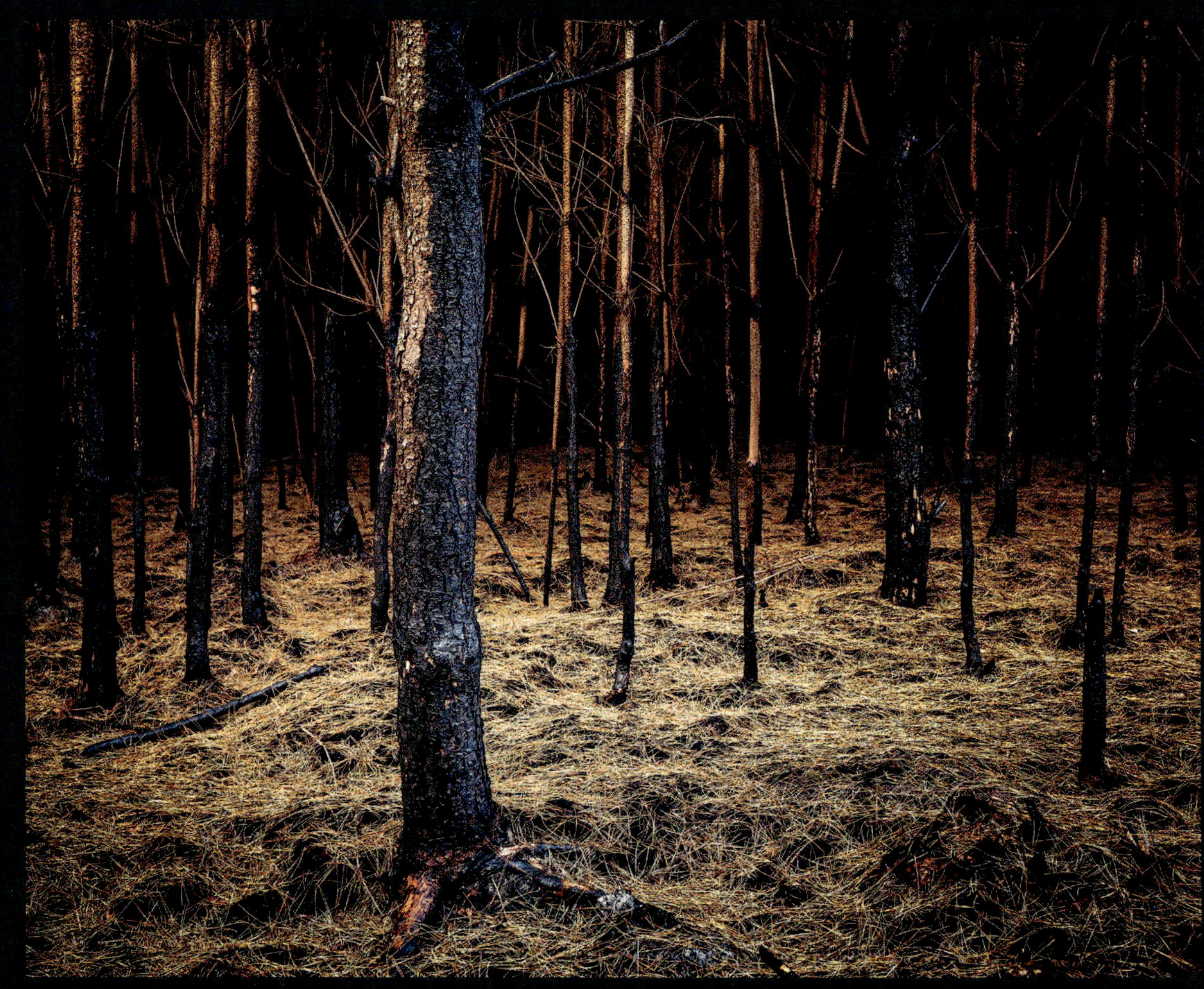

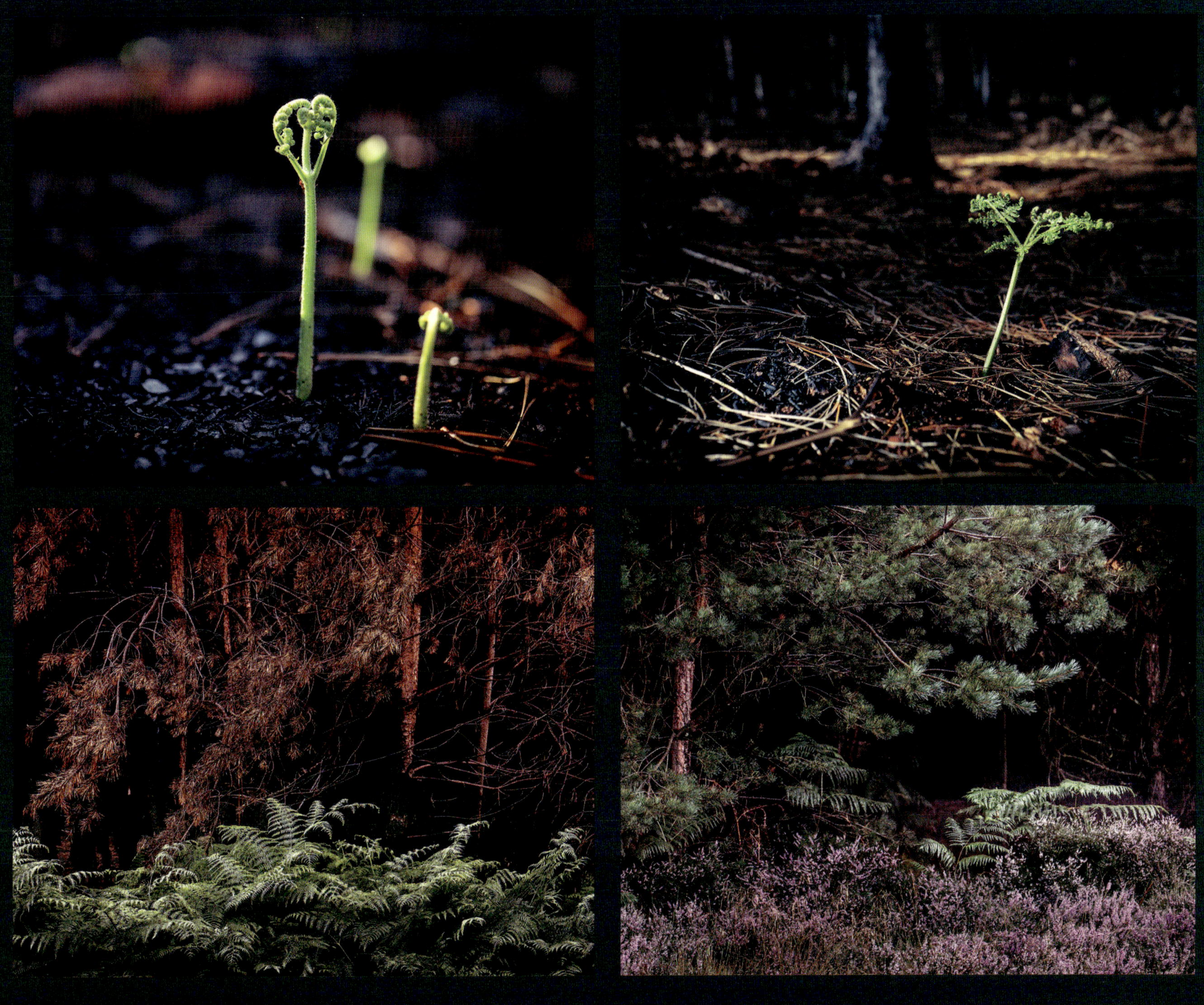

MINGHUI YUAN   3RD PLACE, WILDLIFE IN THE GARDEN
THE ROYAL PHOTOGRAPHIC SOCIETY BRONZE MEDAL

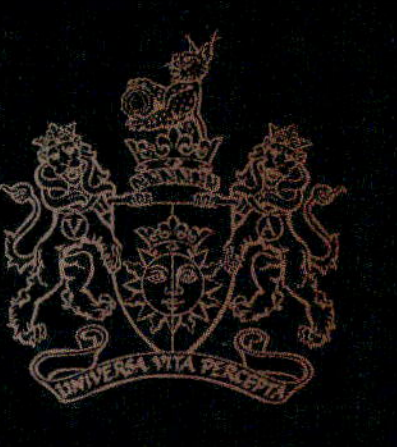

The Miracle of Life
Wuhan City, China

This is a series of images depicting the reproduction of certain insect species in the garden. Life really is full of beauty, wonder and joy and capturing key parts of this cycle helps us feel closer to nature. Every year new life will appear, expressing its own form of beauty and dignity, bringing the garden to life and reminding us we are not alone.

Canon EOS 70D + Nikon DS3 + Nikon D7000, Tamron 90mm macro lens, 1/80sec to 1/400sec at f/5.6 to f/9.

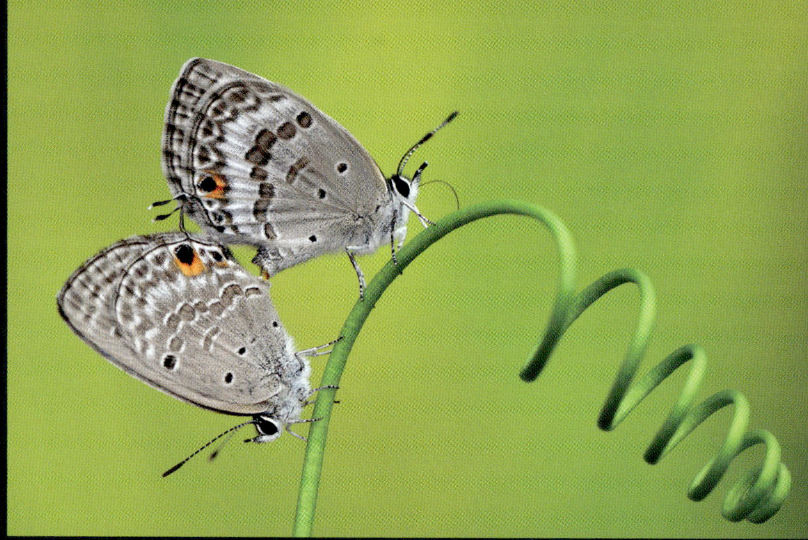

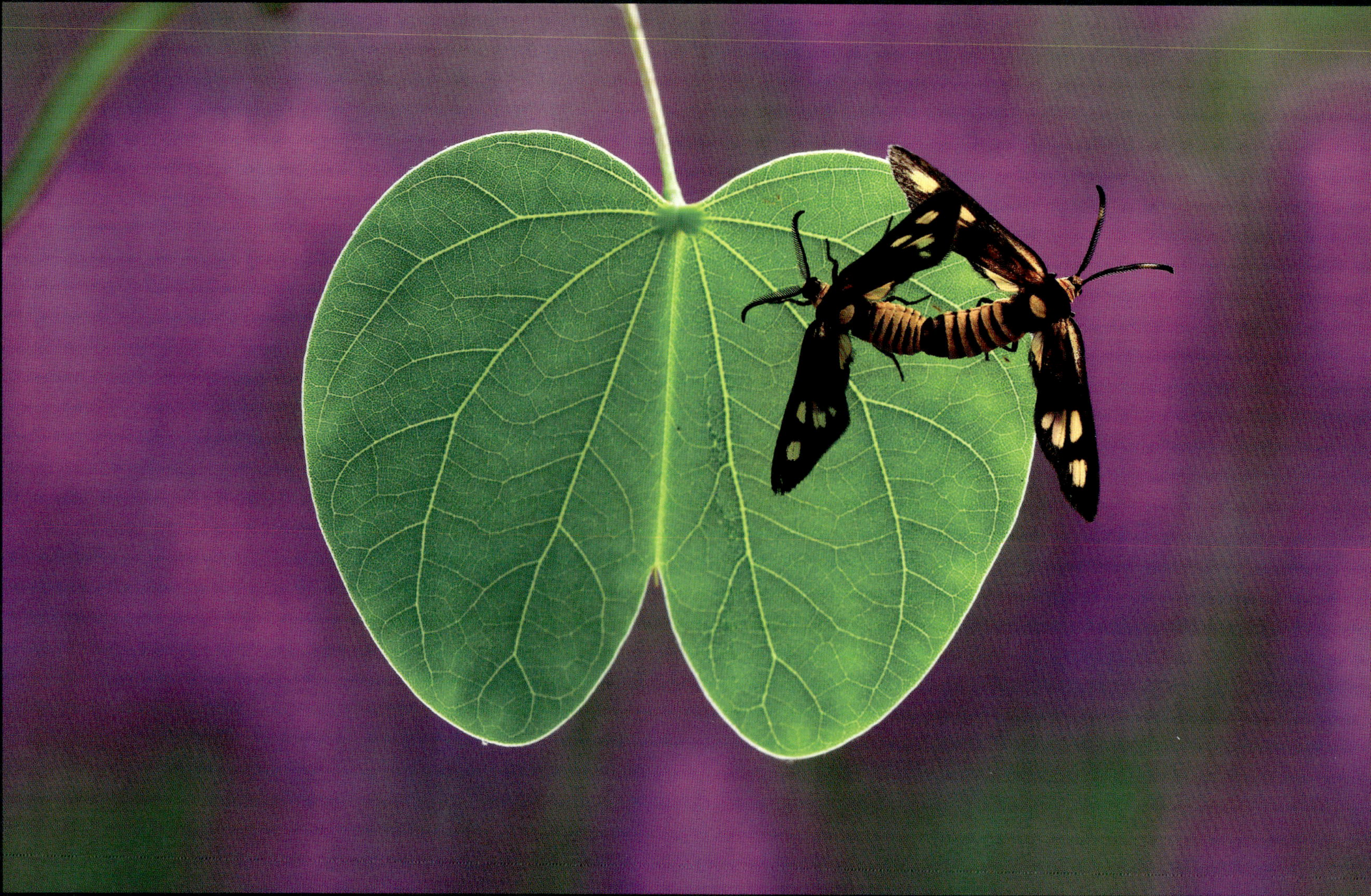

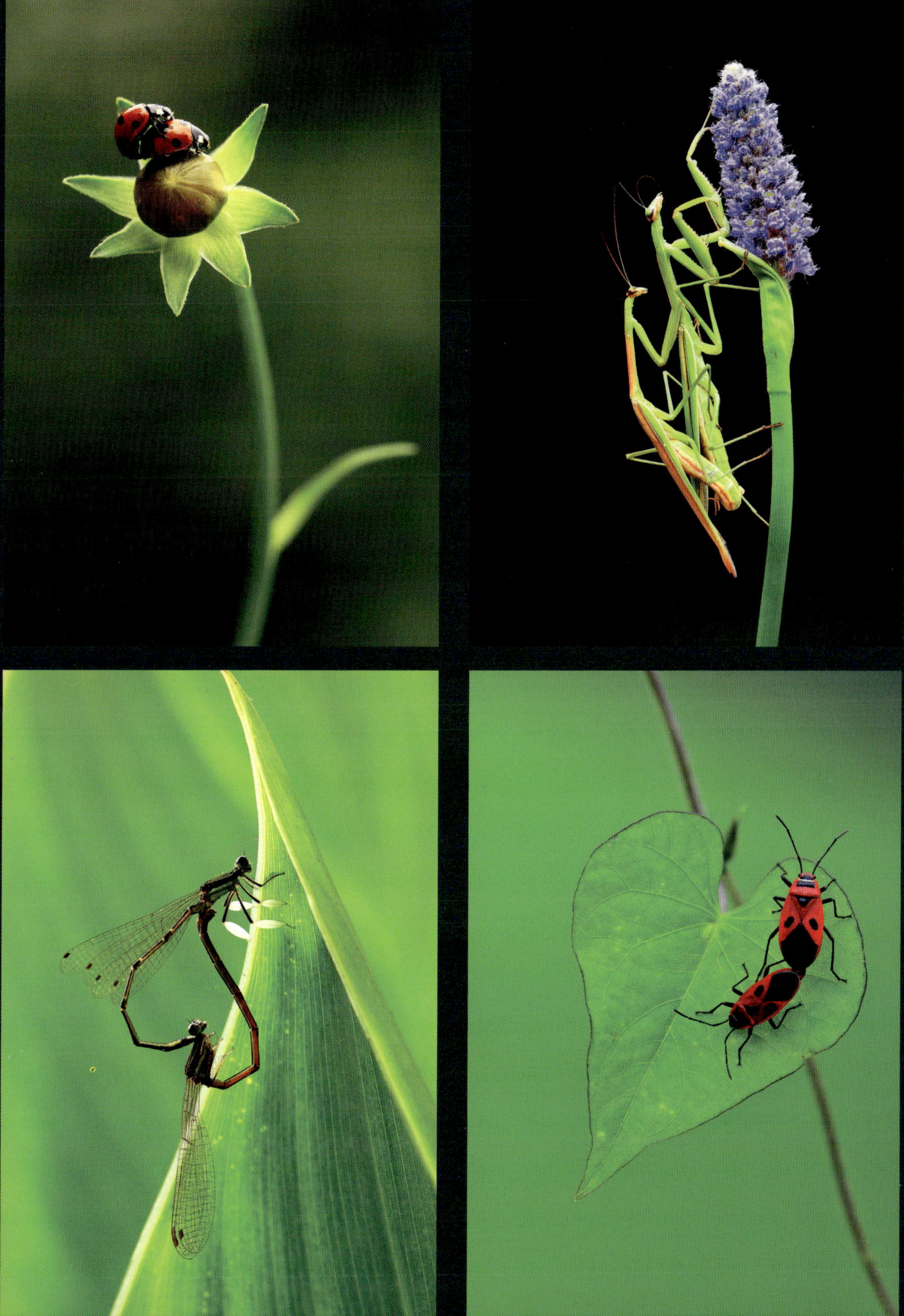

Interface
Dickleburgh, Norfolk, England, UK

This is a series of images that I took in a derelict plastic polytunnel. I was attracted to the interaction of plants, other life forms and plastic together with the natural light shining through. The plastic created a superb textured filter, producing a series of semi-abstract images. Where the plants were touching the surface of the plastic they were very sharp and any plants that were a distance from the plastic were rendered with a soft focus effect, despite often using a wide-angle lens set at a fairly small aperture. The conversion to monochrome completed the abstract effect which I envisioned.

Ricoh GXR, Voigtländer 15mm lens, 1/60sec to 1/250sec at f/5.6 to f/11. Post-capture: converted to monochrome, basic image management.

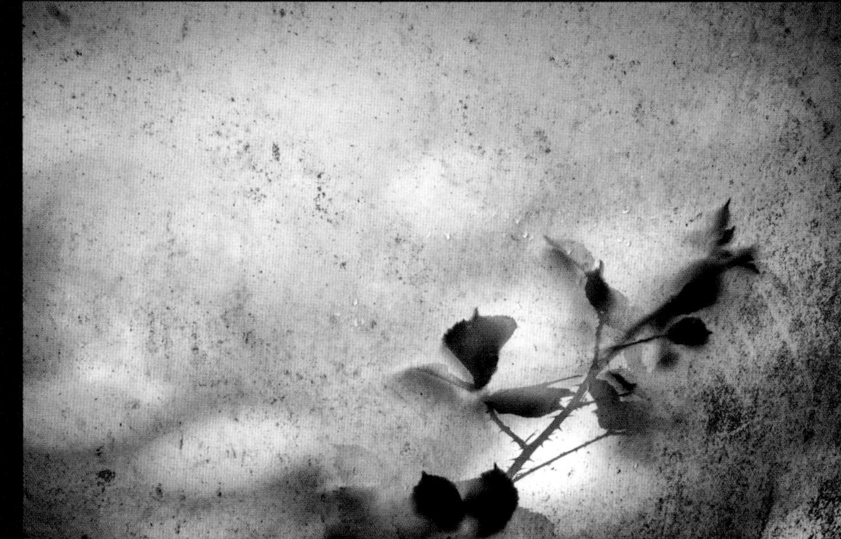

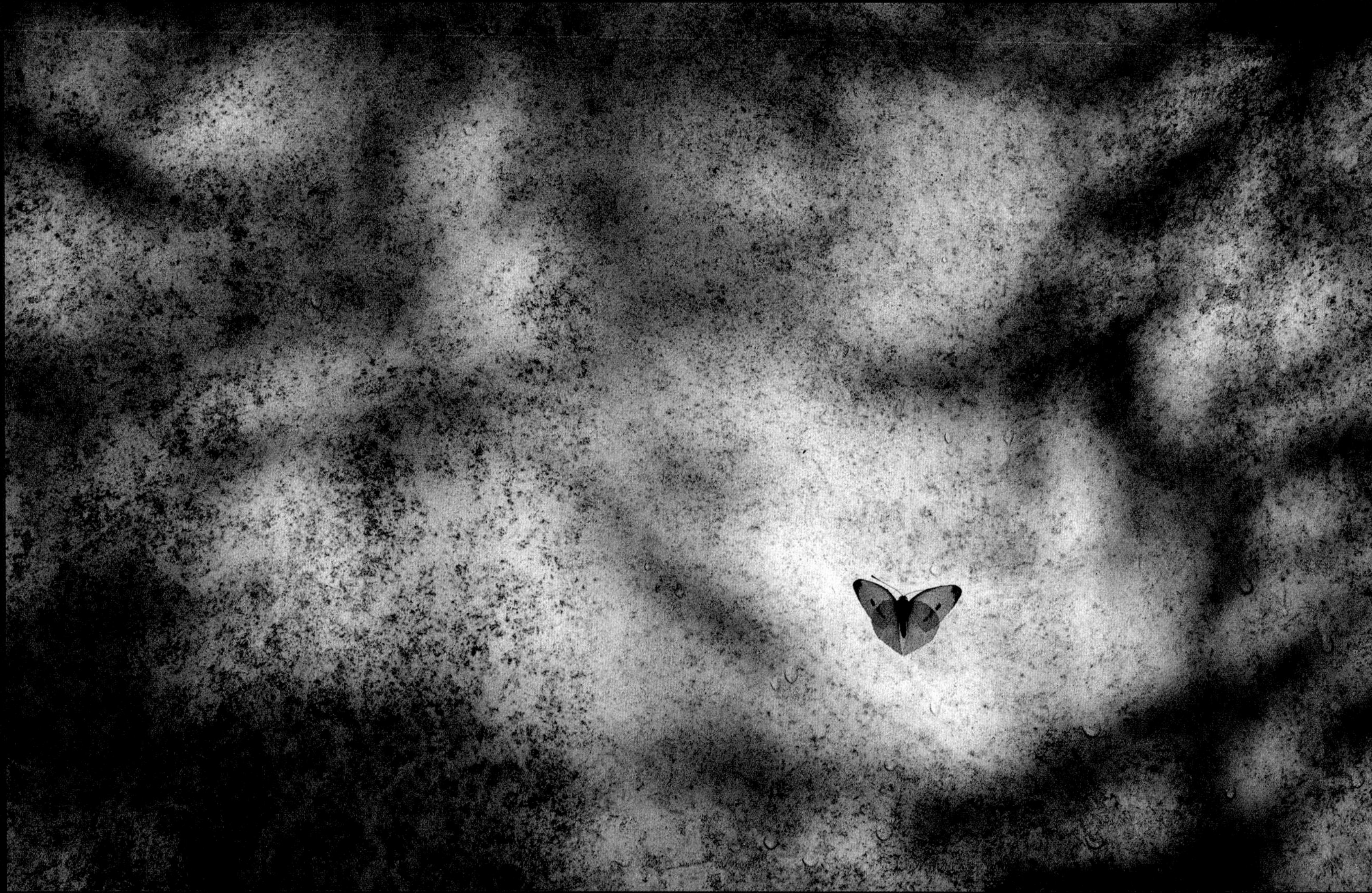

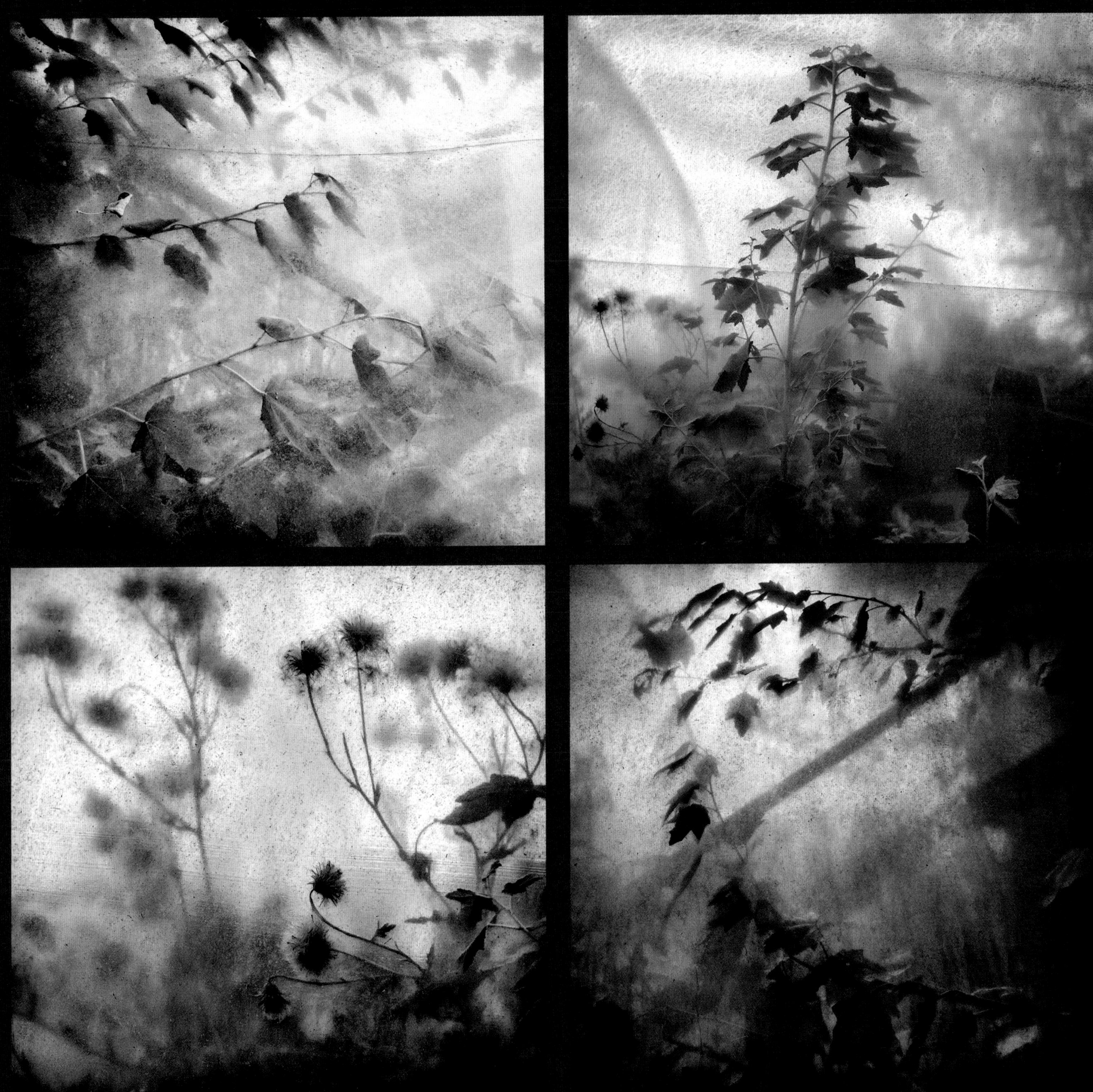

BOB KELLER   Highly Commended, Trees, Woods & Forests

Spreading Limbs
Oregon/South Carolina/Hawaii, USA

I am a tree devotee and photographer of the forest. This group of notable spreading canopy specimens was assembled over a period of almost four years, ending in late 2014. The habitats of these special protective trees with their expansive growth habit range from a tropical island to the high desert, from a rose garden in an inland valley to the High Cascades of Oregon and from the low country of South Carolina to the rain forest of the Pacific north-west. For millennia, large spreading landmark trees have served as important human gathering places and refuges.

Canon EOS 5D Mark II + Nikon D800, Canon 24-70mm lens + Nikkor 24-70mm lens, 1/2sec to 1/40sec at f/14 to f/16. Tripod, cable release. Post-capture: each image is made from two horizontal captures, basic image management.

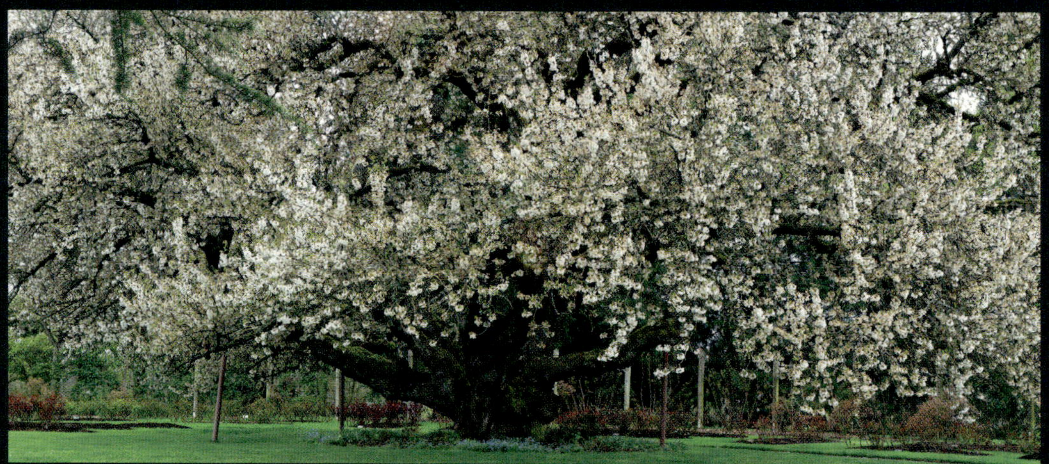

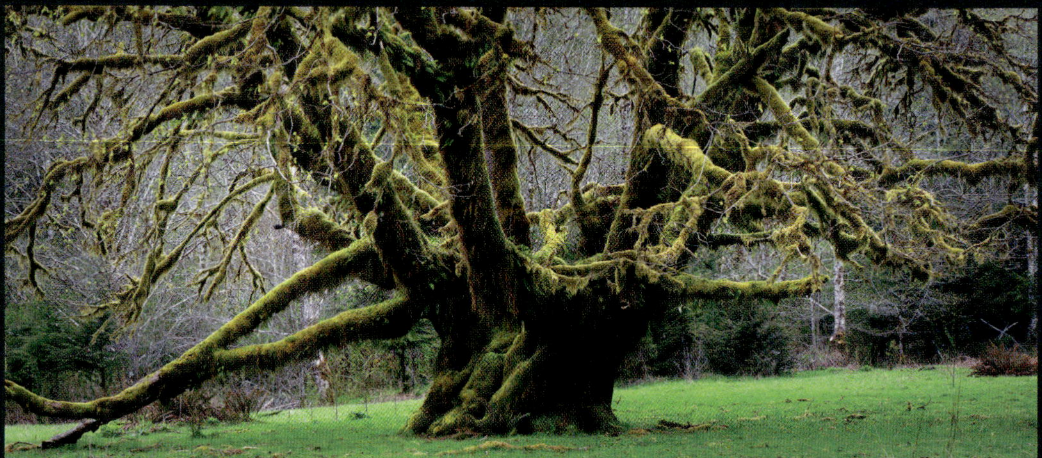

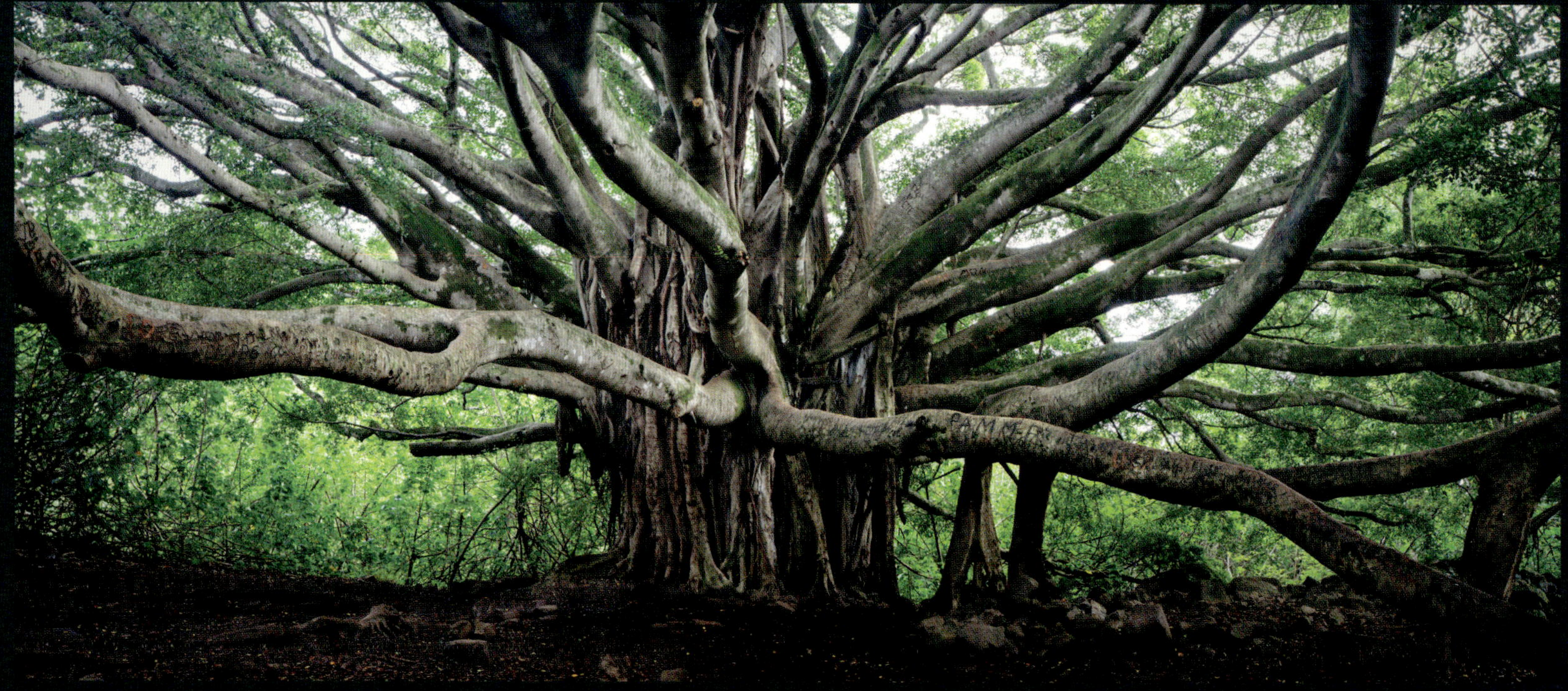

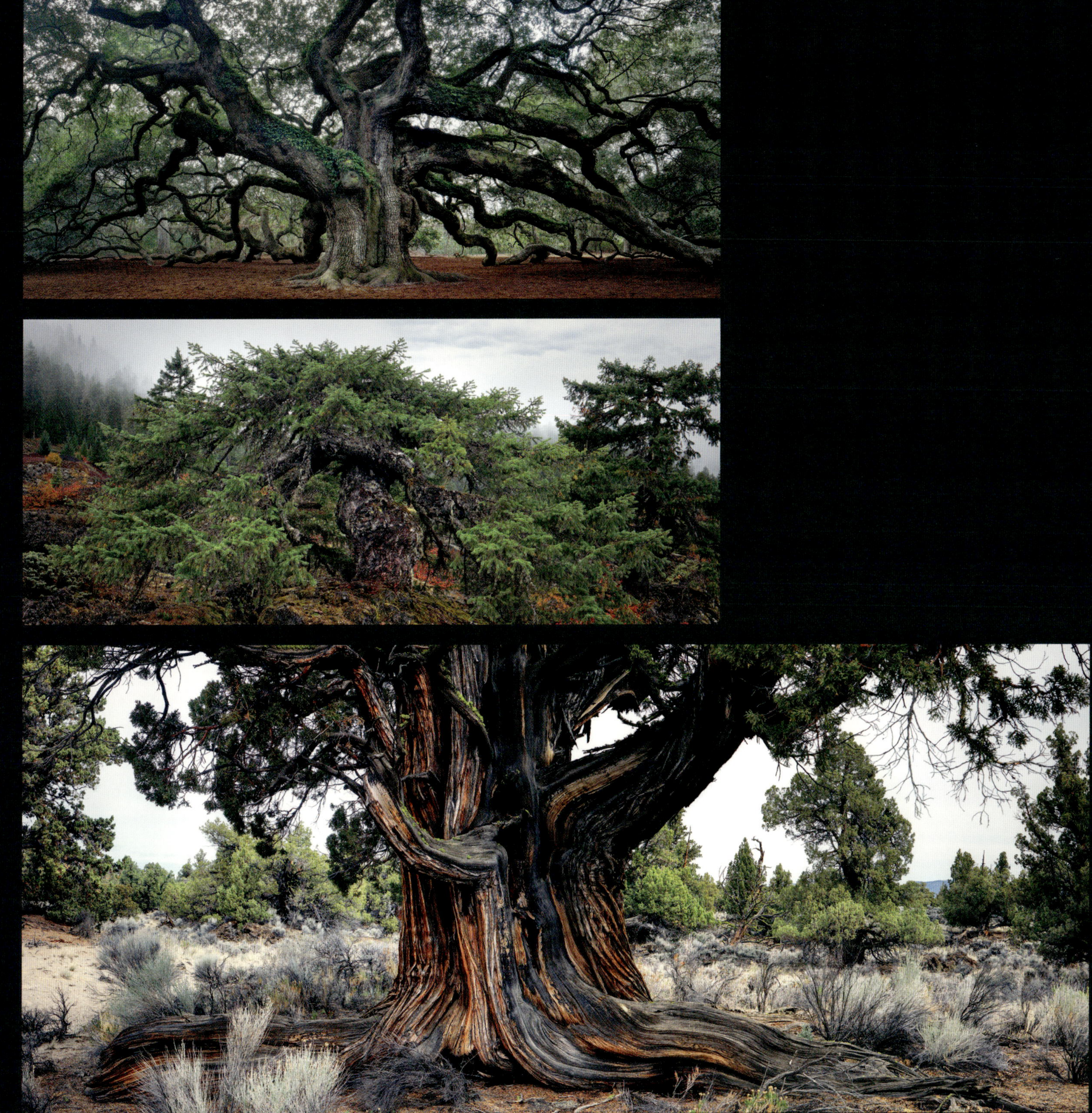

FRANTISEK RERUCHA   FINALIST, THE BEAUTY OF PLANTS

The Mystery of Dry Plants
Pionyrska, Czech Republic

I mainly specialise in shooting macro photography and have been especially interested in photographing dry plants. Throughout the year I collect fresh plants and dry them, arranging them into different compositions; I find the flowers, stems and leaves provide a wealth of intriguing patterns and colours. Although dried plants have an aspect of beauty taken away, they also retain something mysterious which is waiting to be discovered.

Canon EOS 70D, Canon 60mm lens, 1/25sec to 1/60sec at f/5.6 to f/9. Stand, focusing rail, ring light. Post-capture: focus stacking.

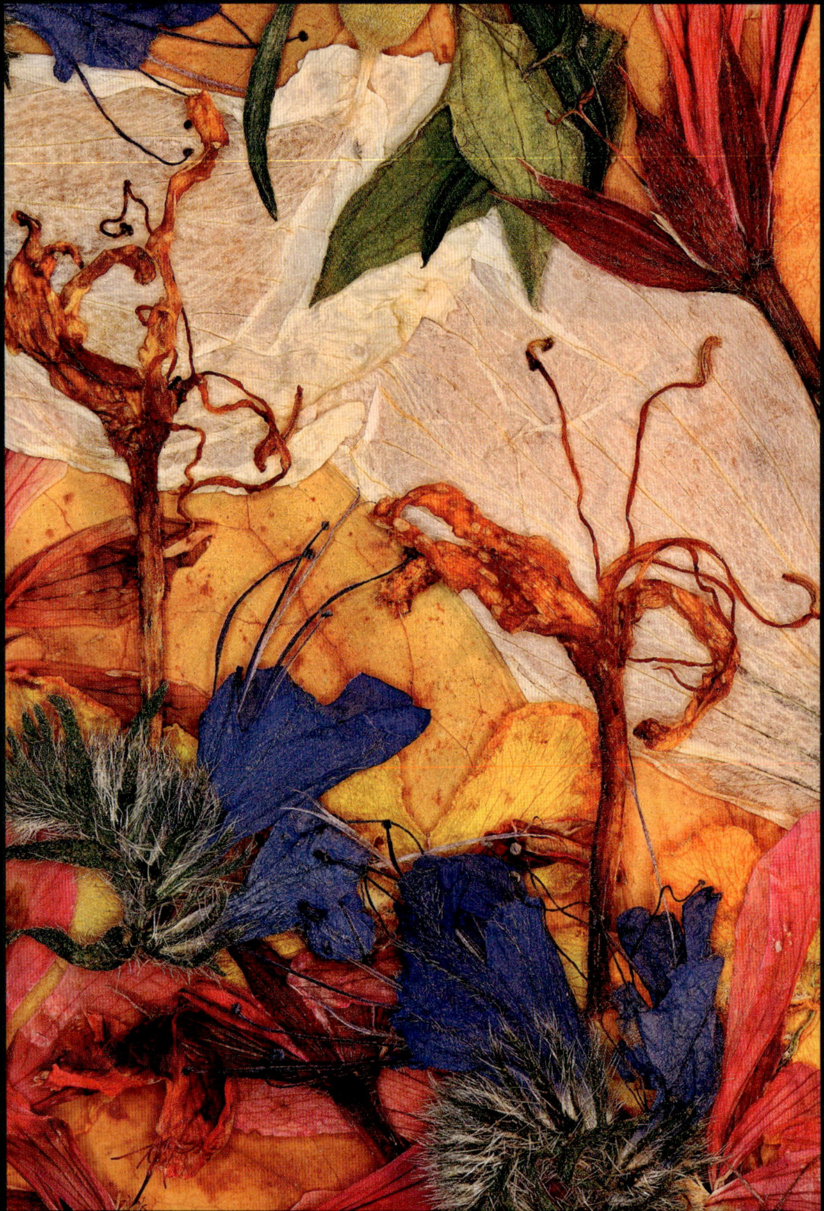

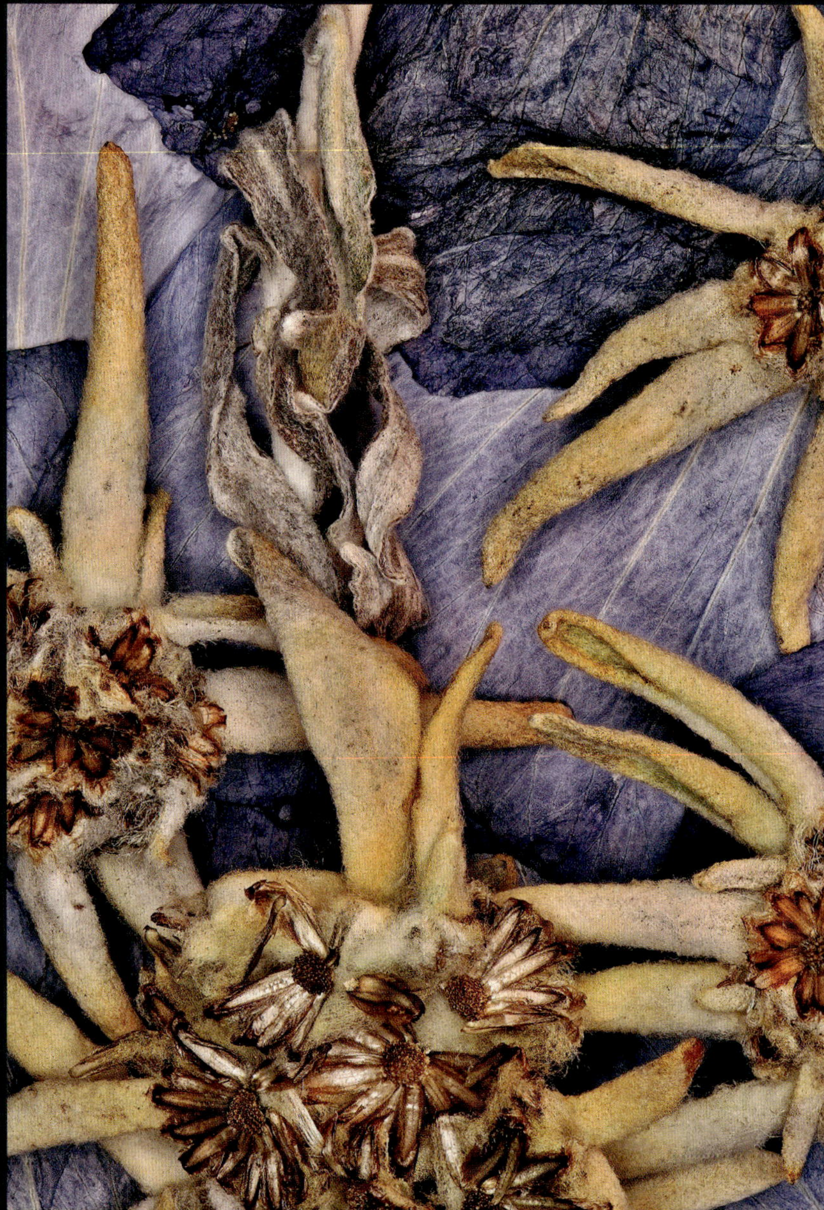

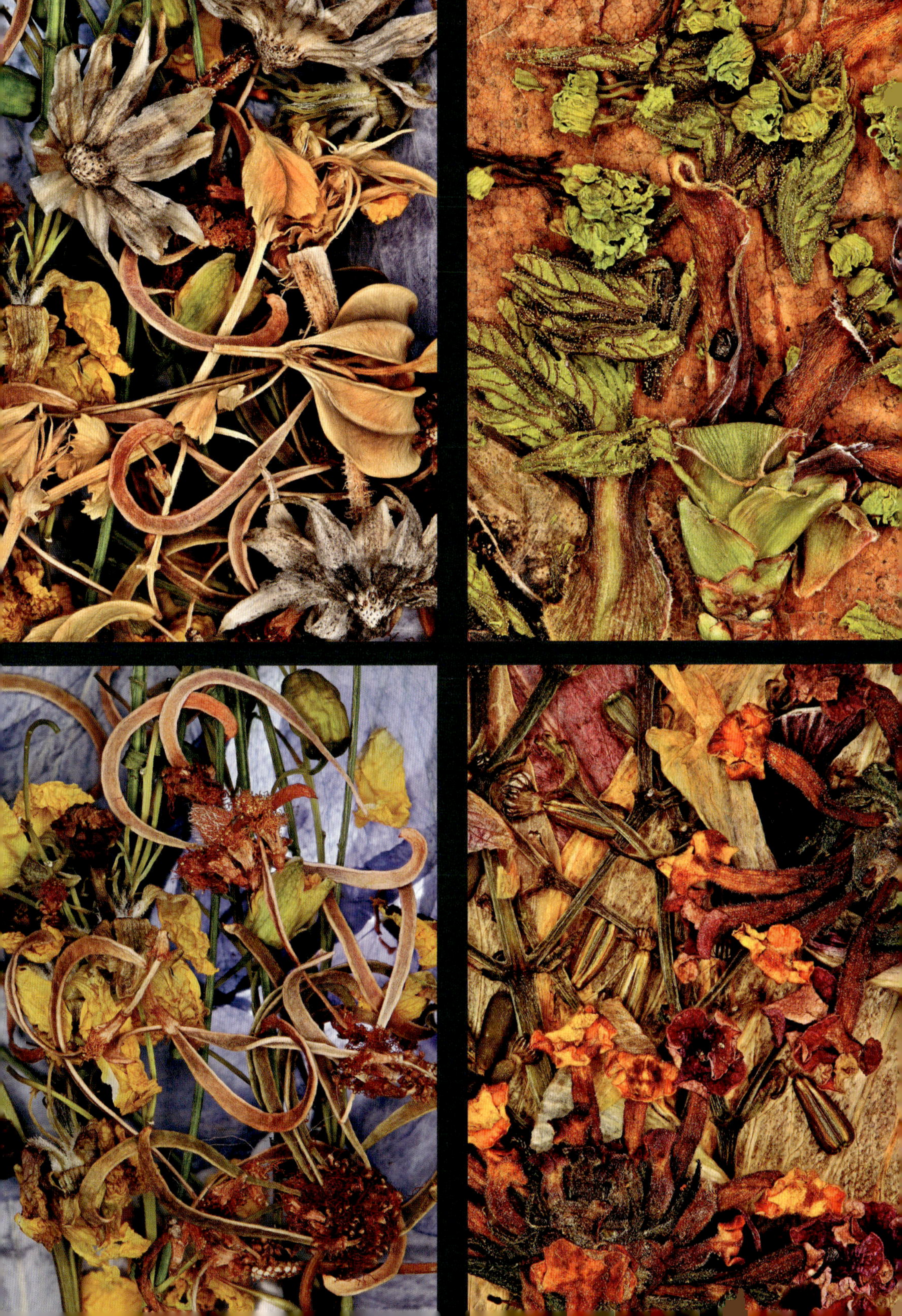

Truncated
Derbyshire, England, UK

For this series, I made frequent visits to photograph the same forest over the course of around three years. My aim was to not only emphasise the ecological importance of trees, woods and forests worldwide, but also to generate an aesthetic appreciation of the beauty of these magnificent trees. For me, woodland is a living landscape, with an endless variety of forms, and I wanted to show something of the mysterious nature of the forest by conveying a strong sense of place. I believe that the environmental importance of trees cannot be overestimated, so I hope I have managed to impart even a small measure of their immense value.

Arca Swiss, Ilford HP5, 150-300mm lens, 1/4sec to 8min at f/16 to f/32. Tripod, handheld light meter, cable release, dark cloth.

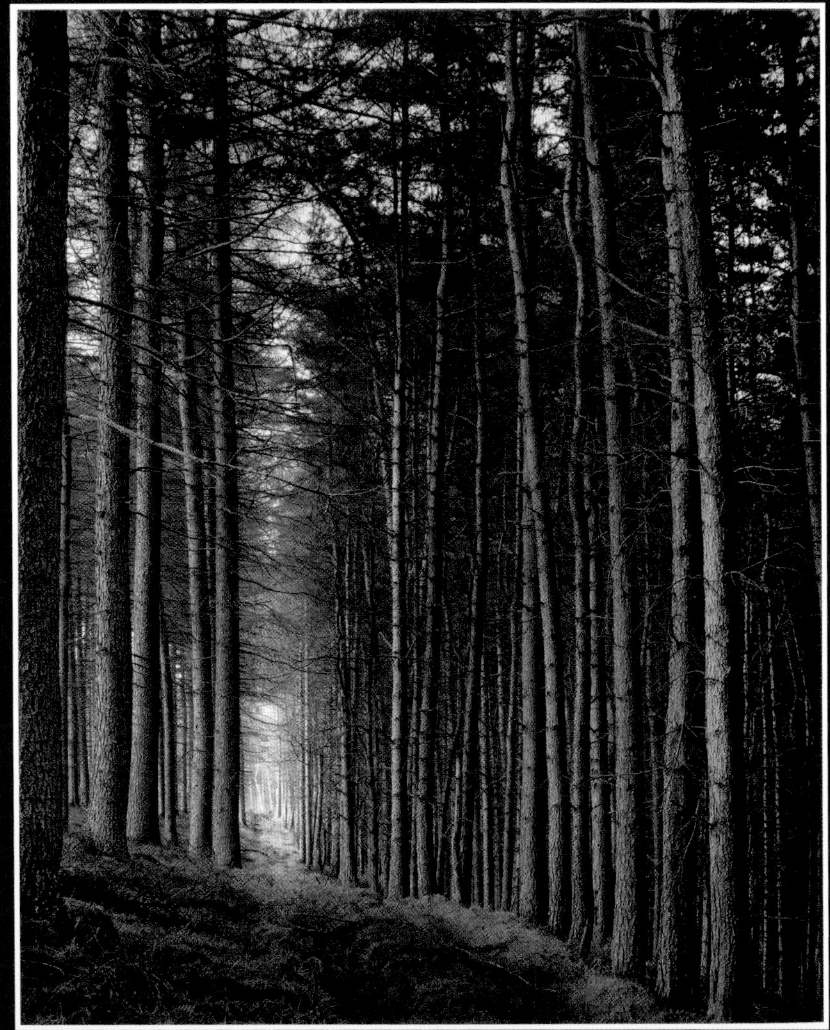

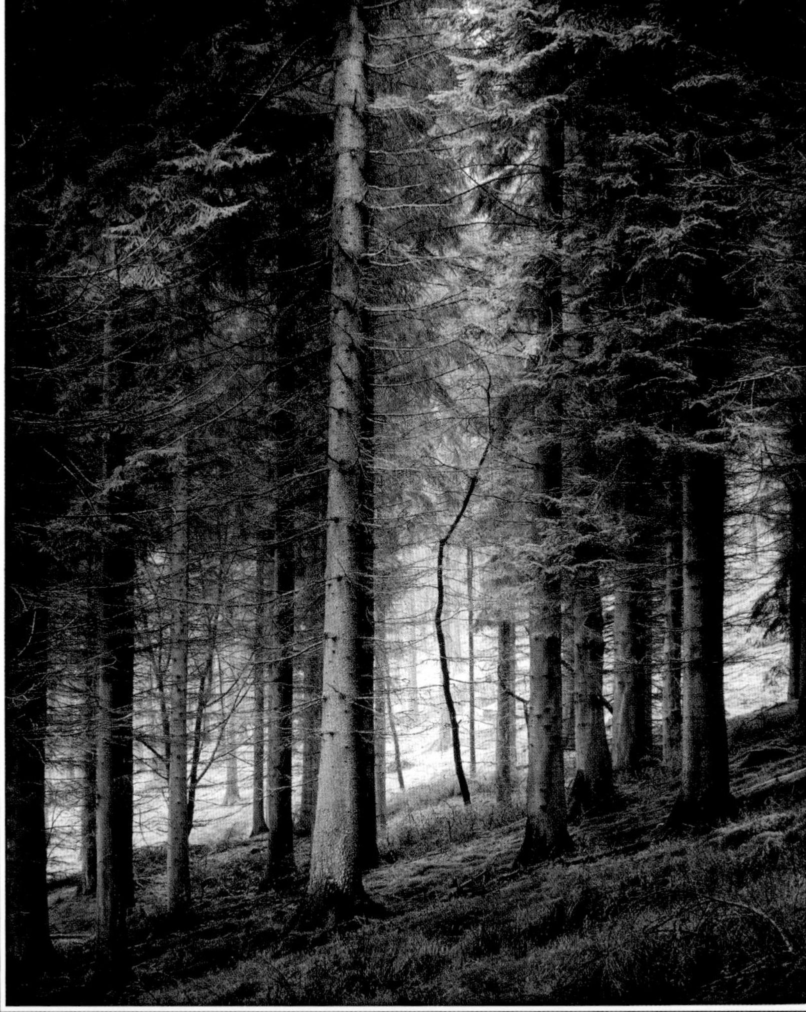

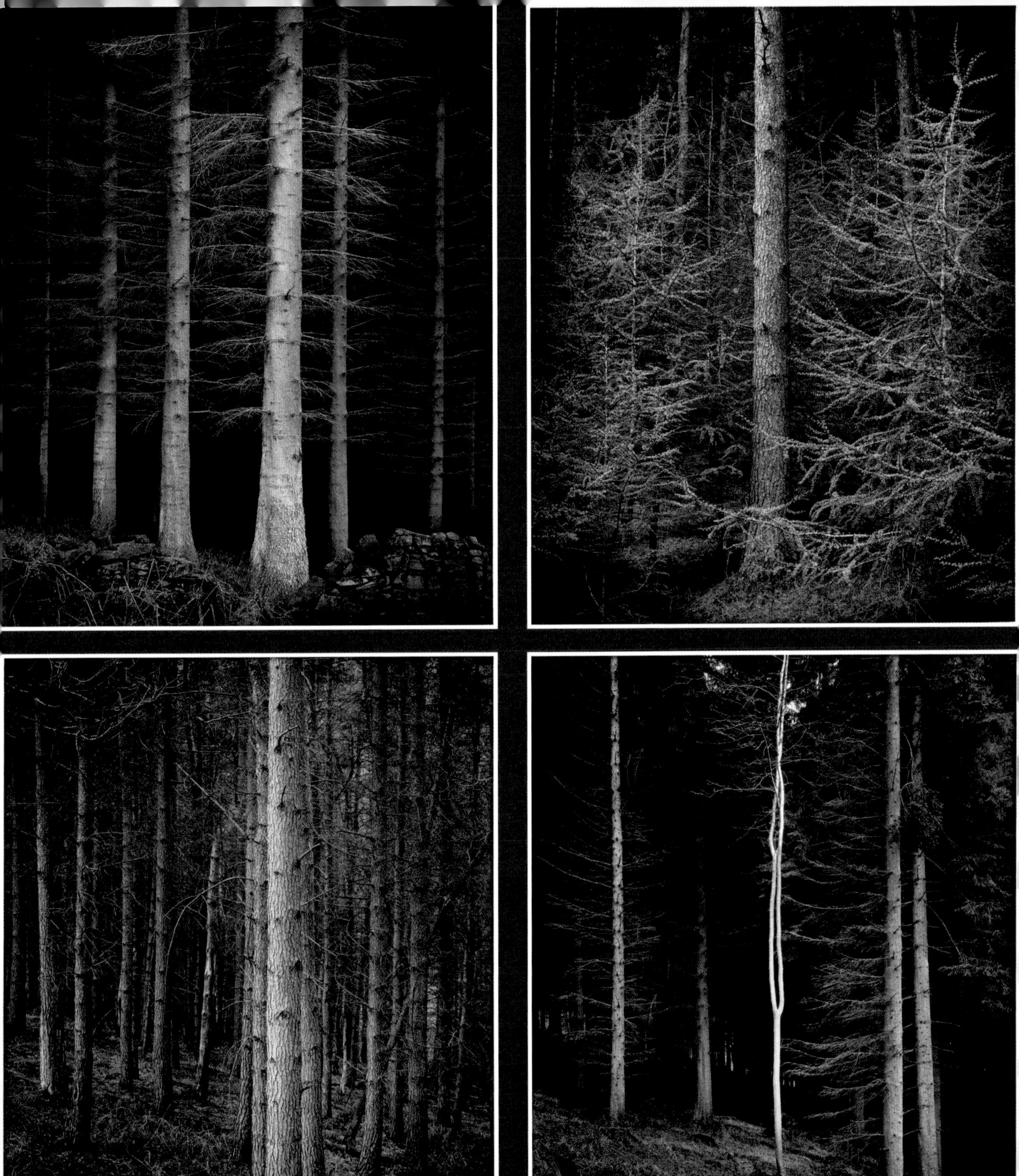

AGNIESZKA KRZYWDZIŃSKA   Highly Commended, The Beauty of Plants

Traces of Light
Bulowice, Małopolska, Poland

I wanted to showcase the colour, shape and shade of fruits from different plants growing in my garden. I decided to concentrate on red fruit from various species such as *Sorbus* and *Viburnum*. To achieve the desired effect, I used a background of semi-gloss glass; on the glass I placed the fruits and leant it on two chairs, I then lay under the glass and photographed the image on the glass, which showed the fruits and their shadows as traces of light.

Canon EOS 7D, Canon 28-105mm lens, 1/200sec to 1/400sec at f/8. Post-capture: basic image management.

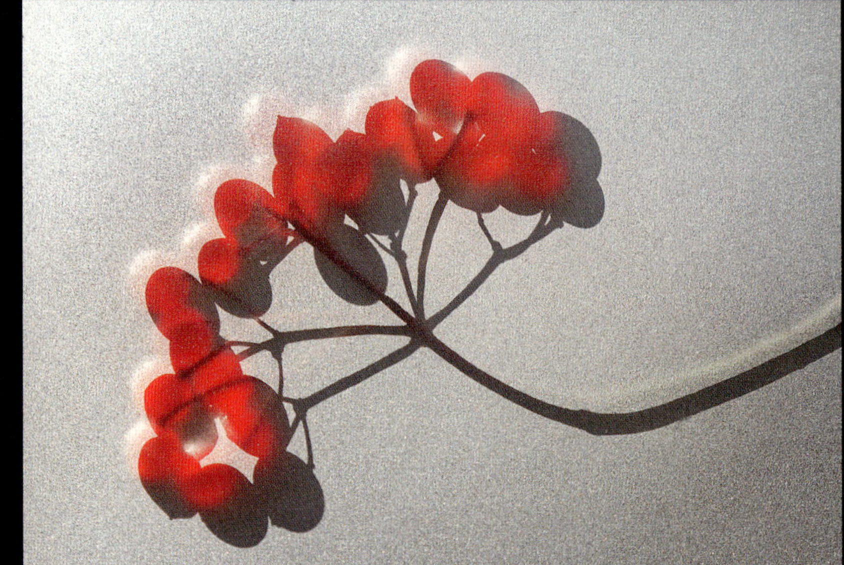

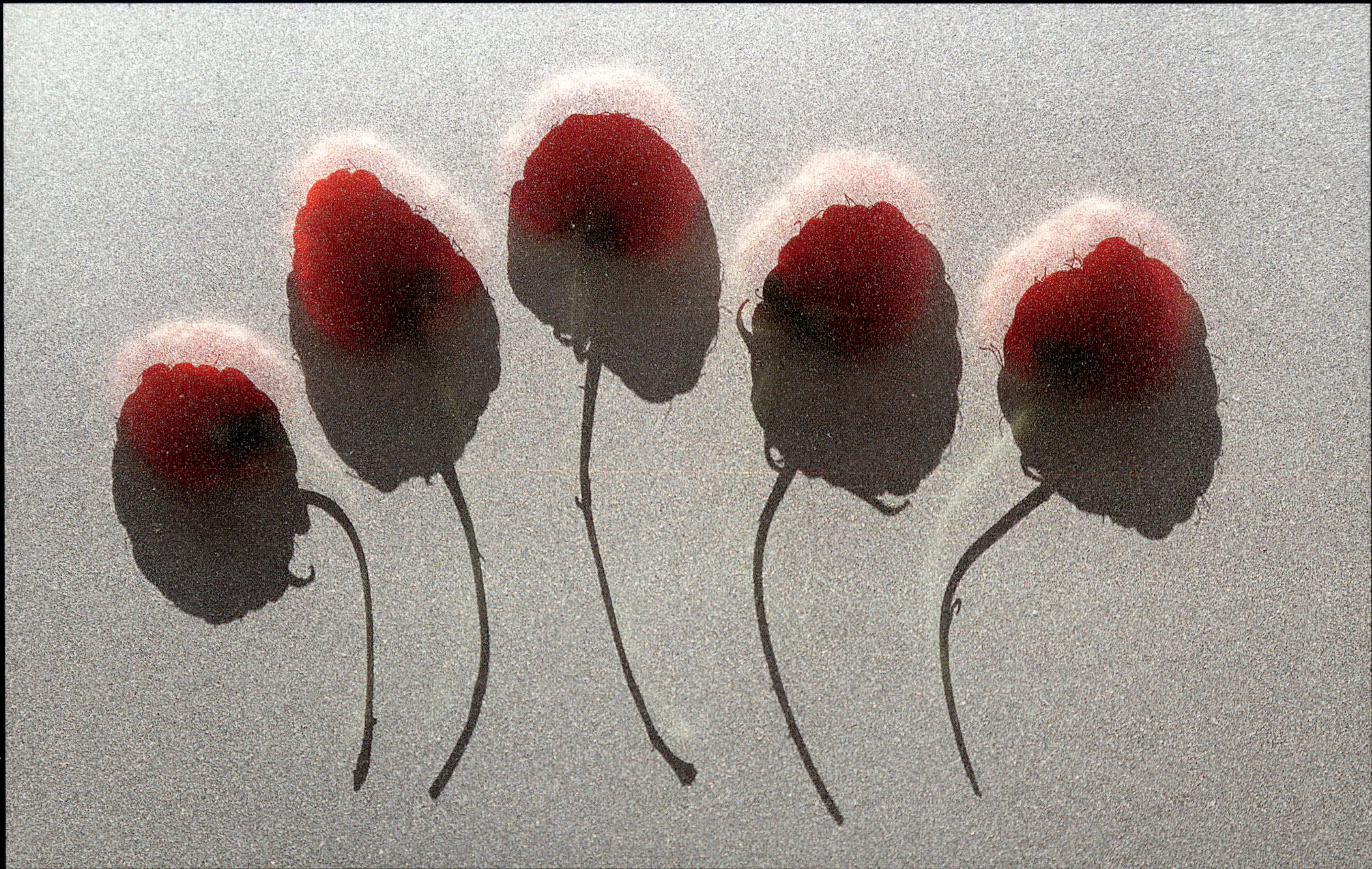

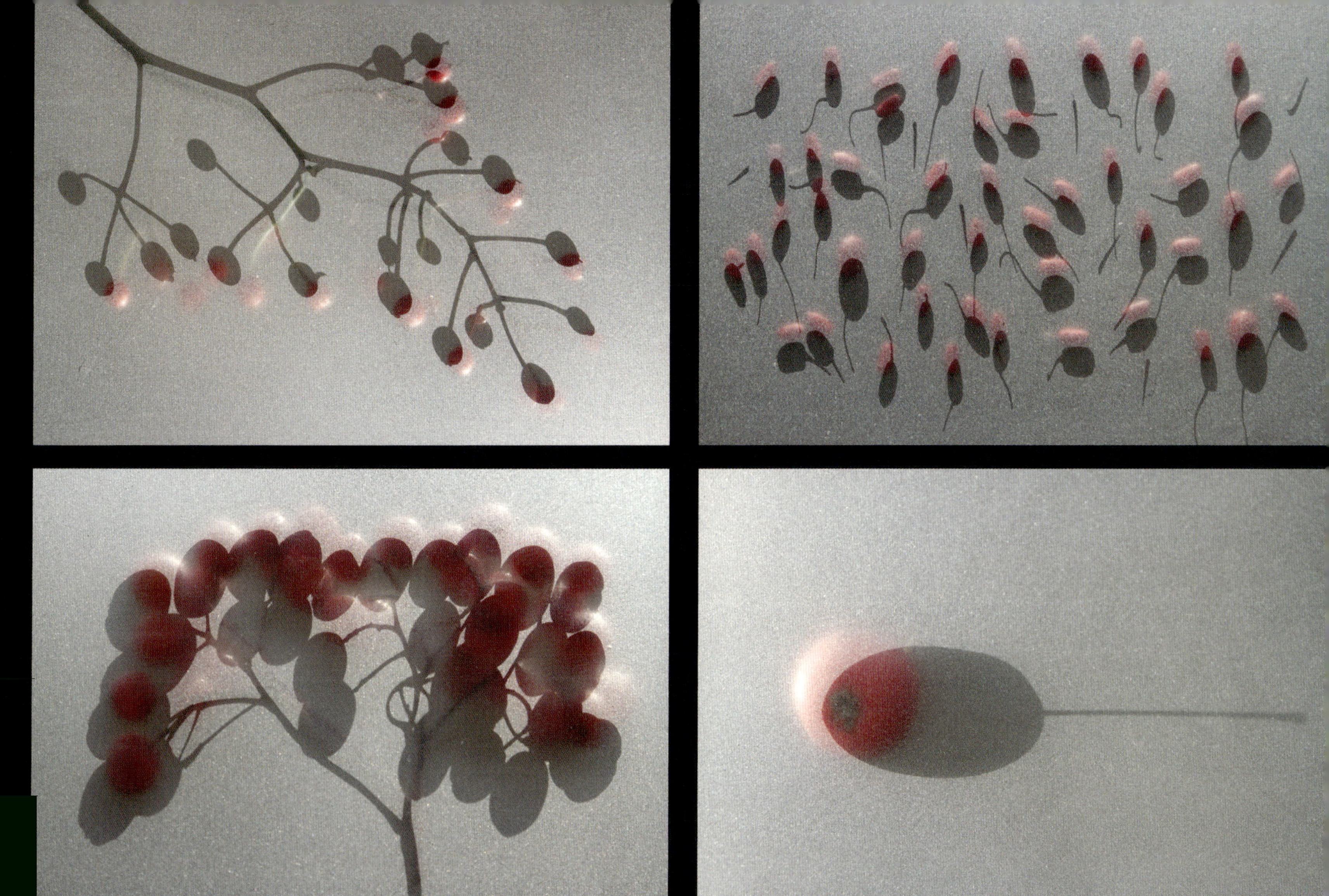

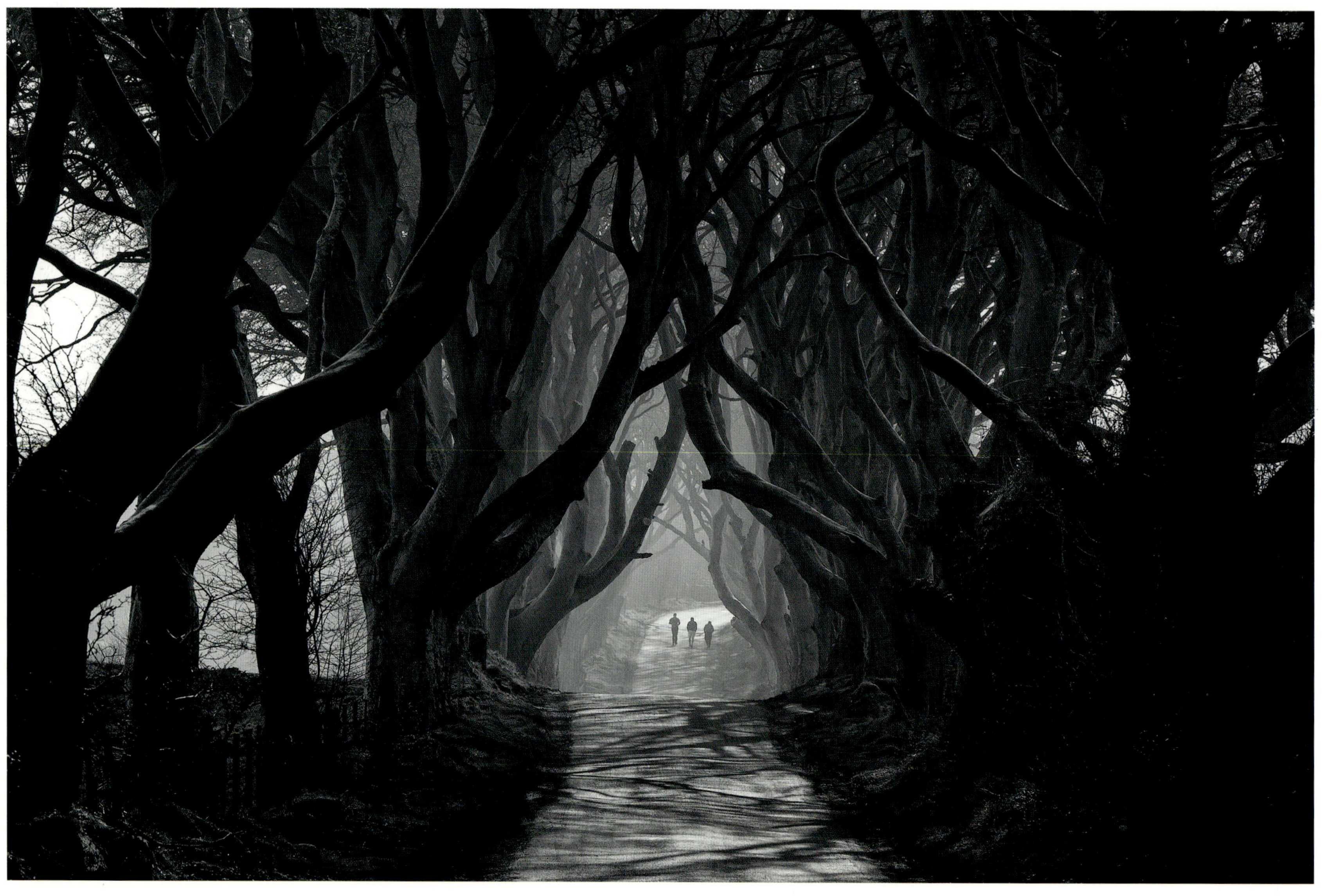

▲ **MATTHEW WOODHOUSE**   1ST PLACE, MONOCHROME

Three

County Antrim, Northern Ireland, UK

'The Dark Hedges', the real name of which is Bregagh Road, is an avenue of Beech trees planted in the 18th Century by the Stuart family with the intention of impressing visitors as they approached the entrance to their home, Gracehill House. I am in awe of this road. The natural beauty of the trees and how they hold each other along the road, I often think that the trees knew why they were planted, to impress, and they have followed that task to this day! I have wanted to capture the road in black and white for quite a time now as I feel the monotones really highlight the tunnel that so beautifully overhangs the road.

📷 Canon EOS 6D, Canon 70-200mm lens, 1/40sec at f/11, ISO 100. Post-capture: converted to black and white, basic image management.

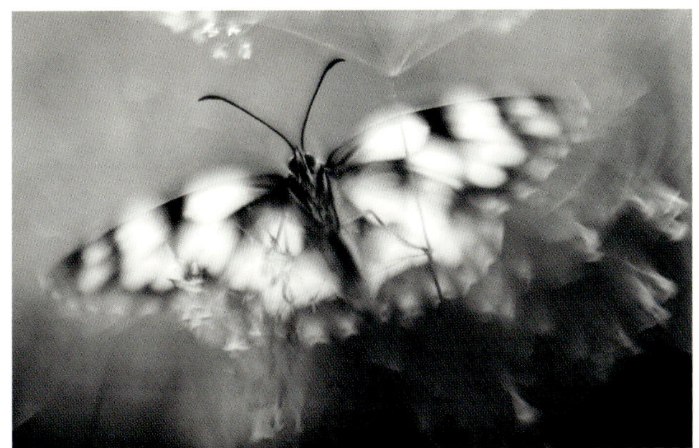

Ephemera
Aveyron, France

Marbled White Butterfly (*Melanargia galathea*) among grasses in our meadow. The inflorescences of the grasses created such drama and movement, yet it all was so fragile and ephemeral. I love capturing these moments. In summer I often get up before sunrise to explore life in our meadow. It took many days of patient stalking before I was able to get close enough with my Lensbaby and macro converter.

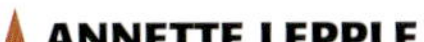 Canon EOS 5D Mark II, Lensbaby Double Glass Optic and macro converters, 1/500sec at f/4, ISO 250. Post-capture: converted to black and white.

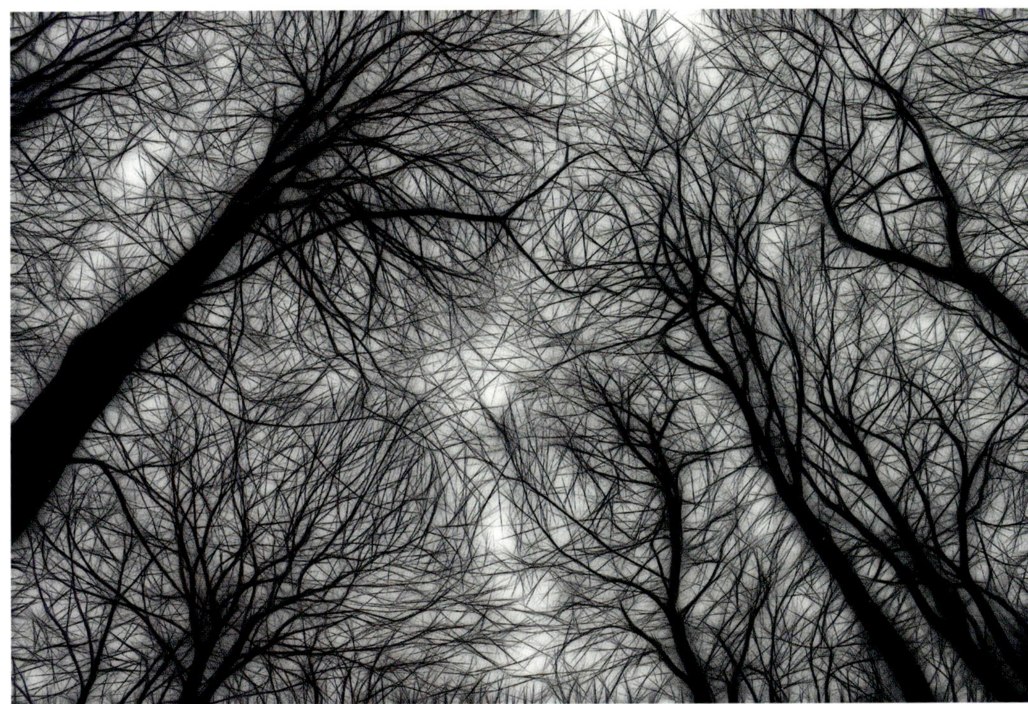

Reaching for the Sky
Oxfordshire, England, UK

Tree branches of the Oxfordshire woodlands during winter. The bare branches depict the harsh but intriguing pattern of the canopy against a winter sky. There is beauty to be found even in the depths of this bleak season.

 Canon EOS 300D, Canon 17-50mm lens, 1/25sec at f/10, ISO 200. Post-capture: the image was simplified using a Redfield plugin which highlights the natural patterns of the branches. Converted to black and white.

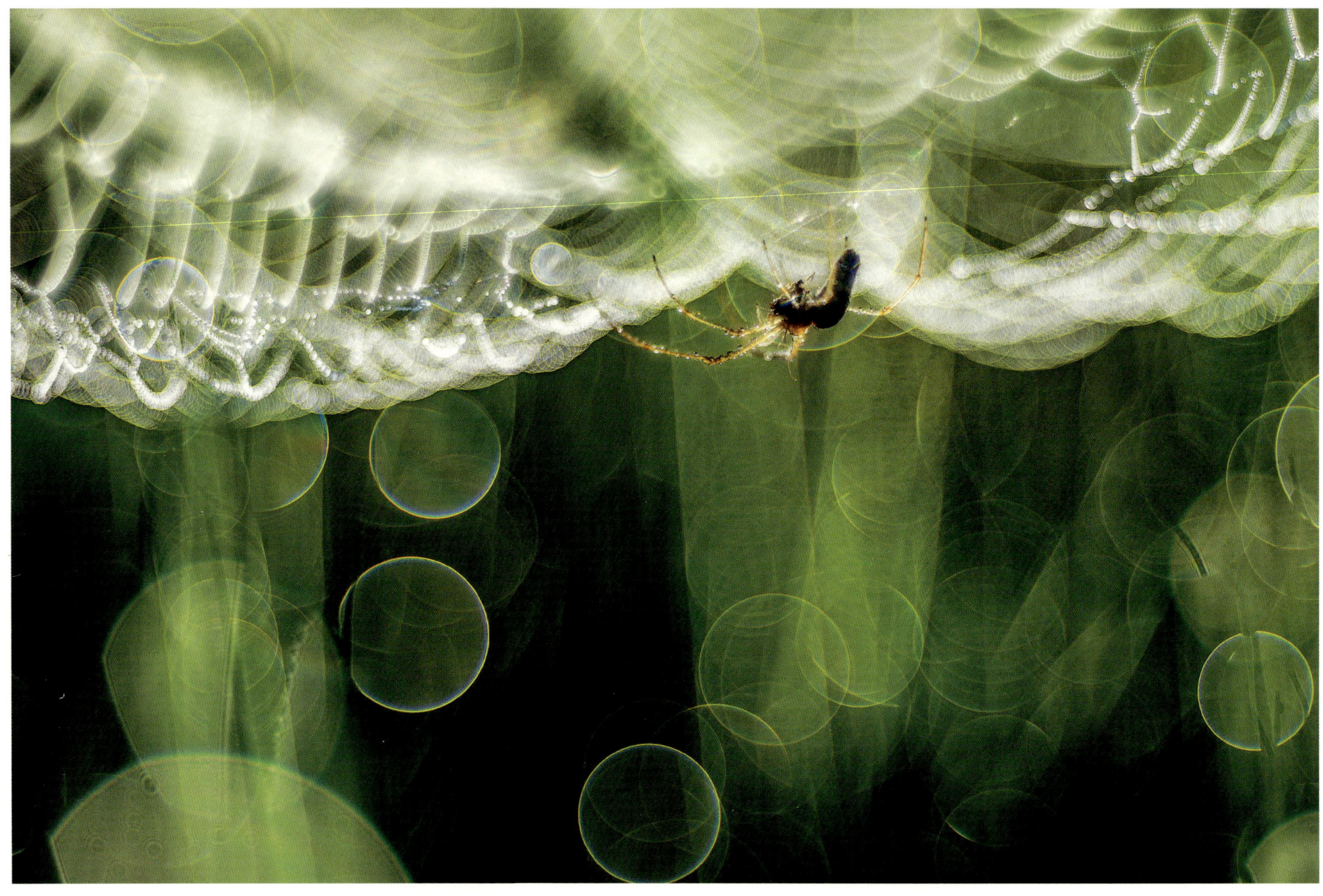

Pearl World

Lake Velence, Hungary

I was hunting for some macro themes at my favourite meadow during an early morning. The grass, flowers and cobwebs were full of dewdrops, which were shining very strongly in backlight. Knowing the very special bokeh of my old lens (Meyer Optik Görlitz Trioplan 100mm f/2.8) I was sure I could record my impressions of this wondrous Pearl World. The angle of the optics to the sun had been carefully set to maximize the optic's special bokeh. I also used a DIY lens shade to avoid the sun hitting the front lens.

📷 Nikon D600, Meyer Optik Görlitz Trioplan 100mm lens, 1/2000sec at f/4.0, ISO 100. Tripod and remote release. Post-capture: basic image management, lens correction, chromatic aberration removal.

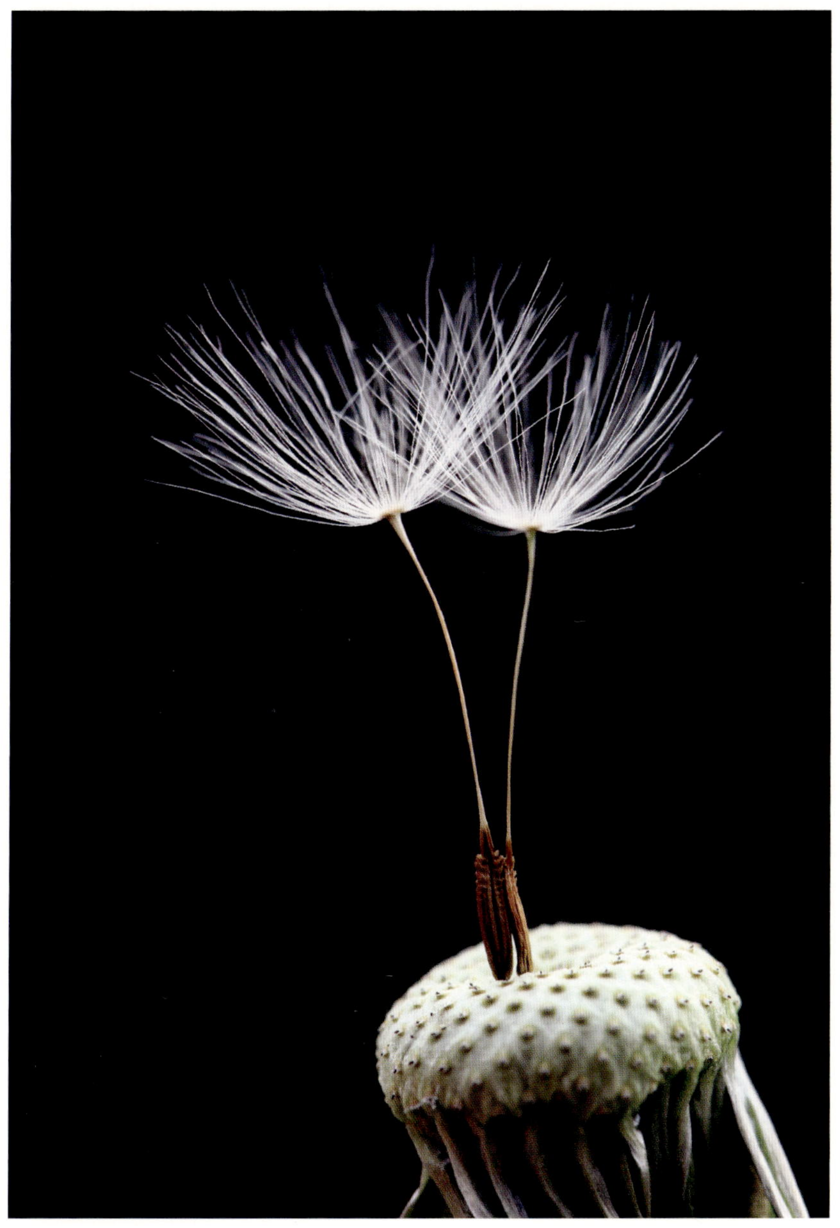

2ND PLACE, MACRO ART

Last Embrace
Wuhan City, China

Dandelion seeds are destined to leave their mother, to fly away in the wind and grow somewhere new; such is their life cycle. There is much inspiration to be taken from this everyday scene: life is ordinary, but ordinary life is also emotional, and even though this depicts a transient event, I wanted keep that important moment of warmth.

Canon EOS 70D, Tamron 90mm macro lens, 1/100sec at f/9, ISO 400.

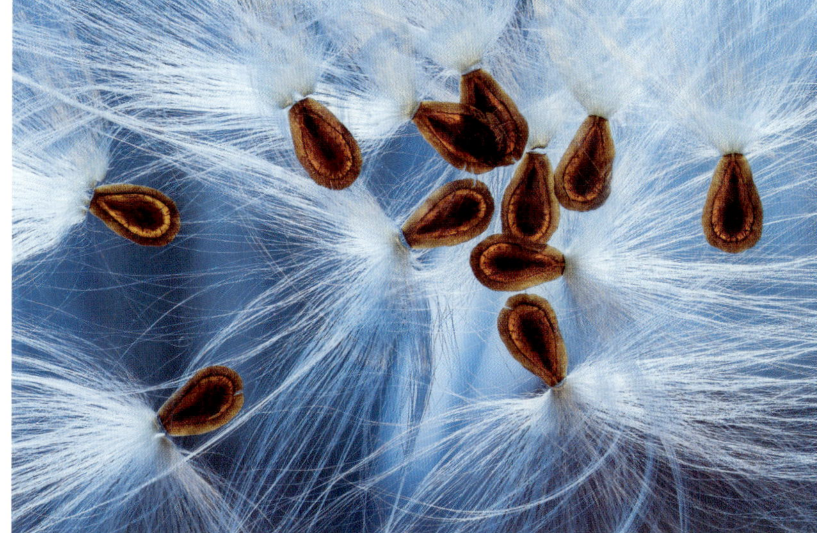

3RD PLACE, MACRO ART

Meteoroids
Stockholm, Sweden

Looking through my macro lens, these strange seeds trapped behind a glass pane magically transported me to their micro cosmos. I had never seen such seeds and was fascinated by their unusual shape. I also wonder a lot about their origin; there was an aura of mystery about them.

Canon EOS 7D, Canon 100mm macro lens, 1/4sec at f/11, ISO 100. Post-capture: added the blue background colour.

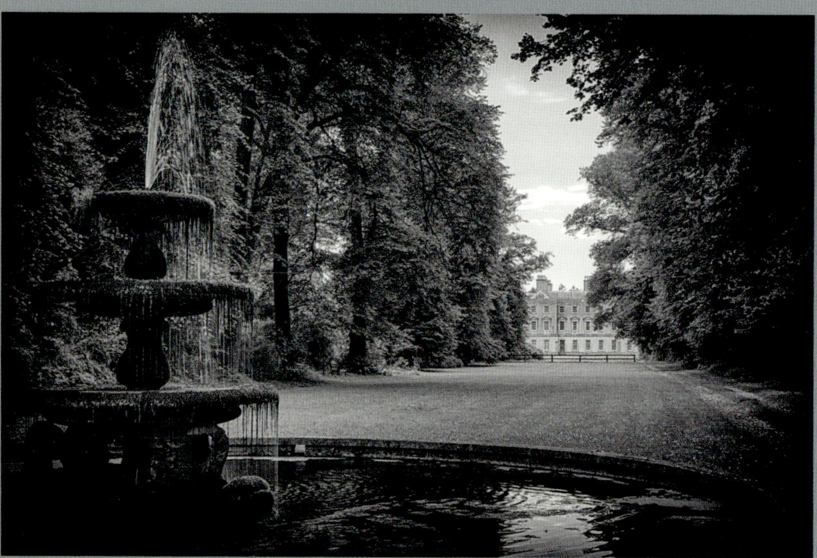

▲ NEIL DAVIES   MONOCHROME

Fountain
Glynllifon Park, Gwynedd, Wales, UK

Glynllifon Hall, built by Lord Newborough in the 1830s and 1840s, can be seen in the distance. The gardens themselves are Grade I listed with an abundance of mature trees and shrubs. Meandering through the park is the gently flowing River Llifon, all the more reason to take a stroll around this picturesque beauty spot. The scale of the mature trees leads the eye from the fountain, in the foreground, to Glynllifon Hall in the background. Although Glynllifon is a beautiful green space, its age lends itself to monochrome photography.

📷 Sony NEX-7, 35mm lens, 1/25sec at f/5.6, ISO 200. Post-capture: added a slight vignette.

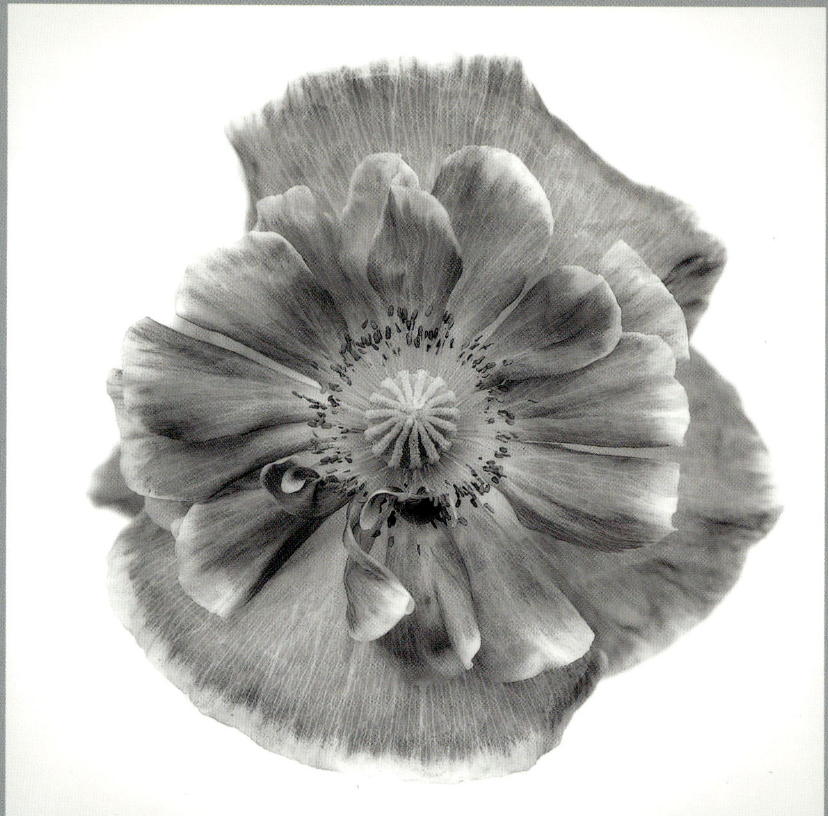

▲ LOTTE GRØNKJÆR-FUNCH   MONOCHROME

Homegrown Poppy
Copenhagen, Denmark

I am in love with poppies and like every stage of the plant's growth. I had planned the photo by sowing the seeds some months before the capture.

📷 Nikon D610, 105mm lens, 1/500sec at f/9, ISO 400.

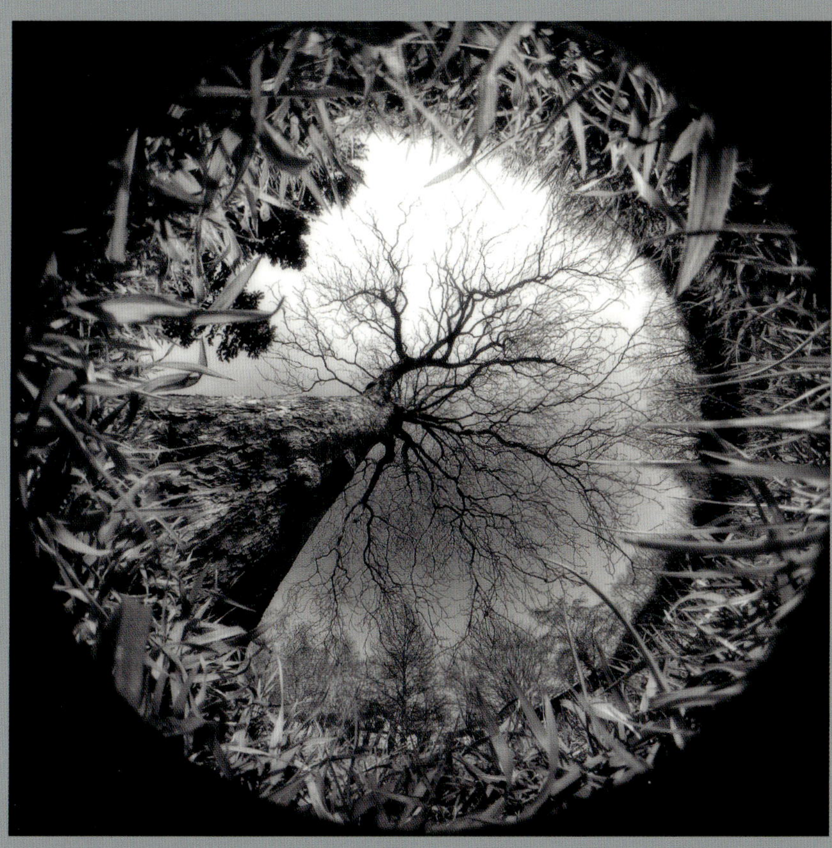

MONOCHROME

In the Eye of an Ant
Parc Floral de Paris, France

Nature inspires me, in all its forms. After working in a 'classic' style for magazines, doing photo illustrations of plants, my work moved towards a more poetic style. With the new technical possibilities, I found it interesting to identify with an ant and imagine his view of nature.

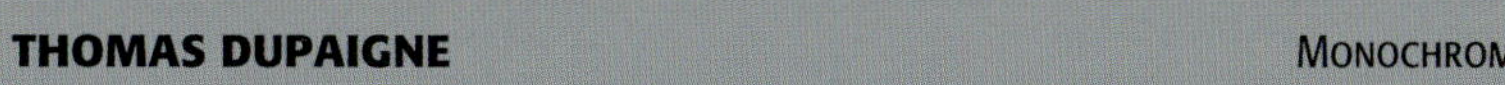

Kodak SP360, 8mm lens, 1/1488sec at f/2.7, ISO 100.

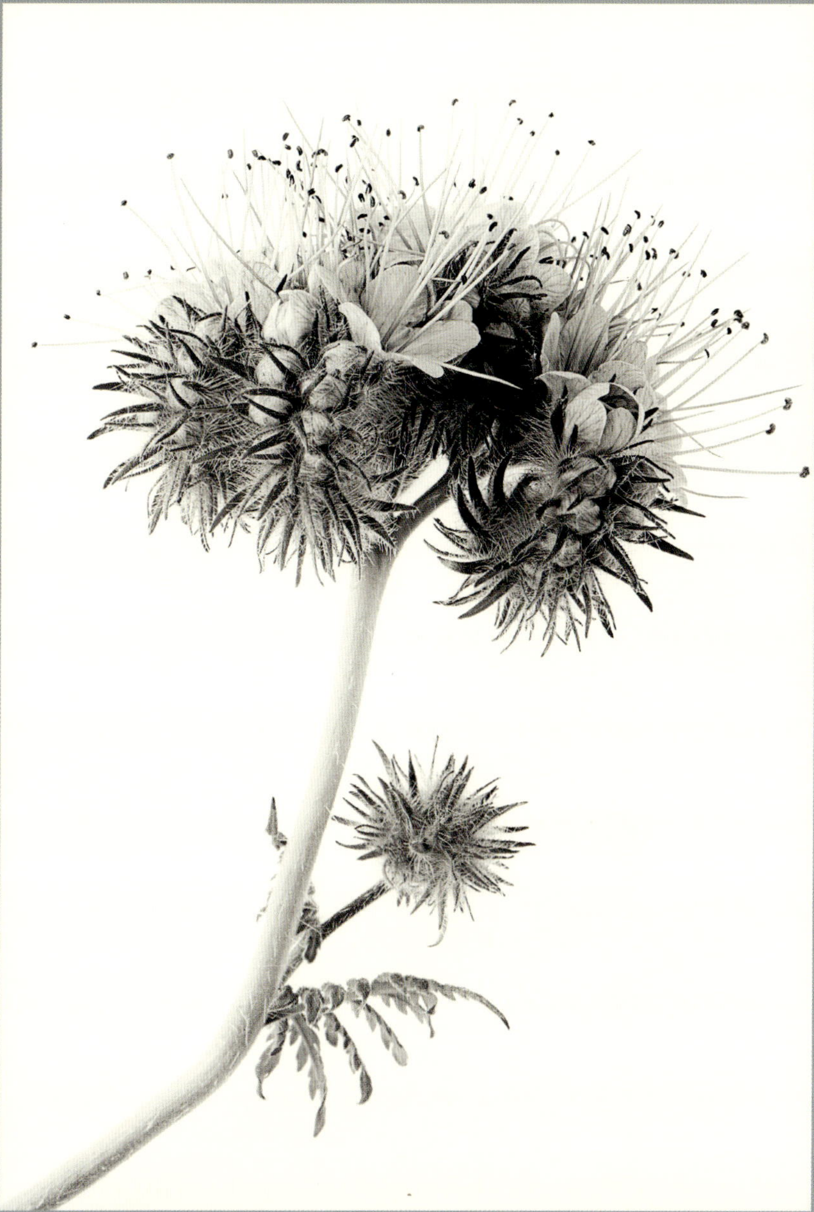

JACKY PARKER

MONOCHROME

Phacelia tanacetifolia
Iver, Buckinghamshire, England, UK

Phacelia tanacetifolia - lacy phacelia or purple tansy, is a hardy annual wildflower used to attract pollinators. I was intrigued how the flowering portion of the stalk is curled, unwinding slowly to reveal the intricate purple flowers.

Nikon D700, Nikkor 105mm lens, 1/2sec at f/36, ISO 200. Post-capture: minor tonal adjustments made before converting to monochrome with software.

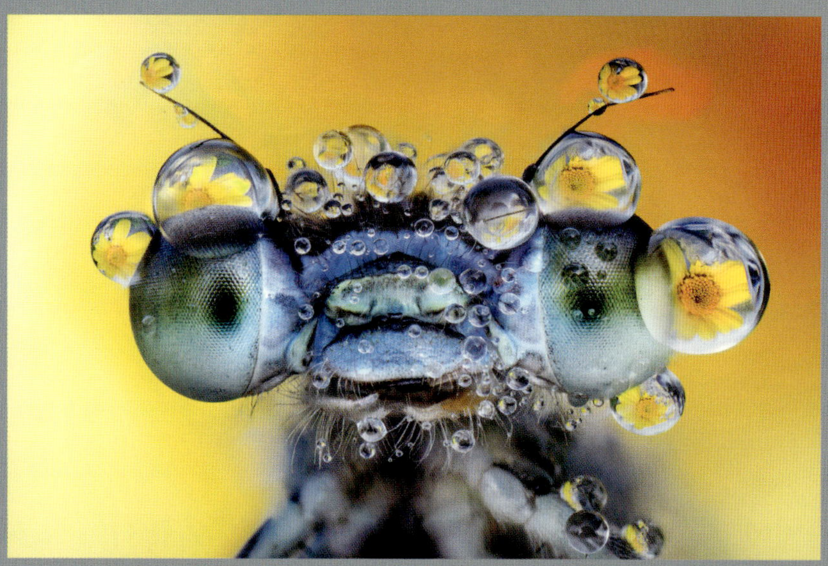

▲ **ALBERTO GHIZZI PANIZZA**   MACRO ART

Adorned by the Dew
Luzzara, Emilia-Romagna, Italy

A portrait of a damselfly with drops of dew resting on its head. The dew is refracting a wild flower behind the subject. I often take long walks between the floodplains and the riverbanks near my town. Here I found my subjects and inspiration.

Nikon D810, Nikon 60mm lens with bellows, 3/5sec at f/16, ISO 64. Post-capture: focus stacking of 25 images, basic image management.

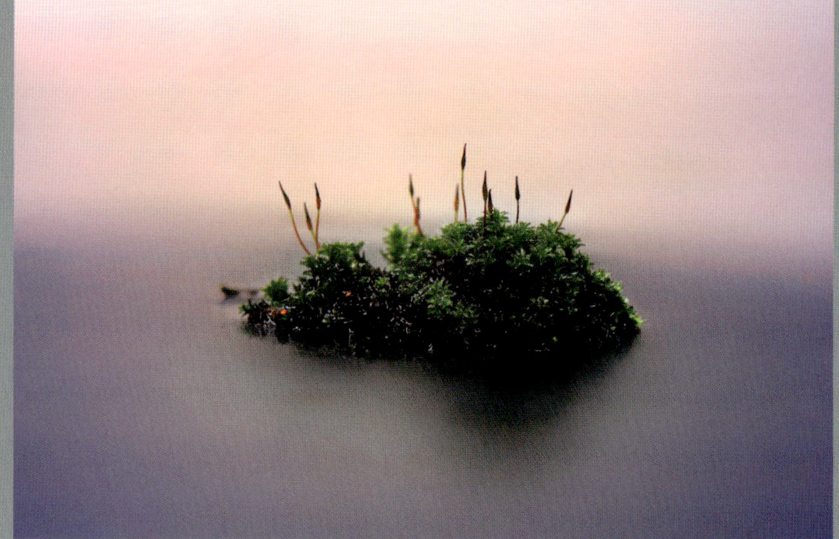

▲ **IAN GILMOUR**   MACRO ART

Moss Island
Hebden Bridge, West Yorkshire, England, UK

Moss grows on the roof of our house and is often dislodged by the wind or by crows. It reminded me of a miniature tropical island with the tiny sporophytes resembling little trees.

Pentax K-5, Sigma 105mm macro lens, 1/13sec at f/8, ISO 100. Tripod. Post-capture: to enhance the tropical island feel, I slightly saturated the colour and sharpened the image.

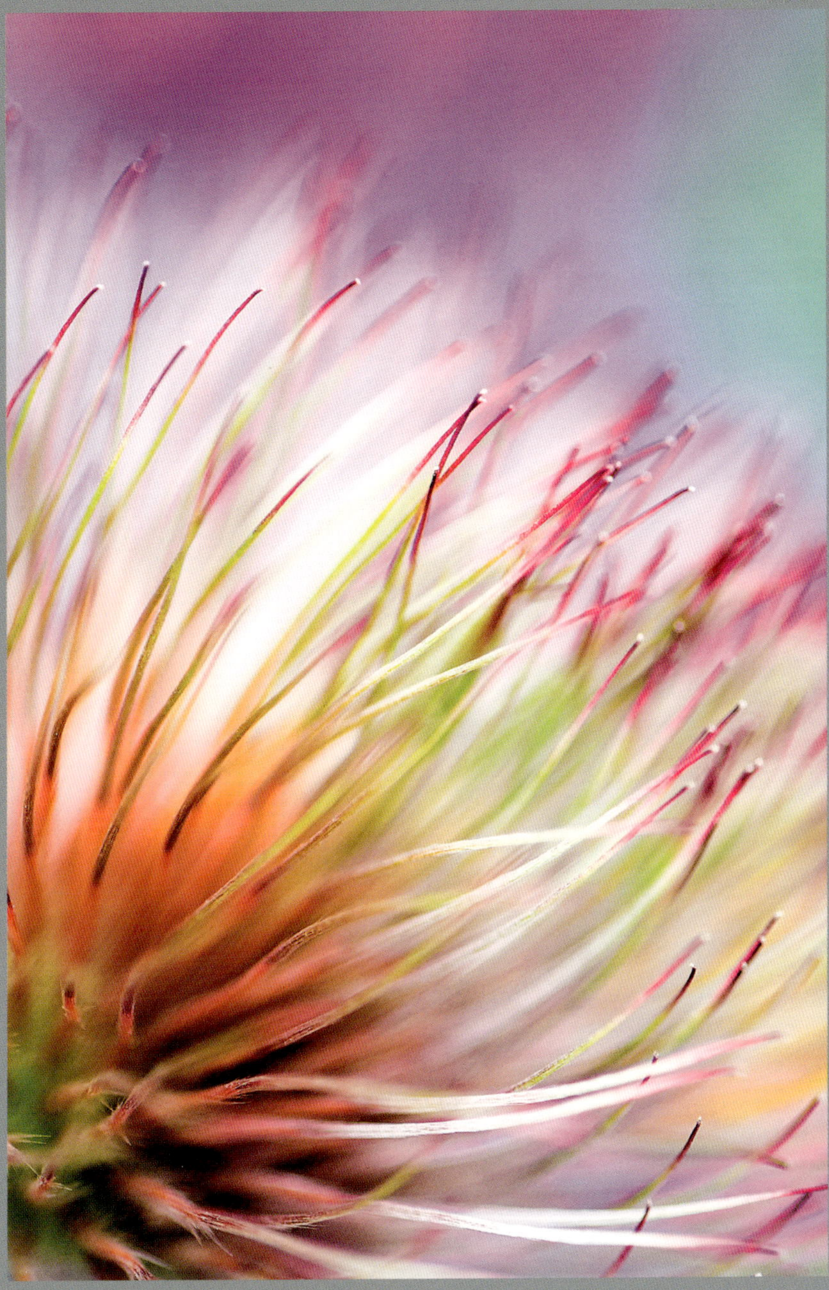

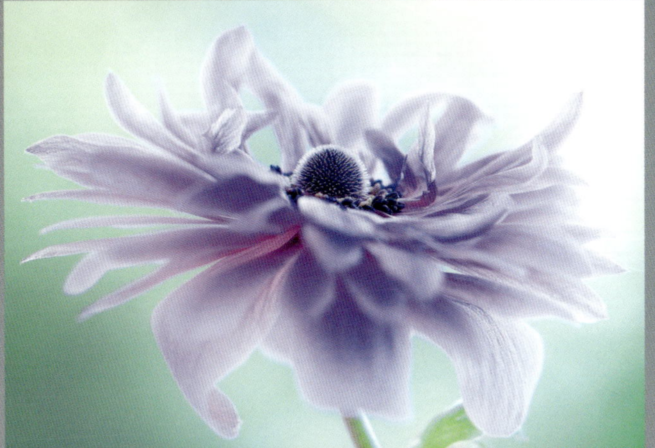

▲ CHRISTL DECKX — MACRO ART

Dancer
Bierbeek, Vlaams-Brabant, Belgium

This is a capture of an *Anemone coronaria* 'Lord Lieutenant', which I was cultivating in a planter this spring. It was too windy to shoot outside, so I took the planter inside and placed it near a big south-facing window. The beautiful double petals reminded me of a dancer so I softened the purple colours of the flower to give it a lighter feeling.

Nikon D5100, Tamron 90mm macro lens, 1/50sec at f/4.5, ISO 100. Post-capture: basic image management.

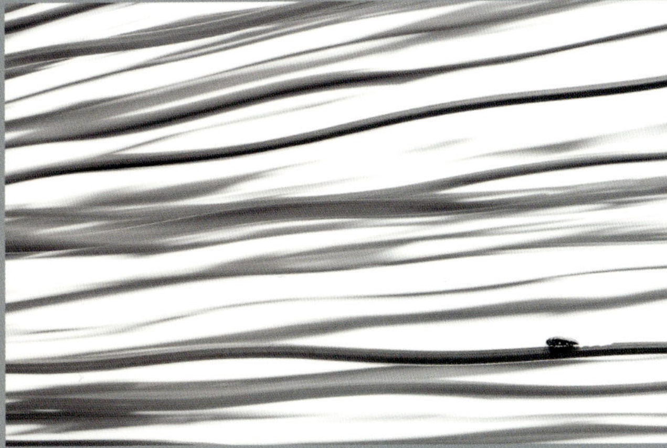

▲ YICAI CHANG — MACRO ART

All Roads Lead to Rome
Australian National Botanic Gardens, Canberra, Australia

The grass stems look like roads. Travelling along just one of them, this creature tells us that there are many roads that can take us to our goal.

Nikon D90, Nikon 105mm lens, 1/125sec at f/5.6, ISO 200. Post-capture: basic image management.

▲ STEVE PALMER — MACRO ART

Filaments
Sheffield Botanical Gardens, England, UK

I had travelled from my home in Cheshire to photograph the flowers and plants in the Botanical Gardens and was lucky to discover this flower head. I was amazed as this was a plant I had never seen before; the filaments and the colours were fascinating and I could not resist taking some shots.

Pentax K-5 II, Pentax 100mm macro lens, 1/500sec at f/2.8, ISO 400. Post-capture: basic image management.

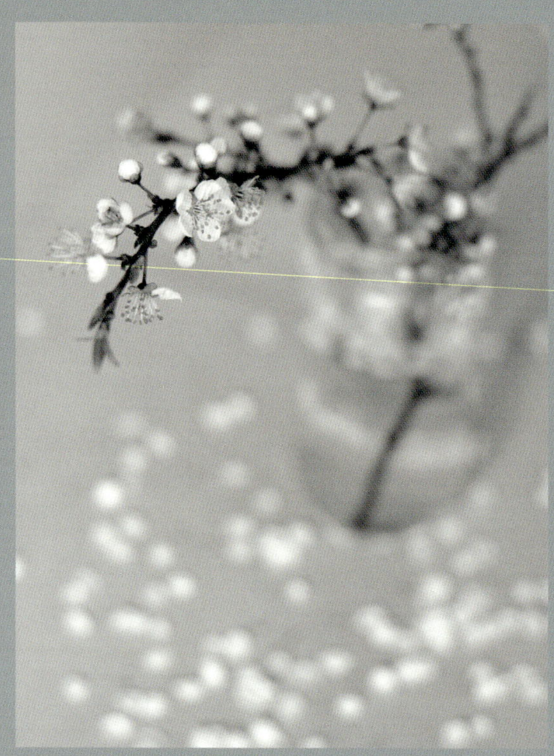

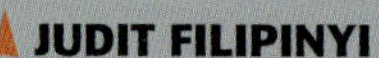

JUDIT FILIPINYI — Monochrome

Spring Is on Its Way…

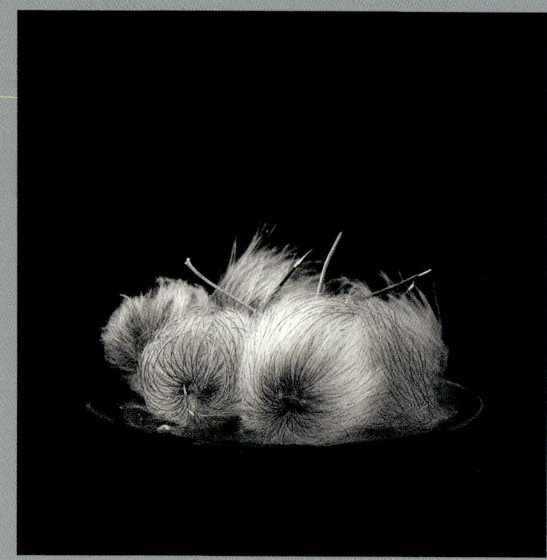

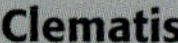

JULIA ROBSON — Monochrome

Clematis

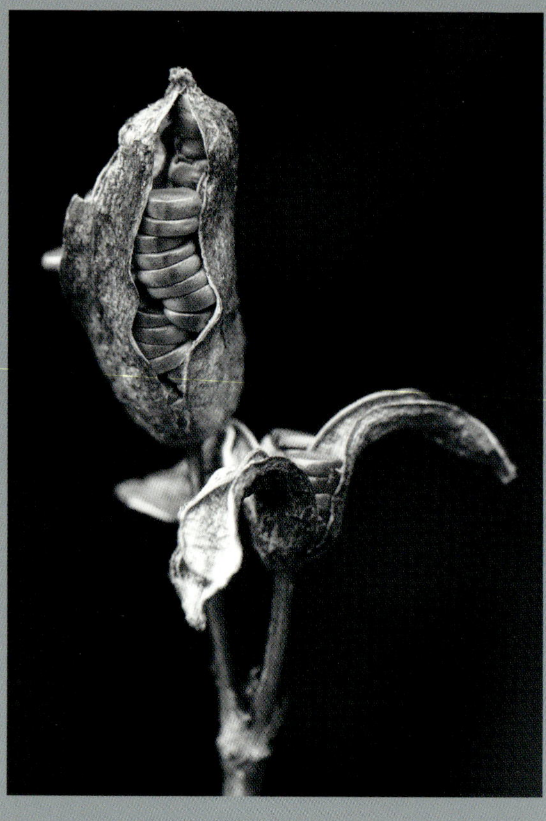

GILLIAN PLUMMER — Monochrome

Seed case

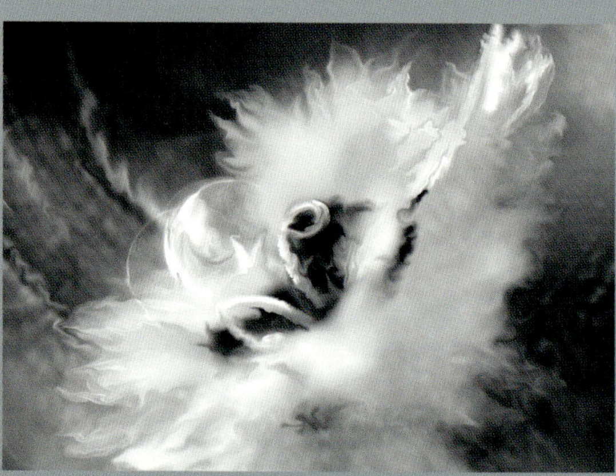

GILLIAN HUNT — Monochrome

The Snow Queen

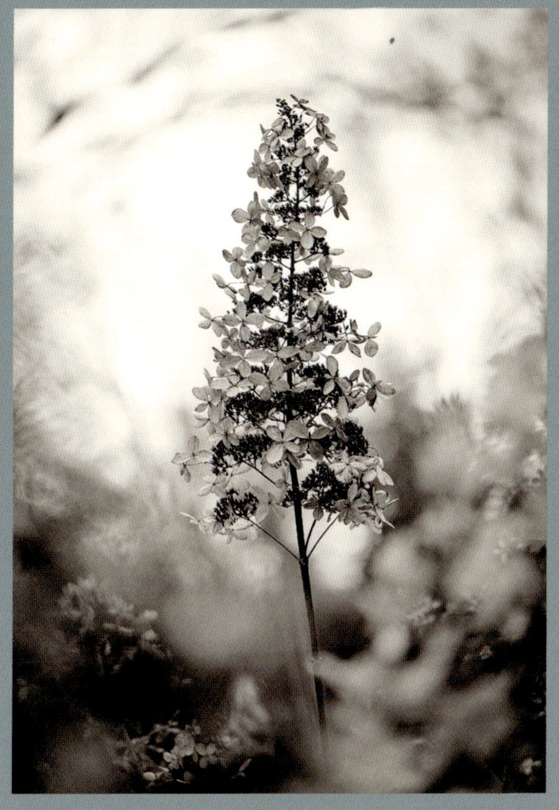

Hydrangea 'Brussels Lace'

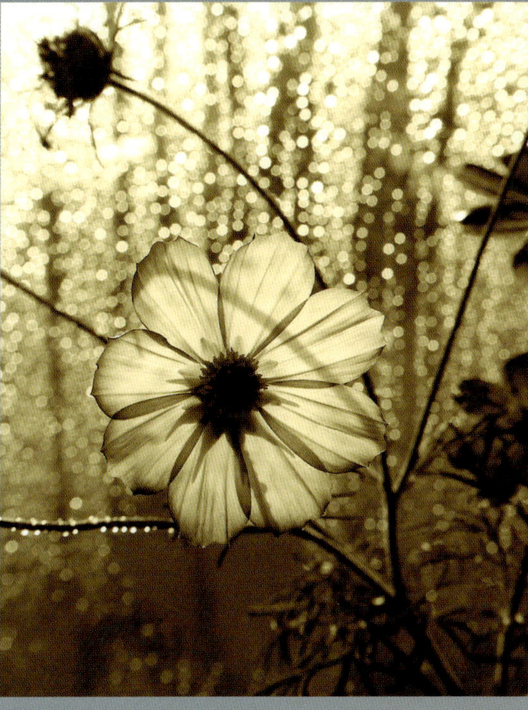

Light and Transparency

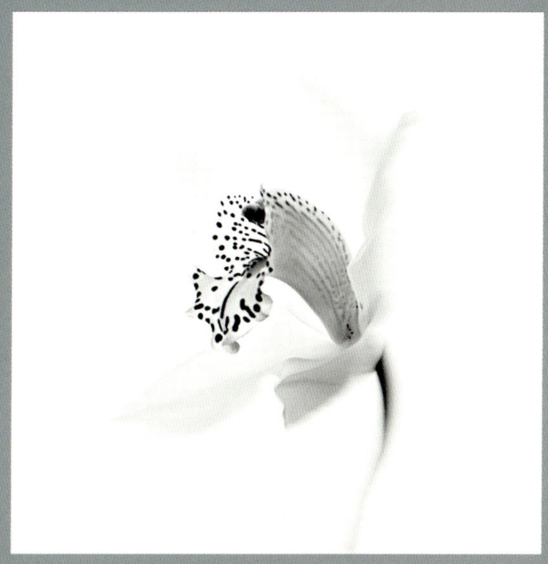

Cymbidium

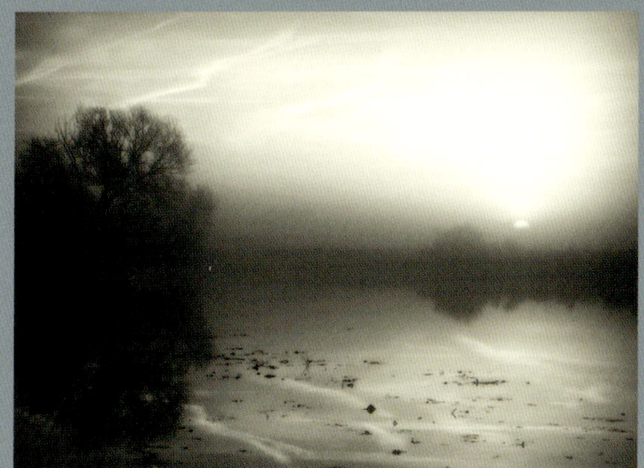

Mystery Moor

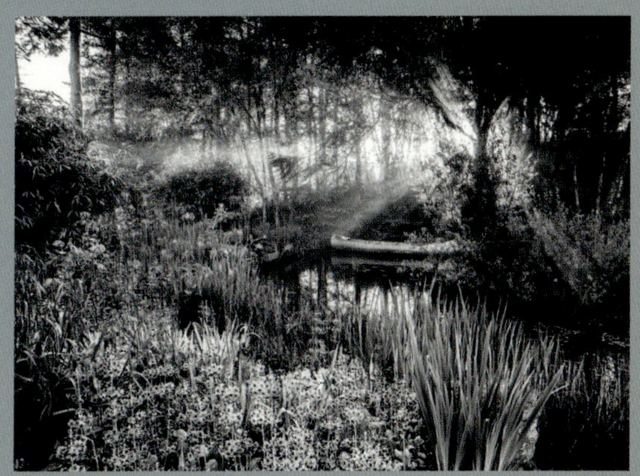

Dawn over the pond

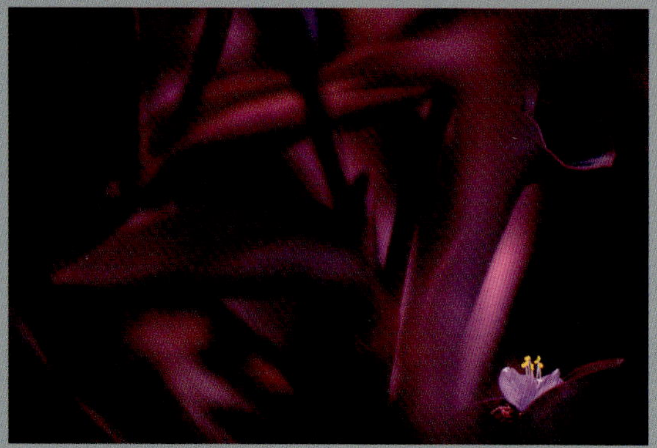

ANDREW GEORGE MACRO ART

Hidden Beauty

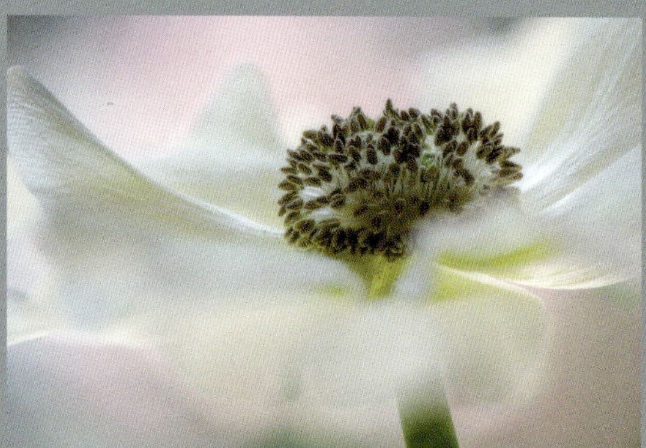

DIANNE ENGLISH MACRO ART

Graceful *Cosmos*

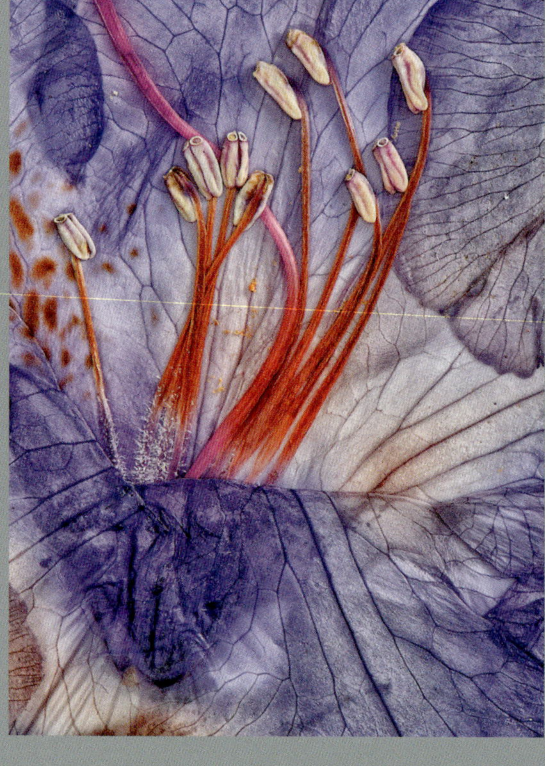

JAMES WOODEND MACRO ART

Androecium

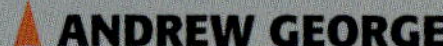

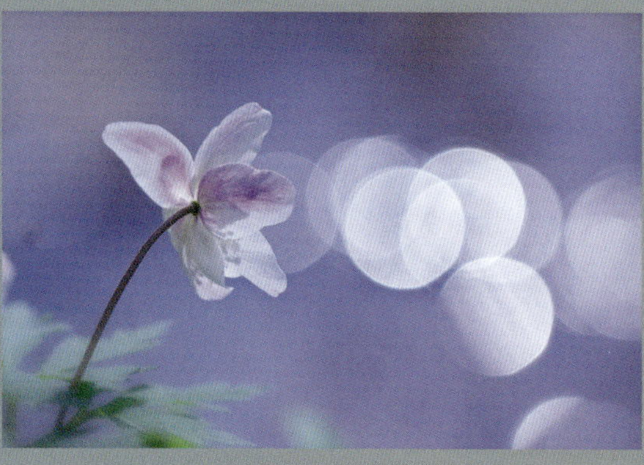

CHRISTL DECKX MACRO ART

Whispers

JANICE KUM MACRO ART

Graceful *Anemone*

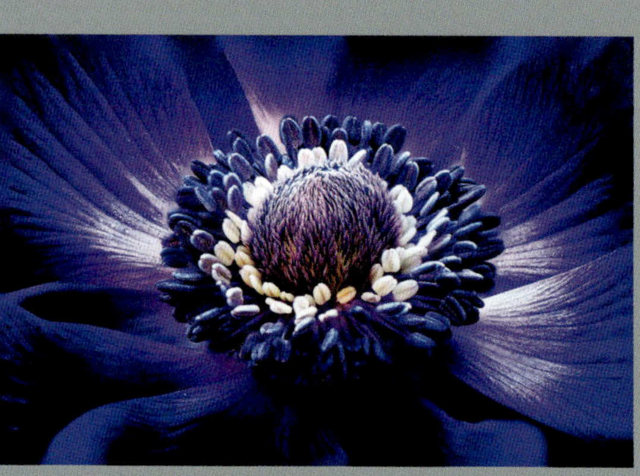

BARBARA GARDNER MACRO ART

Anemone

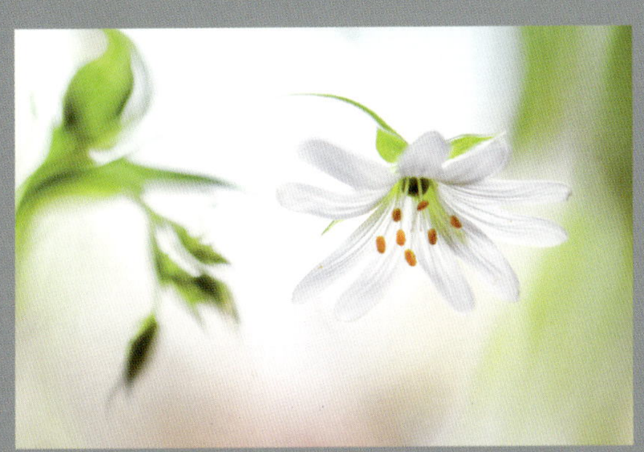

MANDY DISHER Macro Art

Stitchwort

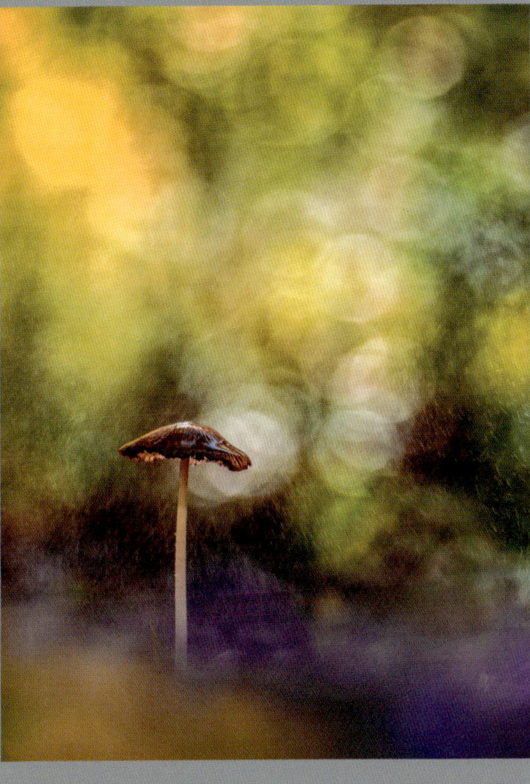

MARCO ZAMÒ Macro Art

Undergrowth

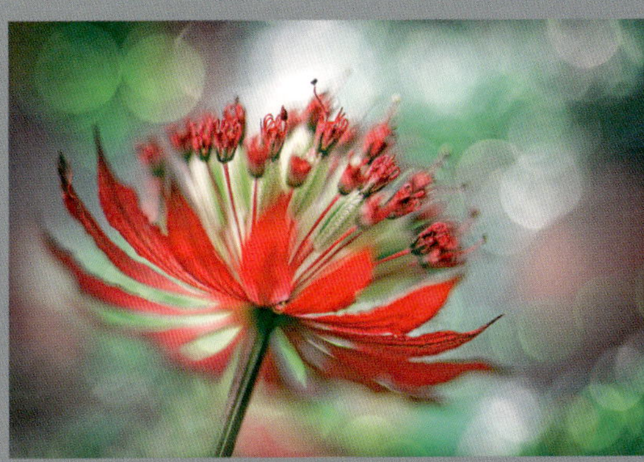

ANNEMARIE FARLEY Macro Art

Dazzling *Astrantia*

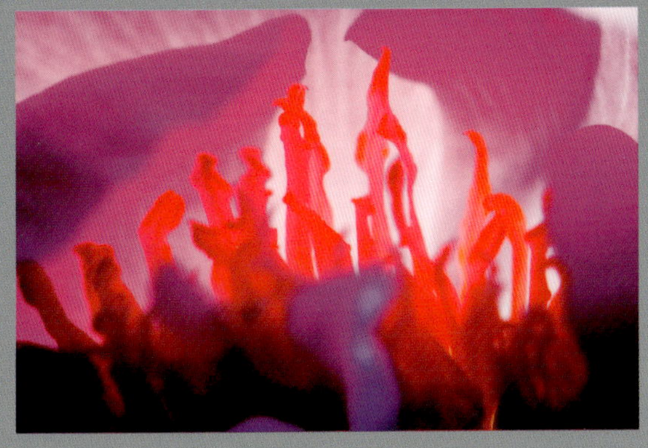

ROY HUNT Macro Art

Bowl of Beauty

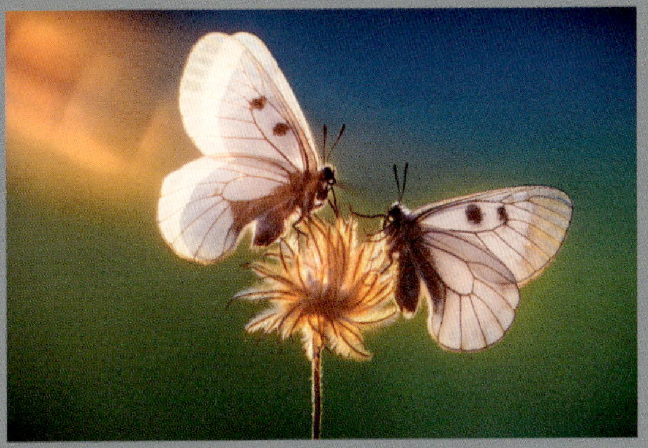

PETAR SABOL Macro Art

God's Rays of Light

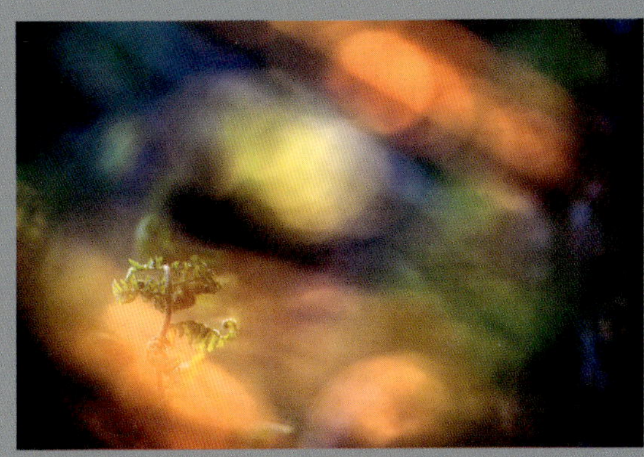

ANNA ULMESTRAND Macro Art

Enchanted Forest

SPECIAL AWARDS

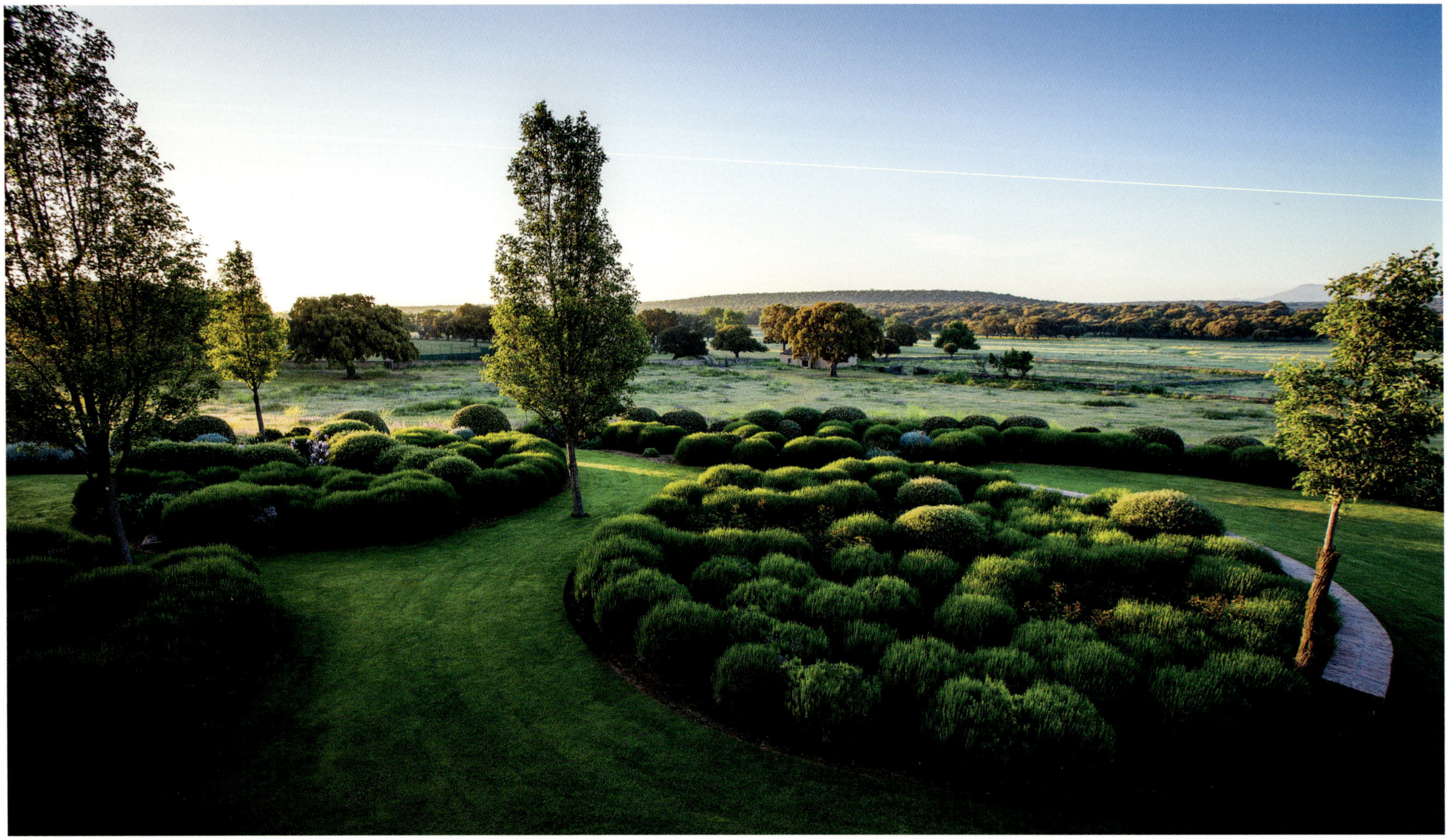

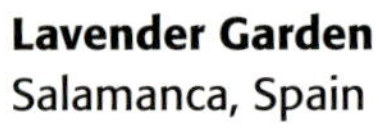

SCHLOSSPARK DENNENLOHE

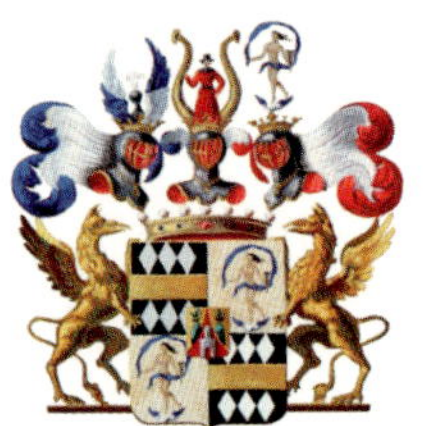

▲ **CLAIRE TAKACS**   1ST PLACE

Lavender Garden
Salamanca, Spain

I loved the way the flowing, circular shapes of the garden blended in beautifully with the surrounding landscape, complementing the gently rolling hills in the distance. The clusters of lavender and grass created a very harmonious garden, well suited to its harsh, dry climate.

📷 Canon EOS 5D Mark III, Canon 17-40mm lens, 1/10sec at f/8, ISO 100. Tripod. Post-capture: blended together two exposures, basic image management.

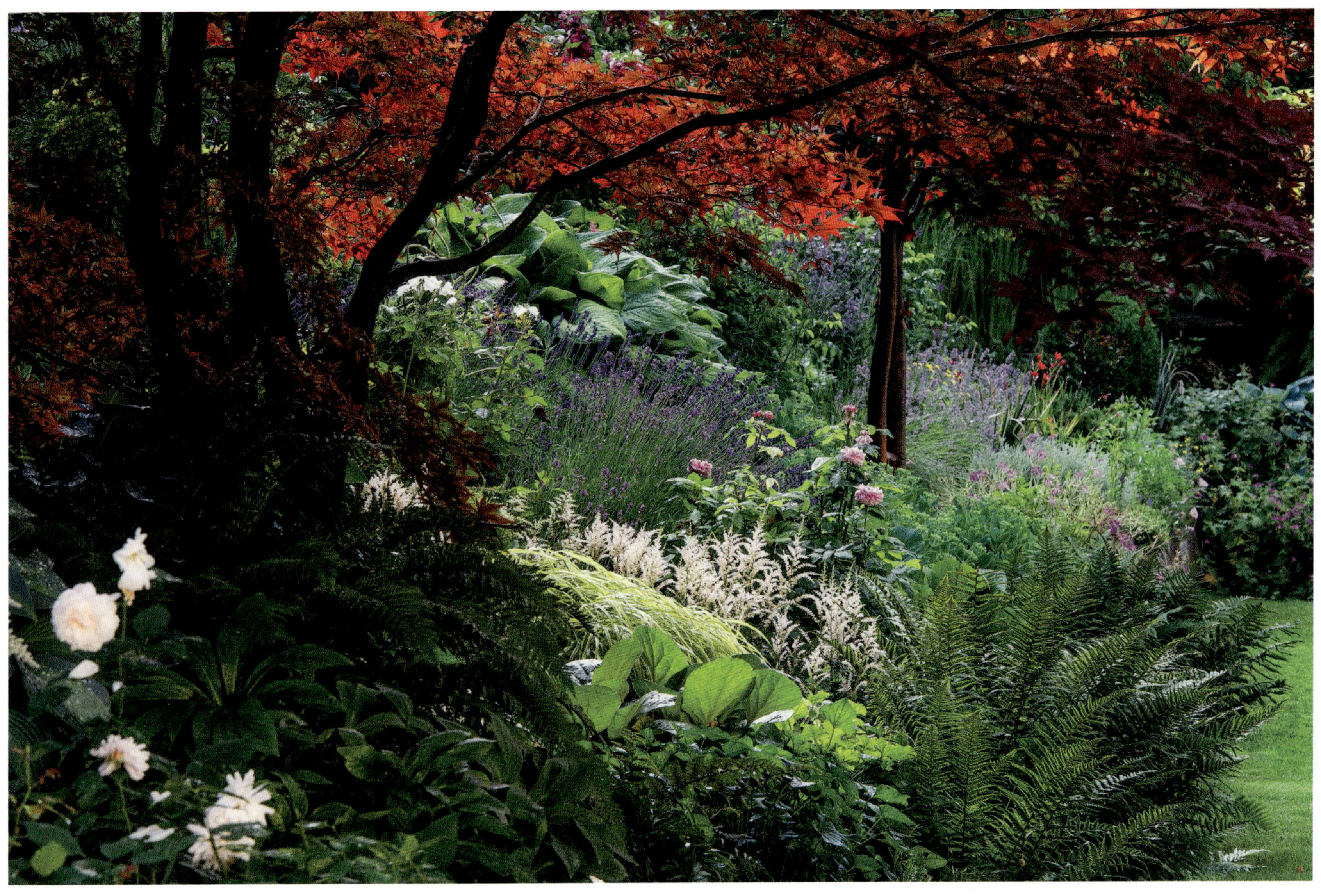

2ND PLACE

Early Summer Morning
Zürich, Switzerland

This photograph perfectly illustrates what my wife and I are striving for in our garden: lush and dense borders where shapes and colours complement each other and where the whole is more than the sum of its parts.

📷 Nikon D4, Nikon 70-200mm lens, 1/200sec at f/13, ISO 1400. Post-capture: basic image management.

EUROPEAN GARDEN PHOTOGRAPHY AWARD

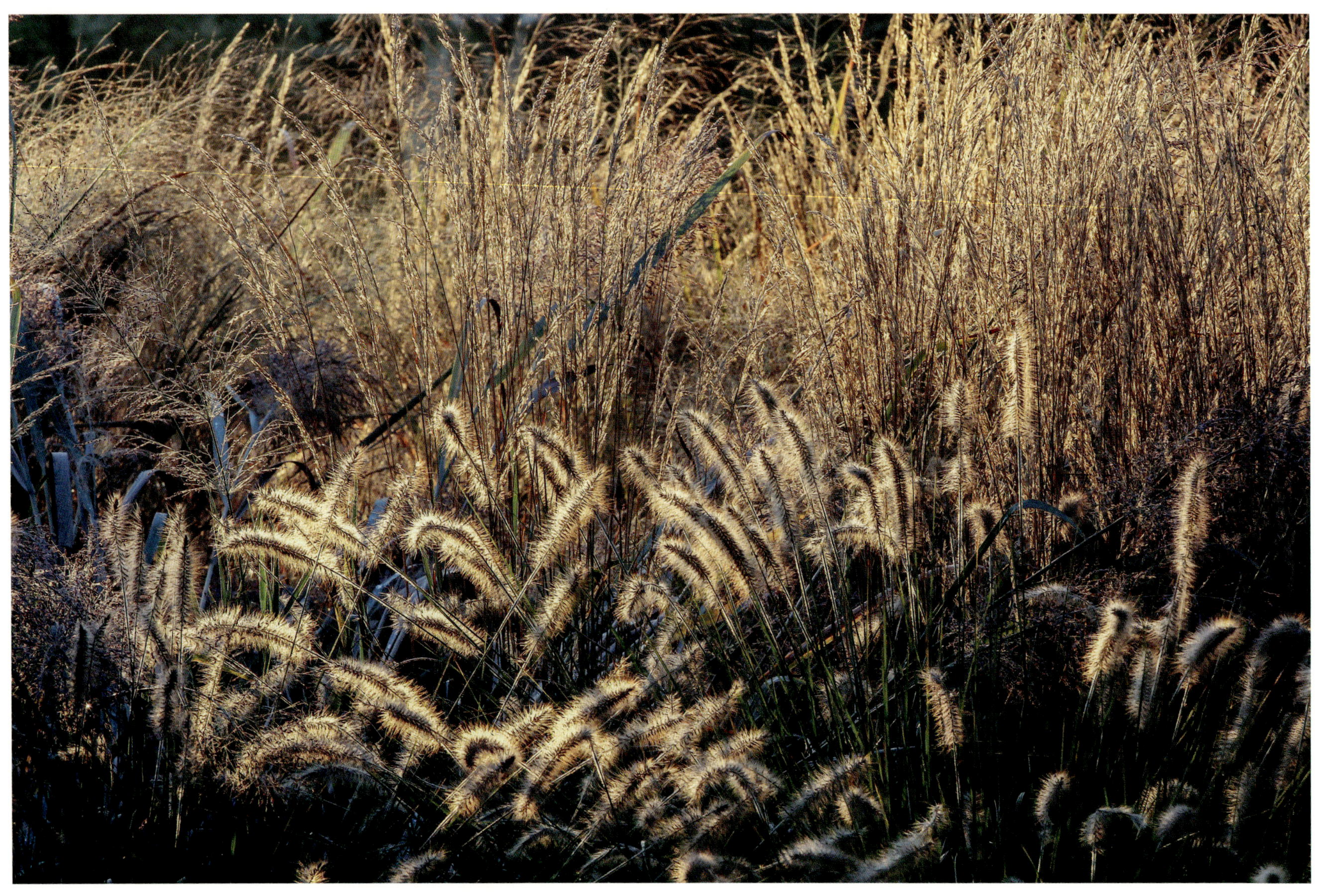

▲ **ROSANNA CASTRINI**   3RD PLACE

Dancing Light
Saluzzo, Piedmont, Italy

This photo was taken in the botanical garden of Domenico Montevecchi, located on the hill of Saluzzo in a temperate sub-alpine climate. I particularly liked the grasses, especially when the sun illuminated the seed heads and emphasised their structures.

📷 Canon EOS 600D, Canon 70-200mm lens, 1/100sec at f/13, ISO 400.

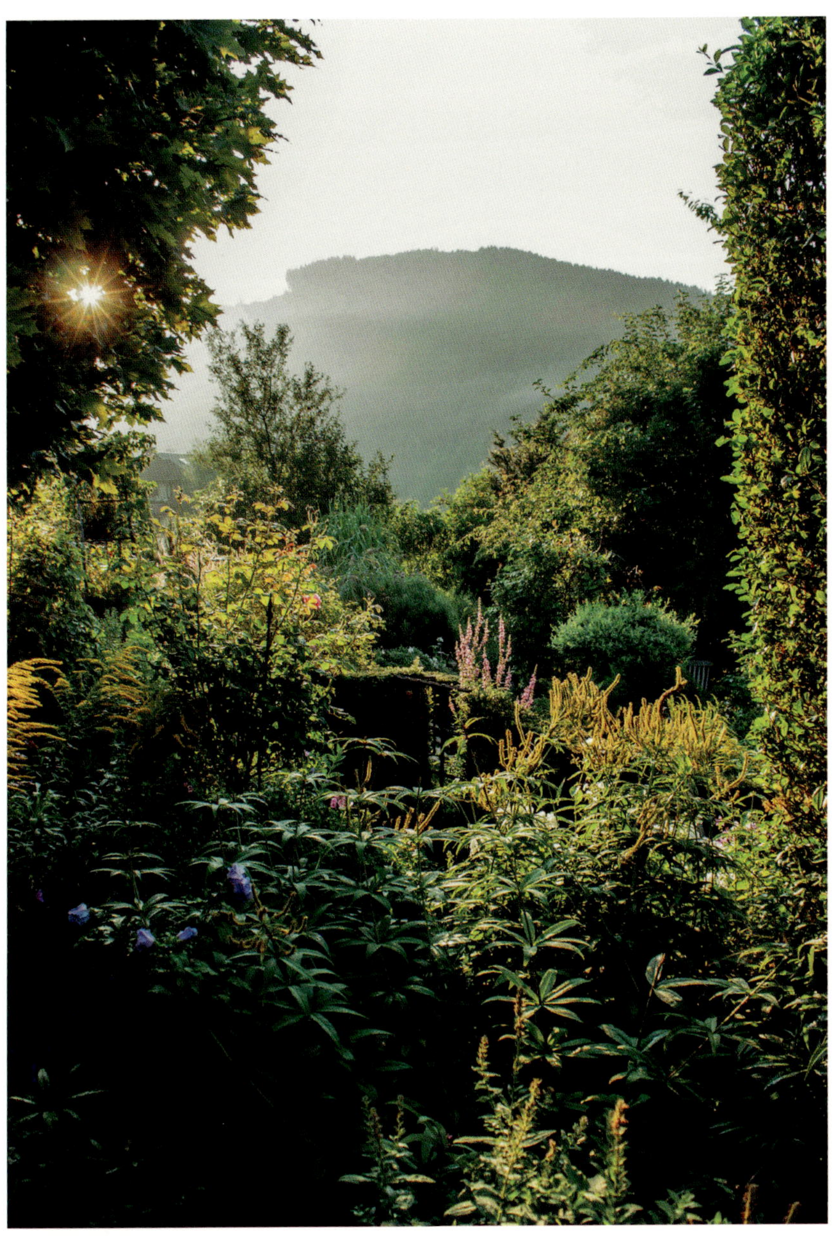

Morning Gold
North Rhine-Westphalia, Germany

Taken on an early September morning in my garden, the birds were singing and the mist was just starting to lift. All I had to do was wait until the sun was at just the right height.

Canon EOS 450D, Canon 18-55mm lens, 1/300sec at f/35, ISO 200. Post-capture: basic image management.

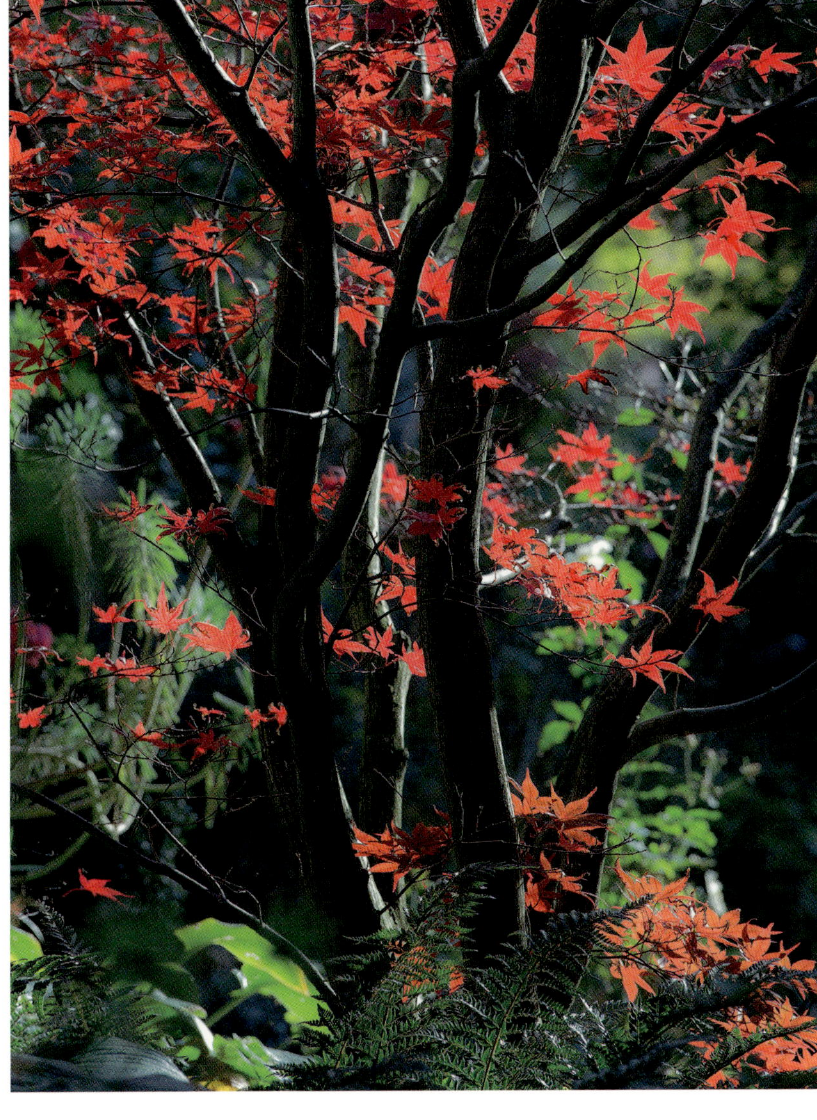

The Show is Over
Zürich, Switzerland

I loved the effect of the red leaves of the maple, lit by the clear morning sun, framed by the amazingly fresh green of the perennials and roses. The picture was further enhanced by the stark sculptural quality of the stems and branches.

Nikon D4, Nikon 70-200mm lens, 1/250sec at f/6.3, ISO 360. Post-capture: basic image management.

SPECIAL AWARDS

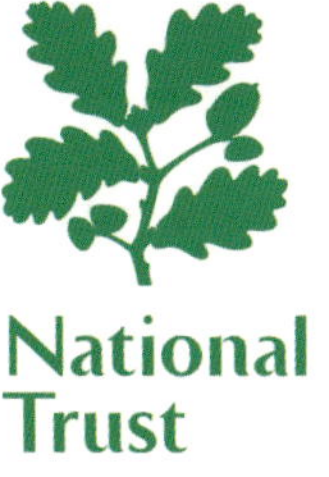
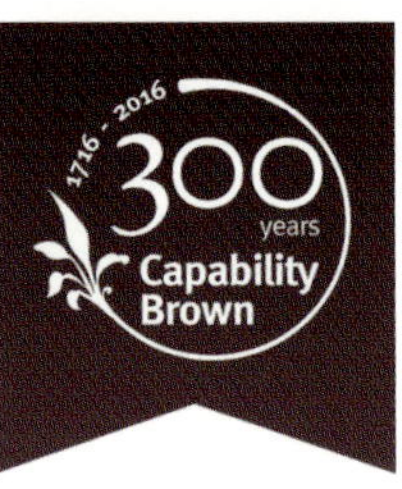

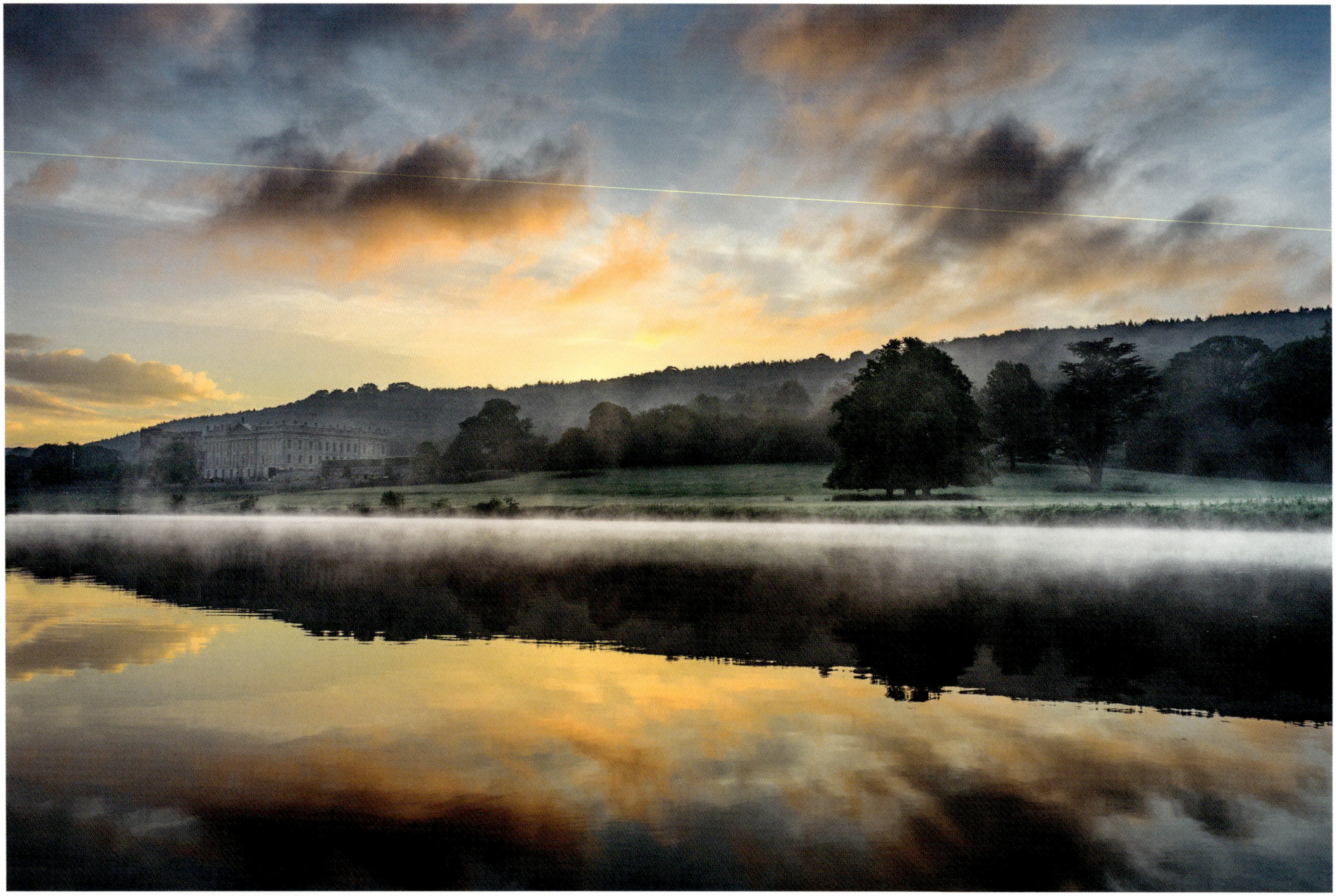

To celebrate the 2016 tercentenary of the birth of Lancelot 'Capability' Brown, International Garden Photographer of the Year teamed up with the National Trust to offer a new special award in memory of his far-reaching influence on landscape gardening.

▲ JUDE GADD

1ST PLACE

A Misty Sunrise in Chatsworth Park
Chatsworth Park, Derbyshire, England, UK

This was taken on one of my favourite kind of mornings, with a hint of mist and some wonderful colours in the sky. I positioned myself right down by the water in order to fill the foreground with the reflections. I wanted to include Chatsworth House as part of the composition but did not want it to dominate the shot.

📷 Sony α7, Sony 28-70mm lens, 1/3sec at f/16. Tripod, soft graduated filter. Post-capture: basic image management.

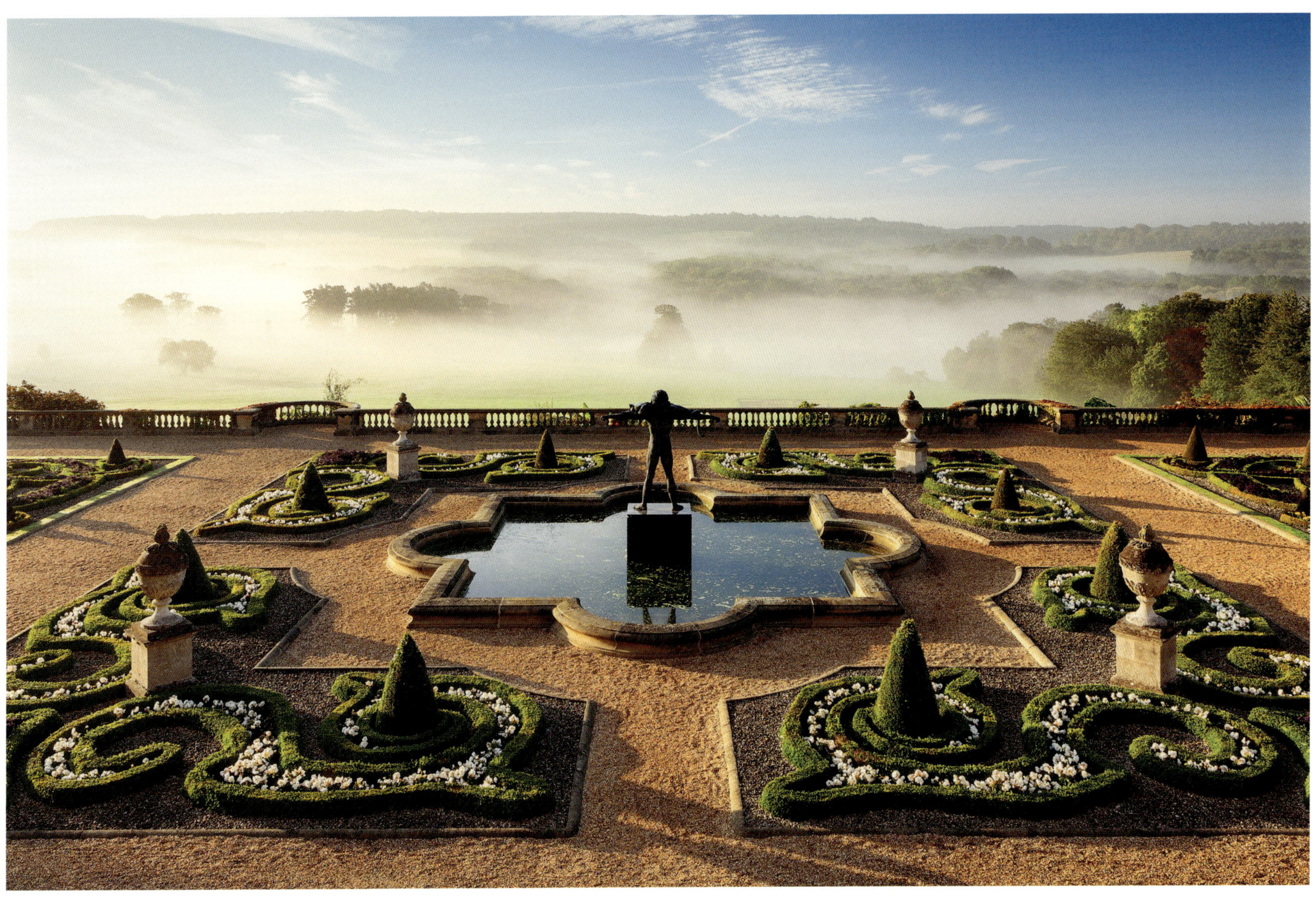

Sea of Mist
Harewood House, Yorkshire, England, UK

This shot was taken on a beautiful misty morning in early September. As the sun rose it bathed the garden in lovely, warm light as the mist ebbed and flowed across the distant landscape. The bright blue sky helped to complete the scene.

Canon EOS 5D Mark II, Canon 24-70mm lens, 1/10sec to 1/40sec at f/16, ISO 200. Tripod, cable release, polarising filter. Post-capture: merged three different exposures, basic image management.

SPECIAL AWARDS

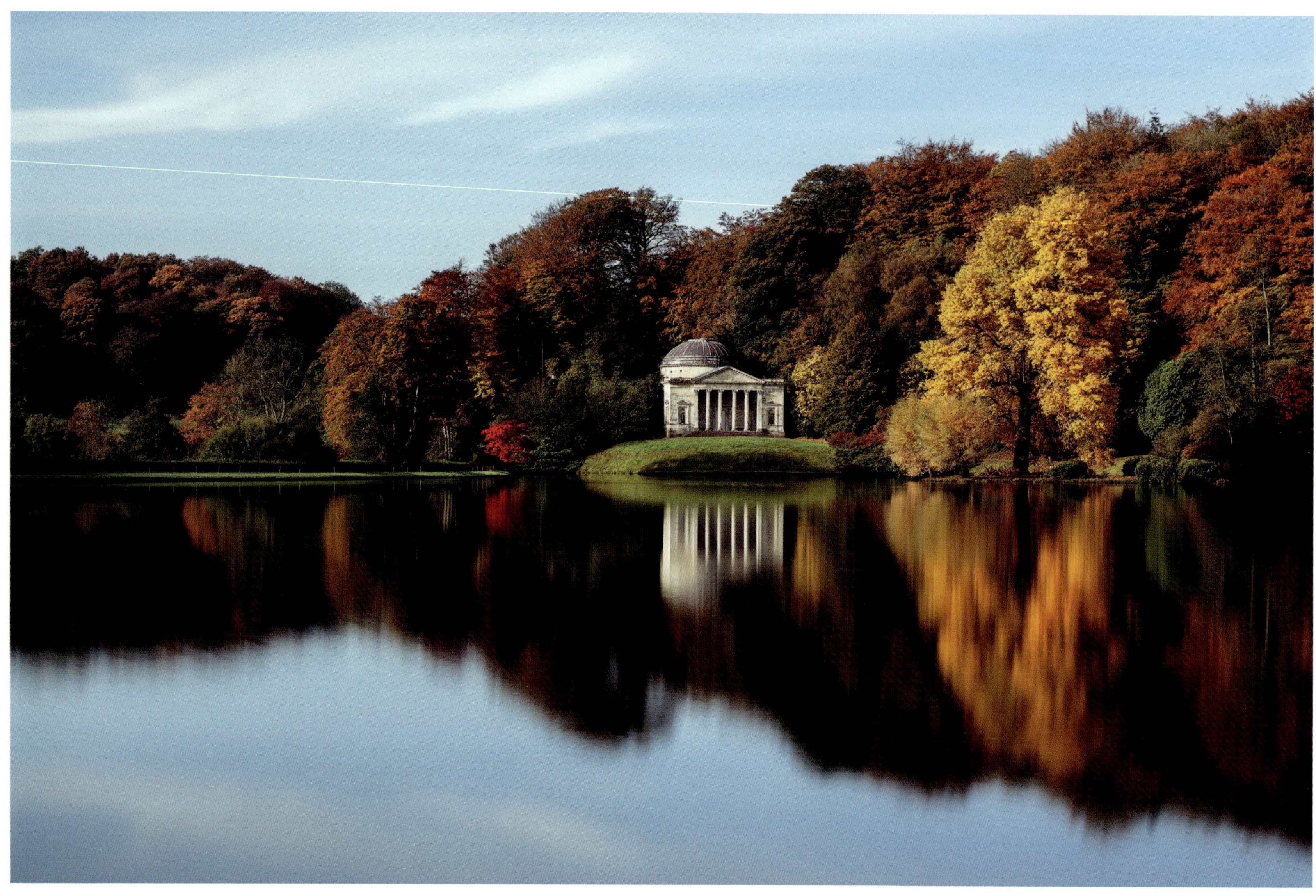

▲ **TONY GILL**   3RD PLACE

Stourhead Tranquility
Stourhead, Wiltshire, England, UK

The view across the lake towards the pantheon at Stourhead comes into its own in autumn; vibrant colours are reflected in the water, creating a majestic landscape.

📷 Canon EOS 5D Mark II, Canon 24-105mm lens, 30sec at f/16, ISO 125. Neutral density filter.

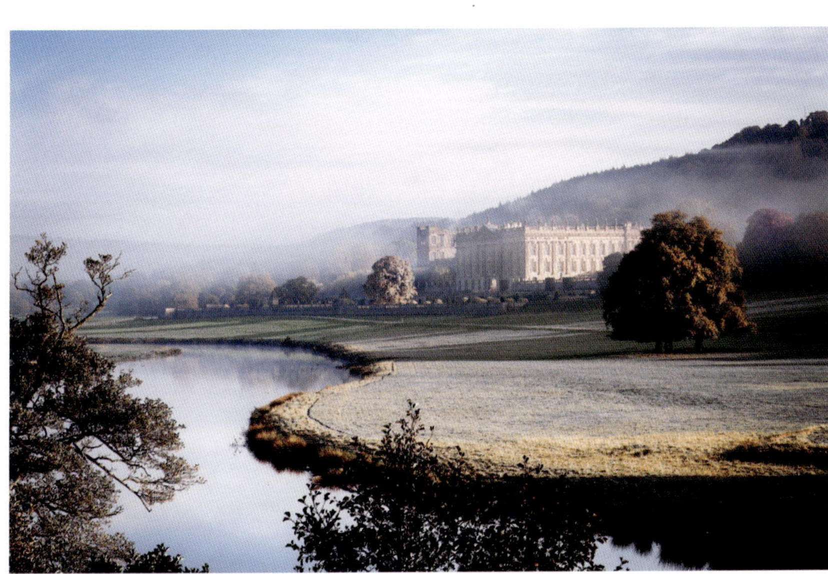

Chatsworth from the River Derwent
Chatsworth Park, Derbyshire, England, UK

Chatsworth House has been photographed extensively but not from this vantage point. This is a magnificent view because the River Derwent and the parkland designed by Brown sweep the eye up towards the house which is shown off beautifully in the early morning sun. There is a charming mix of parkland and grazing land which further enhances the rural setting. Brown transformed most of the working farmlands of Chatsworth to gardens in 1760, leaving aside a small section for its original purpose.

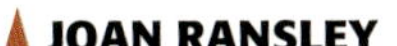 Canon EOS 5D Mark II, Canon 24-105mm lens, 1/25sec at f/11, ISO 100.

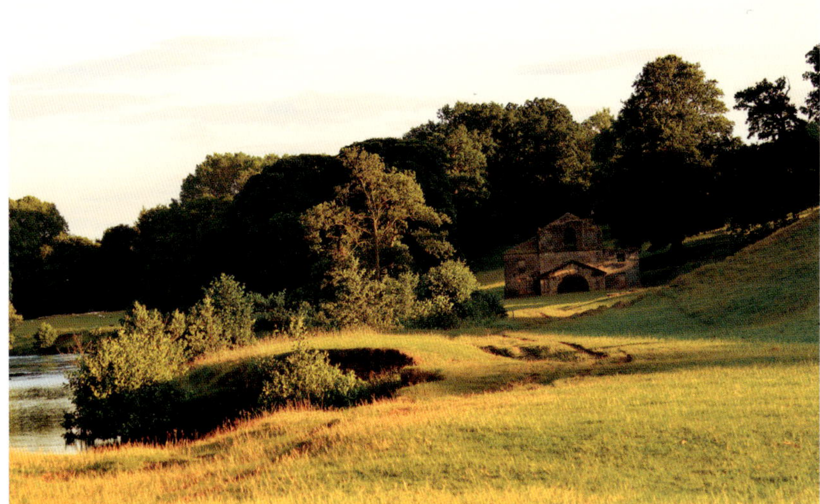

Chatsworth
Chatsworth Park, Derbyshire, England, UK

Chatsworth is one of my favourite places; every vista seems to offer the perfect photo opportunity. This shot shows an old mill beside the river, surrounded by beech trees during a golden sunset.

Nikon D5100, 18-200mm lens, 1/250sec at f/11. Post-capture: basic image management.

CAPTURED AT KEW

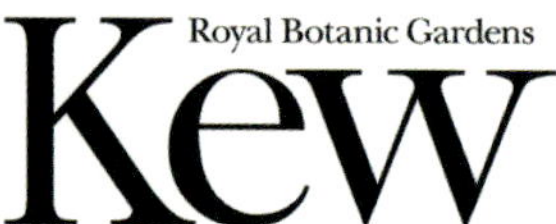

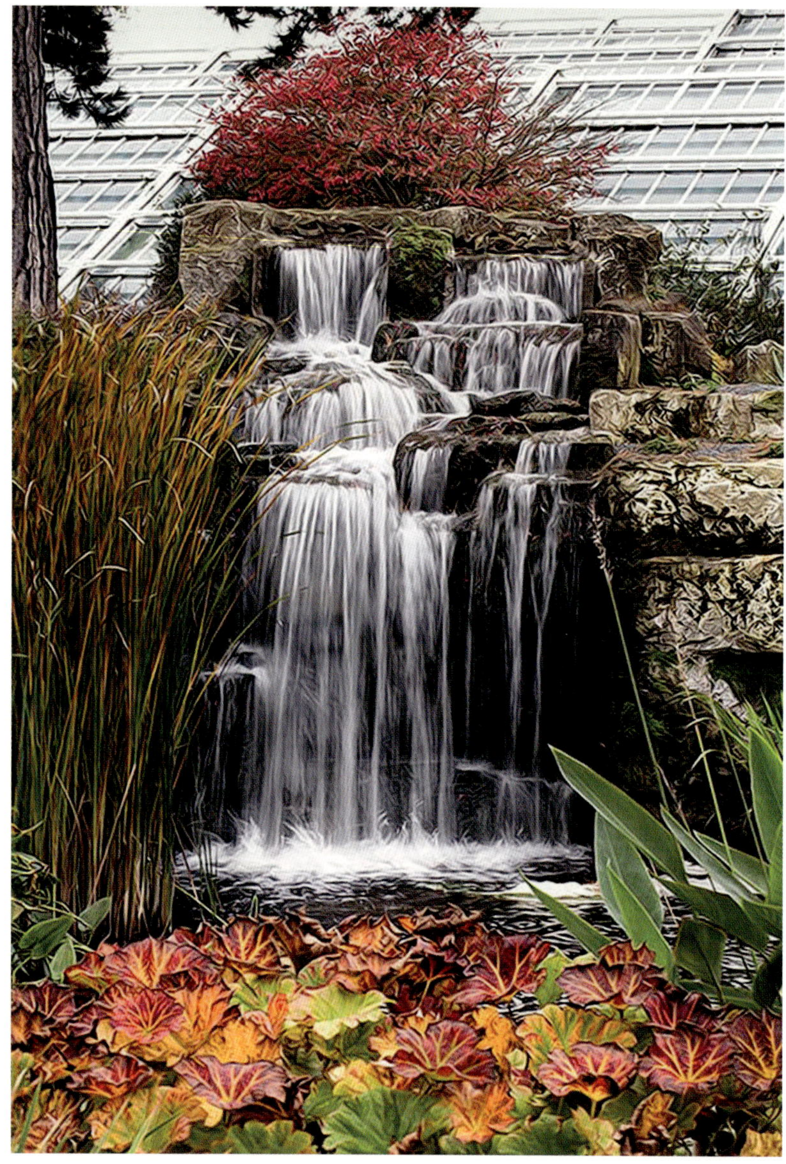

▲ **PAMELA SHAHLAVI**   1ST PLACE

Water Feature

I love the autumn colours at work in this shot, especially the variation in the leaves in the foreground combined with the water feature and rock formation. The cascading shape gives a real depth to the picture and looks like several small waterfalls flowing into each other.

Canon EOS 5D Mark III, Canon 100mm macro lens, 1/10sec at f/10, ISO 100.
Post-capture: applied Topaz filter in Adobe Photoshop.

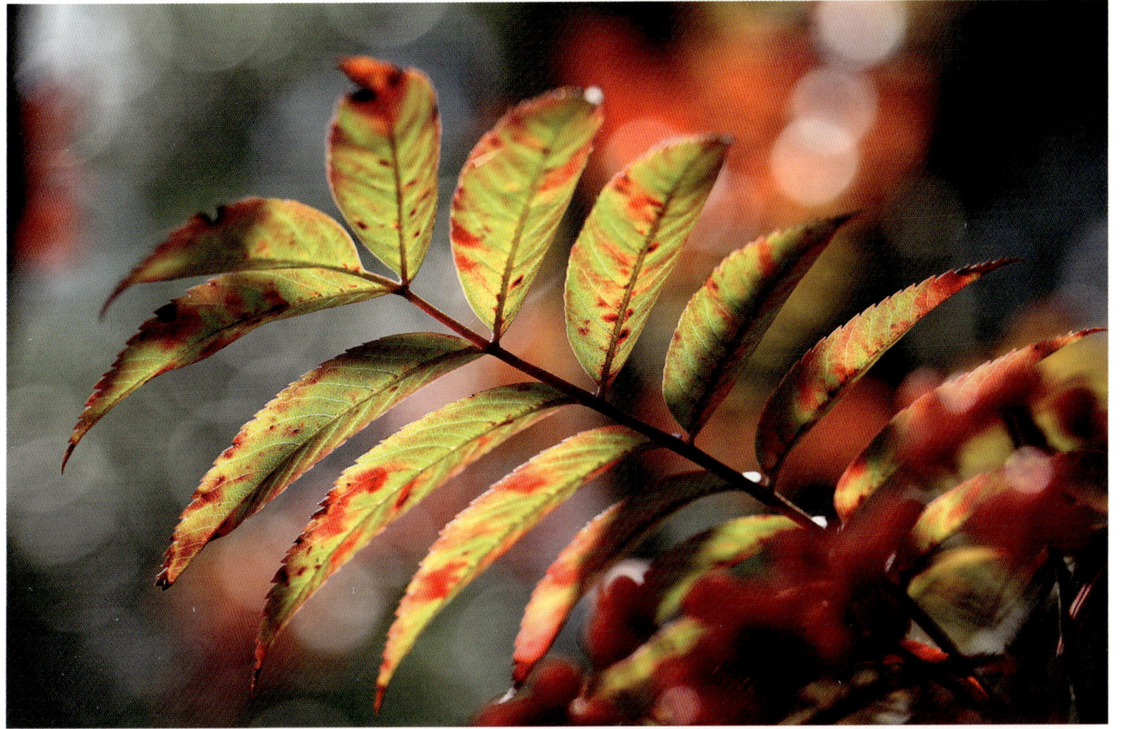

Autumnal Rowan Tree

When I visited Kew the first autumn colours were beginning to spread, giving the gardens a stunning glow. I liked the foliage and the red berries on this rowan tree and had a lot of fun playing around with various depths of field against the sunlit background to achieve the desired effect.

Canon EOS 5D Mark II, 100mm lens, 1/320sec at f/5.6, ISO 100.

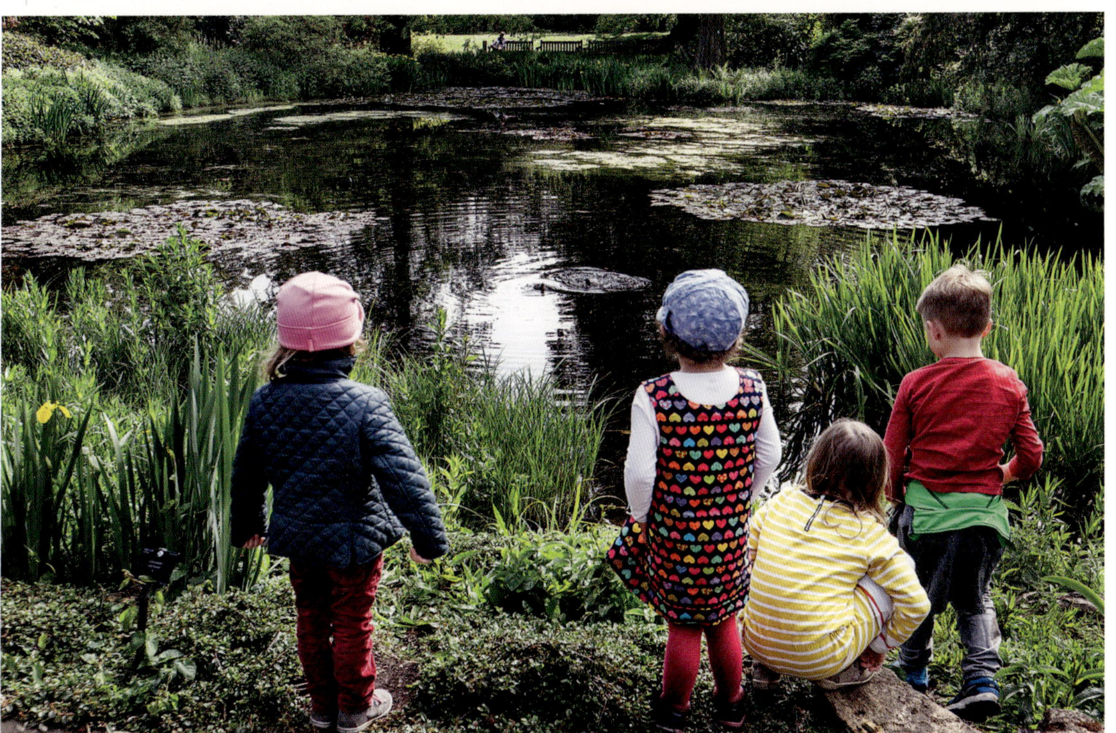

The Pond

I try to stop at the Royal Botanic Gardens, Kew every time I visit England. Last spring, I had spent the day walking through the gardens when I noticed a group of children captivated by some ducks taking a bath in one of the ponds. There was a simple innocence to the scene. I love this photo because it shows that all ages enjoy the open spaces and beauty of the ponds and gardens, as well as the wildlife which inhabits them. It is actually one of my favourite places in the world.

Canon EOS 5D Mark III, Canon 16-35mm lens, 1/500sec at f/7.1, ISO 320. Post-capture: basic image management.

CAPTURED AT KEW

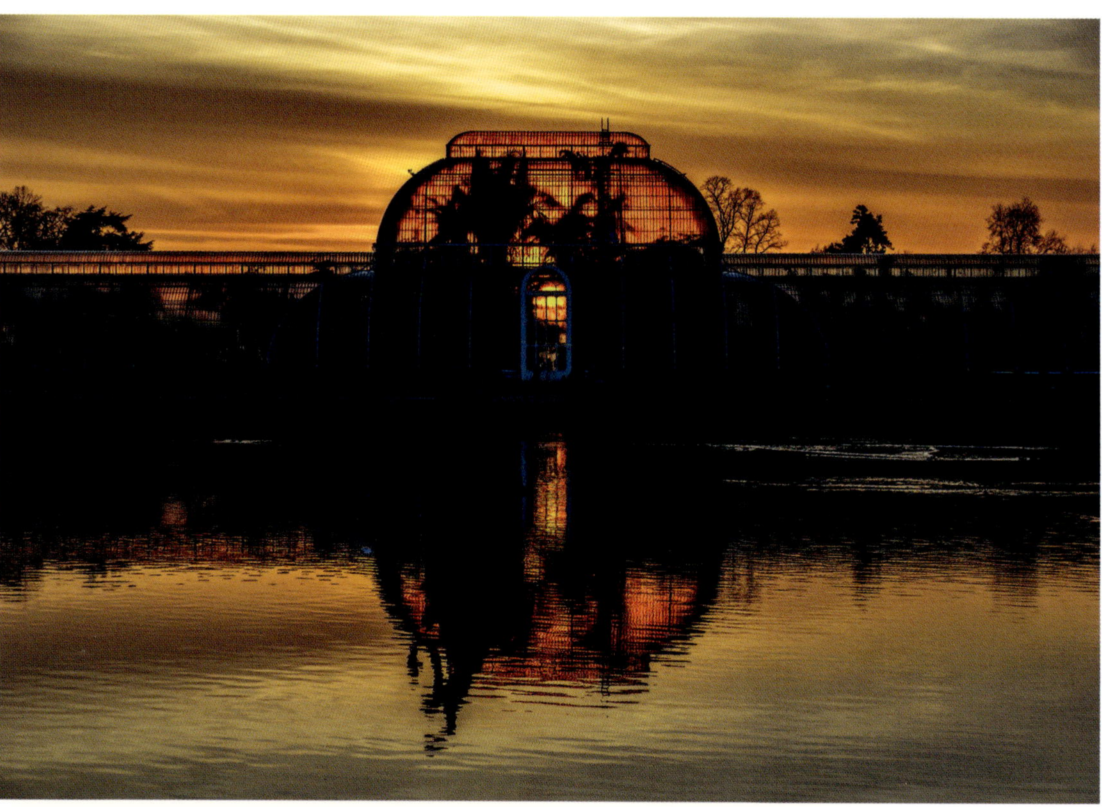

PAUL BATE ▶   Highly Commended

Sunset Kew

During the winter months the sunset behind the Palm House at Kew backlights the palms and glass in warm fiery colours.

📷 Sony α77, 16-50mm lens, 1/640sec at f/5, ISO 100.

RONA BASSETT ▶   Finalist

Victoria amazonica

This was my first visit to Kew Gardens and I remember coming down the stairs of the Princess of Wales Conservatory, seeing these giant circular leaves and being blown away by the scale and beauty of these amazing water lilies. They were much more impressive close up than they are in pictures. I sat and watched the light dancing on the leaves and when I decided to photograph them I went in close to capture the sunlight throbbing across the veins and their reflections shimmering on the water.

📷 Canon EOS 70D, Canon 100mm macro lens, 1/800sec at f/2.8, ISO 100. Post-capture: basic image management.

  HIGHLY COMMENDED

Waterlily House

I was drawn to the contrasts of the Waterlily House – the welcoming warmth inside compared to the brisk September day outside, the strong forms of the ironwork against the lush freeform planting, and the momentary oasis of calm in the middle of a hectic day.

Canon EOS 6D, Canon 11-24mm lens, 1/500sec at f/14. Post-capture: merged two images, minor cloning, basic image management.

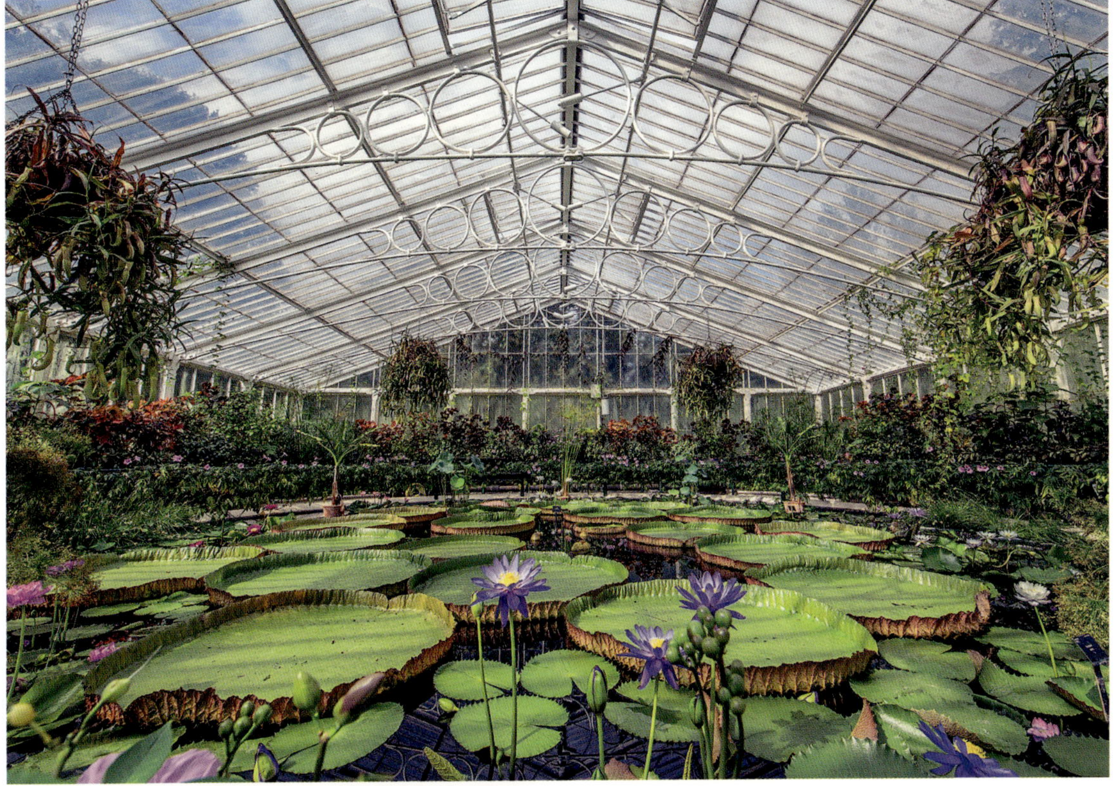

JEFF EDEN ▶ FINALIST

Sunset in the Palm House

I was photographing an evening event in the Palm House and noticed the changing light outside as the sun set. I liked the way the structure of the glasshouse and the plants growing inside became a silhouette against the sunset.

Nikon D600, 16-35mm lens, 1/15sec at f/13, ISO 1000. Tripod. Post-capture: basic image management.

  FINALIST

Kew Palm House Window

In the early morning at Kew Gardens the Palm House windows have wonderful patterns of condensation created from the warmth inside. Through the condensation and the glass, glimpses of the breathing plants can be seen within. Fascinating shapes and shadows, a hint of colour, a suggestion of foliage diffused and distorted – all adding to a sense of mystery and a tropical world waiting to be discovered inside.

Canon EOS 5D Mark II, 100mm macro lens, 1/640sec at f/10, ISO 400. Post-capture: increased colour vibrancy.

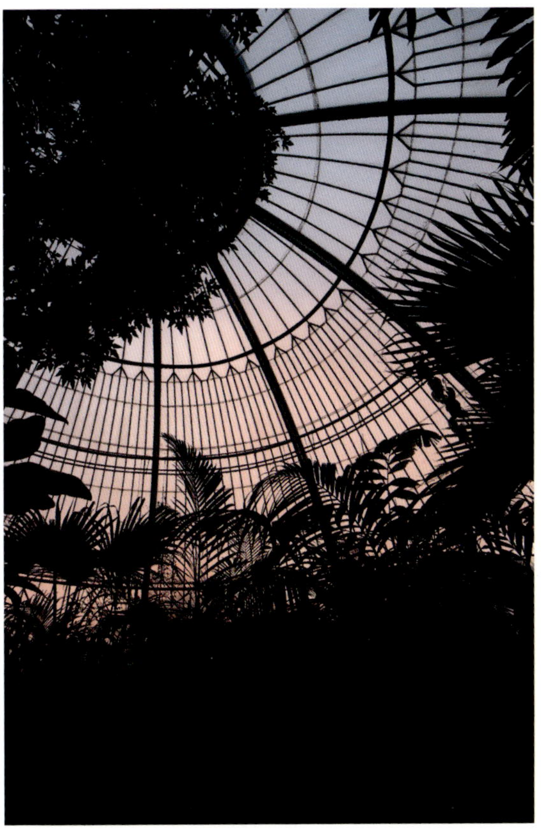

SPIRIT OF SWEDISH GARDENS

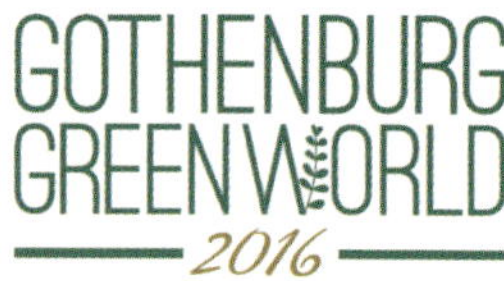

Gothenburg Green World 2016 is a year of horticultural and environmental events to showcase Gothenburg as a premier venue for gardens and parks in Scandinavia. The festival vividly demonstrates the importance of green spaces in the urban environment. One of the events is a summer exhibition of International Garden Photographer of the Year held in the city centre garden of the Garden Society of Gothenburg.

The winning entries in our special award will form the centrepiece of the exhibition. We acknowledge with thanks the support of *Allt om Trädgård*, Sweden's leading garden magazine, and Gothenburg Botanical Garden.

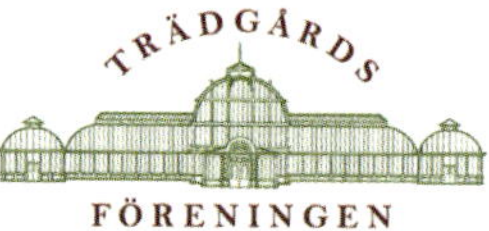

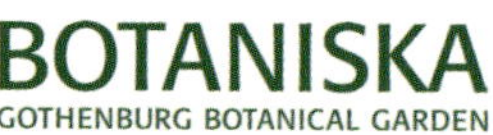

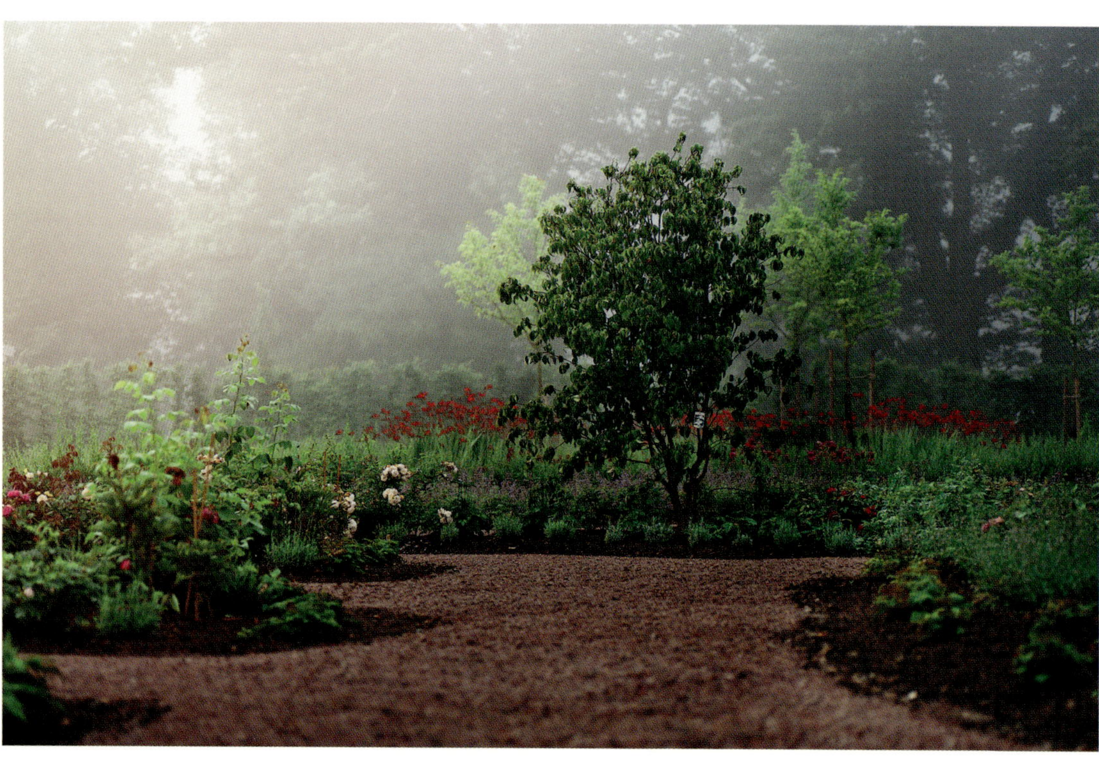

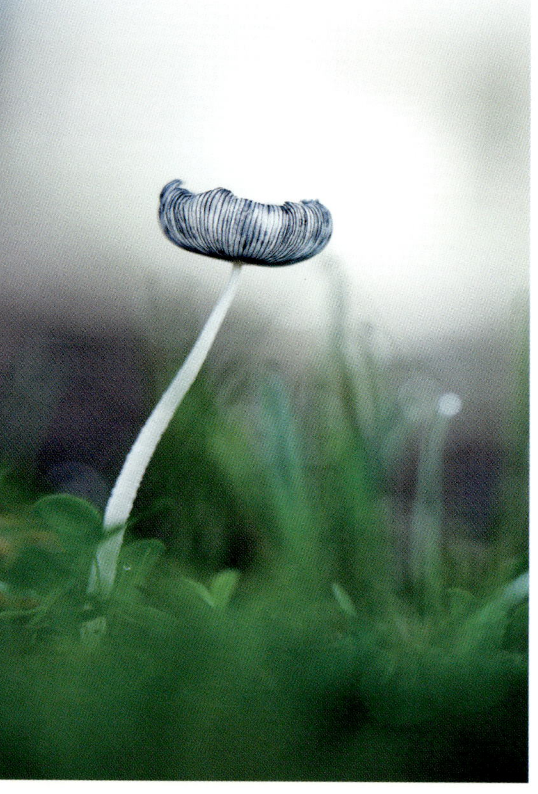

ANNICA CLARHOLM   1ST PLACE, PUBLIC GARDENS

KARIN BJÖRKLUND   2ND PLACE, PUBLIC GARDENS

Early Morning
Jonsereds Trädgårdar, Partille, Gothenburg, Sweden

i took this picture on a very beautiful July morning in Jonsereds, Trädgårdar. This public garden has been designed and planted to resemble its appearance during the 1800s. It is a wonderful old-fashioned garden and a very relaxing space.

Nikon D700, 90mm lens, 1/200sec at f/2.8, ISO 200. Post-capture: basic image management.

Ink Cap
Trädgårdsföreningen, Gothenburg, Sweden

Trädgårdsföreningen is a beautiful public garden in Gothenburg which I visited on an early September morning. This mushroom can be found in short grass, appearing overnight following rain; it also has a very short life cycle – within 24 hours there is no evidence of it having ever existed.

Sony α99, Sigma 150mm lens, 1/125sec at f/2.8, ISO 400.

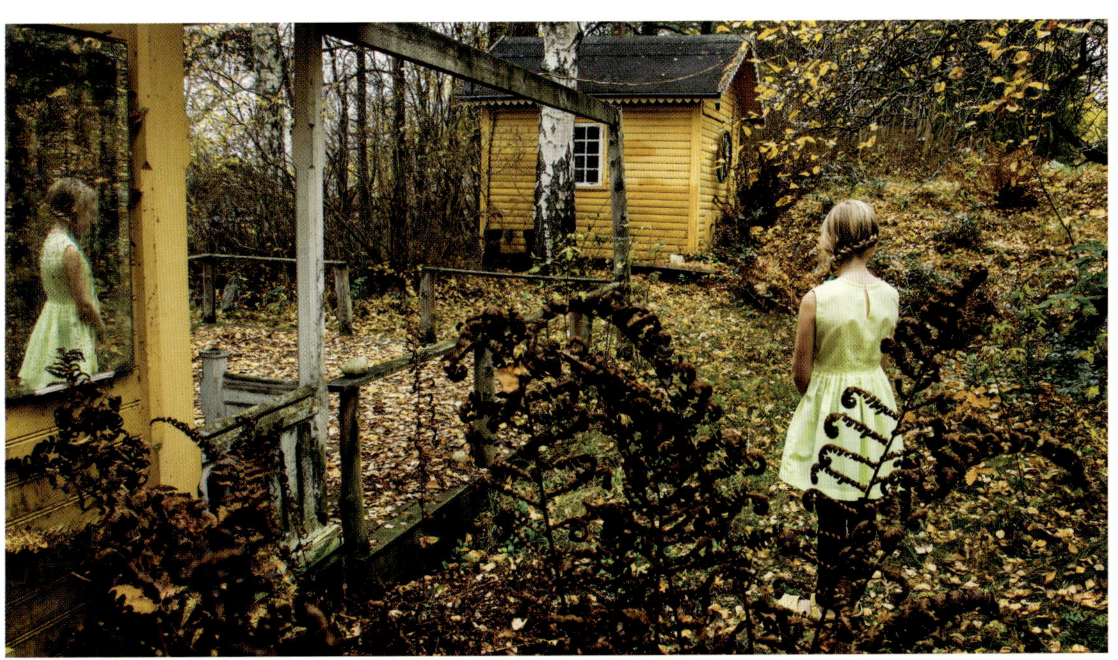

1ST PLACE, PRIVATE GARDENS

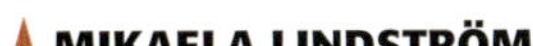

Girl in Yellow
Kvicksund, Lake Mälaren, Sweden

This abandoned summer house dates back to the early 1930s and has been left untouched and open to the elements. I have enjoyed wandering through this garden for five years during all seasons and I have used it as a backdrop for several pictures. I wanted to tell a story of family, nature and passing time. The dress my daughter is wearing used to belong to my mother and I wanted the dress to complement the colours of autumn.

Canon EOS 550D, Sigma 18-200mm lens, 1/25sec at f/10, ISO 800.

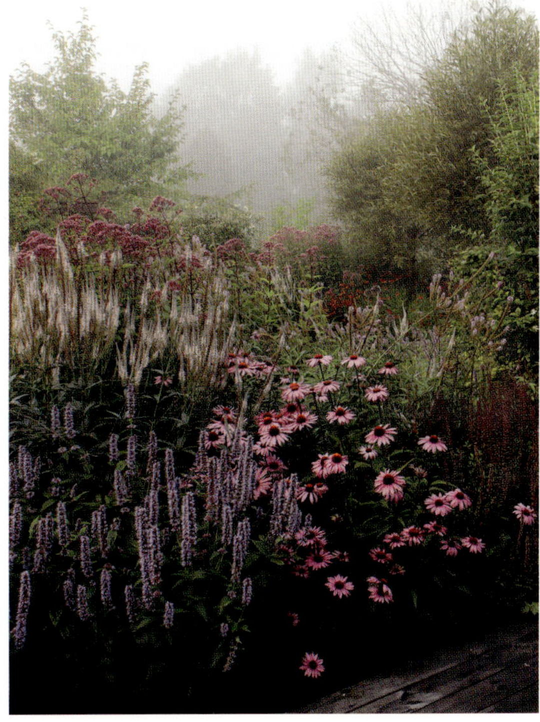

2ND PLACE, PRIVATE GARDENS

Misty August
Gimmersta, Tyresö, Stockholm, Sweden

It was such a magical morning. The mist muted all colours to soft pastels and blurred the borders of the garden. During the autumn months the mist drifts in from a nearby lake and wraps the garden in a soft white blanket.

Canon EOS 600D, Canon 18-55mm lens, 1/125sec at f/8, ISO 200.

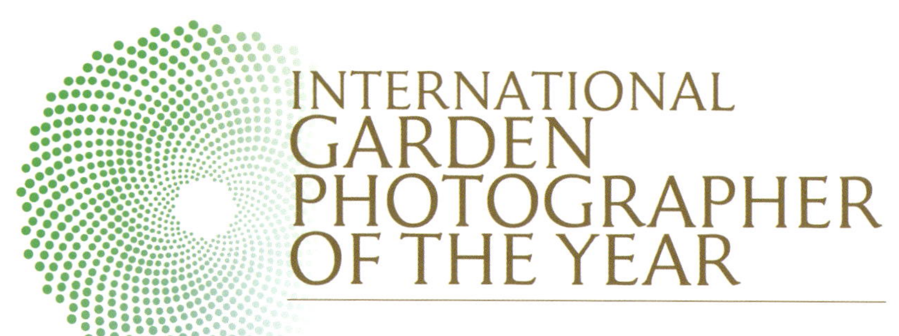

INTERNATIONAL GARDEN PHOTOGRAPHER OF THE YEAR

NEW SHOOTS AWARDS

We are very interested in encouraging new talent as part of the competition. 'New Shoots' awards are open to anyone who has not won an award in the IGPOTY competition.

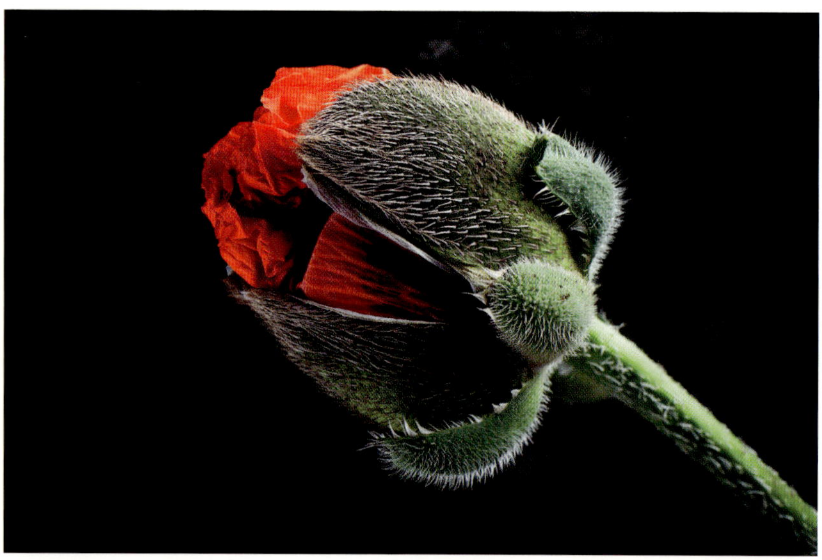

GIANT POPPY **STUART HALL**

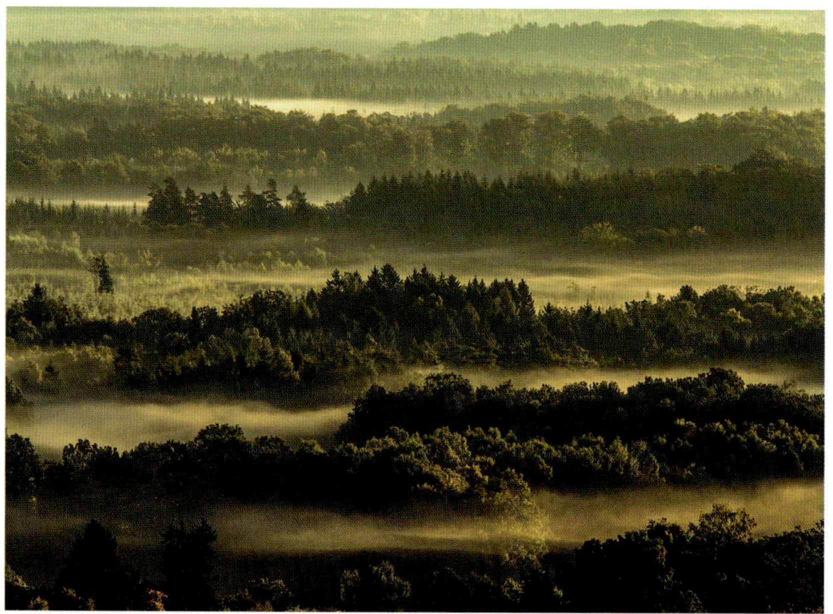

FOREST AND MIST **HÅKAN LILJENBERG**

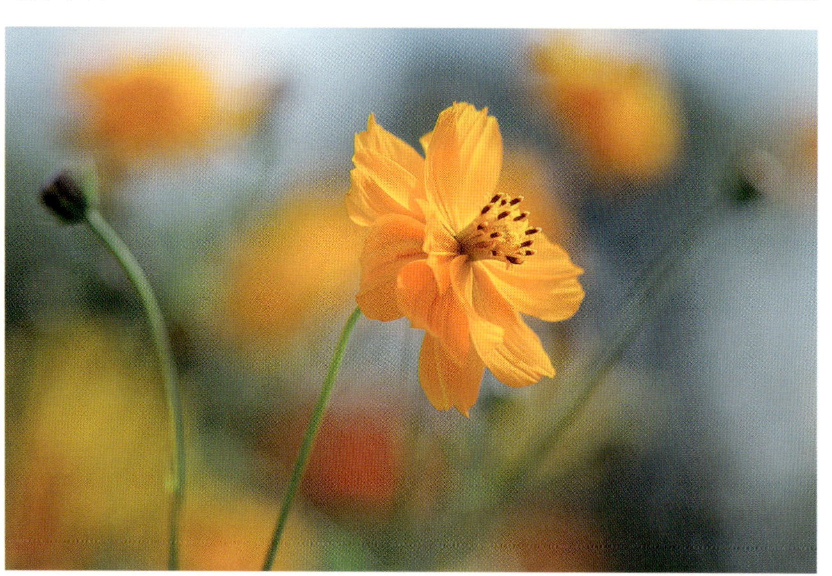

AUTUMN'S GLORY **BARBARA FISCHER**

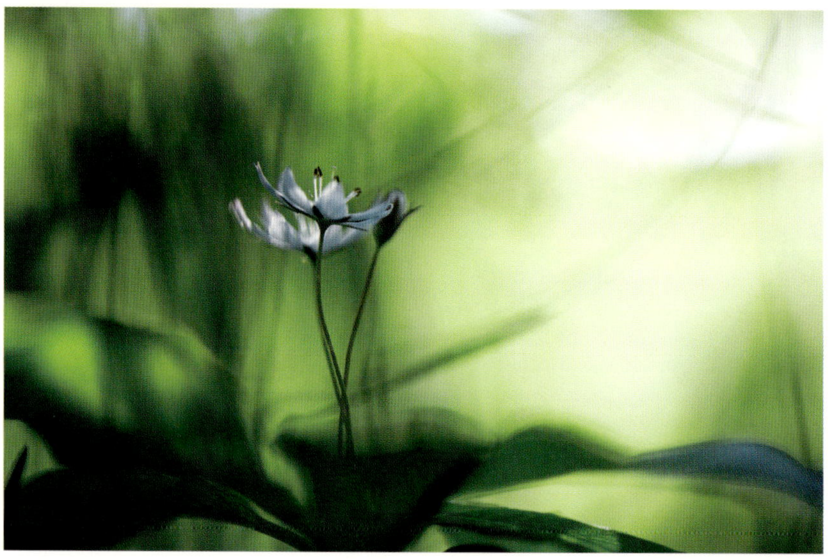

A FOREST STAR **BENTE KLEVENBERG**

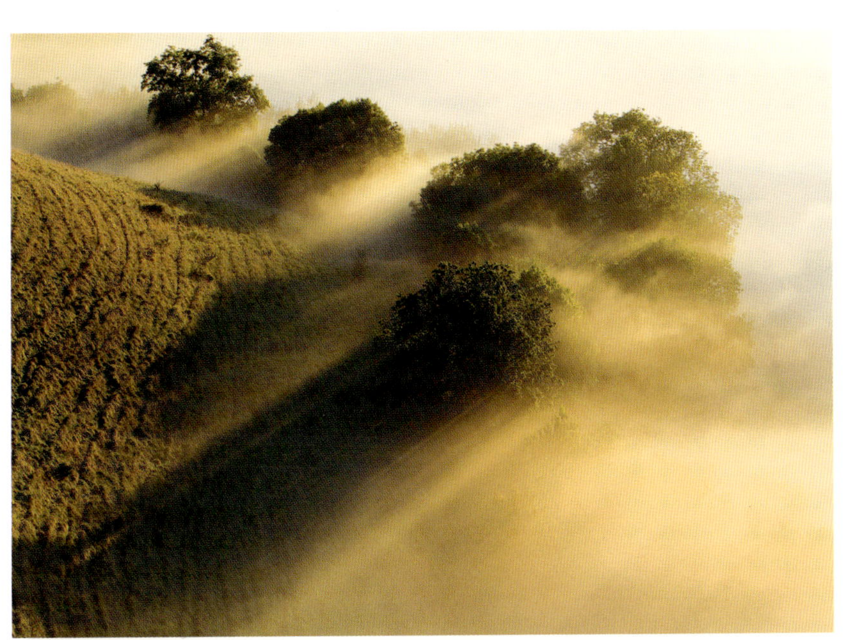

FINGERS OF GOLD   **STEVE DEELEY**

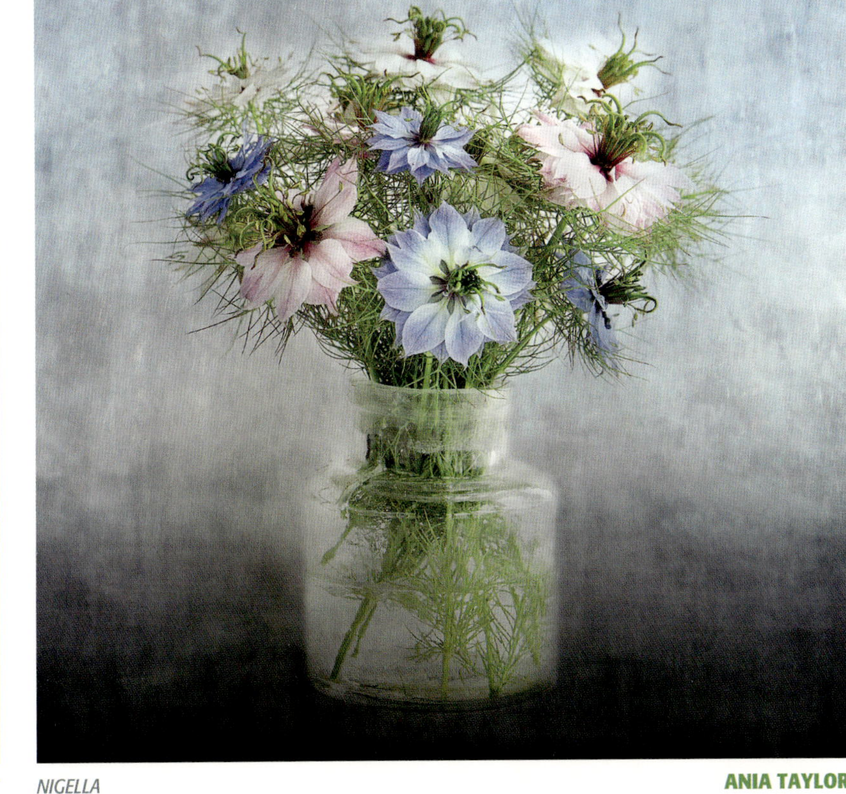

NIGELLA   **ANIA TAYLOR**

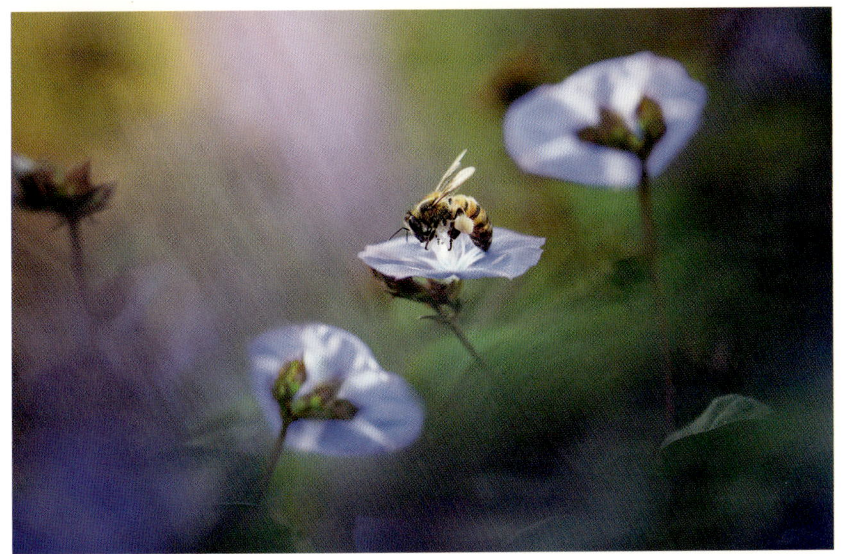

MORNING VISITOR   **PEI LING LEE**

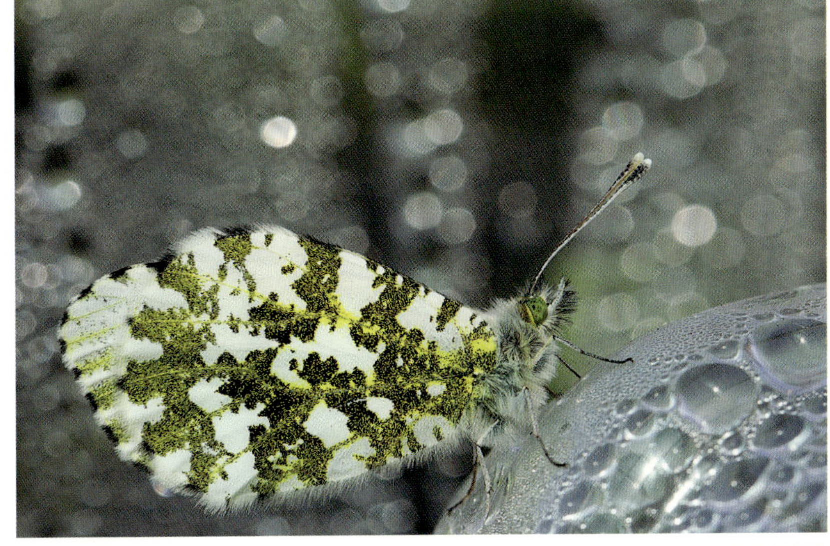

SLEEPING BUTTERFLY   **CATHERINE WALKER**

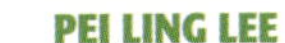

NEW SHOOTS AWARDS

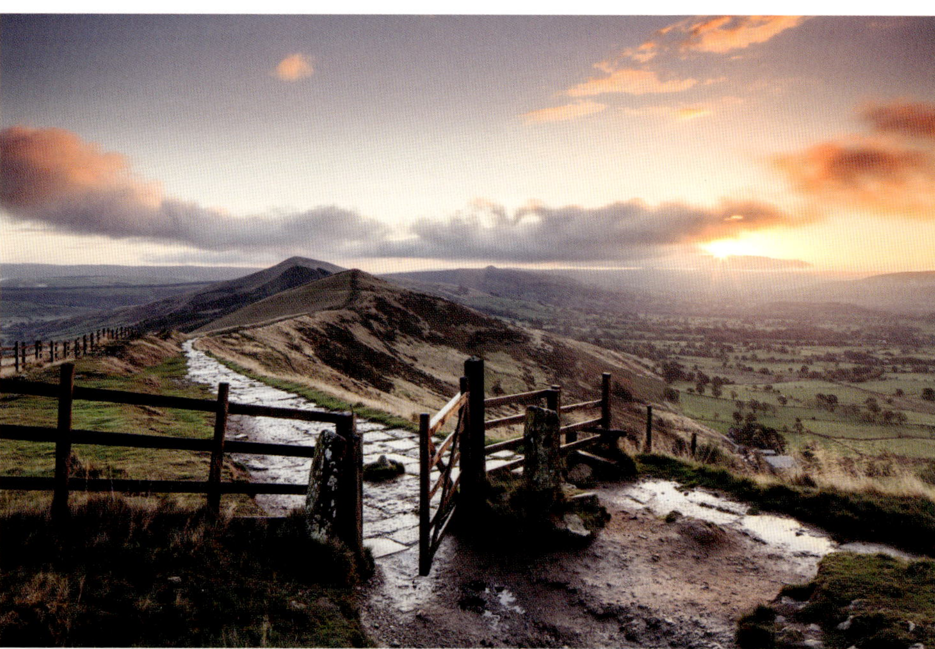

COME ON IN **JULIAN ELLIOTT**

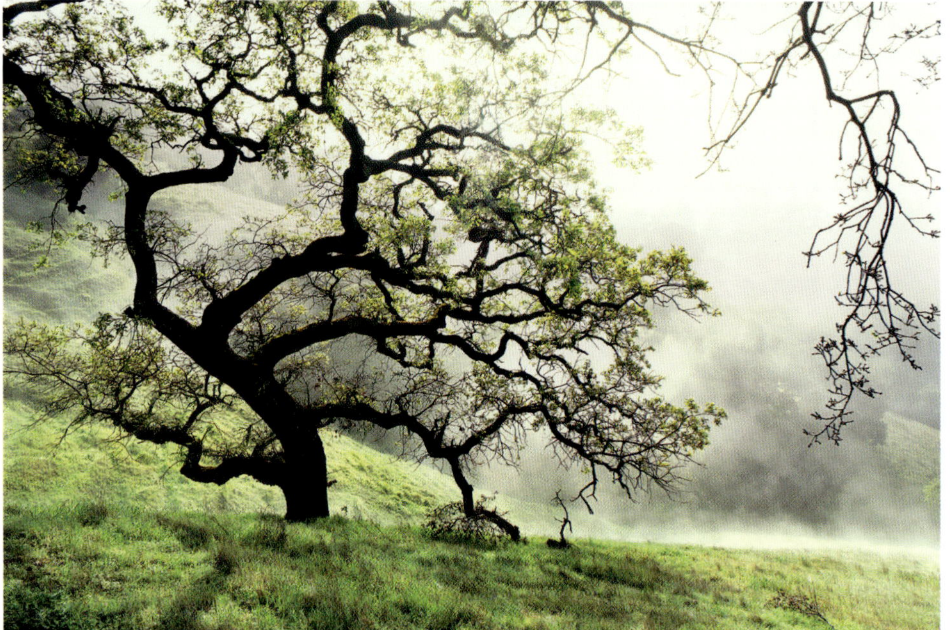

BLUE OAK **SAXON HOLT**

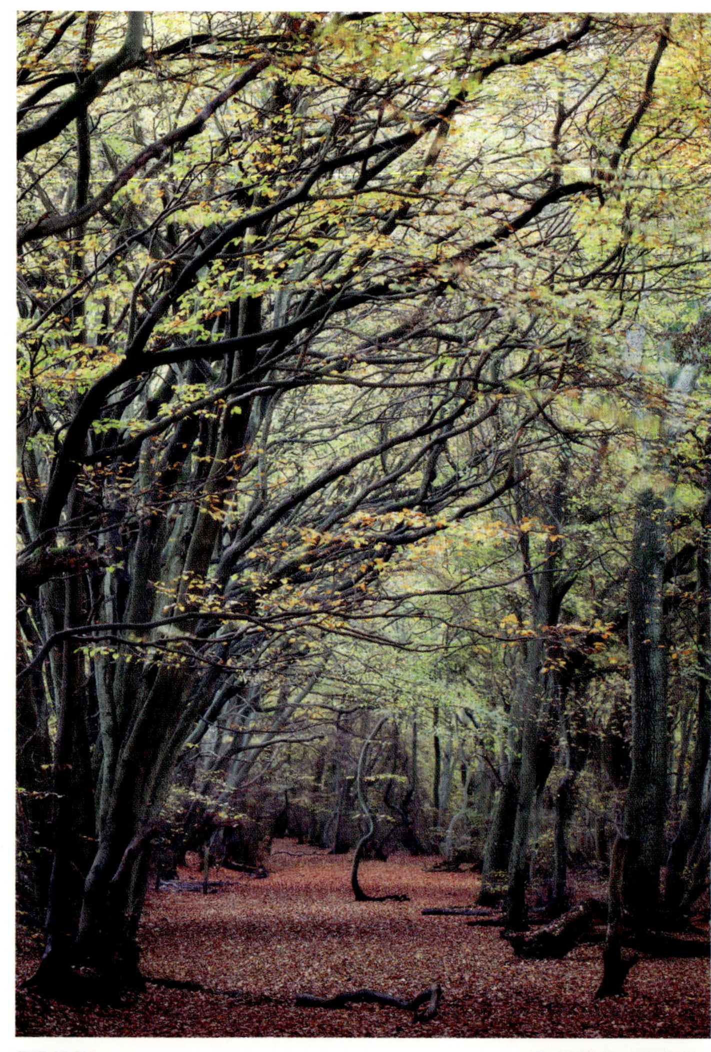

THE ARCH **CLAIRE McCONNELL**

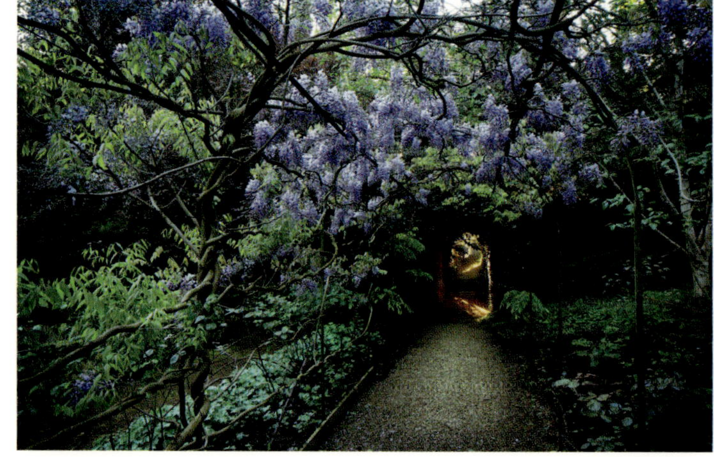

WISTERIA ARCH **SUE FLOOD**